Peter Levi

Just city delicate as a hare-bone
'For Colin Macleod', *The Echoing Green* (1983) 29

Peter Levi

OXFORD ROMANTIC

Brigid Allen

Signal
Signal Books
Oxford

First published in 2014 by
Signal Books Limited
36 Minster Road
Oxford OX4 1LY
www.signalbooks.co.uk

A catalogue record for this book is available from the British Library

ISBN 978-1-908493-98-9 Cloth

Cover Design: Tora Kelly
Typesetting: Tora Kelly
Cover Images: (front) courtesy Christopher Barker; (back) courtesy Elizabeth Chatwin; Photo of Oxford by DAVID ILIFF. License: CC-BY-SA 3.0

For Nancy Sandars

CONTENTS

LIST OF ILLUSTRATIONS

Preface and Acknowledgements

This biography is intended as a portrait of a life rather than a scholarly or critical assessment of its achievements. It does not attempt to adjust Peter Levi's literary reputation or identify him with a particular movement or group. The term 'Oxford Elegist', coined by Fiona Sampson in *Beyond the Lyric: a map of contemporary British poetry* (2012), could have been devised especially for him but for the fact that the small number of poets to whom Sampson applied it were still living at the time she wrote. 'Romantic', especially when linked with Oxford, is a vaguer, more all-embracing term, suggesting Shelley, Matthew Arnold and generations of student poets ranging from the sensitively observant to the emotionally overwrought. Few academics would admit to being romantics, but Peter Levi was an unusual kind of academic, much of the interest of whose life lies in the number of borderlines it crossed.

In 1958, as a final-year undergraduate destined for the Jesuit priesthood, he published his first poems in the *New Statesman* and the *Times Literary Supplement* and had his first collection accepted by André Deutsch. The next few years were a period of high-minded political anxiety among left-leaning English intellectuals. Levi, although isolated from the world by his vocation, yearned to understand Eastern Europe, and through an Oxford friend became the co-translator of the Penguin volume of Yevtushenko's *Selected Poems*. His gift for friendship led to one introduction after another, to a part-time life in Greece with the passionate political involvement that entailed, and eventually to his marriage. From his thirties to his fifties he was a member of the classics faculty (as well as, latterly, Professor of Poetry) at Oxford, but he never received more than a token salary, and after leaving the Jesuits had to rely on casual tutoring and steady writing for a living.

My reasons for undertaking Peter Levi's biography are not easy to explain. As a *New Statesman*-reading adolescent in the early 1960s I was struck by the atmospheric melancholy of two or three of his short poems, and surprised that a Jesuit could be so self-revealing. Somehow, without being told, I realized that he was still young. More than twenty years later I was enchanted by his memoir *The Flutes of Autumn* and the wit of his published, rhyming lecture *Goodbye to the Art of Poetry*. It was several years after his death, however, when I came across a diffident letter he had written to Sir Isaiah Berlin about his versions of Yevtushenko's poems, that I knew at once what I wanted to do. Happily, his widow and other family members agreed to help me, and I found that half a dozen of his close friends had kept large collections of his letters. Among his papers at Boston College, Massachusetts I found valuable correspondence and notebooks. The rich complexity of the literary, social and emotional life that emerged from these and other sources far exceeded anything I could have imagined in advance.

My chief debt has been to Peter's widow Deirdre for her enthusiasm, helpfulness, hospitality and forebearance during the years it has taken me to produce this book. I should not have been able to write it without her support. Her son Matthew Connolly has also helped me greatly with loans or copies of printed and manuscript material and film, together with extracts from his own diaries. William Charlton, John Fuller, Peter Granger-Banyard S.J., Julian Mitchell, David Pryce-Jones and Nancy Sandars have shared memories of Peter with me and kindly allowed me to make use of their collections of his letters. David Pryce-Jones has given me permission to reprint the address he gave at Peter's memorial service in an Appendix. The late Sister Mary Anthony, Peter's sister Gillian, entertained me at her convent at Hyning, Lancashire with sparkling accounts of her and Peter's early life. My brother Hugh Allen, a patient reader of the text in draft, has offered advice on religious subjects as well as general encouragement.

I have been most grateful for conversations and correspondence with, and other help from, the following: John Berger, Brendan Callaghan S.J., Elizabeth Chatwin, Cressida Connolly, the late Zoë Dominic, the late Kevin Donovan S.J., James Fenton, the late Sir Patrick Leigh Fermor, the late Clarence Gallagher S.J., Roger Garfitt, Martin Haddon, the late Paul Haddon, Denise Harvey, June Henman, Billy Hewett S.J., Frances Heywood, Adrian House, George Huxley, P.J. Kavanagh, the late Maurice Keen, James Knowles, Brendan McLaughlin, Robin Milner-Gulland, Anthony Mitchell, Brian Mountford, Anthony O'Hear, Craig Raine, Miranda Rothschild, Michael Schmidt, Mischa Scorer, Mrs Geoffrey Tigar, Iain Watson and Duncan Wu.

Institutional archivists and others who have helped me include staff members of the Oxford University Archives, the Special Collections Reading Room, Bodleian Library, and the Jesuit Archives in Mount St, London; the Secretary of the Prior Park Past Pupils Association; Judith Curthoys at Christ Church, Oxford, Margaret Davies at St Catherine's College, Oxford, Penelope Hatfield at Eton College, David E. Horn and Justine Sundaram at the John J. Burns Library, Boston College, Massachusetts, Amanda Ingram at Pembroke College, Oxford, David Knight at Stonyhurst College and Miriam Rodrigues-Pereira of the Congregation of Spanish and Portuguese Jews in London. An enquiry about letters from Peter Levi among the papers of Cyril Connolly at the University of Tulsa, Oklahoma resulted in the unexpected but most welcome arrival of a complete batch of photocopies.

For permission to quote from Peter Levi's poems I am grateful to Anvil Press poetry of 70 Royal Hill, London SE10 8RF (www. anvilpresspoetry.com), who have kept most of his poetical works in print from *Collected Poems, 1955-1975* (1976, reissued 1984) to the posthumous *Viriditas* (2001). I am grateful to Penguin for permission to quote from his translation of 'Birthday' in Yevgeny Yevtushenko's *Selected Poems* (1962), and to Marion Boyars for permission to quote from George Reavey's translation of the same poem in *The Poetry of Yevgeny Yevtushenko, 1953 to 1965* (1966). The editors of the *Isis* magazine have permitted me to quote from poems of Peter's published in 1956, from the 'Isis Idol' profile of him in 1957 and from his 'Isis Idol' profile of Dom Moraes in 1958. I am grateful to The Random House Group Ltd. (U.K.) for permission to quote from his prose works *The Hill of Kronos, The Flutes of Autumn* and *The Light Garden of the Angel King*, all published by Harvill.

The portrait photograph of Peter Levi on the book-jacket and at p. 352 is reproduced by kind permission of Christopher Barker. The portrait photograph from the *Isis* of 30th October 1957 is reproduced by kind permission of Studio Edmark, the editors of the *Isis* and the Bodleian Library Imaging Service, Oxford (Per.G.A.Oxon. 4° 145, p.21). The photograph of Peter in Afghanistan is reproduced by kind permission of Elizabeth Chatwin. The portrait photograph of Nancy Sandars is reproduced by kind permission of Nancy Sandars with the help of Mike Tomlinson. Other photographs are reproduced by kind permission of Deirdre Levi.

A few foreign place-names in my text, such as Euboea rather than Evia, will be found in the traditional form Peter Levi used rather than the modern one.

Charlbury
January 2014

INTRODUCTION

That was the terribly hot summer when the elm disease had ravaged England, but dead elm trees were still standing up like giant skeletons in every hedge.

The Flutes of Autumn (1983) 153

It was the hottest summer in London most people could remember. For two months the exhaust smog in the streets covered the western sky in a dull, grey-pink haze by evening. Kebab fumes, odours of grilled dog-mess, stale beer-smells and the cabbagy detritus of open-air markets blended with the sweat-reek from buses and the parched breath from Tube-station mouths. Hollyhocks grew tall and rank among the rubbish of abandoned plots. As the waters of the Thames receded, the layer of exposed mud on the foreshore baked solid and cracked under a metallic sun. Houses subsided and developed cracks as the London clay under their foundations compacted and shrank.

Urban marriages were also cracking up, encouraged by the newly permissive divorce laws and an uncertain atmosphere of liberation. It was 1976, when the backwash of the sexual revolution, mingled with the sudden insecurities of inflation, upset many people's assumptions about how life ought to be lived. House prices were shooting up, leaving new owners struggling with mortgages and bridging loans. Bankruptcies, dispossessions and unemployment were on the increase. Settled couples, who had until then behaved normally, began to embarrass their children by competing with the long-haired student young. There were street parties with hummus and sangria, wives in see-through cheesecloth smocks and whiskered husbands in flared trousers and shirts open to the navel. Gay men emerged wearing Greek shoulder-bags and caftans. Small children ran naked round the climbing-frames and paddling-pools of town gardens, while their parents experimented with cannabis and knocked back quantities

I

of cheap red wine. Women talked of banishing their husbands to bedsitters, dividing the matrimonial home in half, or moving to Ibiza or Somerset to grow organic vegetables, breed donkeys or weave rugs. Anything seemed possible in that unreal weather, with the sun blazing off bricks and melting asphalt from the early morning onwards, and the solid afternoon heat simmering down into rackety open-air evenings and humid, sleepless nights.

Peter Levi was experiencing a crisis of his own that summer. He was forty-five, the same age as some of the men who were starting second families or marrying divorcees with ready-made broods of children. Yet even bachelors cocooned by work and friendships were not proof against the doubts that could attack men of his age. 'One is not usually conscious of such a crisis,' he wrote later of Edward Lear's depressive fit at forty-five '– the male menopause as it is called – in one's own case, at least until it is over.'[1]

As a Jesuit priest, he was spending much of that summer in Brixton Prison. The Provisional IRA's terror campaign on the English mainland showed no sign of letting up. Explosions in shops, cars, offices, Underground trains and pubs had killed dozens of people in the past few years and injured hundreds more. London attracted most of the bombing, and the top security wing at Brixton was full of terrorists who had been caught. They were all officially Catholics, so it was his job to try to minister to them, as well as to ordinary Catholic prisoners, as holiday relief for their usual chaplain, his tough Jesuit friend and contemporary Tony Lawn.

Some of the smarter London priests were known to enjoy a quick brush with prison life. Peter, too, had once found the prospect of a real man's job exciting. 'How have I never been to prison in my life?' he had written jauntily to a friend three years earlier.

> Arrested yes, in Foustat (Cairo), on the steps of the Cathedral (Benghazi), held (Corfu & Athens), deported, summonsed

(as a boy with an airgun in the woods), & arrested at sea by Admiralty marshals (Cowes 1973), but never once in jug. Can we all be more adequate than we think?[2]

He had been introduced to the inmates of the top security wing in stages before dealing with them alone, but this period was the most exhausting he had ever spent. Up and down the long, clanging, openwork staircases he toiled, along caged-in walkways layered with smells of rancid food. His back ached from too little sleep, his feet from the burning of the iron staircase treads through his shoes. The soul-crushing hideousness of the buildings and futility of the regime seemed all the worse for the unremitting heat, which affected life inside the prison as much as it did life outside. Discipline cracked up as the men lay down to sunbathe in the sticky tarmac exercise yards, then climbed on to the roofs of the prison and stayed there, refusing to come down. The place was crammed with remand prisoners from all over London, banged up in twos and threes in high-windowed cells in the stink from slop-buckets and abandoned meals, the vegetable smell of sweat and the thick, unventilated air.

In some moods he found the challenges enjoyable. Sympathetic towards the hot-weather rebels, he did his best to try to mediate between them and the decent, hard-pressed prison staff. Although shocked in principle by terrorists, he learned to read the difference between the hardened ones and the innocent young men they had recruited as stooges. One or two of these even reminded him of boys he had known at school; if he had been Irish, he might have gone the same way. It even surprised him that ordinary prisoners seemed so hostile to the Provisionals, who seemed to imagine they were engaged in the same revolutionary struggle as the British working class.[3]

Yet, as summer shrank into autumn and drought-curled plane leaves littered the pavements, he felt that these weeks had been a waste of time. What difference could you make to men who were so densely evil or stupid that they ought never to be let loose in the world? To murderers numbed by the knowledge that they had been sent down for life? To their desperate visiting wives and girlfriends, bringing in wafts of stale frying-oil, cigarette smoke, exhaust fumes and cheap shampoo? He had no impersonal religious love to offer, of the kind he was expected to carry round with him like a portable Mass-kit. What cheered him most was the realization that he had learnt 'the art of liking people in place of the theology of loving them,'[4] and that a few of the prisoners, instead of fearing him as an authority-figure, actually seemed to like him back.

For his dark good looks, dark suit and clerical collar hid an unconventional kind of Jesuit. Although rarely asked to perform pastoral duties, he had always felt for sufferers when he came across them – meths-drinkers living rough in a Manchester winter, neglected families of political prisoners of the Greek junta. Because it was not his job to offer them practical help, much of his sympathy had gone into intense, sometimes apocalyptic poems. Given to preaching impassioned, deeply personal public sermons in verse, he did not fit the pattern of the clever, smoothly spoken priests at the church of the Immaculate Conception in Farm Street, Mayfair, from whose clergy house, the English Jesuit headquarters in Mount Street, he went daily to work at the prison.

Somehow, since entering the novitiate at seventeen, he had hollowed out an idiosyncratic cave for himself within the mountain of Jesuit discipline. Craving love, recognition and attention, he had lavished his interest on friends in the outside world, dedicated poems to them and encouraged or sought encouragement from fellow-poets. Nearly every poem he had published had reappeared that spring, with new additions, in his *Collected Poems, 1955-1975*. His determination to assemble everything in one volume, while assuming that half his creative life still lay ahead, showed how seriously he took his own achievements. 'If a poet wants to be believed, not to be applauded, he must inevitably wish to present the whole corpus of his writings,' he had declared in a self-justifying prefatory note. It would be 'gratuitous' (he had added) to limit the circulation of his poems by letting any pamphlet or collection remain out of print. Perhaps, having reached the point in life at which most men had families and a stake in the future, he was indulging the need of a published monument of his own.

Most of his fans were gentle, romantic or contemplative types. Some had felt curious about his earliest poems, with the byline 'Peter Levi, S.J.', in *Encounter* and the intellectual weeklies. Jesuits with Jewish surnames were unusual in England, as were members of religious orders with a pointedly secular presence in the literary world. Others had come across him at Oxford, where he taught classics at the Jesuit house of studies, Campion Hall, or through his book reviews or the collections of poetry he had published from 1960 onwards. They enjoyed his sensitivity to landscape, sharp-edged imagery, flowing rhythms and bursts of experimentation or naked feeling. His more indulgent seniors liked to call him 'our other poet', as if to compensate for the wretched life and premature death in exile of the nineteenth-century Jesuit poet Gerard Manley Hopkins. A few years earlier Frances Horovitz, just emerging as a finely observant lyric poet, had been told 'with bated breath' (as she recounted) that Mick Jagger, at the peak of his fame, had seen a pamphlet of her poems and would like to meet her. She had been unimpressed. 'Now, if it had been Peter Levi...'[5]

He had been lucky in his poetry publisher for the past eight years, Peter Jay, the founder and editor of Anvil Press. William Cookson's magazine *Agenda*, to which he often contributed, supported him consistently in reviews. The hardest criticism came from the camp of Ian Hamilton, a sparingly published poet and notoriously savage critic. Hamilton and his disciples scorned the fact that, while so many of Peter's poems suggested yearnings for intimacy with friends, he hid those feelings behind meditations on landscape or outbursts of moralizing. They were irritated by his copious output, and by stylistic quirks such as lines that began with a verb but contained no subject. They cringed at his religious rhetoric and found his left-wing posturing feeble. That July, the *New Review* carried a full-on attack on the *Collected Poems* by Colin Falck, condemning their 'mannered obscurities', 'unpoetical abstractions' and failure to engage authentically with real life. By becoming a Jesuit, Falck asserted, Peter had censored his imagination and so destroyed his own future as a poet.

This was not the first time someone had sneered at his celibacy in print. His friend and literary hero Cyril Connolly had done so several years earlier, to his embarrassment, in a *Sunday Times* review. It was as if those critics gave him a choice: join the sexual swim and grow up, or stop pretending to have anything of poetical value to say.

℀

From London he returned at weekends to Oxford, in its own bowl of greyish-yellow summer smog. The parched stubble-fields of the Thames valley were dotted with newly industrial-looking straw bales that made him feel the whole countryside was changing. Gaunt remnants of hedgerow trees killed by Dutch elm disease had been left to rot where they stood, unlike the felled Broad Walk elm avenue in Christ Church Meadow. Change had been rampant in Oxford in the past few years, obliterating streets and squares of nineteenth-century workmen's houses to erect the hideous Westgate shopping centre at one end of the street where he lived. But Campion Hall was still the secretive, priestly institution he had known since the 1950s, where he expected to continue living and teaching until superannuated to a Jesuit retirement home.

The room in which he slept, wrote and sometimes tutored was on

6

the first floor of an old house adjoining the twentieth-century main building. It was crammed with books in nine or ten languages: Greek and Latin texts and scholarly commentaries on them, history, novels, religion, philosophy and poetry, and his vital notebooks. Books had colonized the bed, which he had decided was too short, preferring to sleep on the floor. On a westerly wind, with the window open over the garden, he could smell the nourishing scent of malting from the breweries in St. Thomas's and hear the hooting of diesel trains from the station. Ten minutes' walk away was the Bodleian Library, with its collections of precious manuscripts and early printed books. A little farther, across Christ Church Meadow, was the Botanic Garden, where he loved to see the leaves of the actinidia against the wall near the north-west corner turning pink, white and green like a Neapolitan ice cream in early summer. As he limped up St. Aldates and along the High Street, recognizing the odd familiar face among the crowds of tourists and summer-school students, he was at home.

Or partly at home, since for several months each winter he lived as a poet, scholar and friend of poets in Greece. At first he had maintained a balance between the two parts of his life, but things had become unstable lately. Personal and political impulses had pulled him first one way, then another. His long, exuberant, confessional letters had dwindled into enigmatic postcards. Four years earlier he had told his oldest Jesuit friend that he felt 'like an out of control bicyclist enveloped in a bee swarm.'[6] He had taken on too much, but was not yet ready to give anything up for fear of losing part of his life he might regret.

Towards the end of that drought-stricken August he began to wonder where his true vocation lay. He had written no poems for months and felt no new ones stirring. Perhaps the *Collected Poems, 1955-1975* would be the tombstone, not the half-way marker, of his career as a published poet. His ambitious Greek scholarly project seemed to have backed itself into a ditch. His experience in Brixton that summer had convinced him that he was useless as a priest. Despite the growing exodus from the religious life of priests, monks, friars and nuns, he regarded his own vows as cast-iron. Yet something in his life needed to give way, even though so much of its substance rested on decisions his father had made before he was born.

1
CONSTANTINOPLE

My grandparents were called Moses and Sultana: he was from
Istanbul but she was from Leghorn.
A Bottle in the Shade (1996) 199

Bert Levi, a divorced Sephardic Jew with a family business importing
oriental carpets, was forty-four when he married his much younger
second wife Mollie Tigar at the Uxbridge Registry Office on May 12,
1928. His first marriage had taken place just over sixteen years earlier
at his family's traditional place of worship, the Bevis Marks Spanish
and Portuguese synagogue in the city of London, just round the corner
from his warehouse and offices in Houndsditch. His bride, Katie
Brighton, a twenty-year-old tobacconist's daughter from Croydon, had
converted to Judaism to marry him and taken the name of Ruth. Bert's
parents, Moses and Sultana, also lived in Croydon, and the couple's
two children, Maurice and Pamela, were born there in 1915 and 1917.

After the First World War, in which Bert served briefly and not
very gloriously in the Royal Flying Corps, he had moved Katie and the
children to join his widowed mother and siblings in a scattered colony
of Levi households in Cricklewood and Kilburn. His marriage had not
survived the move, and after the break-up he had retired to a bachelor
flat in Frognal, looked after by a devoted manservant who (as Mollie's
ex-stockbroker father noticed) fiddled the household accounts.

Mollie, an ardent, twenty-five-year-old cradle Catholic, resisted
suggestions from Bert's family that she might take up Judaism. Ignoring
the fact that the Catholic Church did not recognize registry office
weddings and would have refused to marry her to a divorced man
whose former wife was presumed to be still alive, she was married, not
from her widowed father's house at Harrow, but from the house Bert
had bought for them to live in, 61 Kings End, Ruislip. Within a year

Bert was also a Catholic, and from that point onwards their household was fiercely, observantly religious. Mollie saw to it that their marriage had a Catholic blessing, and Bert liked to joke about the way in which she kept dragging him off to church to get married again. Generally, however, he was devout, as he had learnt to be during his Jewish childhood. The house bristled with crucifixes, holy-water stoups and statues. 'It wasn't enough for my parents just to practise their religion, they had to let it hang out of the window,' said their daughter Gillian, a nun.

Bert was not only a middle-aged father with a complicated past; he was also the youngest of at least ten children, five or more of whom had been born in Constantinople before Moses and Sultana moved their family to England in 1878. Bert and Mollie's three children, Anthony, Peter and Gillian, never knew their Levi grandparents and barely met any of their father's siblings. The 'St John's Wood aunts', famous in the family for their Turkish rose-petal jam, were in fact the children's first cousins, being the unmarried daughters of Bert's eldest sister Victoria, who had died before he and Mollie were married. And once Peter had made friends in his late twenties with another first cousin in her late fifties, the satirical novelist and theatre-writer Caryl Brahms, he told David Pryce-Jones that he had 'an aunt *whom you must meet.*'[1]

'Because my father was quite well off then,' he wrote sadly about his childhood, 'and a Jewish businessman who had made his friends long ago, we knew rather few people in Ruislip; but because he was also a Catholic, we had very few Jewish friends, and saw only a few of his vast family.'[2]

Not surprisingly he knew little about Bert's background, guessing vaguely that he had been born 'probably in Croydon or in Hackney.'[3] He knew that Croydon was where Bert had grown up, but sensed that North London came into the story somewhere. Discouraged by Mollie from dwelling on his earlier life, Bert had let fall only scraps of reminiscence – about a Yiddish street game a small girl had taught him in some Jewish neighbourhood; about the old man who used to go round the oriental warehouses in the City of London selling *halva, pistachio nuts, loukoum*.[4]

Imagination filled in the gaps. Peter was thrilled that, in the office of Levi Sons at 58 Houndsditch, his father still had a business letter-heading with the words 'and at Constantinople'. As a child he yearned for the city his grandparents had left, with its carpet-traders and foreign steamers, its Turkish coffee and Latakia tobacco, and its polyglot babble of Armenian, Greek, Arabic, Ladino, Bulgarian, Turkish and French. Passing through Istanbul in 1969, he chatted in French to a cosmopolitan carpet-repairer in a small shop in a back street, and persuaded himself that his grandfather must have had one like it.[5] Moses, however, had been an importer and wholesaler of carpets, with a warehouse but probably never a shop. As a young man he had travelled between Constantinople, the carpet-trading cities of the Near and Middle East and the burgeoning market for oriental luxuries in London. In Moscow in 1989, Peter thought his imposing, old-fashioned hotel must be like the ones his grandfather had stayed in.[6] And in Greece for the last time, buying sweet, seedless grapes (*soultania*), he thought once again about the grandparents he had never known, whose genes had given him his olive colouring, his catarrhal reaction to English winter damp and his love of dry, intense summer heat.[7]

For centuries, Eastern Mediterranean merchants like Moses Levi had moved between Athens, Salonica, Smyrna, Constantinople, the Black Sea ports and the cities of Syria and Egypt. Other Sephardic communities, especially those in Italy and Holland, had sent merchants to England from the middle of the seventeenth century, after Cromwell's government lifted the medieval ban on Jews. In 1701 the newly built Bevis Marks synagogue became the spiritual centre of the Sephardic community in London. Later, with steam navigation, rail travel and the growth of commerce and industry, England attracted ever larger numbers of Sephardic and Ashkenazic Jews. The Sephardim moved westwards from the City into Bloomsbury, Bayswater and Marylebone, while the poorest, mainly Yiddish-speaking Ashkenazim filled up the East End. Even before the Anglo-Ottoman alliance and its involvement in the Crimean War, Jewish merchant families in the Ottoman Empire had begun to name their daughters Victoria and their sons Victor, while looking towards England, the most prosperous and stable country in Europe, as the place for opportunity and a new home.

Both Moses and Sultana Levi had been born in Constantinople. Sultana belonged to a Sephardic mercantile family, the Jourados, from which her daughter Victoria's husband Moses presumably also came. As the London censuses from 1881 onwards give her birthplace as Constantinople (apart from that of 1901, which mistakenly gives it as Bishopsgate), Leghorn must have been a family myth. She may have married at fourteen, or possibly two or three years later.* In the 1881 census her eldest child Isaac's age is given as twenty, and hers and her husband's as thirty-five and thirty-eight – if this Isaac was indeed their son and not one of many visiting cousins and nephews who used the house as a base for establishing themselves in the carpet and textile trades. A fourteen-year-old Isaac Levi, also born in Constantinople, and perhaps the twin of fourteen-year-old Victoria, was boarding at that time at a Jewish academy in Northwick Terrace, St. John's Wood.

Caryl Brahms, who loved tall stories, perpetuated a myth about her grandparents' arrival in England which many people seem to have accepted without question. Born Doris Caroline Abrahams, she was the only child of Moses and Sultana's third daughter Pearl, who had

---

* Accounts of their ages vary. Moses was said to be 70 when he died late in 1914, and Sultana to be 77 when she died early in 1922. But the censuses from 1881 onwards suggest that Moses was probably born in 1842, and so lived to be 71 or 72. In the 1901 census he and Sultana were said to be 59 and 57, although previous censuses had made Sultana three or four years younger than him.

briefly enraged her mother by marrying an Ashkenazic East End Jew. As a child she had often stayed with the grandparents at Croydon, practising the piano in the hope of reaching concert standard. After failing at this she reinvented herself as Caryl Brahms and began to write musicals, plays and joky historical fiction. Tiny, hook-nosed, sharp-chinned and witty, she liked working with male collaborators but never married. Light comedy was her speciality, and telling wildly exaggerated stories about her family her idea of fun.

In her version of the story, Moses had moved to London as a carpet importer on his own, leaving Sultana in Constantinople and fathering sixteen children on annual visits home. Because he had a mistress in London he did not tell Sultana where he lived, but she knew that he worked for Maples in the Tottenham Court Road. Exasperated with her situation, she chartered a ship, filled it with her sixteen children, rose-bushes and household goods, and arrived without warning in England. Depositing herself on Maples' doorstep, she summoned the manager and demanded to be taken to her husband.[8]

More prosaically, Moses and Sultana probably arrived in England together, with their children Isaac, Victoria, Sarah, Pearl and Nissim (later Ned). Their first home was at 2 Newton Villas, Finsbury Park, then a leafy, spacious area between Green Lanes and the Seven Sisters Road, soon to be redeveloped as the late nineteenth-century Brownswood Park. A sixth child, Rosie, was born at 2 Newton Villas, followed in the next six years by Laura, Lewis, Lionel and Herbert Simon (Bert). Although Rosie seems to have escaped registration, all the censuses confirm her birth year as 1878, the year in which Moses became a signed-up member of the congregation of Bevis Marks.

By the 1890s the Finsbury Park neighbourhood was beginning to go downhill. Bevis Marks was also losing much of its congregation as Sephardic Jews moved westwards into Bayswater and Maida Vale. Moses resigned from Bevis Marks in 1884, probably on moving his family to 31 Warrington Crescent, Maida Vale, a tall terraced house which required a young staff of six (a Swiss butler, a governess, a nursemaid, two housemaids and a cook) instead of the two maids of all work they had managed with in Newton Villas. Their nearest Sephardic synagogue was in Bryanston Street near Marble Arch, until a big new replacement opened in Lauderdale Road, Maida Vale in 1896.

By the mid-1880s Moses was managing his own business, Levi Brothers, at 13 Bury Street, St. Mary Axe. As an importer of 'Turkish & Persian rugs, carpets & oriental articles', he aimed to profit from the huge demand for such things from the furnishers of large to medium-sized houses, common-rooms, boardrooms, private libraries, mess-rooms and gentlemen's clubs. His first partner may have been his elder brother Abraham, who was staying with him in Maida Vale when the census-taker came round in 1891. By then, however, Victoria had married the Constantinople-born Moses Jourado, who was employed, probably by her father, as a commercial clerk. Within a few years the firm had become Levi, Jourado & Co., based in 1895 at 21 Bevis Marks, in 1899 at 29 St. Mary Axe and in 1905 at 19 Camomile Street, all within the same small part of the City, with other carpet-dealing firms nearby.

Bert seems never to have mentioned Maida Vale to his children, although he must have spent half his childhood and part of his adolescence there. Perhaps he suppressed the memory of a family crisis in June 1898, when Sultana brought a divorce petition against Moses. Nothing seems to have come of that, except that she, Moses and the younger children left Maida Vale for a surprisingly modest house in Morland Road, East Croydon, re-attaching themselves to Bevis Marks. Isaac, probably finding the climate intolerable, had left England to work as a photographer in Italy. Victoria, Sarah and Pearl had all married and left home. Not long after the move to Croydon, Laura was married at Bevis Marks to a member of the carpet-dealing

Behar family from Constantinople. Ned's girlfriend Lettice, already the mother of a year-old daughter, Sultana, took the name Leah for their belated Jewish wedding at 28 Morland Road. Rosie was cast out by her mother for becoming a Christian and died in 1909 as an Anglican nun. Meanwhile the Levi-Jourado alliance had come to a sticky end. Victoria and her husband, who had named one of their North London houses 'The Bosphorus' and had eight Anglo-Turkish children, seem to have separated soon after the youngest was born. Jourado left the family firm to run his own West End carpet business, while Victoria kept their house in West Hampstead before moving to a mansion flat in Cricklewood soon after the end of the First World War.[9]

Moses, dapper and neatly bearded, with an oriental fluidity of movement and a seductive twinkle, looks handsome and confident in a portrait photograph that probably dates from just before the family crisis. Sultana was pale and elegant, while her daughters, like craggy Ned, were generally stocky and strong-featured with black or iron-grey hair. Bert inherited smooth good looks from both parents. As the reliable youngest son, he went to work for the family firm as soon as he was old enough to leave school. This did not simply involve dull clerking; Ned, the firm's commercial traveller, went regularly to Constantinople and other carpet centres such as Tabriz, and in 1898 was said to have shipped beer up the Nile to the British troops at Omdurman.[10]

When Bert was in his early twenties Moses ordered him to Malaya to sort out the affairs of a rubber plantation he had acquired. Bert blamed the experience for his premature baldness, wrecked digestion, chronic ill-health and proneness to sudden violent fits of rage. In 1911, when Moses was nearly seventy, the company changed its name from Levi & Co. of 20 Camomile Street to Levi Sons of 58 Houndsditch. With his three elder brothers as sleeping partners, Bert eventually took over as managing director. Moses, who died in the autumn of

1914, spent his short retirement in comfort at 9 Park Hill Rise, East Croydon, which Caryl remembered as 'a huge house with a large room for a bath-room... and the apple-trees in the garden with Grandpa's special apples'.[11] Bert had lived there until he married Katie, and may sometimes have spoken of it nostalgically as the home of his carefree youth.

❧

While Moses and Sultana were filling 2 Newton Villas with children, a wholesale draper's clerk, Joseph Decimus Tigar, his Roman Catholic wife Anne and their family were living in the same road in north-west Kentish Town as Karl Marx. Maitland Park Road, with its flat-fronted terrace houses, slants north-eastwards uphill from the lower end of Haverstock Hill, while its grander offshoot Maitland Park Villas runs north into Southampton Road, Gospel Oak. The Dominican Priory in Southampton Road, built in 1867, and its big parish church, finished in 1883, must have been central to the lives of Joseph's wife and her children, one of whom Peter remembered from his childhood as an ancient former Dominican missionary living in a friary in Leicester.[12]

Both the Marxes and the Tigars had moved into Maitland Park Road in the 1860s after renting in a scruffier neighbourhood nearby. Rescued from poverty by an inheritance, Marx and his wife Jenny moved in 1864 to a large, detached house at the Haverstock Hill end of the road, where Marx reworked much of his failed critique of political economy, publishing the first volume of *Das Kapital* in Hamburg in 1867. For the last eight years of his life, however, with most of their children grown up, they lived at 41 Maitland Park Road, near the Tigars at 27. Both Marx and Peter's great-grandfather Joseph Tigar lived well into their sixties and must have recognized one another as neighbours, if no more.

In 1890, the year after Joseph died, his Catholic stockbroker son Walter married Mary Agnes Clarke. The couple settled with Walter's mother and his unmarried eldest sister at 23 Maitland Park Villas, where they had five sons. Two of the boys were killed in the First World War and one died at home during the war. In 1902, when their sixth and last child, Edith Mary (Mollie), was on the way, Walter and Mary left the urban grime of Kentish Town and followed the Metropolitan Line to a new, northern suburban development on the Wealdstone side of Harrow.

Peter's friends knew the bare facts of his family background: the pious household in thrall to his mother, who seemed responsible for setting him on course for the priesthood; the bluff, amiable, alcoholic, Jewish-turned-Catholic father. Other stories about his ancestry were as liable to be invented as true, being based on family myths that he casually included in his memoir *The Flutes of Autumn*. Obituaries attributed his dark good looks to Spanish or Cornish blood, on the basis of a story that the Tigars were descended from a Spanish sailor who had been shipwrecked off the Cornish coast and named Tigar after the ship's dog.[13]

Tigar, an Old English name mystifyingly interpreted as 'people-spear', in fact belonged to a group of families who, until the early nineteenth century, lived almost entirely in a small area of East Yorkshire. Tall, fair-haired, solidly built types like Mollie, with distinctive local surnames, still populate the area around Beverley and Hull. Joseph Decimus was the fifteenth child, and apparently the tenth to survive, of William and Elizabeth Tigar, Nonconformists of Beverley. His father seems to have died at about the time Joseph was born in 1821. His mother appears in a directory of 1823 as a straw-hat maker. Four of her unmarried children either stayed in the town or returned there, including a daughter who sold spirits and a son who was a hosier and hatter. Their prosperous uncle Pennock Tigar, a grocer and chemist and founder of a local paint-manufacturing firm, was buried at the big town church in 1851. Other relatives, some of them Dissenters, lived in Hull. Joseph worked briefly in Hull as a living-in draper's clerk, then moved in his early twenties to London, where he married Anne Mary Borchert, a Catholic of partly Continental, possibly half-German descent.[14]

A single marriage between a Catholic and a non-Catholic could change a family's history for generations. Most children of such marriages were automatically brought up as Catholics and discouraged from marrying non-Catholics. Even if they ignored this advice, they often did so to the Church's advantage. Sermons in Catholic churches against the evils of mixed marriages, like those against the evils of Communism, were largely pointless. Many non-Catholics became converts after marriage, and cradle Catholics who lapsed did not always do so as a result of marrying outside the faith.

Joseph and Anne Tigar had two daughters, then six sons, two of whom died young. All four of the surviving sons remained staunch Catholics. The Dominican, Herbert, served for years in the South African missions. The stockbroker Walter became Peter's maternal grandfather. The two eldest, Edward, a minor Treasury official, and Joseph, an art-dealer, married sisters from Beverley, Clare and Florence Wharton, and settled near one another in Stroud Green and Crouch End, North London. Edward and Clare's youngest child, Clement (1892-1976), was schooled by the Jesuits at St. Ignatius's College, Stamford Hill, and became the popular Catholic apologist Father Clem Tigar. Joseph and Florence's eldest, Gilbert (1890-1942), was the family's second Dominican friar.

It was through Gilbert that Bert Levi, representing the heavily pregnant Mollie, attended the consecration of the new Blackfriars chapel in St. Giles, Oxford in the spring of 1929. The solemn, welcoming charm of the Dominicans and the simple numinousness of their chapel, with its barrel-vaulted, light-filled ceiling and Perpendicular chancel window, acted powerfully on Bert and made him decide to become a Catholic, too.

❧

How did Bert and Mollie meet? Their daughter Gillian never knew. Nor did her cousin, Lionel's daughter, the theatrical photographer Zoë Dominic, who was a child when her Uncle Bert remarried. Perhaps Mollie had done a secretarial course, as nice suburban girls did, and gone to work for Bert in Houndsditch. Even her middle-aged Tigar maiden aunt had described herself in the 1901 census as a literary typist. Perhaps, in a quiet corner of the office, Bert had put his arms round the tall, shy, awkward virgin and told her about the wife who had walked out on him, taking the children. Or perhaps they had met through Mollie's father Walter, who had lost his stockbroking business when caught out with foreign securities on the outbreak of the First World War. Peter wrote that his grandfather never worked properly again, but could still offer private advice, as he did when he noticed that Bert's domestic accounts showed unusually large outgoings one Christmas.

The North London Levi colony had almost dispersed by the time Mollie came on the scene. During the First World War Ned and Pearl had moved their families from the Essex coast to Cricklewood and Kilburn. Lewis also lived in Cricklewood; Sultana moved there from Croydon; and Bert and Victoria joined them after the war. But Sultana died in 1922, and Victoria five years later. Perhaps she and her sister Pearl, an embroidery enthusiast, who later retired to the Mediterranean and died, trapped, in Vichy France, had been the sharp-eyed, deaf, elderly-seeming ladies, with an equally deaf servant and a garden full of Turkish roses, whom Gillian placed farther south, next to the Abercorn telephone exchange, as the original generation of St. John's Wood aunts. Clumsy young Mollie met these relations of Bert's and was intimidated by their critical glances as they sat upright, beadily stitching floral cushion-covers in *petit-point*. To her they seemed alarmingly foreign in the stuffiness of their crowded sitting-room, whereas Bert, with his elegant charm and jovial manner, was the complete, relaxed Englishman.

The most helpful member of the Levi family was Ned. His younger brothers, the antique-dealers Lewis and Lionel, were absorbed in their businesses. Ned, sea-loving, rugged and generous, had kept his wartime refuge in Cricklewood but returned to live on Canvey Island in a large house he called Kismet. His wife Lettice either became a Catholic convert or returned to practising her original faith, and Ned was sympathetic towards it. In 1922 he sent their fifteen-year-old son Maurice to finish his education with the Jesuits at Beaumont College in Old Windsor, and sixteen-year-old Pearl to a convent at Namur. Well-disposed towards the Catholic priest of nearby Leigh-on-Sea, Father Francis Gilbert, who was responsible for the Canvey Island Catholics, Ned gave him space to hold Masses at Kismet, and contributed to the cost of building a Catholic church on the island after he and Lettice retired to Poole.

Brought in by Ned to help Bert and Mollie, Father Gilbert advised them to go ahead and marry in a registry office. From an orthodox Catholic viewpoint Mollie would be putting her immortal soul in danger by living in sin with a divorcee. From a practical point of view, he thought there would be nothing as effective as a *fait accompli* for persuading the hierarchy that, rather than being excommunicated for life, she should be forgiven and her marriage should be blessed.

2
CATHOLIC CHILD

Gardens and roads when I was three
first lured my wandering sense to spin
these crystals of maturity
to expose imagination in.

'For Peter Hacker', *Agenda May-June* 1962

The builders were in when I reached the former 61 Kings End, Ruislip. Most of the houses in that road once had both names and numbers, and many front gates still had small plates attached to them bearing the names of British beauty spots, or proclaiming 'No Hawkers', 'No Circulars' or 'Beware of the Dog'. Number 61, which the Levis knew as Wardington, had gained an integral garage and been renumbered 61A, since a neighbouring house had been inserted into the space where Bert's garage used to stand. Similar thrifty reuses of space were happening all down Kingsend (as the name is spelt now). Several houses had been demolished, and their boarded-up sites with scalped gardens were waiting to be filled up with new homes. Cars and vans sped up and down a rat-run that was once a quiet, leafy road, along which Peter, aged five, used to take himself home from school, chatting affably to any adult neighbour he met. In his cap and tiny tweed uniform jacket with an intertwined SD on the pocket for St. Dominic's Convent, Harrow, he must have looked as he does in a set of Polyfotos taken at that time: alert, button-bright and confident, with a different amused, dark-eyebrowed, quizzical expression in each shot.

Nice ladies smiled enquiringly as I passed them in the road, but 61A looked shabby, its white-painted brickwork discoloured by a slick of green mould. Someone had replaced the small-paned Edwardian casements with doubled-glazed ones enclosing imitation glazing-bars. Squeezing past the clutter of skips and vans round the open front door, I followed the side passage into the back garden. Between old apple trees and a broken concrete path, the grass had been left to grow long. There was a stack of old bricks, a pile of ripped-out planks, a bonfire heap of smaller wooden pieces, two dilapidated deckchairs and a scatter of dumped conservatory furniture. Above the ground-floor back windows a new, verandah-like roof was being built, perhaps replacing the roof of the sun lounge that Bert added after the war as his private retreat for afternoon rest and prayer. The builders were drilling in one of the rooms below this, and it wasn't long before I heard a rap on the glass and an enquiring shout of 'Oi!'

⁊

That suburban road was twenty years old when Bert and Mollie's middle child, Peter Chad Tigar Levi, was born at home on May 16, 1931. Ruislip was classic Metroland: a place for new starts, rootless but respectable upbringings, families from anywhere and everywhere. Not all the Catholic congregation was Irish ('We have no Irish in our family,' stressed Mollie); a near neighbour, Anthony's godmother, was a French lady who worked in Selfridges' hat department.[1] Although the country began nearby, the local vowel-sound was the outer London ee-ow, which Peter claimed he never entirely lost. The dazzling white concrete of the Uxbridge Lido, to which a nursemaid used to take the children by bus, typified the modernity of the area, along with Bert's favourite watering-hole The Orchard, a Tudor-style roadhouse conveniently near home at the crossroads at the top of Kings End, and Ruislip High Street with its large red-brick cinema and parade of mock-half-timbered, gabled shops.

Peter's elder brother, Anthony Herbert Tigar Levi, was born on May 30, 1929. He took after Bert and was Mollie's favourite. Big, solid and dark-haired, he became a coping, efficient boy, drily intelligent and ambitious. Peter was a quicksilver, more feminine child, with his slight, thin figure, Sephardic olive skin and dark eyes, and long English nose like the tall, fair, long-nosed Mollie's. Gillian Mary, three years younger than Peter, inherited the olive skin with a chubbier version of Mollie's long, thin face. All three, especially asthmatic Anthony, were prone to chest complaints. Like other controlling mothers of her time, Mollie believed in keeping children in bed for several days' recovery after any temperature, rash or other symptom of illness had disappeared.

The family attended Mass together, at first at the tiny, makeshift Catholic church in the High Street, then from 1938 at its new, Romanesque replacement, the Church of the Most Sacred Heart in Pembroke Road. Both Anthony and Peter were sent to a small Catholic kindergarten before moving into the lowest forms of the girls' convent day-school at Harrow, the usual pattern for middle-class Catholic boys who were too young to go away to prep school. They caught a bus to Harrow from Ruislip station, opposite the bottom of Kings End, and dawdled home from the station bus-stop on their own.

Catholic children made their first communion aged seven or eight, in white dresses and veils for girls and neat, short-trousered suits for boys. On each occasion Mollie gave a lunch party at The Orchard, inviting her brother Fred and his family from Wimbledon and probably also her cousin Father Clem. It was one of the many gatherings from which Bert's relations were absent, and he may have slipped away to the bar with a wry sense of being outnumbered.

The Levi children were pious and good. The entire household deferred to Mollie's simple, strong convictions, despite Bert's occasional, man-to-man murmurs of 'Don't tell y'mother'. Family solidarity was important in that suburban setting, and the Levis set an example to laxer members of the Catholic congregation through their consistent attendance at confession, Mass, Benediction and the all-age parish socials at which Anthony did conjuring tricks and Peter, at ten or eleven, recited his own poems.

Bright Catholic boys, especially from lower middle-class backgrounds, were often marked out early as future priests. Anthony would take over the business and the headship of the family, leaving Peter to pursue a different career. And Mollie, with her family background, was unquestioningly in favour of the priesthood. Father Clem Tigar, a priest of stridently simple, sentimental faith, was principal of an austere Jesuit seminary for late vocations, Campion House at Osterley, and leader of a devotional organization called The Knights, Handmaidens and Pages of the Blessed Sacrament. His cult of the Elizabethan Catholic martyrs, in whose honour he led pilgrimages, shared the same spirit, to Mollie, as the commemoration of the dead in battle.

> They were like the Catholic martyrs. They were like her brothers. Courage was so automatic one never questioned what it was... Faith was absolute and tranquil. She breathed gallantry like a dragon breathing fire.[2]

A priest's devotion to the faith would shed glory on his family, while his celibate, self-sacrificing existence would preclude all rivals to his mother's affection, earning him an almost guaranteed place in heaven on his death.

It was not all Mollie's doing, however. Peter had begun to play at being a priest long before the age of ten, by which time (he wrote in his late twenties) he had 'wanted to be a priest and expected to be a poet.'[3] To a small Catholic boy a priest was the supreme authority-figure, mysterious, untouchable and holy. He could channel divine forgiveness even to the invented sins of seven-year-olds, and at the moment of consecration at Mass could transform the bread and wine into the body and blood of Jesus Christ. Every day he would say his office and recite the Latin liturgy of the Mass, whose rhythms and incontrovertible statements were engraved on Catholic children's minds long before they were able to translate them into English. As soon as he could remember the opening lines of the Mass, sprinkle his congregation from a pretend holy-water bucket and clank an imaginary thurible, Peter used to dress up in robes and officiate in front of a makeshift altar to a congregation of Gillian and her dolls. Although girls were not allowed to serve Mass he appointed Gillian as his server, but when she turned out not to know the responses he said them for her and pretended the dolls were answering him.

ɛ৲১

By the time Anthony reached his eighth birthday and had outgrown the top mixed form at the Harrow convent, the whole family needed a change. Bert's irritable shouting-fits were on the increase, which made Anthony's asthma attacks worse. Perhaps the strain of supporting two families, keeping the business going during the Depression and being forbidden by the Church to use artificial contraception was more than Bert could bear. Certainly he was drinking more, spending weekends at The Orchard and stockpiling his garage with bottles. The family doctor suggested that Anthony might do better if sent away to prep school. Where Anthony went, Peter insisted he must go too, so Bert and Mollie had to find a school in a healthy area with a junior form that would accept a boy as young as six.

Until then they may have avoided thinking much about the boys' education. All the best Catholic schools were outside London, and none of the middling ones was within easy reach. After moving from Kentish Town, where the Dominicans had a school next to the Priory, Mollie's brothers had attended the non-denominational John Lyon grammar school in Harrow. Fred's sons went as day-boys to the Jesuit-run Wimbledon College, but that was a long way from Ruislip. Ned's lively, athletic son Maurice had got into trouble at Beaumont, which seemed to rule out both that and its preparatory school, St. John's. Then, again, the whole question of prep schools was tricky. You were expected to choose the right one if you wanted your son to go to Downside, Ampleforth, Beaumont or Stonyhurst at thirteen. Bert and Mollie hadn't a clue where to begin, and even Father Clem, whose seminarians came mainly from humble backgrounds, may have known very little about the Catholic public schools.

Bert, in his big Buick, made a tour of those schools and decided they looked like prisons. He may also have met with a little mildly anti-Semitic condescension from masters whose grandest pupils were the sons of Catholic peers, Spanish princes or Polish counts. Then he thought he had found the perfect compromise, a school in a Palladian mansion in elegant parkland with a dazzling view of a city far below. It consisted of a junior school, St. Peter's, in one wing and a senior school, St. Paul's, in the other, so there need be no fuss about changing schools at thirteen. It was sporting rather than academic and not obviously smart, with a large number of pupils from upwardly mobile Irish families who were not long established in

England. Many old boys, however, achieved solid careers in business, medicine, the army or the priesthood. Mollie was delighted with the level of hygiene, mistaking the boys' urinals for little footbaths. She and Bert also misguidedly assumed that the air there would be good for Anthony's asthma. Because some parents lived overseas or simply could not cope with their young children, the junior school had a Tiny Tots' form supervised by a friendly Irish matron. The school was Prior Park College, just outside Bath, at that time owned by the local Catholic diocese and run by a notoriously brutal teaching order, the Irish Christian Brothers.

❧

When James Joyce arrived as a boarder at Clongowes College in County Kildare, he was asked his age and lisped 'Half past six'.[4] Joyce's father, although he could not afford it, had chosen the Jesuit-run Clongowes to give James the best possible classical education. He would never have sent his six-year-old to the Christian Brothers, since in Ireland their bog-standard day schools were notorious for bullying and violent beatings. In England they seemed comparatively respectable, especially in the setting of Prior Park; yet most of the teachers there were products of the Irish system, and traces of its savagery came out among both boys and masters in the rougher ambience of the senior school.

As adaptable as any other bright six- to eleven-year-old, Peter seemed unquestioningly happy during his first five years at the school. He liked Brother Hayes, the gentle, intelligent housemaster of St. Peter's. Being clever, he was placed in a form of boys two years older than himself, so he raced ahead in Latin, French and Maths without being held back by his age-group. In a photograph of the Tiny Tots he looks quite the tiniest in his Eton collar and long-trousered suit, with neatly combed and flattened hair, almost overwhelmed by the beefy matron in a billowing white headdress next to him. Towards the end of his first year he was cast as the heroine in a form play called *No, John,* looking sweetly sexless in a sunbonnet, short white dress, dimpled knees, white ankle-socks and pumps, demurely dangling a small handbag. There was something inevitable, as he would find in the next fifteen years, about being chosen for willowy female parts in all-male institutional plays.

In the holidays he had Anthony and Gillian for company. He went bicycling with Anthony and played imaginative games with Gillian. Lovingly protective towards her, he called her Donk, short for donkey, and enjoyed the softness she brought into the family, which mitigated Mollie's triumphalism as a mother of boys. He invented stories for her about fairies dropping messages down the nursery chimney, then upset her by telling her that fairies did not really exist. '*Let's pretend* they exist,' he said, and fairies at the bottom of the garden remained their private joke until after they had both grown up.

Passing through Ruislip later, he wondered how they could all have fitted into such a modestly sized house. It sheltered not only the five of them but the three sisters who were their living-in maids: Cissie, Elsie and Aggie Rigg, whose parents sometimes visited from Tyneside, squeezing into odd corners to sleep. Uninhibitedly fond of the family and each other, the Riggs diffused a soothing ordinariness that counteracted Mollie's bossiness and Bert's alternate moods of joviality and rage. Elsie and Cissie looked after the children and did the housework, while grumpy Aggie, the eldest sister, did the cooking. Mollie, free from domestic chores, learned to drive her own small car, which she used for shopping or to take the children to run with the dog on the common or have picnics in the nearest part of the extensive Ruislip Woods.

Ruislip at that time was as far out of north-west London as you could get. Beyond the twentieth-century network of suburban roads radiating from the Metropolitan Line station lay the nucleus of a medieval manorial village which had once belonged to King's College,

Cambridge. There were green lanes and waste spaces, dense woodland to the north, and villages like Ickenham and Harefield, barely touched by development, to the west. From high ground you could look across an expanse of tiled roofs, industrial sprawl and patchy greenness towards the Harrow gasometer, shimmering in the distance like a Norman castle keep. Life in Ruislip depended on regularly travelling somewhere else: to the shops in Harrow or Uxbridge, to the mysterious near-Constantinople of Houndsditch, or to grown-up entertainments in the West End. Peter had a nostalgic, middle-aged fantasy about living there in 1929:

> *somewhere beside the Uxbridge line,*
> *just out of sight,*
> *we would have travelled up to town*
> *and bought orchids for half-a-crown*
> *and danced all night.*[5]

As soon as they were allowed out on their own, the two boys went as far from home as their heavy, gearless bicycles would take them. In the summer there were farm or seaside holidays in Devon, Sussex, North Wales or the Isle of Wight. Peter loved these for the sight and smell of real country, and because Bert relaxed and played cricket and the whole family made discoveries together, forgetting the nervous edginess and prohibitions of suburban life.

When late September came, Bert made a family expedition of driving the boys back to school. Most boarding-school children had to go by train, seen off by their mothers at Paddington or Euston with Protestant murmurs of 'Chin up' or bracing Catholic cries of 'God bless'. 'One thing that made us very jealous of the Levi brothers,' said an older Prior Park pupil, Richard Hudson, 'was the way in which they always arrived back at the beginning of term in a large American car.'

High up to the south of Bath, Prior Park stood out as a backdrop in all the beauty of its deep gold limestone. Built originally for Ralph

Allen, a local magnate and friend of the poet Pope, the house stood in grounds that reflected Pope's taste for manipulating nature. Flanking the porticoed main building, the two wide, nineteenth-century wings that contained the senior and junior schools embraced the prospect of a grassy hillside flanked by woods, plunging exhilaratingly down towards the city. Eighteenth-century tourists used to flock out from Bath to admire the house and the grounds, with their terraces, lawns, embryonic blocks of woodland, sham castle, Gothic temple, grotto, Palladian bridge, serpentine lake and cascade. By the time the Catholic diocese leased the estate to the Christian Brothers in the early 1920s, many of the best features had disappeared or been covered up. But the bones of the place were still there, as were the twenty-foot-high mounds around the playing-fields on Combe Down Hill, which might or might not have been prehistoric defences

As Peter took in the scale and grandeur of Prior Park he realized it was unlike anything he had ever seen before. He also realized that it owed nothing to the Christian Brothers, who were simply its temporary occupants, bringing with them a miniature Ireland of religious authoritarianism, rough games-playing, toothlessly decrepit servants, punishments with a strap on the outstretched hand, and *Hail, Glorious Saint Patrick* and shamrocks on St. Patrick's Day, March 17.

Small boarding-school boys are not usually allowed to stray far even inside their school grounds. Prior Park revealed itself gradually to him, often during afternoon games, when he preferred skulking round the edges of fields to pretending to be a team player. In the summer term there was the sensuous abandon of crawling through tunnels in the thick, seedy grass round the edge of the cricket field, when he was supposed to be fielding on the boundary. In those hiding-places he and his friends went to ground and ate secret feasts of whatever scraps they had hidden in their pockets from breakfast or lunch. Forty-five years later he remembered eating cold left-over sausages in the brilliant summer of 1940, 'while France I suppose fell but never Ireland.'[6]

☙

What makes a poet? On winter evenings early in the war, in the vast, high-ceilinged Round Room full of boys scratching inkily away at their prep, he began to read Scott's poems and ballads, then to imitate their compulsive rhythms. *He is gone on the mountain,/He is lost to the forest,/Like a summer-dried fountain,/When our need was the sorest.* He was in love with the idea of Scotland, of galloping over the heather with dirk and claymore at the ready. When he was reading privately, after finishing his prep, it did not matter that he was the smallest in his class and hated games, or that nobody around him shared his literary passion. Poetry could make him a hero of the imagination.

Like every other small boy in England he was also fascinated by the war. At home he collected bomb fragments and pieces of broken fuselage, and sat up with the family and their howling dog when the sky shook as Hurricanes and Spitfires took off from the Northolt airbase. To train himself for stalking the invader, he joined a scout troop run by a friendly bachelor who later became a Dominican friar. 'At the age of eleven I was a one man Dad's Army.'[7] Fantasizing about hand-to-hand combat with Germans, he took to prowling round the woods with an airgun, ostensibly shooting birds but hoping to meet the odd crashed airman trapped in a tree and take him prisoner with a shout of *Hände hoch!* Instead he got into trouble and the police confiscated his weapon.

> *It was the chestnut tree by the fire station*
> *that used to colour; nutting in August,*
> *shooting at birds in intricate bushes*
> *while the fruit fell and the rough leaves hung on:*
>
> *we used to move by instinct and a smell:*

31

stubble was time, afternoon was airguns
and earth, hedges, it can't have been clouds
were the only thing in life that ran well.[8]

He still wanted to be a priest, but the war made it imperative to be tough and brave as well as clever and good. Although the Irish were neutral, Prior Park boys were fiercely patriotic. One of them, after joining the RAF, looped the loop in a Spitfire over the school; soon afterwards they heard that he had been killed. Admiralty officials in Bath, who had taken over a classroom block for their secret work, fielded teams against the school's first cricket eleven, who always won. The boys knew that heroes of the playing-field would soon be fighters, like the handsome Richard Hudson, a future relation of Peter's by marriage, whom he hero-worshipped for his Englishness and kindness as well as his brilliance as captain of cricket.

Once the raids came very close indeed. Bert's London warehouse escaped the Blitz, but on the night of Saturday, April 25, 1942 the Luftwaffe bombed Bath and destroyed several dormitories in the St. Paul's wing of Prior Park. It was three weeks after Easter, and the summer term was just about to begin. If it had already started, Anthony, in St. Paul's, would almost certainly have been among the dead.

The war drew the family closer together. During the Blitz Uncle Lionel Levi, his wife and their twenty-year-old daughter Zoë took refuge in Kings End from their home in St. John's Wood. The children of Bert's marriage to Katie also paid visits. Maurice ('Boy'), solid and self-reliant, had nearly died of pneumonia after the evacuation of Dunkirk. Bert's anxiety about him stepped up his sentimental patriotism, his tendency to reminisce about the First World War and his reliance on the bottle. At The Orchard, where he had set up his air-raid warden's post, he enjoyed treating the Northolt airmen, and sometimes rolled home with friends for more drinks. Decorous Saturday night dances were laid on for the airmen, at one of which sad, awkward Pamela pushed little Gillian into the Ladies' Excuse-Me, where a massive Pole trod so hard on her foot that it went septic.

Mollie put her car away for the duration, learned to drive an ambulance, do her own housework and wear trousers, and even allowed Anthony and Peter to teach her to bicycle in a lane behind Kings End, until she wobbled and collapsed into the hedge. The three children learned to ride horses, hiring them by the hour from a riding-school and cantering on the Eastcote Grub Grounds or ambling up Ladygate Lane, off the northern continuation of the High Street, where the horses stretched out their necks to snatch at greenstuff in the hedges. Peter, delicate and games-shy, turned out to be a natural, courageous rider, as he appears, smiling and turbaned, between a soldier-guide and Bruce Chatwin, in a photograph in his Afghan travelogue, *The Light Garden of the Angel King.*

3
THE DARKEST PLACE

Who can break loose without a sense of sin?
There was no discipline except living
reason confused, what was obscure was free,
drumbeat of words was the one discipline.

Suburban streets are a kind of forest,
in which religion is the darkest place...

Collected Poems (1976) 151

Thirteen was the usual age for moving up from the junior to the senior school at Prior Park. Peter made the move at eleven, at the beginning of the autumn term of 1942. 'From eleven to fourteen I prayed for death. At fifteen I left,' he said, peering into a dormitory at Prior Park (by then a co-educational Catholic school, no longer run by the Christian Brothers) in his 1989 television series, *Art, Faith and Vision*.

The bullying came first from tough, pubescent, bored thirteen-year-olds, who longed to be fighter pilots and resented having a precocious, airy-fairy small boy among them. One or two of the more bigoted Brothers dropped snide hints about Jews who were too clever for their own good. Serious games became a torture.

Hockey was worse than rugby because of the freezing wind and the showers of hailstones in which it was played. Also because you were hit more suddenly and harder, and the ball, the unwelcome centre of action, was harder to avoid. The plum-faced Irish Brother would scream at you, the other boys would yell derision... The smell of unhappiness is the smell of the bootroom at Prior Park in the 1940s.[1]

To get out of games Peter joined a group who were allowed to help the groundsman, Mr. Haskell, level some of the mounds with pickaxes to make space for more playing-fields. Too small for that kind of work at eleven, he found the tools too heavy, while a biting Cotswold wind lashed the oaks and beeches on the stony hill. But he liked Mr. Haskell, an earthy, sensible Wiltshire countryman, and added him to his collection of working-class heroes together with the Riggs.

He found school work as easy in St. Paul's as he had in the junior school. The Brothers provided a limited but disciplined education, which even included learning some poetry by heart. Boys were beaten if they did not work, and were trundled dutifully through examination syllabuses. At twelve, Peter gained distinctions in French and Maths in the Oxford Junior Locals. At fourteen, still two years ahead of most other boys, he was awarded his School Certificate in seven subjects, with 'A' grades in English Language, Latin and Maths.

Because the Brothers did not aim to turn out classical scholars or intellectuals, they did not include Greek in the curriculum. They sent boys to medical schools and seminaries, but hardly ever to university except to read for vocational degrees. They did, however, lay on elocution lessons to iron out regional and Irish accents into the kind of English that might help people to get good jobs. The teacher was Hedley Goodall, a lively, bearded young man who worked for the BBC in Bristol, sometimes acted in radio plays and later ran his own drama school. This friendly, civilized person, with his pure English intonation, encouraged Peter in his love of poetry and Shakespeare and in his confidence in his own speaking voice, which became ringing, rich and precise. For the Paulites' Christmas Concert in 1945, the fourteen-year-old P. Levi wrote and delivered his own Prologue.[2]

Religion, the 'darkest place' in Peter's poem about his boyhood, was ineradicable from his life. Twenty years later the Brothers' bigotry might have turned him into an atheist, but that rarely happened in Catholic schools of the 1940s, in which doubt was regarded as sinful and conformity was strong. There was pride in the glorious, defiant history of the Catholic recusant martyrs, rousingly evoked in the Victorian hymn *Faith of our Fathers* with its description of deaths by 'dungeon, fire and sword'. The moral burden of the martyrs' example, the fear of Hell, or at least punishment, for backsliding, and the enforcement of religious observance at home and school kept most Catholic children as obedient churchgoers, making weekly confessions and communions and never missing Mass on a Sunday or holiday of obligation unless ill.

So juvenile Catholic rebels like the poet Christopher Logue were rare. Several years older than Peter, Logue briefly overlapped with him at Prior Park, and when he wondered later why they had never been friends Peter replied with teasing anecdotes about an Anti-Logue Society to which he had belonged.[3] The friends he made in St. Paul's were mainly devout, hard-working boys like Patrick, James and Brian Murphy O'Connor, three of the five sons of an Irish doctor and his wife in Reading. In 1944, when Peter was thirteen, he and Brian joined the Sodality of Mary Immaculate, a prayer-society for senior boys of which James was President. James became a rugby-playing doctor, Patrick, Brian and their younger brother Cormac became priests, and Cormac ended his career as Archbishop of Westminster and a cardinal.

Young men who entered the Church sometimes did so because they admired their parish priest. Peter, however, once past his phase of saying Masses in front of a home-made altar, must have noticed that Ruislip presbytery life looked uncomfortably boring and drab. It would be more romantic, he thought, to become a missionary and spend his life converting a tribe in Tibet. A visitor of Bert's, half-way to slipping him the tip that men traditionally gave their friends' schoolboy sons, dropped the half-crown back into his pocket when Peter told him what he wanted to be when he grew up.

After realizing that the Tibetan idea was as unachievable as Shangri-La, he began to think seriously about the Jesuits, whose seventeenth- and eighteenth-century missionaries had indeed reached

Tibet. One obvious role-model was Father Clem, a blunt instrument of the faith with a strong influence on Mollie and her children. But other, remoter Jesuits were known to be subtler and cleverer, especially those attached to the church of the Immaculate Conception in Farm Street. The elderly Father Cyril Martindale had made many ordinary converts through his persuasive radio broadcasts and writings. The glamorous, wickedly handsome Father Martin D'Arcy, Master of Campion Hall in Oxford, had specialized in fashionable converts such as Evelyn Waugh. For centuries the Jesuits had imposed a rigorous form of Catholic education on vast areas of Europe, the Americas, south-east Asia and Japan. They had produced theologians, linguists, scientists, mathematicians, astronomers and missionary explorers and written ground-breaking works of geographical description and natural history. There could be no doubt that they were a cut above the Christian Brothers, from whom Peter longed to escape.

Searching for literary heroes among the books in the senior school library, he came upon Oscar Wilde's *De Profundis*, a lushly aesthetic autobiography of the kind most likely to appeal to a lonely, questing young Catholic. In prison Wilde had begun to read the Gospels in the original Greek. Although they were familiar in this form to most public-school men of his time, Wilde found the language a revelation, as if he were 'going into a garden of lilies out of some narrow and dark house.' He believed that Christ must have spoken Greek as well as Aramaic, and that the simple, repetitive Greek text must be a record of some of his actual words. That was enough for Peter. He longed to begin learning Greek, not as a grudging exception from a half-educated Irish Brother, but from masters who knew the subject and would teach it properly.

Anthony's schooling at Prior Park ended in the summer of 1946. With his School Certificate and years as a senior pupil behind him, he was ready to join Levi Sons. Self-motivated, self-sufficient and largely self-taught, he was fluent in modern languages and good at coping with the practical details of life. At first he lived at home in Ruislip, until Bert packed him off to a branch office in Sheffield. Mollie adored him as her elder son and the perfect product of a Catholic upbringing. Like many self-conscious young Catholics who considered themselves unready for marriage, he remained fiercely chaste. Instead of becoming involved with girls, he put his spare energies into voluntary work for the Society of St. Vincent de Paul, looking after ex-prisoners and tramps. One of the St. John's Wood aunts (perhaps his fifty-year-old cousin Dorothy Jourado in Abercorn Place, or her sister Sultana in Eyre Court, near St. John's Wood station) lent him a key to her flat so that he could sleep in her spare room after evenings out in London.

'And you can bring back a girl-friend if you like,' she offered.

'I most certainly will not.'

'I can't think why not,' she said, amused. 'Your cousins always did.'

❧

To Peter, at fifteen, the end of Anthony's schooling brought the chance to break free from Prior Park. Bert and Mollie had long since lost faith in the Christian Brothers, and as the war was now over they no longer had the excuse for allowing things to muddle on somehow. Persuaded that Peter must learn Greek, they overcame their long-standing objection to Beaumont College and arranged that he should start there that September, to join a small, elite group in the classical sixth.

Beaumont was not a Catholic Eton, although it was a near enough neighbour at Old Windsor, across the buttercup-rich Thames flatlands, to play regularly against Eton at games and compete with its eights on the river. Predominantly middle-class and high-minded, it was smaller and more unassuming than its northern counterpart Stonyhurst. Not many Beaumont boys went to university, and the school had none of

38

the self-indulgent sophistication of pre-war Eton that Cyril Connolly had described in *Enemies of Promise*. Yet to Peter, after nine years of the Christian Brothers, it was heaven.

While Latin is a lapidary language, Greek can be as fluid as the flicker of a lizard on warm stone. To Peter, it became one of the most defining accomplishments of his life. In only a year he gained his Higher School Certificate in Latin, Greek and Roman History, with a consolation-prize pass in Greek History at ordinary level. Outside lessons, he polished his oratorical skills in the Higher Line (senior school) Debating Society. At an OTC training camp at Aldershot, seeing a lieutenant-colonel of the Parachute Regiment galloping round the racecourse on horseback followed by his two dogs, he was so impressed with his dashing style that he decided he would rather be an officer in that regiment than a priest. He fell in love with Windsor Great Park and the ceremonial of the Castle. 'We hung out of our windows on summer evenings to hear the last bugle calls floating over the oak trees as if the year were 1911.'4

The school had begun in 1861 in Beaumont Lodge, a white, eighteenth-century mansion which until then had been a seminary for Jesuit ordinands, on the edge of the park between Runnymede and Datchet. For a time it had been as smart as Stonyhurst, with cosmopolitan and military traditions as well as scholarly and religious ones. Former pupils included foreign aristocrats such as de Salises and de Zuluetas as well as judges, senior military officers, civil servants, priests and academics. The walls of the boys' refectory were hung with stags' heads, a tiger skin and a pair of furled, crossed banners above an array of sporting cups. Important figures like Father D'Arcy, who had left Campion Hall to become Provincial, or administrative head, of the English Jesuits, came down on visits from the Jesuit clergy house in Mount Street, round the corner from the Mayfair antique shop in which Lionel Levi sold choice eighteenth-century furniture.

Towards the end of term there were visits from Jesuit undergraduates at Campion Hall, who fraternized cautiously with the senior boys and were allowed to take informal classes.

Many of the masters were laymen. There was young Maurice Bond, the head of history, who also worked as parliamentary archivist and helped the boys to understand their place in the history of the country by organizing trips to the Houses of Parliament and Westminster Abbey. There was Mr. Brinkman, possibly a visiting Jesuit scholastic, 'who had advanced views about Aeschylus and Bach, and told us to read *Horizon* and Evelyn Waugh.'[5] There was the classics master, Arthur Mayhew, whom Peter remembered foggily as 'a very old Wykehamist... born in the 1860s', adding at least ten years to his age.[6] 'Dear old Mr Mayhew' was in fact sixty-eight when Peter joined his group of four classicists at Beaumont, having been a master at Eton in the 1920s between spells of teaching overseas. A genial old thing with a liberal, open-minded outlook on life, he loved the poetry of Horace with the Housmanesque wistfulness of his generation. Later, Peter placed the 'high water-mark of English Horatiomania' in the 1920s, when even Kipling had been 'crazy about Horace'.[7] Spellbound by Horace's elegance and rhythms, he developed a lifelong passion for the Odes.

But the master who had the most burning influence on him was a Jesuit priest. Christopher Devlin was a vulnerable, chaotic, saintly, poetry-writing, forty-year-old teacher of English literature. Once Peter had gained his Higher Certificate and could do more or less as he liked, he joined Devlin's English classes, impressing him with the quality of his writing. 'In his private character,' Peter wrote 'he recalled Shakespearean comedy, but in the classroom he was sometimes King Lear.'[8]

Grief-stricken by a wartime Catholic chaplaincy in the RAF, when he had cradled dying airmen in his lap, Devlin taught passionately, with the maxim 'Love your boys'.[9] His own long-term biographical subject was the melancholy Elizabethan recusant priest-poet, Robert Southwell, who had been tortured, hanged, drawn and quartered for the faith. Peter responded eagerly to Devlin's stories, and when asked by Father D'Arcy why he wanted to become a Jesuit replied that the 'cloak and crucifix' aspect of the Elizabethan martyrs appealed to him most.[10] But what he probably most wanted was to become another Christopher Devlin, whose deep romanticism was illuminated by religion and intensified by the mysterious demands of Jesuit discipline.

ल্জ

In keeping with Jesuit tradition, the classes at Beaumont were Figures, Rudiments, Grammar, Syntax, Poetry and Rhetoric. Back at school for his second and final year, in Rhetoric, Peter looked forward to a carefree three terms of Latin, Greek, English literature and debating. In the classical set he made friends with Kevin Donovan, an attractive, half-French boy in the year below him, with cornflower-blue eyes, full lips, an open, French peasant's face and an impulsively eager manner. Kevin had almost made up his mind to become a Jesuit, but revelled sensuously in the love-poems of Catullus. Peter invited him back to meet the family at Kings End, and one evening Anthony took the pair of them out to dinner and a theatre in central London. If being a Jesuit meant one could remain friends with people like Kevin, perhaps it would be an emotionally rewarding existence as well as one of tough self-sacrifice.

'I stuck it,' said Kevin sixty years later, smiling and screwing his eyes up against the sun in a Kensington convent garden, while elderly nuns in wimples and habits pruned the scrambling wall-shrubs from ladders. 'One never knows what God plans for one.' Wiry and still bright-blue-eyed, with rebellious hair, a white beard, thrift-shop clothes and an informal manner, he looked more like a hiker or an elderly radical demonstrator than a priest. Half-retired and a recovered alcoholic, he still lectured at Heythrop College, a specialist university centre for theological and philosophical studies which had developed out of the Jesuit seminary of that name in Oxfordshire, and now occupied the London premises of a former Catholic teacher-training college. He was also an assistant priest at the church of the Sacred Heart, Wimbledon, where he regularly interrupted his own sermons with passages on the flute.

Kevin spoke of his fifty-eight years in the order, the changes that he welcomed and his many Jesuit friends who had left. Although life had become easier for intending priests, who no longer even needed to know Latin, their numbers had shrunk drastically since his time, when (he now thought) there had been too many. Like Peter, he had gone into the novitiate straight from school.

☙

At the beginning of the autumn term of 1947 Christopher Devlin, as chairman of the Higher Line Debating Society, had a chance to admire Peter's public speaking style, since he had been elected Prime Minister for that term. He had spoken confidently, even cockily, in debates in the previous school year, and two days after his sixteenth birthday had won joint first prize in a debating competition, opposing the motion that war brings out the best in man.

> The speech of the Hon. Member for Chelsea (P. Levi) was well thought out and delivered with only very occasional reference to his notes. War breaks civilization, severs friendships and disrupts families. The man who gains the V.C. is hardly ever fighting for his ideals. War only breeds blood lust, and it only leads to the downfall of civilization. The speaker's manner is, however, uninspiring [the report ended rather sourly] and the odd question is apt to throw him completely off his train of thought.[11]

On Sunday, October 12, Peter moved a popular anti-Communist motion 'that this house would rather be the nephew of Uncle Sam than of Uncle Joe'. The motion was carried by twenty-three votes to eight, since Communism was anathema to most Catholics and its evils were a standard subject for tub-thumping sermons at Sunday Mass. Then, two weeks later, he was absent and another boy stood in for him. At the end of the meeting the society passed a unanimous motion that 'this House is deeply grieved at the loss of the Prime Minister, and hopes that he will soon return'.[12]

The first major English epidemic of poliomyelitis, then still called infantile paralysis, had killed or crippled thousands of babies, children and adolescents during the hot, dry summer of 1947. The epidemic ran on into the autumn, when boarding-schools, with their cramped conditions, mass catering and shared lavatories and bathrooms, became breeding-grounds for infection. Peter caught a mild form of polio at Beaumont that autumn. His legs were temporarily paralysed, leaving him with a limp that an accident nine years later would worsen, so that limping became part of his personality which some people suspected him of putting on for effect. He occasionally joked about his 'cork leg' but never needed supports.

Bedridden in a Maidenhead hospital for the rest of the term, he distanced himself from the mind-numbing ward routine by translating Latin verse into Greek, Greek verse into Latin, and *Times* leading articles into both. He liked to tease thirteen-year-old Gillian about her difficulties with Latin grammar, and when Bert brought her to the hospital from her convent boarding school at Slough he made Peter do her Latin homework for her. Gillian's innocent, cheerful brightness encouraged him to get better quickly. On a family holiday at Lyme Regis in the summer of 1948 he strode ahead of her on long, powerful legs to the top of Golden Cap as if to prove that he had conquered the infection which might so easily have left him a cripple in irons.

By late February he was back as Prime Minister in the Debating Society, moving a successful motion that 'This House could not care less about the Falkland Islands'. Argentina had challenged British sovereignty over the islands in a United Nations debate, but had failed to provoke a serious international crisis. In the summer term he served as Hon. Leader of the Opposition, having changed the name of his constituency to Ruislip and Ickenham as if acknowledging the existence of the suburb that he was about to leave for good.[13]

Jesuit masters at Beaumont sometimes prompted boys who were undecided about their future to think about vocations to the priesthood. Peter needed no such urging, since he had joined the school with his mind already half made up. Once the Parachute Regiment was out of the question he fell back on his earlier ambition, strengthened by the example of Kevin's piety and Chris Devlin's descriptions of the sufferings of Elizabethan Catholic martyrs. He was excited to read John Gerard's early seventeenth-century account of how he had survived torture and escaped from prison to join fellow-Jesuits abroad. Even if martyrdom was unlikely, he would emulate the recusant priests as best he could.

Yet his chief reason for wanting to become a Jesuit, he told Father D'Arcy, was that he admired his teachers at Beaumont, thus suggesting that he knew next to nothing about life outside the school. What he did know was that the Church demanded priestly vocations, that the world (as he had been told in countless sermons) was a vale of tears, and that by submitting himself to lifelong obedience and renouncing sex, money and possessions he would not only become holier and wiser but might earn eternal bliss after death. In the short term it would free him from making decisions about the future, since training for the Jesuit priesthood would be like a very long extension of school; and it would gratify Mollie, who still exercised a powerful influence over his life. Religion lured him into its forest, while all around he could see only a huge halo of promised happiness.

4
LIVING IN LATIN

It was in these unrecallable conditions, in this strange wonderland, that I got to know my first coalminer and university lecturer and Prussian nobleman and bank clerk and lower-deck sailor, all on terms of more intimacy and equality than even military service at its luckiest could have afforded.

The Flutes of Autumn (1983) 63

At breakfast on September 8, 1948 at Manresa House, Roehampton, the thirty-odd new Jesuit novices were still shy of one another. The night before, as instructed, they had trooped up to their cubicled dormitories in silence and said their prayers kneeling by their beds. A bell had woken them, as it would every day, at six. Over their ordinary clothes they had buttoned the shabby, handed-down novice's gown, a black, sleeveless affair with ribbon-like wings trailing from the shoulders. Clumping along corridors and up and down flights of stairs, past dramatically posturing, eye-rolling, lacerated and bleeding life-sized statues, they had stumbled into the chapel to pray, then returned to their cubicles to examine their consciences in silence. Back in chapel at half-past seven, they had joined the second-year novices and a group of juniors in the next year up for Mass. By then the sun was well up; but on fine days between October and February the rising sunlight would pour in through the east window above the altar during Mass. That radiance, seen clear-headed on an empty stomach, remained for Peter the most transfiguring experience of his Jesuit years.

At breakfast the silence continued after a Latin grace. Chairs scraped, eyes were lowered, cutlery clattered. Some novices exchanged stiff, self-conscious signals. Then Peter caught the eye of a round-faced boy opposite him who was restrainedly trying to squash a wasp in his marmalade, and they both laughed out loud. From that moment he and Peter 'Bertie' Granger-Banyard were best friends, and 'wasp day' was one they would still remember near the end of their joint lives.

Undergraduates in their first few days at university laugh a lot, and bubbles of the same light-headedness kept breaking through the surface of discipline at Manresa. Once the novices were allowed to talk they began to exchange life-stories. Friendly, fatherless Bertie, like Peter, was seventeen and straight from school. After his father died he had had to leave Belmont, the Benedictine public school near Hereford, for humbler day-schools of the De La Salle Brothers in Ipswich and Upper Norwood. Like Peter, he had a devoted younger sister who would soon become a nun. A keen, expert rugger-player, he made no claim to be intellectual, but responded to the beauty of landscape and was a willing explorer of literature. He admired the amount of English poetry Peter knew by heart, and became the audience Peter demanded for his own, conventionally pious adolescent poems.

Eighty years earlier, Gerard Manley Hopkins had broken more drastically with his past by burning most of his copies of his own poems after deciding to join the novitiate at Manresa. Converted to Catholicism at Oxford, at a time of high Victorian religious turbulence when many graduates became Anglican clergy as a matter of course, he chose the long, exacting path through Jesuit obedience as the logical next step. Although as a novice he returned to writing intense visual descriptions in his notebooks, seven years passed before he broke into poetry again with his magnificent ode 'The Wreck of the Deutschland', followed by several exuberant sonnets.

At that stage Peter disliked Hopkins, feeling frightened by the complexity of his poetry and the gloom of his late, terrible sonnets. He felt more interest in his own contemporaries than in as remote a predecessor as Hopkins, assuming that he must have led an impossibly grim and self-punishing life at Manresa. Both he and Bertie belonged to a loose, bright, sociable group of 'brethren' who took a relaxed view of the more demanding Jesuit precepts, such as that everyone should treat everyone else in an equally detached, impersonal way. 'How odd it is,' he wrote later, 'to think that one will never again be so close to anyone, except one's innermost family, as one was to Jesuits around one's own age before one was twenty.'[1]

There was a sprinkling of converts among them: clever Alexander Eaglestone in the year above, who had become a Catholic as a boy at Winchester, and twenty-eight-year-old Charles Praeger, who had been received into the Church while in the army in Palestine before finishing his degree course at Oxford. Most, however, were cradle Catholics of various ages and social classes. Peter and Bertie made friends with Tony Lawn, an athletic ex-Stonyhurst pupil who had joined the army towards the end of the war, and big, slow Willie Forrester, a former elementary schoolteacher from Glasgow, who told hair-raising stories of violence and destitution in the Gorbals. They played up to both of them as teenage innocents, giggling at Willie's snort of amazement when Peter asked if he believed in fairies and teasing Tony for his martial manner and love of tough outdoor pursuits.

Robert Butterworth, a serious Lancastrian a few months older than Peter and Bertie, reckoned that more than half their year, ranging in age from late teens to mid-thirties, had fought in the war, been to university, done National Service or held some kind of job. There were men from the Commandos, the Merchant Navy and the RAF, some of whom had been crammed with Latin at Father Clem's remedial seminary at Osterley. Not all of them, Butterworth felt, made ideal companions for naive, middle-class ex-schoolboys. Years later he complained about the afternoon walks in threesomes, in the supposedly random order in which the novices left the chapel after lunch, with people 'who would hardly have known, or even looked at, one another in the ordinary world.'[2] Yet, with a certain amount of pre-arrangement, friends usually stuck together, even if chaperoned by an unwelcome third.

In a pious farewell letter to Kevin, Peter had written that he could not think of a better way of spending his life than to give it to God. His teachers had given their blessing; Mollie thoroughly, and Bert more passively, approved; and he would be sheltered for life in an order he already knew from Beaumont. Even moving to Manresa meant exchanging one large, classical villa on the southern edge of Windsor Great Park for another on the eastern fringe of Richmond Park. The whole novitiate had made the same move in 1861, when Beaumont, its home for the past seven years, had become a school. Instead the Jesuits had bought Parkstead House, built in the 1760s for the second Earl of Bessborough as one of the upper-class pleasure-palaces and play-farms that encircled the outer edge of London, beyond the market gardens, onion fields, drying-grounds, squatters' settlements and uncultivable heaths. Renaming it after a town near Barcelona where St. Ignatius had seen a vision, and filling it with religious kitsch, they had maintained the strict routines that applied in Jesuit novice houses everywhere.

Discipline had changed little between Hopkins's day and Peter's. Novices were allowed to sleep until six in the morning instead of half-past five, but in most respects their routine was like that of the 1860s. Everything had a set time, from the hour of private prayer and meditation before early Mass to the hour of strictly limited recreation (talking, reading, or writing the weekly letter home) between supper and evening Benediction. The only books provided for them were a limited selection of devotional works, together with small quantities of fiction and poetry by safe, dead Catholic authors such as G.K. Chesterton, Hopkins and the poet Francis Thompson of 'Hound of Heaven' fame. They had not been allowed to bring books with them, and any that came into their hands were presents, which they circulated unofficially among friends.

In the autumn term they had their first long retreat, a month of intensive meditation, conscience-searching, sermons and readings in the *Spiritual Exercises* of St. Ignatius. This began half-way through October – not, as in Hopkins's day, straight after the beginning of the novices' year in September. Like Hopkins, however, they were sent into London on Sundays to give catechism classes after mid-morning Mass. Peter's were in an Irish parish off the Harrow Road, where the rough children terrified him like a foretaste of the Brixton inmates, giving him his first intimation that he could not love people unless it was also possible to like them.

Then there were the punishing long walks: across Wimbledon Common in the rain, along the bleak riverside settings of Isleworth, Mortlake and Barnes, or all the way into central London, stopping off, as instructed, in as many Catholic churches as they could, with just enough money for the tram-fare back or a cup of tea and a bun. While not herded in soutaned crocodiles like Italian seminarians, they still formed a conspicuous gaggle at a time when most eighteen- and nineteen-year-old men were in uniform and few Londoners walked from choice.

Outside the walls of Manresa they dutifully lowered their eyes on meeting anyone apart from priests, fellow-Jesuits, bus-conductors and the children in their catechism classes. They had no contact with former friends and were allowed to write only to their families, leaving letters to be censored on the way out. They received only occasional, prison-like parlour visits from close relatives, and had no home leave in twenty-four months. Some quietly cracked up, and their names were crossed off the printed lists on which they had appeared as Antonius, Petrus, Paulus, Jacobus or Patritius. Most, however, accepted the privations as a means to an end. To men who had faced blind parachute jumps or smelt singed and rotting flesh in fire-bombed cities and death-camps, the antique rules promised peace. To idealistic boys too young to have served in the war, they meant a quicker route to adulthood than they would have known as university students spending half the year at home, or even National Servicemen in local barracks with their forty-eight-hour leaves.

Seminarians were exempt from National Service. ('Tonse the lot of them,' a government minister is supposed to have said, referring to the tradition that tonsured clergy should not bear arms.) Once their call-up papers arrived, soon after their eighteenth birthdays, the youngest members of Peter's year were escorted to the Putney labour exchange and signed off. Instead of military or naval discipline, they were subjected to a routine designed to focus their minds and emotions on religion, keep their consciences scoured clean and break their wills. Morning lectures from the Novice Master on St. Ignatius's *Constitutions of the Society of Jesus* were interspersed with bouts of wordless domestic skivvying – floor-washing, mopping, polishing, dusting, scraping out residues of breakfast porridge, carrying buckets of swill to the pigs or scrubbing vegetables (*olera*) for lunch, often in the way of the silent, scurrying lay-brothers (*coadjutores*, 'helpers') who did most of the practical work of the house. They also had classes in patristic and ecclesiastical Latin to prepare them for their six years as scholastics, when, in keeping with the international character of the order, most of their philosophy and theology lectures and their textbooks, known as codexes, would be in Latin.

Like seventeenth-century schoolboys or students, they became used to receiving instructions in Latin and using Latin terms for household objects. Lunch, like breakfast, was eaten in silence, against a background of swooshing and clattering from washing-up in wooden sinks, while a novice read out loud from the Bible or a stupefying sixteenth-century Jesuit classic, Alfonso Rodriguez's *Practice of Perfection and Christian Virtues*. After post-lunch prayers in the chapel, when they went for walks or worked in the grounds, they were expected to remain silent for the first half hour or talk Latin. For the classically educated this could be a chance to show off, while others struggled to improvise.

'*Habesne buckshee hoe?*' ('Do you have a spare hoe?') one ex-military chap was heard asking another.

In compensation for those hours of repression, the more schoolboyish novices enjoyed sniggering at sexual embarrassments and innuendos. They joked about their monthly self-examination sessions with the general confessor or Spiritual Father, about 'pious ejaculations' (a serious expression for short, exclamatory prayers), and about the discipline, the little string whip they were supposed to use to suppress their carnal instincts. Sexual roles were allocated, with the usual camp clerical use of 'she' for unpopular members of their year. Pairs of friends who seemed particularly close were referred to as 'Mr. and Mrs.' Yet it seems unlikely that any of the novices can have joined from consciously homosexual motives, since the vow of chastity that lay ahead was too solemn to be cynically flouted in advance. To eradicate non-religious love altogether was harder, as Peter would find when it burgeoned in his poems.

ℰℐ

Beyond the western boundary of Manresa House lay a golf-course, and beyond that Richmond Park. Peter claimed that, in hard winters, deer used to come up from the park to the kitchen door to be fed.[3] He and Bertie revelled in the beauty of the setting and the tree-surrounded quietness of the grounds. The blocks of Alton Estate council flats which would loom over them in the next few years were still sketches on the London County Council architects' drawing-boards. There were shrubberies, pigsties, a walled kitchen garden, an orchard, and wildernesses inhabited by nightingales and pheasants. A wartime bombing raid had blown out part of the library, and charred and sodden remnants of old books could still be salvaged from under cindery debris and leaf-mould. Lay-brothers tended the kitchen regions and managed parts of the garden, while an outside man looked after the pigs. Years later Peter remembered him.

Dick Wernham,
in 1948 like a jockey to look at
He had ten pigs and a pensioned off horse
and one heroic sow,
moon-backed, hairy-backed, heavy,
she smelt sweet and she used to kiss him.
The roads smelt of tar and leaves —
she was the nearest pig to Westminster.[4]

The spring and summer of 1949 were extraordinarily fine and warm. Families packed into seaside boarding-houses, tents and caravans, while the novices were allowed to picnic and make hay in the Manresa grounds. In the outside world, seeds from rosebay willowherb drifted in through grimy open office windows from the bombed sites. In the parks, the horse chestnut leaves turned colour early. Trams and buses, fogged inside with tobacco-smoke, swept past the gaggles of novices, who for once felt no desire to board them while out on their long walks.

Then, on September 7, the Jesuit calendar clicked forward and everyone moved on. The second-year novices took their first vows of poverty, chastity and obedience, put on shiny clerical collars and newly tailored black suits, spent a few days with their families and then returned to Manresa as juniors, or, in a few cases, went straight to Heythrop College in North Oxfordshire to begin their three years of philosophy.

Peter's group provided 'guardian angels' for the first-years who had just arrived. Among them were Kevin Donovan and the twenty-year-old Anthony Levi, who had decided that a life in business was not for him. Peter welcomed them both into his gang of brethren, while keeping Bertie as his closest friend. When former school friends, brothers or cousins met again as novices, this created fresh, unofficial links between them, once again frustrating the Jesuit intention that all members of the order should treat one another in exactly the same way.

On Anthony's twenty-first birthday, during the 1950 Whitsun break, he, Peter and Kevin had a day out in central London. Peter described this fully in a letter to his parents, after instructing them how to dispose of his books after he had taken his first vows in September, then rhapsodizing about a Whitsunday broadcast of Solemn Vespers from Buckfast Abbey, followed the next day by Beethoven's Ninth ('which Anthony thinks is a bit low, but which I love.')

On the Tuesday morning the three young men set off. They lost their way walking to the tram-stop in Wandsworth, but 'that didn't matter as it gave us time to do our ½ hour's meditation'. From Lambeth Palace they crossed on foot to the Tate, where Anthony enjoyed the work of 'frightful modern painters nobody but he can understand – Picasso, and Matisse, and Rouault, & Degas and Pisarro', while Peter raved about a roomful of paintings by William Blake. He especially loved Blake's visionary *Death of the Virgin* with its rainbow background, flanking angels and central, standing figure of Christ, who had returned to Earth on his mother's death to carry her soul to Paradise, 'clear and sudden and splendid, above the dim blue-draped body like the first moment of eternity, – "the dayspring from on high"'.

After examining their consciences in silence for fifteen minutes, they found a bench under a tree in the Embankment gardens.

'So we had lunch, sandwiches & malt-currant-bread, and cake, and chocolate biscuits (the big sort, like a bar of chocolate, & wrapped in silver paper) and an orange, and lemonade out of a Cointreau bottle. It was a bit astonishing for a 21st birthday lunch, but I don't expect you can imagine how pleasant it was or how we enjoyed it, & enjoyed one another.'

Too short of time to revisit the Tate, they wandered into Westminster Hall, which Peter thought beautiful and impressive, then into the Abbey, where he admired Chaucer's tomb ('That's my favourite corner'), but objected to the *'appalling'* bad taste of the monuments to 'some shocking old rascals of the 18th century, who didn't even have the merit of being picturesque'. And so to Westminster Cathedral, Hyde Park, Kensington Gardens and Hammersmith, all on foot, before taking a bus most of the rest of the way home. At five o'clock dinner, which was ham, Peter 'ate & ate & ate, having an appetite like half the hunters in Leicestershire.'

ᔥ

'When I'm Rector of Beaumont,' he once said to Gillian, 'and you're Reverend Mother of St Bernard's, then we'll put the family on the map.' It was easiest to imagine himself back at Beaumont, perhaps teaching sixth-form classics in place of dear old Mr. Mayhew, while writing poems and exciting the more impressionable boys with the intensity of a second Christopher Devlin. The fact that, under obedience, he could be packed off at the whim of his seniors to teach in any of their boarding or day schools, or to a mission in South Africa, Rhodesia, British Guiana or Japan, seemed pointless to worry about when he had a decade or more of preparation ahead.

Most ordained Jesuits taught in schools. Few, in the early 1950s, had degrees, and fewer still had been formally trained to teach. Once they had completed the novitiate and the one-year juniorate they spent three years studying philosophy, two years teaching in a Jesuit school and then a further three years studying theology before ordination. Only a small elite, chosen to be possible future cardinals, administrators, seminary professors or distinguished scholars, fitted three or four extra years into their training by reading for degrees at Campion Hall in Oxford. For all the uniformity imposed on the novices, the upper reaches of the order were steeply hierarchical, and promotions and demotions could take place swiftly and often without warning.

With ex-servicemen joining the novitiate, its numbers had swelled since the war, and senior Jesuits believed that the drive for more Catholic vocations, boosted by the unpopularity of National Service, would mean that applications could only continue to go up. Partly to accommodate the expected influx of recruits they purchased Harlaxton Hall, a large, florid, neo-Jacobean country house in southeast Lincolnshire, which was on the market cheaply after wartime requisition by the RAF. Having transferred the novitiate there, they moved it back and forth between Harlaxton and Manresa for the next twelve years, until forced by shrinking numbers to sell Manresa to the London County Council to become part of Whitelands teacher-training college, later the University of Roehampton.

Early in Peter's second year plans were being finalized for Harlaxton while the damage the airmen had done to it was patched up. One additional reason for the move was a fear that the Labour government might nationalize the private schools, or at least demand that their secondary-level teachers had the same kind of training as those in state schools. The Jesuits therefore thought it prudent to give all scholastics a teaching qualification, which for the time being would be recognised as equivalent to a degree. A teacher-training (in Jesuit-speak, pedagogy) course, licensed by the LCC and directed by Peter's old Beaumont teacher Chris Devlin, was established for the fourth-year scholastics after they had completed two years of philosophy at Heythrop and a third year of philosophy at Manresa. To make room at Manresa for these third- and fourth-years, all the novices were moved to Lincolnshire on August 20, 1950, less than three weeks before Peter and the rest of his year took their first vows.

5
A LICENCE TO SMOKE

How old were the field names, I wonder? How old was the name Foxbury Wood? It was an entangled place with some very old trees, felled now most of them; you could smell the foxes in the river-bottom, a penetrating, unmistakable smell like rotten cabbage.

The Flutes of Autumn (1983) 72

In the 1950s, people living in a scattering of small villages on the Oxfordshire edge of the Cotswolds often saw black-suited Jesuits out and about in the fields and lanes. Sometimes they were on bicycles, property of the archdiocese of Birmingham, which they were lent to take catechism classes for local Catholic children. Usually they were on foot, plodding along the footpaths like so many giant crows. Sometimes, on free Thursdays, you would see them huddled against a hedge on the southbound side of the A44, then a main route from Birmingham to the south, illicitly thumbing lifts into Oxford or beyond. If they took a short cut over the fields that brought them out north of the Heythrop College drive gates, they were unlikely to be seen by emerging members of the staff. They could ask for the bus-fare into Oxford if they had a legitimate reason for going there, such as a dentist's appointment, then keep the fare and hitch-hike in and out, which would at least give them a tiny sum of money to spend on themselves.

On its writing-paper, Heythrop College described itself as: 'Nr. Enstone: 5 miles from Chipping Norton. Telephone: Enstone 38. Station: Charlbury (W.R.) 6 miles.' A handsome slab of a much altered, early eighteenth-century mansion, the house looms solitarily on its high, stony plateau, surrounded by arable fields, winter mist and woods. In the 1870s it was drastically remodelled for the Brasseys, the family of a successful railway engineer. The Gothic lodges and village labourers' houses were Brassey additions, as were the shrubberies above the chain of ponds that ran through woods below the house. Peter wrote that the oblong bulk of the main building struck him at first as a 'gigantic abandoned railway station in the middle of a field'.[1]

The estate was in famous foxhunting country, which an early nineteenth-century Duke of Beaufort had preferred to his own country around Badminton, leasing the house from the Earl of Shrewsbury as a hunting box. From the neighbouring villages of Heythrop, Enstone and Great and Little Tew, farm labourers and their families rarely ventured farther than windy, hilltop Chipping Norton a few miles up the road. In the winter, a menagerie of circus lions and elephants occupied stables in a remote part of the Heythrop grounds. Vixens screamed their harsh mating-cries on early spring nights, and the clamour of the Heythrop Hunt hounds, kennelled a few miles away, echoed thrillingly in the autumn and winter woods.

> We lived in the country all right, but without... that sense and presence of a village that even the grandest private houses have. We pumped our own water and generated our own electricity. The ugly and comforting noise of rams and generators speaks about peace in my recollection much as an old threshing machine... does to others. There was a ram I used to pass sometimes at night; that ram, and a vixen barking near what were called the Gas Cottages, whose only light was oil-lamps, and the steady chewing noise of cattle in the ground-mist, almost abolish thirty years, and I can feel the wetness again soaking through my shoes, I can smell the mist and see that night's piece of moon and few stars.[2]

Peter had not expected to go straight into philosophy at Heythrop. Several older, better-educated members of his year went at once, while the younger ones were expected to kill time for another year at Manresa. Then, in one of those sudden Jesuitical calculations, he and Robert Butterworth were selected to read classics at Oxford after a further three or four years. With almost no notice they were pulled out of the juniorate and packed off by train one sunny September afternoon. Chaperoned by a trusty, older Heythrop first-year, who bought their tickets in a steam-filled Paddington Station and stood them tea in the dining-car of the Cathedrals Express, the two nineteen-year-olds were whisked through Oxford, catching a glimpse of the domed Radcliffe Camera, the spire of the Methodist church and the tall campanile of St. Barnabas by the canal. Then the train carried them up the Evenlode valley to Charlbury station, from which most approaches to Heythrop began.

Robert Butterworth later complained that he had found the Heythrop country bleak and empty, and had felt lonely as one of the youngest students there. His account of his Jesuit training mentions Peter only in connection with the move to Heythrop, although they both belonged to the same loose group of friends from their year.[3] Peter, meanwhile, was busy absorbing new impressions, persuading himself that scholastic philosophy fascinated him, writing torrential letters to Bertie and falling in love with the high, open, north-west Oxfordshire country, its amazing skyscapes and clear blue views towards the Chilterns and Berkshire Downs.

He was good at being the youngest, and had already made friends at Manresa with several members of the year above. The chaperonage rule about threesomes no longer applied; philosophy students, being vowed to chastity, were allowed to go about in pairs. They were firmly separated, however, from the theologians, men in their late twenties or thirties in the final stage before ordination. At coffee-time in the central hall, the two groups stood at opposite ends of the long room without mingling. They ate separately, swam separately and, as at Prior Park, slept in separate wings attached to the main building. The only contact between them took place in formal 'fusion' sessions on major feast days, or through organized outdoor activities such as football or scouting.

After the cultural starvation of Manresa, Peter began to catch up on English classics in the philosophers' library. But his most impassioned discovery, lent to him by a fellow-scholastic, was *Brideshead Revisited*. The ornate, triumphalist, country-house Catholicism, the romantic but tactfully de-sexualised friendship between Charles Ryder and Sebastian Flyte, and the fact that the Flytes frequented Farm Street when in London, made him feel that he had half a foothold in its world. He loved the lapidary dialogue, the melancholy aestheticism of Charles's outlook, the potent rhythms of Waugh's style and the way in which each of the main agnostic characters submitted to Catholicism in the end. He may even have seen traces of Anthony in the priggish Lord Brideshead and of Mollie in the manipulative Lady Marchmain, with her fondness for tame priests and perpetual mourning for the heroic brothers she had lost in the First World War.

Gushing over *Brideshead* to Bertie, Peter admitted that one or two things in it had struck him as distasteful. Within a year or two, however, they had read all Waugh's novels and discussed Sebastian as if he were a cherished but difficult friend. Once, Peter wrote that he had heard that *Brideshead* was 'the Bible of all Catholic undergraduates' in Cambridge. They began to use expressions like 'proud-making' and 'shame-making' from *Vile Bodies*, and 'Goodness how sad' ('G. how s.' or variations) from the short story 'Cruise'.

Optimistic, naive and cushioned by the system, Peter had little trouble with the day job of absorbing Thomistic philosophy through the medium of Latin. He found the idea of philosophy glamorous, even when it amounted to the driest form of Aristotelianism pushed through a medieval sieve. At first he did not question the relevance of spending two or three years on this stuff; it was simply part of the Catholic Church's accumulation of historic dialectical clutter. At least one of the philosophy professors, Frederick Copleston, was a scholar, not a hack; the second, medieval volume of his eleven-volume *History of Philosophy* came out in 1950, two years before he left Heythrop to teach at the Gregorian University in Rome. But that book, being in English, was meant for a wider public than Jesuit seminarians, whose own intellectual hamster-wheel consisted of dull textbooks in Latin. Half-docile, half-impatient, Peter longed to graduate to the theologians' library, which was full of rare, sixteenth-century volumes of Biblical exegesis. Although it was out of bounds to philosophers, he once climbed out of a bathroom window and over a roof to reach it, meeting an intoxicating smell of damp, musty, largely unread books.

So far, Oxford excited him only in the pages of *Brideshead*. He had no reason to join the illicit hitchhikers and went there only on special occasions, such as his former Ruislip scoutmaster's ordination as a Dominican in June 1951. Meanwhile, he was happy to take country walks with Alexander Eaglestone, another high-flyer intended for Campion Hall.

All around the high ground on which Heythrop stood were trees: saw-toothed evergreen plantations and drooping larches, shelter-belts of spruce and Scots pine, the ancient oaks in Ditchley Park, the wellingtonias at Great and Little Tew, and the long, undulating, buzzard-circled skyline of Wychwood to the south. On foot, on free Thursdays, scholastics could explore as far as the broad upper Evenlode valley on the borders of Gloucestershire and Warwickshire, or the lower reaches of the river in murky pools under hanging woods. Nearer home was the Glyme, which rose below Chipping Norton, fed the chain of ponds at Heythrop, then flowed down past Enstone, Kiddington, Glympton and Woodstock to meet the Evenlode on the edge of Blenheim Park. How Peter would have enjoyed a still undiscovered poem, 'Of a little River in Oxfordshire neare Kiddington', that Philip Sidney's sister the Countess of Pembroke wrote at Ditchley, exactly describing the meanders of the Glyme through the little sheep-grazed valley between Enstone and the hamlet of Radford downstream.[4]

In the Heythrop grounds non-games-players did outside work, clearing undergrowth, cutting back rhododendrons, coppicing woodland, mending fences, keeping bees or cleaning out the ponds. In between times they relaxed in huts scattered through the woods, each of which had a stove, a kettle, a frying-pan, plates, mugs and rudimentary seating. On Thursdays, bacon, sausages, eggs, bread, butter and jam were put out for lunch and tea. They could fry up greasy lunches, adding mushrooms in the autumn, make elderflower wine in spring (sugar could be scrounged from the kitchens or bought with the half-crown Whitsun pocket-money), or just huddle in a group, smoke and talk.

Lonely, middle-aged Jesuits sometimes became whisky priests. The Heythrop scholastics had the barest acquaintance with alcohol – half a pint of the local Hook Norton bitter at lunchtime, and a glass of cheap port with their pudding after dinner on feast days. Many, however, like the senior Jesuits, smoked. Any scholastic who claimed that his nerves needed calming could apply to the Provincial for a smoker's licence, and every month would receive tins of Capstan tobacco and packets of cigarette papers. Preparing themselves for a future of fogged-up staff-rooms, they enjoyed the ritual of rolling their own and coughed heroically through the winter like so many Marlboro County cowboys.

'Oh! What a house this is!' Peter exclaimed to Bertie after his first Christmas at Heythrop. The emotional high of a group celebration, with a pantomime, decorations, a broadcast concert and cards and letters from friends at Manresa, replaced the family life he barely noticed he had left.

He was immature and knew it. When Peter Whittall, the trusted scholastic who had brought him and Robert Butterworth from London, told him he was suffering from depression, Peter felt helpless to give advice. He and Bertie remained innocently happy, exchanging solemn sentiments in their letters about the peace and joy and love and blessings of Our Lord Jesus Christ. If they wrote on a Jesuit feast-day they were allowed to do so in English; otherwise they were expected to use Latin. All letters were theoretically censored, although that did not stem the undercurrent of ribaldry about pious ejaculations and passionate kisses. Between describing events at Heythrop, retailing community gossip and making schoolboy jokes about their friends, Peter fretted that he was unable to help Whittall, but concluded that, being in God's hands, he must recover soon.

At nineteen he was happy because everything good seemed to hang together: God, nature, the beauty of springtime, music (he loved Brahms's thumpingly triumphant variations on a theme of Haydn's *St. Anthony Chorale*), and the promise of becoming one of God's elect. In exaltation of spirit, and with that impulse towards self-sacrifice that sometimes shapes the lives of young Catholics, he saw himself as part of a crusade to rescue civilization from the post-war ruins. Testimonies from the Holocaust even made him consider himself a Jew, although the Catholic view of history he had grown up with left little room for Jewishness. After joining the Heythrop scouts he told Bertie, in Father Clem-like language, that 'Rovering' was about the 'knighthood' idea of conserving the countryside, maintaining public-school values in the face of dereliction, '& regarding one's life as held in trust for the service of God our Lord, & one's country, & all the people one meets'.[5] It was also, of course, about having fun out of doors and meeting some of the remote theologians. Catholic scout troops from the Birmingham archdiocese camped at Heythrop every Whitsun, and the theology students built a venture course which Peter helped to test in advance. One of the older members of his year was in charge of the local Hook Norton scouts, whose earthy humour he would enjoy when leading them himself.

He was physically fit, swimming in cold water in spring and summer before 'Morning Ob.', as they called community prayers in chapel soon after the rising-bell at six. The swimming season started in April, with separate ponds for philosophers and theologians and scheduled turns in a purpose-built, unheated swimming-bath. In the summer vacation, recruited as unpaid labour by members of the Oxford University Archaeological Society, he helped to uncover a mosaic pavement at the Roman villa site at Beaconsfield Farm, just below the Heythrop plateau. Describing that summer later, he did not say what it had felt like to meet undergraduate diggers of his own age. What he chose to remember was the pleasure of cycling out with a bag of sandwiches in the early morning, the relaxing daytime life of the farmyard with its sunlit smells of dung and straw, and the ride home in the evening through Enstone or the butterscotch-coloured ironstone village of Little Tew.[6]

Once, he and a friend got permission to ride the archdiocesan bicycles across the Cotswolds as far as ruined Hailes Abbey, way to the Severn estuary. It was his first view of that part of distant Gloucestershire, whose sweeping lines, translucent views and swan-flights would fill the poems of his last years. Then it was time for the fortnight's villa or July holiday by the sea. For nearly a century the 'Jesuit gentlemen' had been using the same holiday home at Barmouth in Merionethshire. The plain, bleak sandstone buildings, between the foothills and the sea, did not seem depressing to Peter, and he was thrilled to find some foreign scholastics in the party. He sent Bertie a blissful catalogue of swimming, boating, climbing, cycling and adventure films with 'Ours of various nationalities', as if the brethren, in their more athletic moments, could have been a company of holy boy scouts.

Early in September he travelled to Harlaxton to see Anthony take his first vows. Then, back at Heythrop, he welcomed Bertie and other members of his former year. A few, to his disappointment, had chosen to study philosophy at French or German seminaries. Anthony, a fluent German speaker, was about to skip the juniorate and go straight to the

Berchmanskolleg at Pullach, just outside Munich.

In spite of his enthusiasm for the foreign brethren, Peter hated the thought of friends disappearing abroad. Bertie shared his patriotic love of England, and he enjoyed showing him the country he had rhapsodized about in his letters. He also introduced him to the one local family he knew. A struggling, middle-class Catholic mother with three sons under seven was allowed to live in one of the Heythrop lodges. Peter had been asked to give catechism lessons to the eldest, and found all three boys attractive and fun. Even in the drab surroundings of the tiny lodge he enjoyed being in a family atmosphere, took an interest in the fatherless boys and hoped that money might somehow be found to send them all to good Catholic schools.

Once Bertie was back with him, Peter no longer needed to write to him. Instead he was writing for him. He and Bertie would tease one another later about their piety at Heythrop, but at that stage much of his poetry was conventionally religious. His twenty-first birthday offering to Bertie was a poem about God the Father, faintly echoing Newman's 'Praise to the Holiest in the Height'. A few months later he wrote a florid address 'To Earth':

> *God knows I have desired you, loved each fair*
> *Tumultuous veil that shines upon grey skies*
> *While lucent dawn hangs splendid on the air,*
> *And the world wakes her thousand melodies.*
> *I too have loved the dark blush of the rose,*
> *Scent of forgotten Summers, & the Spring,*
> *When on one wind all Hebe's magic blows,*
> *And in bright trees at eve, the thrushes sing:*
> *Black thunders shattering thy clouds like smoke,*
> *White mist upon the sea, and golden wheat*
> *With flaring poppies, these are one in me.*
> *Since first upon my wondering soul they broke*

I strove that this, our oneness, be complete:
Pray God I may be one with Him, and thee.[7]

As summer advanced, however, he changed his tone in the poem 'I Heard You Laughing':

My head was hot and I was sick for sleep,
I crept up slowly to my room to hide;
And heard you laughing on the grass outside,
As well contented as those stars that keep
On summer nights the early watch; you seemed
Made holy, touched with splendour, crowned and free,
Eternal and forever far from me.
There's nothing I have thought of you or dreamed,
Can take the breath of that more spacious day
Where you have strayed. Beyond love's patient thought
There's something in you deathless: you shall be
Part hidden from me. I can only say
That deathlessness is in your laughter caught
And that I love you everlastingly.[8]

❧

After a happy Barmouth holiday in July (photos have survived of stocky Bertie, skinny Peter and four friends, all bare chests and angular shoulders, elbows and knees, smiling into the sun in shorts and boots on Cader Idris), Peter's two years at Heythrop were over. For the next two years he moved back to Roehampton to finish philosophy and do a year's teacher-training, which only a few brilliant scholastics were excused.

Manresa was largely unchanged, and he fell in love with its beauty again. Freer of restrictions than when a novice, he was also more confident. Soon after his arrival he and a friend went 'up to town' to inspect his uncle Lionel Levi's antique shop, then dropped in for tea at the clergy house in Mount Street. Within the next few days (he told Bertie) he planned to go in again twice, to hear a sermon by Monsignor Ronald Knox and a lecture on translating poetry by Cecil Day Lewis.

There were intermittent cultural treats. The winter play was James Elroy Flecker's *Hassan*, in which he had a female part: 'It had to be cut... but the only line censored was "and her hips are like water-melons in the season of water-melons". I am the she referred to, Yasmin, v. alluring, & *awf'ly* fast. Goodness how blush-making!'

Full of undirected literary energy, he wondered if his poems would seem truer to themselves in Latin. He practised translating poems from one language to another, and considered writing a play, an epic poem, a book about philosophy or 'my Brideshead'. After a Jesuit in the pedagogy department asked him to write a serio-comic playlet, to be performed by a small group of men at the Borough Road Training College, he attempted a serious verse play, *The Hostages*, and submitted it to his old elocution teacher Hedley Goodall at the BBC in Bristol, who sent it back it with a kind rejection letter.[9]

As always, he was keen to see his poems in print. One undemanding outlet was *Stella Maris*, a monthly Catholic family magazine that Father Clem edited from Campion House. Bertie criticized him for not aiming higher, but Peter thought it better to be published somewhere than not at all. Chris Devlin, the head of pedagogy, gave him useful advice, and he recited many of his poems to Clarence Gallagher, a new member of his year, who had moved to Manresa from the Scots College in Rome after choosing to become a Jesuit rather than a diocesan priest. Like Peter, he had been selected to read classics at Campion Hall. The two of them took Greek lessons together and went for bicycle rides along the Thames towpath. Father Gallagher remembered Peter as an avid reader and enthusiastic declaimer. He found the poems he wrote at that time straightforward and simple, although later (he wrote) 'he lost me'.[10]

Once or twice that year Peter managed to meet Bertie and other friends at a romantically significant halfway point between Heythrop and Manresa, near the Dashwood family's house, West Wycombe in Buckinghamshire. On one of the monthly 'Blandykes' or whole leave-days, named after a former Jesuit villa in Flanders, they would hitchhike from London or Oxford along the A40. Then they let themselves into the church tower, as anyone could in those days, and climbed up into the tiny, ornate dome called the golden ball. In the 1760s the depraved Francis Dashwood, Lord Le Despencer, was said to have held punch-fuelled orgies there with his fellow Medmenham Monks. That touch of ecclesiastical naughtiness just suited the playful tone of their friendship, as well as Peter's growing fascination with eccentricities from the past.

> *Over the roof, high in among the gloom*
> *you come to a remote, airy room,*
> *a hexagon resting on pure light,*
> *where mind can shoot to any height*
> *or in a ripe curve down the leaden dome*
> *dissolve in mere formality*
> *of that grave, simple century*
> *that here for a mind at peace hung this home...*[11]

❧

After years of seeing almost nothing of his parents he was drawing closer to them again. Early in 1953 Bert came down with pneumonia and Peter was allowed home to see him. Then at Easter he went home again for special Levi treats of meringues and champagne. Finally, on May 12, he went back for his parents' silver wedding anniversary. Bert, suddenly frail at sixty-nine, was about to close down the business, which he had left in the hands of a manager for some time. He and Mollie planned to sell the house at Ruislip and retire to a comfortable Eastbourne flat.

Gillian was in her first year studying French and German at King's College London. Keen on operas, plays and all the cultural richness she could cram in, she also belonged to the college Catholic Society and sold Catholic newspapers on Friday evenings outside Temple Bar underground station. That summer in Munich, where she went to practise her German, Anthony lectured her sternly about turning up late for Mass and failing to take life seriously. Two years later she graduated, passed her driving test, thought about taking a secretarial course, then entered the novitiate of the enclosed order of nuns at St. Bernard's Convent, Slough, where she had been at school.

∾

In 1953, the year that Stalin died, English Catholicism was enjoying a post-war boom. Irish immigrants, middle-class converts, displaced East Europeans and former prisoners of war and their families swelled the congregations in many areas. A few of the smarter churches resembled private chapels for the rich, with a pewful or two of the poor at the back. Small boys served Sunday Masses in white lacy surplices over little cassocks, ringing bells, clanking thuribles and chiming in with the Latin responses by rote. Most paedophile priests and schoolmasters relied on their positions of authority and the sanctity of priestly bachelorhood to go through life unexposed.

Helping out at a vocations exhibition at Olympia, Peter was entertained to lunch by Bertie's sister Clare, who was preparing to become a nun. Very much the busy, suave young Jesuit, he chattered away to Bertie about the crowds who had thronged his stall: nuns, Anglican clergymen, the Dominican Provincial, the mothers of Jesuit novices and a Beaumont boy who was about to join – 'A magnificent fellow, you would like him very much.'

At Manresa he had been mooching solitarily, scribbling down in a notebook his impressions of April blossom and the sweet smell of meadow grass. He regretted the lack of enthusiasm for cricket that year, although men were still kicking footballs around in late April and many were playing tennis or running. Attracted since his schooldays by the beautiful sight and rhythm of cricket-matches, he told Bertie that he would even play himself if he thought it would please anyone.[12]

> *We will not last, football will swallow all,*
> *cricket needs the sewn ball the crack-willow*
> *that the old women brewed up into tea,*
> *it needs the wicket and the willow bat,*
> *football is coarser, they play all day long.*[13]

But in late May he spent a brilliantly hot day on the river, discovering a pub at Long Ditton with poignant First World War photographs of a young man in cavalry uniform and a group of soldiers with crucifixes resting on their tattooed chests. 'I think this Summer will last for ever. God bless. God save the Queen.'[14]

Coronation Day, June 2, was pouring wet but a jubilant success. The philosophy examination results came out at the end of July, and Peter found that he had done respectably, although not brilliantly. One man achieved *summa cum laude*; five failed. Bertie had done poorly in his second-year exams at Heythrop and would be moved to the easier 'short course', which was the same length as the long course, for his third year. Nobody was sacked outright for failure, but some hares overtook others. Robert Butterworth, who had spent his third year of philosophy at the Berchmanskolleg, was allowed to skip teacher-training and go straight to Campion Hall that October. 'It's good to see Bob again! Goodness how kiss-making!' Peter enthused to Bertie, not seeming to resent that he had been overtaken, if indeed he was aware of it. So many Jesuit administrative decisions were made at the last minute, depending as much on chance vacancies as on elusive academic merit.

In September, after another Barmouth holiday, Peter began his teacher-training with direct practice. Typically of the Jesuit presumption that scholastics could do both anything and nothing, the students had to go out in pairs, unprepared, to face their first lions. In Peter's case they were tough secondary modern schoolboys at the Mawbey Road school in Peckham. The daily journey was tiring, across London from Roehampton and far down the Old Kent Road. But at least the experience was brief, and he was unlikely ever to have to teach in such a hopeless school again. Both he and the pupils were older than they had been during his catechism class ordeals in the Harrow Road. After years of recognizing the varieties of Jesuit-induced boredom, he sympathised with the misfits and rebels when they played up to their teachers, and with most of the teachers for being stuck in an educational dead end.

> One thing worked on the senior boys like magic; it produced perfect peace and quiet for at least two hours. Half way through the afternoon, when the oldest teacher was fed up with teaching, he had only to lean back and say 'Get out your paints boys.' The snakes slept on the heads of the furies.[15]

The following autumn, aged twenty-three, he was at last ready for Campion Hall. Poised at Heythrop in early October, as if about to plunge from a slippery diving-board into the cold-water swimming pool, he looked about him:

> 'One more evening & then Oxford tomorrow. I am looking forward to it tremendously. It's the most superb afternoon now, as if to celebrate – of a very fine Autumn. I think among my eccentric ancestry there must be a vegetation god, because Autumn always moves me extremely in a hundred directions at once. Heythrop is glorious just now... God bless. Peter S.J.'[16]

6
OXFORD POET

Campion Hall was... a smart, grim parody of an ecclesiastical building, designed by Lutyens and created or conjured like a rabbit out of a top hat by Father D'Arcy, who had left it to its own devices long ago. It stood in an obscure lane that ran outside the Oxford city wall, in the town ditch, not far from Pembroke and Christ Church.

The Flutes of Autumn (1983) 81

The Oxford of the mid-1950s has now vanished as irrevocably as the Oxford of *Brideshead Revisited*, thirty years earlier. It was a city of uncrowded pavements, in which undergraduates stood out with their confident voices, height, haircuts, tweed jackets, flannel trousers and bicycle clips, and dons with their shaggy untidiness or sleekly tailored suits. Lorries still rattled up and down St. Giles, Cornmarket Street and St. Aldates on journeys between the Midlands and the south. Every street contained small shops selling anything from second-hand furniture, books or pictures to buns and lardy cake, fountain-pens, raincoats, typewriters or cigars. There were a few department stores but no pedestrian shopping malls. Undergraduates arrived by train, shouldering their trunks or reclaiming them in college as luggage sent on in advance. The huge majority were men, nearly all aged twenty and upwards, since nearly all of them had done two years' National Service after leaving school. The tiny handful of Benedictine monks, Franciscan and Dominican friars and Jesuit scholastics were a little older, but since their clothing and manner set them apart from the rest any difference in age seemed irrelevant.

The rules at Campion Hall were more relaxed than those at Heythrop or Manresa. Scholastics would have found it impossible to chaperone one another, so they were allowed to go about alone. Unlike monks and friars, who had to slip out of evening meetings early to be back in chapel in time for Compline, the Jesuits were on their honour to say their office by themselves. They socialized in a limited way, frequenting the most respectable societies and avoiding the publicity-seeking cliques, the raucous parties they overheard when taking short cuts through Christ Church, and of course the women. Most of them spent hours in libraries, went faithfully to lectures and were conscientious about writing essays. Pressure to conform was exerted gently within Campion Hall through the mutual watchfulness of a small, tight community who knew a great deal about one another. When a new friend invited Peter to dine with him early in his second year, he excused himself reluctantly. 'We're not supposed to dine out terribly often, and I have been out rather a lot lately, so I don't think I ought to; but may I simply postpone it and come some other time?'[1]

His first two Oxford terms were cautious and low-key. He told Bertie, early on, that he saw a lot of Bobby Butterworth, Clarence Gallagher and a couple of other brethren from Heythrop and Manresa, but knew hardly anybody else. The idea of making real friends in any of the festively lit-up colleges, or even at lectures, seemed remote. In his clerical collar and black suit he stood out as someone of whom non-religious undergraduates might well feel shy. He found, however, that he already had one ready-made college friend. Alexander Eaglestone had had a crisis at Campion Hall the year before, left the Jesuits and begun again at Magdalen College that autumn. Missing his years of closeness to the brethren, and nervous that Campion Hall men might cut him dead in the street, he was grateful for Peter's eager friendliness, which helped to bridge the gap between his two Oxford lives.

Peter worked enthusiastically at his Greek and Latin texts, finding a hero at once in Oxford's most distinguished Latinist, Eduard Fraenkel. One of the great refugee scholars of his generation, Fraenkel had been Professor of Latin until he turned sixty-five the year before. A crustier version of the terrifying and inspiring figure he had been in the late

1930s, when Iris Murdoch had been the star pupil at his seminars on the *Agamemnon* of Aeschylus, he continued to hold seminars in retirement, and for a time believed Peter might be another Iris. On the first Tuesday of term at five o'clock he had wandered uninvited into the seminar room at Corpus Christi. Most of the twenty or so people crammed round the table were either graduate students or second-year (he wrongly thought third-year) undergraduates. Fraenkel glared at Peter's clerical collar, raised his eyebrows at his Jewish surname and invited him to read. The subject was Horace, of whom Fraenkel was writing a critical study. Peter, who loved Horace, went away exhilarated at the end of two hours. He soon read all Fraenkel's published textual commentaries and learned the right moment to offer scholarly doubts about the authenticity of a passage. Fraenkel would beam and exclaim 'Ah, Mr. Levi, you and I, alone in the world, understand this.'

Classicists studied Greek and Latin for five terms, taking Honour Moderations (Mods) for the first part of their degree examination in the second term of their second year. In Peter's time they had to read the whole of the *Iliad* and *Odyssey*, the *Æneid* and other literary set books in Greek and Latin. They had to be able to write Latin and Greek prose compositions and (optionally) verse, and to have studied a special subject such as Homeric archaeology, classical philology, Greek vase-painting, the comedies of Aristophanes or the histories of Thucydides. This usually led on to Literae Humaniores (Greats), a further seven terms spent on ancient history and the whole of western philosophy, from Plato, Aristotle, Descartes, Leibniz, Kant and Hegel to the analytical philosophers who dominated the contemporary Oxford scene.

Hardly any teaching took place in Campion Hall, although Peter had a tutor there, Father Vincent Turner, who arranged his outside tutorials and gave him general advice. More of a religious dormitory than a college, it was one of the fringe institutions that were only affiliated to the university. English Jesuit scholastics studied there, together with a few foreign priests. The senior members, who came and went as the Provincial decreed, consisted at that time of a dean, two tutors who were both philosophers, and the Master, the wise and kindly Father Thomas Corbishley. It had a common room, a library, a refectory, an ornate chapel in an upper room, and tall, gabled rear quarters filled with study-bedrooms. The clean-lined Clipsham stone front designed by Lutyens looks impenetrable, with leaded, mullioned ground-floor windows set high above pavement-level and double entrance doors under a receding arch, facing north towards the blackened stone rear walls of Pembroke College in narrow, tunnel-like Brewer Street off St. Aldates. The people who pass through those doors are usually alone and move briskly. Inside, footsteps clack back from the surfaces of tiles and varnished wood.

The clever and energetic Father D'Arcy, the Master and guiding spirit of Campion Hall from its creation in 1935 until he left eleven years later to become Provincial, had been more interested in making it a centre of brilliance than in importing worthy academics. He had filled it with works of art and fashionable dinner-guests, some of whom were his personal converts. A remnant of that tradition lived on in the shrill male gossip that filled the refectory on guest nights. 'There is no ladies' night in this miserable institution,' Peter apologized twelve years later, '& we must suffer hideous feasts of all-male & clerical wit.'[2] Prominent visiting Catholics often stayed or dined at Campion Hall when invited to speak at the Oxford Union or at the Catholic Chaplaincy just down the road in St. Aldates.

It was perhaps at a Newman Society meeting or after-Mass gathering at the Chaplaincy that Peter met Denis Bethell, his first non-Jesuit Oxford friend. 'A medieval historian... enchanting, humorous, kindly, and brave',[3] Denis was one of the few people he portrayed in *The Flutes of Autumn*, the intriguingly evasive autobiography he wrote soon after Denis's death from cancer at the age of forty-six. Discreet about Oxford friends to the extent of excluding them from his account, he made that one exception in a chapter that is effectively a prose elegy for Denis.

Big, hairy, untidy, sexless, joky, learned and deeply serious, Denis was in his first year reading history at Lincoln College. His Anglican, public-school, official background was tainted with sadness: his father had committed suicide as colonial treasurer of Gibraltar when Denis was very young. A much older brother had been a wartime fighter pilot who took part in the mass break-out from Stalag Luft III. On National Service in Germany Denis had made friends with John Clanchy, an Ampleforth-educated Catholic, and decided to become a Catholic too. Joyfully ascetic in the pursuit of his interests, which included medieval manuscripts, antiquarian byways and ancient buildings, he seemed indifferent to physical discomfort. In his first long vacation he persuaded a friend to drive him on a tour of Spanish cathedrals, insisting that they ate all their meals and slept in the small, squalid car. He romanticized hunting and introduced Peter to beagling, which kept them both happily exercised on winter Saturday afternoons. Following the Christ Church beagles across stretches of country outside Oxford, they pushed through thickets and squeezed through gaps in hedges, splashed through streams, stood around in icy hilltop kale fields watching for elusive hares, and sometimes ended up being given tea with the field at a nearby country house.

Bold and enterprising, Denis led explorations of parts of Oxford that Peter would never have thought of penetrating on his own. At the Bodleian, he introduced him to the fifteenth-century Duke Humfrey's Library, where scholars read manuscripts and early printed books against the dotty chatter of elderly genealogists and the learned comments of the librarian, Dr. Richard Hunt. He taught him to look at stained glass, carvings, monuments and rare library treasures whose existence few undergraduates had heard of. The two of them explored museums, the vault underneath the Castle, the well inside the green castle mound, and the hill-country of Matthew Arnold's poems *Thyrsis* and *The Scholar-Gipsy* between the Hinkseys, Chilswell Farm, Cumnor and the Thames at Bablockhythe. Imposing themselves on Dr. Hunt's graduate palaeography seminars, they learned how texts descended from one manuscript copy to another from the Dark Ages onwards. Intoxicated with seventeenth-century culture, they swapped quotations from George Herbert, John Aubrey, Andrew Marvell and Izaak Walton. Towards the end of his first year Peter wrote an essay, 'Study to be Quiet', on the longing for peace and refuge in seventeenth-century literature, showing the influence both of Christopher Devlin and of long conversations with Denis.[4]

But Denis was a scholar, not a poet, and Peter soon discovered the noisy swaggerers and quiet dabblers of the Oxford poetry world. An introduction to the friendly Constantine Trypanis, who was Bywater and Sotheby Professor of Byzantine and Modern Greek, gained him a place at Trypanis's Friday evening poetry-readings for groups of six or seven at his Norham Gardens home. A poet with vast literary interests, he had taught classics at the University of Athens, fought through the Second World War, then moved to England to devote himself to medieval and modern Greek literature and English poetry. The readings at his house were usually from classic poets such as Spenser or Marvell, but Trypanis, whose small department of the Modern Languages Faculty did not keep him overstretched with work, also read his own poems at Tuesday meetings of the University Poetry Society, where the contributions were sometimes aggressively cutting-edge.

In those days most ambitious literary undergraduates saw themselves as poets before developing into novelists, playwrights, journalists, publishers or academics. Poetry at its best still attracted high cultural respect, and Eliot, Auden and Edith Sitwell were regarded as national eminences. The University Poetry Society, while relying mainly on its own senior members as guest readers at its meetings, provided a forum for undergraduates to make friends with fellow-poets and admire or bitch about one another's work. In a tradition begun in the 1940s by Kingsley Amis, Philip Larkin and John Wain, it was dominated by the ironical, modernist tendency which had recently been defined as the Movement. Socially egalitarian and anti-romantic, it aimed to reproduce the flat tones and commonsensical, low-key forms of everyday speech. The president of the society in Peter's first term was the future left-wing performance poet Adrian Mitchell, and a recent office-holder was George MacBeth, who antagonized Peter a few years later. ('That terrible man MacBeth I should like to strangle him in his beard,' he wrote, after MacBeth had attached himself to a similar, London-based tendency, the Group.)[5] Trypanis, a close friend of John Wain, had been influenced by the Movement, while its founder members included Elizabeth Jennings, a fervent Catholic and intermittent depressive, who had stayed on in Oxford since graduating with a job in the city library. But Peter had no quarrel with cliques; to meet other poets was enough.

Half-way through the autumn term he struck lucky. At a pot-luck reading chaired by Elizabeth Jennings, a twenty-four-year-old American Rhodes Scholar, Richard Selig, stood up to introduce the poems of Theodore Roethke, his former literature professor at the University of Washington, Seattle. Roethke, a lyrical, highly sensitive romantic poet, was still almost unknown in England and quite alien to the Movement. Reared as the child of an immigrant German father among vast commercial greenhouses in Michigan, he wrote autobiographical poems with strong, musical rhyme-schemes and Yeatsian rhythms. Peter was enchanted and at once made friends with Selig, who adopted him as a companion spirit in the American way. Himself a dedicated romantic, whose work with the halibut fishery off the north-west coast had given a glittering, masculine edge to his poems, he was confident enough to stand out as an independent figure in the Poetry Society and to try out big poems with triumphantly rolling, long lines. When he and Adrian Mitchell edited the 1955 volume of *Oxford Poetry*, it included two of Peter's poems.

Freed from the pious atmosphere he had shared with Bertie, Peter had outgrown hymn-like exercises and derivative, clichéd expressions of emotion. 'Mrs Hanratty Wept', the neat, ventriloquistic piece of fantasy Selig liked best, reflected his cautious venture into a modern, mildly humorous mood. Peter thought it didn't entirely come off, but conceded that it seemed 'to have *something*'.[6]

That white mare flicked up her heels as nimble as ninepence,
when she was young. But now she never stirs more
than from one leg onto the other, the old mare. She'll die
but she was a lovely creature. That ragged dog
went mad in the spring with the smell of so many rabbits,
and had to be shot, poor dog. Oh but they all
die, all grow old, the snorting gryphon and the tiger
in the young woods, the untamable salamander,
and the gentle beast, the dear white unicorn -
who was buried in a meadow in Calvados, and the birds
come to sing him there, but never will wake him, lulled
in his meadow of poppies. But Mrs Hanratty wept,
and said it was a lovely creature. A lovely creature, she said.[7]

❧

Like an ordinary college, Campion Hall ejected its undergraduates for the vacations. Being forbidden to go home to their families, they had to stay at other Jesuit houses. Peter usually chose Beaumont, since he liked being close to London and, despite having friends at Manresa, had no wish to revisit the scene of his teacher-training year. In his first term at Oxford he promised Bertie, who was suffering there, that he would try to get into his 'hell-house' for Christmas, but for the Easter vacation he went to Beaumont, fraternizing with the cleverer sixth-formers and doing a little light teaching. The spring term at Oxford had been its usual trying self, with dull weather causing energy-slumps and academic work becoming a grind. Beaumont revived him, and well before Easter Sunday, on April 10, he had already been swimming and rowing on the river, was thinking of having a run and had promised to dig a ditch. 'Vive le sport!'[8]

In Easter week he and a gang of Campion Hall friends bicycled to Manresa and back to visit Bertie, then set off for Oxford by way of Maidenhead and Henley. With Denis, and sometimes other companions, he would walk back along the river from Oxford to London at midsummer for the sheer romantic pleasure of the journey, telling stories from the Odyssey in a conversation that lasted all night.

We drank port and ate bacon sandwiches,
light found us washing in the empty Thames.

Sharing the same innocent outlook, he and Denis chose to place most human experiences in a literary context. When they came on a pair of lovers in a field they thought of them as figures in a poem by Donne, unaware (Peter reflected later), of *what human weight/John Donne dragged after him as poetry.*[9]

For people who take Schools after three years, the first long summer vacation can be a cultural or career opportunity, a blissful playtime or an agonizing, aimless void. Classicists, however, need to devote much of the time to preparing for Mods. After consulting the Regius Professor of Greek, Eric Dodds, about his special subject, Peter chose the comedies of Aristophanes, and at Dodds's suggestion wrote to Fraenkel asking if he would supervise him. Fraenkel's tired response, from a hotel at Pesaro, already contained a thinly veiled put-down. He would not comment on Peter's suitability for Aristophanes, since both Dodds and Peter himself seemed to believe in it, but hoped that Peter's 'uncommon energy and enthusiasm' would see him safely through. He did not finally refuse, however, since Peter was writing a paper on *The Birds* for him before the end of the year.[10]

Richard Selig went to Ireland that summer and met the love of his life, a beautiful young harpist and singer from Sligo, Mary O'Hara. They planned to marry in Oxford after Richard had taken his finals the following June. Then they would sail to New York, where Richard intended to finance his writing with an office job. As a token of his friendship, from a Jew to a half-Jewish Catholic, he invited Peter to be best man at their Catholic wedding.

Peter had no hope of a foreign holiday until after Mods, when Campion Hall classicists spent their Easter vacation at a Jesuit house in Italy, France or Germany. He worked at his books and fretted about the kind of poetry he ought to write. He may have performed some duty at Farm Street on August 4, when Edith Sitwell, magnificently swathed in black, was received into the Church by Father Philip Caraman and Father D'Arcy. Although he was not one of the small group of people Evelyn Waugh noticed at the ceremony, he wrote to Edith soon afterwards telling her that he had discovered a precedent for the famous Sitwell Egg, a kind of Scotch Egg invented by her father with a yolk of smoked meat, a white of cooked rice and a shell of synthetic lime. Edith sent him a charming reply, wondering if eccentrics differed much from one another through the ages and adding that her father had looked like a 'huge, mad bird', which added interest to the invention.[11]

After that he went through a brief Sitwellian phase, publishing a painfully syncopated pastiche, 'The Black Girl and the Girl with the Unicorns' in the 1956 *Oxford Poetry*.

The black girl jangled
her golden bangles
and said, I am as beautiful
as the apricot blossom
in the garden of the unicorn
at the end of the ocean...

But eighteen months after the ceremony he wrote sadly to Bertie that, while Edith Sitwell thought he had a lovely and loving nature and spirit '(obviously, she says)... my poetry, qua poetry, she doesn't understand.'[12]

Bertie, teaching games at Wimbledon College, was inclined to think, like Clarence, that Peter's poems were veering in the wrong direction. Why couldn't he simply stick to the familiar, traditional stuff? With time on his hands at Heythrop in late September, Peter sent him a long manifesto. He wanted his poems to be 'white-hot, Apocalyptic, or... *strongly* written, like Dryden, or... beautiful in the fantastic & yet simple way of Andrew Marvell.' He believed that one *must* write in modern English, without pulling out familiar emotive organ-stops. Yet he also wanted to learn more from the Greek classics, since half of what they taught did not seem ever to have been learnt.[13]

℘

A shake of the academic kaleidoscope in October brought new Jesuit scholastics to Oxford and new twenty-year-old freshmen into lectures and society meetings. Anthony Levi arrived to read Modern Languages at Campion Hall, and Willie Charlton, an Ampleforth-educated Catholic with an impish smile and a dry sense of humour, came up to New College to read classics. He had just published a book, *Travelling Hopefully*, describing a European hike from one Benedictine monastery to another on the model of Hilaire Belloc's *The*

Path to Rome. John Clanchy introduced him to Denis, who decided to share him with Peter.

> One evening in my first term [Willie wrote] he appeared in my rooms with a strikingly handsome and unexpectedly youthful-looking dark figure in clerical dress. I found Peter slightly awesome but utterly charming. I immediately started seeing a lot of him, usually in company with Denis. We went for walks together along the canal and round Port Meadow. We also often dined together. Denis and I being on a tight budget and Peter vowed to poverty, we did the rounds of the cheapest eating places: the Oxford Union, where Peter or Denis, I forget which, said the dining room was like the inside of an iced cake, the Café de Paris, the Roma, and a small hotel possibly called the Bridge where the road crossed the canal near the station.[14]

With Denis Willie argued about medieval theologians, a subject that interested both of them far more than it did Peter. With Peter he talked classics, playing a favourite game of Peter's of inventing sequels to the *Odyssey*. Peter found him clever and sympathetic and enjoyed feeling protective towards him. He introduced him to Trypanis's poetry evenings as a published writer, and, like Sebastian in *Brideshead Revisited*, offered to show him the Botanic Garden.

Between them, Peter, Denis and Willie planned a discussion club of twelve members, to be chosen for their wit and broad cultural interests. An informal, private version of an old-fashioned college essay society, it would attract their most intelligent friends. They decided to call it the Opimian Club after the Reverend Dr. Opimian in Thomas Love Peacock's *Gryll Grange*, who took his name from a legendary ancient Roman vintage. Peter invented the rules, that members must 'possess as much Latin as Shakespeare and as much science as Dr Johnson'. Willie, in the guise of Cellarer, took responsibility for the minutes, which he wrote with a playful touch.[15] The first meeting took place in Denis's rooms in Lincoln College on May 10, 1956, in the term after

Peter's Mods.

As soon as their exams were over in early March, Peter and Clarence left by train for Italy. Peter, on his first foreign holiday at the age of nearly twenty-five, was about to see Venice and Florence from the chilly shelter of Jesuit houses. Reading the March issue of *Encounter* on the journey, he was fascinated by an unfinished country-house murder story by Cyril Connolly, who at once became his literary hero in place of Evelyn Waugh. 'Shade Those Laurels' struck him as brilliantly sophisticated and original – reminiscent, he told Connolly later, of Petronius's *Satyricon*. Its clever, mannered, Peacockian echoes appealed to his burgeoning Opimian Club sensibilities. Years later, after Connolly's death, he would republish the story with his own ending, too late to attract much serious attention.

Venice can be cold, damp, and grey in March, and his few days there left Peter unmoved. He sent Bertie a disaffected postcard of tourists outside the Doge's Palace, complaining about the food and joking about a bare-shouldered 'loose-looking female' in the picture. Florence, however, enchanted him. The Duomo and Battistero had not yet been blackened by a hundred years of exhaust-fumes, and still gleamed with white, green and red marble among the red-tiled city roofs. Visitors could get into the Uffizi to see Botticelli's *Primavera* without queuing for hours in the sewage-smelling loggia outside. Peter and Clarence spent a few days at a Jesuit house in the city, then moved out to the country retreat-house at Villa Machiavelli, Settignano, in the hills just north-east of the city. Threatened with convalescence there years later, Peter referred to it as 'a terrible ecclesiastical icehouse overlooking Florence from a great distance'.[16] The Jesuits' most famous neighbour was the art historian Bernard Berenson at the villa I Tatti, and the visitors were sent into his garden to see the anemones, although not to view the master's famous art collection inside the house.

Denis, immersed in twelfth-century history, sent notes of things

Peter ought to look at: an ivory crozier in the Bargello bearing a carved head of Ivo of Chartres, and the Codex Amiatinus if it was on display.[17] From Hunt's seminars, Denis knew that the Codex was the earliest whole surviving manuscript of St. Jerome's Vulgate version of the Bible, copied at the Northumbrian monastery of Jarrow-Monkwearmouth in about 700, and preserved for over a thousand years in an Italian monastery until transferred to the Laurentian Library in Florence. Peter dutifully turned up at the Library and asked to see the Codex, imagining a 'slim, pretty New Testament', not an outsize volume.

It took two men to carry, and eight volumes of an encyclopaedia to prop up. I did not dare move from it all day, and I think that was only volume one... It was a gigantic Bible of awe-inspiring beauty and rigorous plainness. Of all the mistakes I could have made, that one was the most rewarding. As dusk fell, I crept away, having had a long read of the Bible in Latin.[18]

ஒ

Back in Oxford he found he had a first in Mods, while Clarence had a second. Now he could relax and enjoy the intellectual high jinks of the Opimian Club. Between them he, Denis and Willie had recruited nine other members, including Maurice Keen, a scholar and future medieval history fellow of Balliol, Brian Brindley, a flamboyantly camp Anglo-Catholic in his last term at Exeter, and Denis's friend John Clanchy at Trinity. ('Nearly all of us got firsts,' explained Willie.) Peter's rambling inaugural paper traced the progress of pastoral from Theocritus to Virgil, then downhill from the classically idyllic to the sixteenth- and seventeenth-century bucolic. Willie, in sprightly Cellarer mode, called it 'a lugubrious chronicle... brightened by the occasional successes of Ben Jonson, Drayton and...Gray, and enlivened by the portentous shuffling of Mr Levi's notes.'[19]

In his other life as a poet, Peter was ecstatic. Two of his poems came out at the end of May in a new magazine, *Oxford Opinion*. One was a romantic evocation of dead cities; the other a Blakean celebration of summer in the open air, its terraqueous imagery suggesting walks through a buttercup-filled Port Meadow towards the Perch at Binsey or the Trout at Godstow.

> *I am the child of earth and of the sun,*
> *I watch him godlike in the fields of air*
> *running up heaven with loose golden hair*
> *to hang there flaming when his height is won.*
>
> *Sometimes I lie all day in seas of grass,*
> *where silence is, and cows like riding fleets*
> *anchor in sunlight; but no water beats*
> *on those still shores; the ripples pass and pass.*

Richard Selig was occupied with work and writing love-letters to Mary, but Peter had a new poet friend in Julian Mitchell, reading history at Wadham after National Service in submarines. A sharply critical, classically educated Wykehamist, he persuaded Peter that the Poetry Society was a waste of time. Defiantly romantic, he hated the ideology of the Movement and mocked the proletarian poets as 'flying jackets' for the Ted Hughes-style leather coats that some of them wore. 'We were obsessed with class in those days,' he said. 'U and Non-U, and all that.'

'Middle-class' was still used as a disparaging term by people who aspired to be upper-class and smart. Peter's charm, wit, eagerness, good looks and mysterious Jesuit apartness transcended his suburban background, so that smart or would-be smart people began to collect him. Brian Brindley, already fascinated by young clergymen, invested him with a certain exotic glamour, claiming that he gave the impression of having arrived from some Tibetan Shangri-La. He invited him to his

Oxford dining club and enjoyed the sight of him sitting innocently among rubicund, white-tied, sporting grandees.[20]

'I'll endeavour to return to Beaumont unwedded,' Peter joked to Bertie in July, on the point of leaving to act as Richard's best man at St. Aloysius, the big Jesuit church next to Somerville. As the pair walked up the aisle, however, the celebrant took fright. Mary was a minor celebrity whose wedding might make a newspaper story, and the Provincial might be horrified to learn that one of his scholastics had been involved. He demoted Peter to serving on the altar, and Richard's tutor stepped forward to be best man. Peter told Bertie that Mary had looked stunning in a dress of lace over satin and a coronet of baroque pearls. The dozen or so guests piled into punts on the Cherwell for a picnic wedding lunch. One of them, with a punt of his own, was the well-off Alec Eaglestone, who (Peter reported) had become engaged to a delightful and suitable Catholic from Lady Margaret Hall.[21] Neither Richard nor Mary told anybody that Richard had been diagnosed with the Hodgkin's lymphoma that would kill him in just over a year.

In August, the Campion Hall brethren spent their fortnight's seaside villa at St. Christopher's School, Heanton Punchardon, near Braunton on the North Devon coast. The men let off steam in their shared dormitory with some puerile rough-housing and jokes about bottoms being beaten. One Saturday Peter, Bob Butterworth and Tony Lawn went otter-hunting – a sport which was still encouraged in those days to protect the salmon fishery in rivers. Like beagling, it was mainly an excuse for the followers to scramble on foot across country and get thoroughly dirty and wet. No otters were caught, but the scholastics had a wonderful day following the Teign upstream from Chudleigh behind a Master in a grey hat and breeches who turned out to be a woman. The hunt staff invited them to come back any Saturday and spend the night at the kennels. Then Tony drove them in their hired Ford Zephyr at a daring forty miles an hour through the nocturnal mid-Devon country with its wooded valleys, small branch-line railways and fields full of baled hay. The next day there was wind, rain and sun, and they swam in a sea 'like cold champagne with waves like hedges breaking & booming all over the place'.[22]

Early in October Peter wrote to Willie that he was looking forward to an Opimian Club term. They would have to find a new twelfth man since Brian Brindley had gone down. He passed on a gossipy rumour that John Clanchy had been seen in Florence wearing jeans, and suspected that he might have 'gone rather bohemian!'

Oxford Greats men of the 1950s were among the most respectable members of a generally conventional generation. The all-male, port-sipping, effortlessly cultured ethos of the Opimian Club suited Peter's celibacy and his almost Widmerpool-like enthusiasm for academic work. After the rigour of Mods he found philosophy glamorous, not so much because the work suited him but because of the personalities involved. Between them the brisk, fashionable logician Freddie Ayer, the burly Catholic Wittgensteinian Elizabeth Anscombe, Iris Murdoch in her emergent state as philosopher-cum-novelist, Stuart Hampshire and Isaiah Berlin represented a rare blend of sophistication, eccentricity and enigmatic wisdom. Peter longed to describe them with the panache that Ved Mehta, who arrived at Balliol that October, would display in an article for the *New Yorker*, republished in his *Fly and the Fly-Bottle* (1963).

New poetic talent arrived that term. At Magdalen College David Pryce-Jones, dapper, sociable and confident, brought sophistication (Eton and the Guards), cosmopolitanism (his mother was a Franco-Austrian-Jewish baroness), familiarity with the literary world (his father Alan edited the *Times Literary Supplement*) and a talent for absorbing languages and inventing fantastic new ones. At Jesus, that year's freshmen included Ved's friend the precocious, eighteen-year-old Dom Moraes, a poet from Bombay with eyes huger and darker than Peter's and a bluish-black, floppy-haired beauty.

Impressed to learn that Dom was a protégé of Stephen Spender, a friend of his father who had arranged his admission to Jesus, Julian Mitchell invited him to Wadham and asked Peter to meet him. Dom was struck by Peter's odd mixture of gracefulness and gaucheness, his loud laugh, which Julian called the *Brek-ek-ek koax koax* of Aristophanes' *The Frogs*, and his habit of plunging into sudden, meditative silence.[23] Peter was attracted to Dom, as much for his romantic dissoluteness (he drank recklessly and was known to have a mistress in London) as for his melting good looks, engaging childishness and whimsically self-indulgent talent. He had already persuaded David Archer, the generous, nearly bankrupt owner of the Parton Press in Soho, to bring out his first volume of poems, *A Beginning*.

Julian was planning a new Oxford and Cambridge literary quarterly with a former school-friend, Willie Donaldson. *Gemini* would be a classy affair, with an introductory article by Spender and a guest poem by Cecil Day Lewis in the first, spring 1957 number. The other poems were the best that Oxford and Cambridge could offer. Two were by Sylvia Plath, in her second year as a Fulbright scholar at Newnham, three by Elizabeth Jennings and two by Peter. Among the handful of other writers a Cambridge undergraduate, Geoffrey Strachan, contributed a clever verse parody of Kingsley Amis's *Lucky Jim*.

'Elements', the more modernistic of Peter's two poems, suggests the archaic Greek and early Christian image in which a shepherd's muscular arms grip the legs of a sheep slung yokewise round his neck.

> *The ewe's hot body weighted his shoulders,*
> *the road splashed up dust...*[24]

In *Isis* that autumn he published the melancholy, accomplished 'Alcaics',

> *We too have seen them, crooked and water-eyed,*

holy, the old - rain strung from the loaded air -
the terrible old with their coughs and wisdom,
under the trees in the truth and darkness...

and a derivative echo of early Eliot,

In Athens, in Paris, in Rome,
the faces pass and repass in rooms
where often in several directions
mirrors reflect reflections of reflections,
where green opacity
of sheer obliquity
confuses the eye in a trapped contemplation...[25]

which, understandably, did not appear in any of his later collections.

❧

Three weeks into the Oxford autumn term, Hungarian students and workers revolted against the oppressive, Soviet-imposed policies of their government. At the same time Israeli forces, urged on by Britain and France, invaded the Sinai Peninsula, east of Suez, in retaliation for Egypt's nationalization of the British- and French-financed Suez Canal. On the last day in October, after the Egyptian government had ignored an ultimatum to withdraw from the Canal zone, British planes bombed Egyptian military airfields in Sinai and outside Cairo. Within a few days British marines were shooting at Egyptian civilians in Port Said.

Political opinion in England sided strongly with the Hungarians, whom the Russians had mown down with machine-guns and tanks on the streets of Budapest. It split violently, however, over Suez, since many liberal-minded conservatives were appalled by the actions of Eden's government. Peter always claimed to have been a left-wing sympathizer from that time onwards, although a postcard he sent to Bertie, soon after the crisis began, referred unpleasantly to 'wogs' and the solidarity of 'anti-wog' feeling in Campion Hall.

On Tuesday, November 7, he and Denis set out for an afternoon walk down the Thames towpath towards Iffley and beyond. It was damp and cloudy and the light failed early. Striking westwards across sodden fields and watercourses, they climbed through Kennington into Bagley Wood, where they lost their way in a tangle of footpaths. By the time they emerged on to Hinksey Hill, which runs down from suburban Boars Hill to the roundabout north of Kennington, it was dark. At that point they probably abandoned a plan to walk on over the hilltop, past Chilswell Farm and down into Oxford by way of Cumnor or North Hinksey. It seemed easier to walk back down Hinksey Hill and hope to catch a bus coming up from Abingdon.

Through a gap in the hedge, above the dark blot of Christ Church Meadow, they would have made out Matthew Arnold's 'line of festal light in Christ-Church hall'. As their figures blended into the dimness beyond the gap, an elderly lady, driving downhill, glanced sideways at the lights without noticing the two walkers and swerved, momentarily out of control. Thrown to the ground by her car, Peter hit his head on the road and lay concussed in a drift of dead leaves. A report in the *Oxford Times* three days later stated:

> Mr Peter Levi, a student, of Campion Hall, Oxford, was admitted to the Radcliffe Infirmary on Tuesday with head injuries after he had been involved in an accident on Hinksey Hill. The hospital said yesterday that Mr Levi's condition was 'improved'.

7
A HORRIBLE MAD FIT

What if the world were a horrible mad fit,
human reason sand, and God a mere unknown,
and no philosophies could temper it
to shivering flesh and nerve, breakable bone,
but the mind's vigour alone?

The Gravel Ponds (1960) 33

His head ached and he hobbled when he walked. For the first time in his life since early childhood his eyes did not focus on print, and it was obvious that he could not go to lectures or keep up his weekly tutorial essays. A doctor told him he needed six months' rest, which (he realised) would mean repeating the whole academic year, a prospect the Jesuits might balk at if it stretched his time at Oxford from four years to five. When he came out of the Radcliffe Infirmary, up the road from St. Aloysius's Church, they packed him off to a retirement home for sick and aged Jesuits, Burton Hill at Barlavington, a few miles south of Petworth in Sussex. The morning he left he wrote a quick note to Willie, saying that he would love to collaborate with him on a Greek translation, and sending apologies to the Opimian Club. 'Please may I not resign?'[1]

Exactly two weeks after Peter's accident, Bert Levi died in hospital at Eastbourne from cirrhosis of the liver and other ailments. Peter had visited him regularly as he had grown weaker through the summer, and was allowed out of Burton Hill for the funeral, which Anthony organized and Father Clem Tigar conducted. Then the bleakness of bereavement struck home after he returned and sat in pain among the wasted figures of his father's age and older. He had written light-heartedly to Bertie, after visiting Italy, that the thought of not having been there was like the thought of being maimed. Now, among the maimed, halt and blind, he wondered if he would ever lead a normal life again.

After a time he began to feel more at home with some of the elderly Jesuits. A few had shrivelled into uncommunicativeness, but others had shed their former institutional manner for a tranquil wisdom. The most famous inhabitant of Burton Hill, and the favourite public figure of many twentieth-century Catholic converts, was Father Cyril Martindale. From Pope's Hall, which later became Campion Hall, he had won an armful of university prizes and the double first in Greats for which Peter still hoped. After ordination he had returned to Pope's Hall to teach classics before turning to pastoral work at Farm Street. Now he was a frail seventy-seven, with an alert mind and a kindly manner.

A few years after Peter's stay at Burton Hill, Father Martindale saw a review of his first volume of poems and wrote him an encouraging letter. Courteously recalling him as 'our visitor here', he advised him to ignore any carping from other Jesuits about his presumption in writing secular poems. Famed in the past his crisp sermons, he urged Peter to exploit his taste for imagery while he was still young enough to have the descriptive urge.

'You probably find that all created things are sacramental, i.e. contain & convey God. In proportion as you are conscious of their Creator, you will probably want to say less & less about them; but while you want to say something, say it!'[2]

In December Peter started to limp around outside. Not far from Burton Hill was Petworth House, a vast, seventeenth-century classical mansion in a park designed by Capability Brown, which the third Lord Leconfield had given to the National Trust while keeping a family tenancy there. The park contains the oldest herd of fallow deer in England. When alarmed, or sometimes for no apparent reason, deer run together in an undulating, almost silent stream.

In midwinter a wood was
where the sand-coloured deer ran
through quietness.
It was a marvellous thing
to see those deer running.

Softer than ashes
snow lay all winter where they ran,
and in the wood a holly tree was.
God, it was a marvellous thing
to see the deer running.
Between lime trunks grey or green
branch-headed stags went by
silently trotting.
A holly tree dark and crimson
sprouted at the wood's centre, thick and high
without a whisper, no other berry so fine.

Outside the wood was black midwinter,
over the downs that reared so solemn
wind rushed in gales, and strong here
wrapped around wood and holly fire
(where deer among the close limes ran)
with a storming circle of its thunder.
Under the trees it was a marvellous thing
to see the deer running.[3]

From Burton Hill, he went to Beaumont as usual for Christmas. His future was still unclear, he told friends in despairing New Year letters. The Jesuits might not allow him back to Oxford until the summer or even the autumn, and he had no idea whether they would let him go on with Greats. He had set his heart on philosophy, and now it seemed that he might have to give it up. 'Meanwhile I don't know what I shall be doing: probably teaching,' he told Willie. At the end of the holidays he moved to Father Clem's institution at Osterley, a lonelier refuge even than Burton Hill, with a meagre electric fire to sit by and a few books in which he struggled to concentrate on a sentence or two at a time. While there, he probably helped out with the Latin teaching which brought the seminarians up to standard to begin training for the priesthood.

Trypanis responded to his letter by tactfully suggesting that if Greats were 'going to prove troublesome' he could arrange for him to change to a Modern Languages course in his own obscure subject, Byzantine and Modern Greek. It would be easier than Greats, and he thought that some of the literature should tie in with Peter's theological interests. Denis wondered if the Jesuits would send him to convalesce in Italy. Julian imagined him wildly as a 'stark black symbol among the creamy beaches of the Maldive Islands', and passed on praise for his poetry in the inaugural *Gemini* number by that great encourager of the young, Stephen Spender.[4] The Opimian Club minutes formally regretted Peter's absence, echoing those of the Beaumont Higher Line debating society when he had been carried off with polio at sixteen.

Had he known it, he was luckier than a Brasenose freshman of that year, the rugger-playing law student and future novelist J.G. Farrell. Just over three weeks after Peter's accident, Farrell caught a severe form of polio which paralysed his upper body, and spent weeks trapped in an iron lung in the Slade Isolation Hospital at Oxford. Recuperating slowly at home, he missed the rest of the academic year and began again, emaciated, grey-haired and reading a different subject, the following October.[5] A bang on the head should have been less damaging to Peter than polio, yet the Jesuits' response to it was almost the psychological equivalent, as far as he was concerned, of an iron lung.

At some point in January he was summoned to an interview at Wimbledon with the Provincial, Father Desmond Boyle. On the way he managed to call in briefly at Wimbledon College, but the 'ghastly grilling from the Prov' shook him so badly that he broke his promise to go back and tell Bertie how the interview had gone. Several weeks passed before he got in touch, and by then he was back at Campion Hall, where the hated Provincial happened to be staying on his annual visit. He had been forbidden to go on with Greats and was reading Trypanis's subject, with only a year and a quarter until his final Schools. He nurtured a faint hope, perhaps more wishful than anything else, of spending the Easter vacation in Greece. Meanwhile, he was enjoying the February sunlight and the flowering prunuses along the Woodstock Road, where he was lodging 'as the Prov's Mate has my bed'.

On fine February mornings in Oxford, the sun pours in through the south-facing upper windows of the Bodleian Library. It glitters on the wrought-iron fanlight in the archway and on cascading birch twigs in Exeter College garden, and throws tall shadows of pinnacles across the south front of the Clarendon Building, on whose western corner, above the frieze, the trumpeting figure of Clio stands out against the blue. Even in Peter's time, before much of the blackened, blistered limestone had been scraped or replaced, some stone was still clean and crisp enough to absorb and reflect the light.

On his way from Campion Hall towards the Bodleian one day, he jotted in his notebook, with Hopkinsian attention to detail:

> Heavy dark crimson colour of masses of berries on the tree at the end of Brewer St. Sky transparent light blue with clouds like porpoises. Feathery bare trees towards Headington embosoming New College Chapel. Vivifying stripes & masses of stone & still-looking shades.[6]

But the brilliance of late February soon turned into a sullen Oxford March, and he became depressed. The sluggish mechanics of Byzantine Greek grammar and the second-rateness of the literature reminded him painfully of his Mods expertise in Aeschylus, Aristophanes and

Homer. Cramming in as much of the stuff as he could, he fastened on the legend of the folk hero Digenes Akritas as a subject for a poem, which may have owed something to Richard Selig's muscular style:

> That hero was strong,
> outlaw and captain:
> but shaggy Charon
> forced his body down
> wrestling with him...[7]

Trypanis had edited an anthology of medieval and modern Greek poetry, and parts of it stuck permanently in his mind, including the famous poem in praise of Hagia Sophia by the sixth-century Byzantine courtier Paul the Silentiary, whom he name-dropped years later in his Afghan travelogue *The Light Garden of the Angel King*. When Julian accused him of preciousness he retorted 'It is actually how I think.'[8]

Yet for all Trypanis's kindness the change of subject seemed futile. His headaches came back, and with them the kind of despair that cries out to be noticed. Denis was revising for Schools, Willie was in his Mods term and Julian was busy with *Gemini*. Anthony, in his second year at Campion Hall, offered what little support he could, and everyone else in that tight little institution got to know about Peter's disruptive behaviour. One day he lay groaning on the stairs, blocking anyone from walking up or down. Another time he casually announced that he had given up saying his office. The senior Jesuits wondered whether his father's death, following so soon after the blow on the head, might have permanently unbalanced him. They packed him off to a psychiatrist, who (in Ved Mehta's version of the story) asked how often he masturbated. He looked blank. The psychiatrist asked again. Had he done it last night? This morning? The week before last? 'Oh, that,' he said innocently. 'Not since I was quite a small boy.'[9]

Lying awake until shuddering dawn, as the Thames and

Cherwell mists merged over Christ Church Meadow, he fantasized destruction.

> *Three counties blacken and vanish,*
> *rivers run unlighted and silent,*
> *lamp by lamp of the city came, went,*
> *into the utter dark, which was my wish.*
>
> *In my scarred thought this city*
> *burns to a ruin under the visiting air,*
> *among the ashes of whose luxury*
> *the young barbarians shake their scented hair.*
>
> *Bitterer, deeper, in my desolate thought,*
> *a lonely and a self-murdering love,*
> *uninhabitable ashes, every dove*
> *murdered, every winged buzzard caught.*
>
> *The wind rises. At this time of night*
> *condemned men lie quiet in their beds.*
> *Birds start. Vagueness clears to light.*
> *The wakeful old can let fall their heads.*
>
> *The wind rises. A workman coughs in the cold.*
> *It rises. Volleys and lines of mist*
> *push from river to river and find no hold.*
> *Leaves fall. Blood runs cold in the wrist.*[10]

Never keen on the idea of an instinctive leap of faith, he liked to argue that his religion was based on reason, and that it would worry him far more if the principles of mathematics turned out to be untrue than if the Gospels did. ('You can't mean that, Peter.' 'Oh, yes, I can. Everything depends on reason.')[11] But now, in his mood of black failure, unconsoled by metaphysics or logic, the annihilation of reason and the absence of God went together. The phase ran its course, not helped by one psychiatric session after another. For over a year he was subject to headaches, 'ghastly fits of madness' and thoughts of killing himself.[12]

> *Twenty-five years before your time my dear*
> *I have laid my head down on railway lines,*

he later mourned the perpetrator of an Oxford suicide of that kind.[13] 'No one expected me to work, least of all at Byzantine Greek,' was how he glossed over that period. Denis, a historical omnivore with a vast knowledge of medieval and early modern culture, gave him Anglo-Saxon and late Latin poems to read and pointed out the connections between outlaw ballads and Byzantine heroic epics. Despite preparing for Schools he made plenty of time for Peter, encouraging him to read medieval chronicles and seventeenth-century antiquaries for fun. 'Denis and I corresponded in the prose styles of Clarendon or Izaak Walton or Charles I. I sat for hours on end in Bodley reading Drayton's Poly-Olbion, a voluminous and crazy topographic poem.'[14]

That, however, was only part of the story; he had made up his mind to compensate for academic frustration with poetical success.

Greece had never been seriously on the cards for the Easter vacation of 1957, and he spent at least part of it at Heythrop. On a long walk one day, scrambling through thickets and trudging across thistly cow-pastures, he followed the Evenlode from Charlbury to its confluence with the Thames near Eynsham, a few miles north-west of Oxford. As he went he mulled over the idea of publishing a volume of poems. He already knew about Dom's whimsically soft-centred, mildly masochistic first collection, which, coupled with his voluptuous looks, would make a sensation the next year when it became the first book in over a decade to win the Hawthornden Prize. If Dom could publish a collection at nineteen, surely he could do the same at twenty-six. Julian, applauding the idea, urged him to 'put in that marvellous radio play', and offered to bring out the book himself under the *Gemini* imprint. Peter turned down the offer, saying that it would not be good for *Gemini's* image. Secretly, however, he had hopes of better things.

In the summer term he turned from Byzantine to modern Greek literature. Reading nineteenth- and twentieth-century poetry and novels, he gained a sense of the intellectual clarity and cultural rootedness of modern Greeks, and longed to talk to some of them in their own language. Vague promises of a visit to Athens and the islands hung round mistily for most of the term before evaporating. Unable to make travelling arrangements like a normal adult, Peter chafed at his own helplessness. Even a trip to Brighton was impossible because nobody would take him. Poverty might be romantic and obedience a shield against worldly distractions, but he was beginning to resent being broke and always needing permission to travel. Julian had been urging him to come and spend part of the summer vacation at his parents' large house at South Cerney in Gloucestershire. He wanted Peter to meet his brother Tony, a Cambridge aesthete with a passion for architecture, and to charm his father, an old-style military gent who thought most literature was rubbish. Wearily, Peter explained that he was only allowed to stay in religious houses or with his mother. 'The whole position is absurd: a sort of iron curtain with no airlift and no Intourism.'[15]

The position became more threatening that September. Under Pius XII, who had been pope throughout the Second World War and had only a year left to live, Catholic discipline was becoming more stringent. Catholic children had long since been forbidden to attend non-denominational school prayers or Scripture lessons. Any Catholic seen attending an ordinary non-Catholic service was considered to be in danger of giving scandal. The Index of Prohibited Books, a list so huge and obscure that few Catholics had ever seen it, included the novels of Sartre and Graham Greene, while films, television and radio programmes were censured if they threatened to undermine the faith.

Now the nicotine-addicted, travel-happy Jesuits came in for a flick of the whip. At a meeting of the extraordinary general congregation in Rome they were told that they would have to stop smoking and could no longer travel abroad except on church business. 'We are all smoking like furnaces before this Papal bomb hits the earth,' Peter wrote to Julian.[16] But in spite of the elusive Greek trip he still believed that, when the chance came, he would be able to find an excuse to get away.

His summer had been largely frittered between Eastbourne, Beaumont and Heythrop. Mollie had been distressed by an unsuccessful Belgian holiday, a sick-making Channel crossing and threatening letters from lawyers about her flat. Peter had spent most of July with her, ritually doing the *Times* crossword and worrying that it would soon be his turn to give a paper to the Opimian Club. From the Jesuit summer camp in North Devon he wrote to Willie that he knew too little to talk about anything Byzantine, and dared not open his mouth about philosophy. What he would like to do, he remarked rather wildly, was to talk about the history of hounds, but he lacked the books and the time to do it. He did not admit that he had sent an article about Oxford philosophers to the Jesuit periodical *The Month*, whose editor, Father Caraman, had gently remarked that, as far as his readers were concerned, it might as well be in medieval Georgian.[17]

Unable to let go of his obsession with the idea of philosophy, he told Julian, after going up early to Campion Hall in September, that although he was supposed to 'brood over nonsensical Greek romances' for Schools he was furtively scribbling away at articles under the desk. He planned an ambitious, critical philosophical work, which would involve 'wading in the next chapter or two in the blood of Plato and Coleridge'. But when he offered a sample chapter to *Encounter*, Stephen Spender, the editor, was as dismissive as Caraman had been, urging him to stick to a single discipline that he knew.[18]

After remarking high-handedly to Julian that spring that 'the national weeklies and whatnot' just didn't seem worth the bother, he began approaching editors in earnest. A long poem, *Sermon and Lament*, went to the BBC, where it was thought at first to have 'distinct radiophonic possibilities'.[19] A proposal for a verse translation of Euripides' *Cyclops* began to do the rounds. Charles Monteith at Faber & Faber, the most prestigious firm of poetry publishers, suggested he try Erica Marx of the small Hand and Flower Press, who brushed him off, saying that too much poetry was being written in those days. John Lehmann at the *London Magazine* thought his poems lacked intellectual tension. Oxford University Press turned down both his collection of poems and his proposed translation of the *Cyclops*, but invited him to stay in touch. Rupert Hart-Davis conceded that there was a freshness in his imagery that made him feel he was 'unquestionably in the presence of a poet', but had too many other poets on his books. An agent at Curtis Brown declined to handle the poems but invited Peter to meet him, and wondered percipiently if he wrote prose.[20]

A cunning detour he made to Soho, after spending a night at the Shaftesbury convent on his way back from North Devon to Beaumont, probably enabled him to meet Dom and his girlfriend Henrietta. Dom was charming enough, with his egocentric, wise-child cleverness and his doe-eyed beauty. When people saw him and Peter together, they were amazed by their combined good looks. But Peter was also fascinated by Henrietta, a raffishly attractive woman of his own age and the only one he knew who seemed to treat him as a normal man. Imperious, needy and attention-seeking, she reeked of sex, drink and Soho low life. Although the mother of two young children (the elder of whom had been fathered by Colin Tennant several months before she married a minor actor, Norman Bowler), she did not let that interfere with her days and nights on the town. She had slept with Lucian Freud, modelled for him and Francis Bacon and hung out in the French House, the Colony Room and the Greek Street café where she had first met Dom. The homosexual artist John Minton had left her the lease of his house in Chelsea when he killed himself early that year. In that cage she hoped to keep Dom, whom she pursued back to Oxford whenever he got away.

In the autumn term of his final year Peter struck a melancholy pose.

Devastated by Richard Selig's death and the news that both Richard and Mary had known of his illness at the time of their wedding, he wrote to Mary that he and other Catholics were praying that God would reunite her with Richard one day in heaven.[21] He busied himself organizing obituary notices, writing a poetic elegy for Richard and arranging for the posthumous publication of his poems, some in *Encounter*, others in a collection with his introduction which the Dolmen Press in Dublin brought out in 1962.

As 'Isis Idol' in the last week of October he was photographed leaning on one elbow against a bookcase, muffled in a sweater under his suit against the damp autumn chill from the river. Large-eyed, long-nosed, full-lipped, undernourished and pensive, with his quirky dark eyebrows and Roman collar, he looked an irresolute mixture of clergyman, beatnik, intellectual and self-absorbed poet. Julian's description of him was blandly tongue-in-cheek.

> The things he most cares for are all in his poetry: flowers (he is happiest in the Botanical Gardens), animals, the classic writers, Christ, philosophy and children... Whether involved in a punting disaster, or reading his translation of Euripides' Cyclops in a field with no Hock, he always succeeds in getting the best out of those he is with. He responds to people, and they respond to him so that fools feel like professors and hacks like Milton. How he manages to fit everything in - his active ecclesiastical, literary, scholarly and social lives - is a continual astonishment to his multitude of friends.[22]

The truth was that he could not manage. That week he complained in a letter to Bertie of his perfectly useless subject, persistent headache and melancholia.[23] A month later he told Julian that he was seriously thinking of changing to a pass degree. He would drop Byzantine and Modern Greek, in which he did not feel competent to be examined although he did not want to give the subject up, and would take pass-degree papers in English literature and classics. Lower even than the increasingly rare fourth, a pass degree was only marginally better than utter failure. It would be a strangely undignified combination with a first in Mods. In April he wrote bravely to Julian that he was reading Caesar and half of Plato's *Republic*, '(which pass-men regard as *a poem*) and two books of Milton & a rather horrifying stretch of history of Eng. Lit. I think it's a fairly unflying jacketed course and leaves one time for life and art.'[24]

New friends flocked round him as he drew near the edge of his final year. Some were young, like John Fuller, a talented freshman poet at New College, to whom Dom had introduced him after he had asked about the limping clergyman who seemed to be invited to all the parties. John noticed with amusement how Peter loved being taken out for meals, enjoying anything that might pass for an exotic treat. ('*Soupe au pistou!*' he would exclaim in wonder over a bowl of insipid slop in a French-style restaurant.) His poem 'For John', a detached, aesthetic meditation on a Chinese porcelain vase in the Ashmolean Museum, came out in the *New Statesman* on April 26, 1958, as a change from its usual output of satirical poems about nuclear war.[25]

Another literary undergraduate was Alasdair Clayre, who, like his fellow-Wykehamist Julian, filled one of the Opimian Club vacancies that year. Brilliant, musical, impulsive and good-looking, he was said by a contemporary to be the cleverest boy ever to have come out of Winchester or anywhere else.[26] In his second year at Christ Church, he was heading for a congratulatory first in philosophy, politics and economics and a prize fellowship at All Souls. Peter admired his radical, liberationist stance and enjoyed his air of energetic freedom. A poem he addressed to him about the humanizing effect of pleasure ends on a wistful note:

> the democratic young are my heroes,
> the casual voices, air, rain, sun.[27]

But if his friends' affairs made him feel that he was watching life from inside a prison window, he also knew that, to some of them, he radiated a mysterious calm. A six-line poem by Dom described him as a gentle, sorrowful and (by implication) Christ-like figure.[28] Elizabeth Jennings, one of the very few Oxford women he knew, was clearly drawn to him by religion and the absence of a sexual threat. She was preparing to give up her library job after spending months on a scholarship in Rome, befriending priests and writing poetry that glowed with piety, discovery, love and delight. Peter read the poems in draft and condoled with her about Richard Selig's death. Years later, before turning against him, she, too, wrote a poem praising his gentleness and kindness.[29]

At Julian's college, Wadham, that summer, he had met its legendary Warden Sir Maurice Bowra, then Vice-Chancellor of the University, who was entertaining the aged Robert Frost before awarding him an honorary D.Litt. Asked by Bowra to rustle up some poets, Julian had brought Peter along. Although Frost's poetry meant little to him, he was thrilled to meet someone who, fifty years earlier, had been a friend of Edward Thomas. Admiring the old poet's magnificent head as he rambled on about how the young Ezra Pound had started nervously consuming a bunch of tulips when taken out to lunch by his publisher, he thought in an awestruck way how much it resembled Yeats's.[30]

Also at Wadham he met the nobly beautiful, wayward, forty-four-year-old Count Dominique de Grunne, who was helping with history teaching while working towards a research degree. A former Benedictine monk with a family château in the Auvergne, he had resigned from his Belgian monastery but remained a priest, partly for his mother's sake. In that odd position he lodged at the Catholic Chaplaincy in St. Aldates but avoided taking any part in its functions. Kind, hospitable and a gourmet cook, he cherished Peter like a waiflike girl and propped him up with soothing advice. Brian Brindley, now a London lawyer, treated him in much the same way, carrying him off to go beagling in Buckinghamshire with the pack from his old school, Stowe.[31]

Early in 1958 a new byline, 'Peter Levi, S.J.', emerged in the intellectual weeklies. Several months before his poem on the Chinese vase came out in the *New Statesman*, a mannered, staccato piece appeared in the *TLS*:

> *He met her*
> *at the Green Horse*
> *by the Surrey Docks;*
> *Saturday*
> *was the colour of his socks...*[32]

Some critics found this perkiness irritating, and six years later Peter told Julian that he no longer knew anything about the colour of socks, even in Chipping Norton.[33] But the breakthrough gave him courage, and within a matter of weeks the publisher André Deutsch accepted his first collection of poems.

This was largely thanks to Dom and Elizabeth Jennings, who had recommended him to Deutsch's literary editor Diana Athill and her adviser Francis Wyndham. It would be another two years before *The Gravel Ponds* came out, but Peter's morale was thoroughly boosted and he let his degree work go hang. 'One in the joy-stick for the flying-jackets,' Julian exulted. Fantasizing about a meeting in the after-life, he imagined Peter going up to a Heaven in which (he would gently explain) poetry was no longer needed, while he and other literary atheists headed downwards to roast in Hell.[34]

Unsurprisingly, after a year and a quarter of headaches and depression, Peter had begun to feel better. A friendly Harley Street neurologist, who shared his keenness on beagling, diagnosed anaemia rather than madness, and prescribed injections of liver extract in his bottom. These continued through the Easter vacation, which he spent at Beaumont perversely reading Firbank and *Marius the Epicurean*, drawing caricatures in charcoal and defending the doctrine of Original Sin to the sceptical Julian. In a frivolous piece for *Isis* about his eternally unwritten novel *The Artist's Wish*, he name-dropped Firbank, Pater, John Osborne and Evelyn Waugh and suggested comic characters based on his friends ('Mitchell in Kenya with an unsuccessful ostrich farm, Bethell as a female master of foxhounds').[35]

That Easter Dom and Henrietta met the Beat poets Allen Ginsberg and Gregory Corso in a fleapit Paris hotel. They were celebrating a double success: the publication of Corso's collection *Gasoline* with City Lights of San Francisco, and the firm's triumph over a prosecution for obscenity for publishing Ginsberg's hallucinatory homosexual poem *Howl!* Dom and Henrietta urged the pair to visit London, where they lunched with Edith Sitwell at the Sesame Club, read at poetry gigs and ended up stoned and broke in Piccadilly. David Archer, rescuing them, packed them off to Oxford, where W.H. Auden, then Professor of Poetry, who had met Ginsberg in America, welcomed them politely but bemusedly to Christ Church.[36] Dom improvised a reading for them with the New College Poetry Society, exposing it to anarchic Beat culture for the first time. When Corso recited his poem in praise of the Bomb, earnest CND supporters took it seriously and pelted him with their shoes.[37]

Peter found Ginsberg frighteningly extreme, but he was charmed by the vulnerable-looking Corso with his mop of hair and rebellious angel face. A year older than Peter, he was the one-time delinquent offspring of poor Italian immigrant parents on the Lower East Side of New York. Impressed by his charm and rebellious humour and dazzled by his flame-thrower style, Peter tried for a time to write like him.

> *Light dissolving birds into bright air,*
> *light dissolving itself into darkness,*
> *black light streaming from the bodies of dissolving sailors*

> *and running in clear streams...*[38]

and

> *The electric night shuddered.*
> *The sun stank of gin*
> *(and she asking him in)...*[39]

After that, sitting for a pass degree must have seemed more absurd than ever. Peter's ignominious result, like the handful of others in the pass school, did not appear with the honours lists that were published in *The Times* and the *Oxford University Calendar*. Anthony achieved a first in French and German and Clarence Gallagher a second in Greats. Julian, who had given up co-editing *Gemini* that winter to concentrate on his work, took a first in History and planned to start research and take the competitive examination for All Souls. Denis already had his first and was immersed in medieval research and teaching. Almost everybody wanted the cosily glamorous life of a successful Oxford don. But for Peter as for Anthony, the next stop on the Jesuit conveyor-belt was unaffected by degree results. All scholastics had to teach in a Jesuit school, usually for two years, before beginning the theology course at Heythrop. Both Anthony and Peter were ordered to Stonyhurst, the top Jesuit boys' public school near Clitheroe in Lancashire, Anthony to teach modern languages and Peter to take the junior forms for classics.

8
STONE PRISON

In mid-December this huge building
settling to grey composes its sad colours,
its cliff-like hulk, perpendicular force,
into a sleep as gentle as a moth's wing.

...

My mind as if in a stone prison
waits for the young gaolers and the wise,
fearing always violence, dissolution,
the island exiles with wind-haunted eyes...

Water, Rock & Sand (1962) 30

On a clear night, from the railway line between Clitheroe and
Blackburn, you may notice a line of lights blinking in the west against
the dark shape of Longridge Fell. Stonyhurst College stands alone on
that hillside, a little way from the village of Hurst Green, above the
Hodder, a tributary of the Ribble. The sandstone Tudor manor house
which its Catholic owner, Thomas Weld, gave to the English Jesuits
after they fled the Low Countries in 1794, has been extended in several
directions and topped with a heavy, plain parapet over a row of shallow
second-floor windows, making it appear hugely wide and squat. The
late Elizabethan tower of the four orders, one storey lower than the
magnificent Jacobean gate-tower of the Bodleian Library at Oxford,
culminates in a pair of preposterously tall, octagonal cupolas which
create an impression of looming height. Other copper-roofed cupolas
surmount the huge 1870s south range, next to the Perpendicular pierced
corner-turrets of St. Peter's Catholic Church, an early nineteenth-
century imitation of King's College Chapel, Cambridge in millstone
grit.

Peter quailed at the sight of this monstrosity with its overbearing skyline, backed by conifer-clad hills of unfamiliar size and shape. He may even have realized that, once he had been ordained, he could be sent back there as a permanent member of the teaching staff. Most Jesuit priests became schoolmasters, a word which stuck on his tongue with hateful cloyingness as he began to meet the religious and lay masters and spot their shuffling, senile, retired Jesuit colleagues. The seeping rain and glum architecture seemed to have eroded their spirits. Apart from one shy, friendly English master on the edge of a nervous breakdown, they struck him as narrow-minded and depressing. 'Oh God those agonised winter walks of school-masters,' he moaned two years later to Julian. If he had ever confronted his probable fate as a master in a Jesuit school, it was only in the congenial setting of Beaumont, within easy reach of Oxford and London friends.

Early in 1960, in his second year at Stonyhurst, two Oxford freshmen he had tutored for college entrance wrote to tell him how they were getting on. One was a clever, confident, musical and drama-loving achiever, Leonard Ingrams. Later, with a double first and a research degree, he abandoned an academic career to join the family merchant bank, Barings, and in his forties bought Garsington Manor just outside Oxford and created the opera festival there. The other was a more typical Catholic ex-public schoolboy, pious, hesitant, chaste and shy. Conditioned by his education to be nervous about sex, he was warier still of the possibility of being trapped in a marriage without love. Stuck in fatalistic adolescent inertia, he could not see why an 'introverted bachelor' should bother about acquiring a career and supporting a family, when he could just as well stay poor and single and become a novelist like Lawrence Durrell, or, more realistically, a priest. Although he knew that the training would be difficult and had some quarrels with Catholic practices and doctrine, he believed that the reward would be magnificent, 'participating in a miracle every day'.

While Peter was naturally drawn to brilliant extroverts like

Ingrams, he was all too familiar with the conditioning that affected the other man. Over ten years later, when a theology scholastic, Paul Haddon, told him that he would rather leave and find a wife than commit himself to lifelong celibacy, he argued strongly in favour of pursuing his vocation. Once a priest, Paul would realize that he was special. Lay people would flock round him, wondering what he had got that they hadn't got. 'They'll peck at you like crows.'[1] He left all the same, became a teacher and had a happy Catholic marriage, although remaining impressed with Peter's charisma and appearance of deep, strong faith.

Some Oxford friends, however, questioned the genuineness of his vocation. Julian became increasing irritated with his naughty-schoolboyish way of triumphantly bending the rules. Even Denis doubted his commitment, telling Willie that he suspected that Mollie had pushed him into the religious life, and that the Jesuits saw him as a potential shop-window priest, whose celebrity as a second Gerard Manley Hopkins might attract high-status converts into the Church.

After leaving Campion Hall that summer, Peter had been free to write. He had stayed partly at Beaumont and partly at St. Ignatius's, Stamford Hill, before heading north in late August for the ten-day Stonyhurst autumn retreat. Another mannered poem in couplets had appeared in the *New Statesman* for August 16, bringing a letter of praise for its cold clarity from Christopher Logue, now a regular *New Statesman* reviewer, nuclear disarmament campaigner and writer of protest verse. After a rejection letter from Faber & Faber, Peter sent his translation of Euripides' *Cyclops* to the Royal Court Theatre, whose artistic director regretted that his company did not perform classics. The script-readers recalled it for a second look in the New Year, but that, too, resulted in nothing.

Jesuits were allowed to go the cinema and put on domestic plays, but St. Ignatius's prohibition of theatre-going had been enshrined in their rule from the beginning. Even so, Peter felt a new fascination with the theatre after meeting his cousin Caryl Brahms at a London lunch party that summer. Co-author with S.J. Simon of comic play-scripts and humorous novels (*Don't, Mr Disraeli!*, *No Bed For Bacon*), she had found a young replacement for him, ten years after his death, in Brian Brindley's contemporary at Exeter College, Ned Sherrin, with whom she wrote musical comedy scripts, satirical television sketches, light fiction, songs and plays.

Caryl and Peter fell on one another. Caryl, who adored clever, handsome young men, discovered that Peter shared her love of mimicry, exaggeration and wicked gossip. The fact that he was both a relation and a Jesuit made him all the more romantic in her eyes. Stimulated by her interest, he felt a surge of protective love for this frail, witty cousin who had memories both of her Uncle Bert as a Jew and of the grandparents he had never met. He sent her a restrained little poem of mourning for Bert, and she wrote back, reminiscing about staying at Croydon as a child and hoping they would meet again. 'Funny that it should be you and me, out of the vast Clan Levi. So different – so alike. Blessings, Caryl.'[2]

During a visit to Cambridge that summer he had made a day-trip to the Castle Museum at Norwich to see the oil and water-colour paintings by Cotman and Crome. Cotman's massively poised, tranquil, light-infused shapes were a revelation of the numinous in landscape, conveying both mystery and stillness.

> *I reverence John Cotman and John Crome,*
> *Sandby and Cozens. You are my masters, Richard*
> *Wilson and David Cox, but long and hard*
> *schooling of your thoughts you gave me...*[3]

he wrote in a fourteen-liner full of Hopkinsian inversions and word-play, in apparent full retreat from the influence of Corso. 'Did I really see for myself the yellow and green leaves yesterday in a pool of light, or had Cotman taught me speechlessly to see them?'[4]

The Earthly Paradise had been the set theme for the 1958 Newdigate prize at Oxford. Jon Stallworthy had recited his winning entry at Encænia at the end of the summer term, while David Pryce-Jones had enjoyed a moment of unofficial triumph when Auden, as Professor of Poetry, called on him at Magdalen to congratulate him on his poem. Peter circulated privately printed copies of his own, unsuccessful hundred-line poem that autumn. Julian thought it too long with too many 'it was as if's (a recurrent fault in *The Shearwaters*, which he wrote the following year), but conceded that it was very personal and very much in Peter's style.[5]

Julian himself was surging ahead. He had written a novel that summer, and would publish half a dozen during the 1960s. Encouraged by *Gemini*'s success he was planning an anthology of recent Oxford and Cambridge writing, to be called *Light Blue, Dark Blue*. Still keen to become a history don, he had taken up a graduate studentship at St. Antony's College, Oxford.

Peter, intent on writing a novel of his own, made a stab at it in the evenings during his first few weeks at Stonyhurst ('I obsecrate you to try it,' he wrote to Bertie), but it ran into the sand after fourteen pages when he tried to describe his characters making love.[6] He pined for his Oxford friends and fretted to be sent a copy of his anonymous 'Isis Idol' article on Dom. Convoluted in style, it lacks the sparkle of Julian's 'Isis Idol' pen-portrait of him.

> Interesting things always draw his own greater interest, potential bores either dissolve entirely or become transformed, by a powerful mythopoeic faculty, into strange and remarkable creatures. Even to hear him subtly refract one's own fortnight-old news is to experience the difference between Shakespeare and his sources. But the forms of his myths are never predictable,

and never cease to amaze. My own favourite is the one about the nineteen spaniels and the dog-boy...[7]

Julian and Dom promised to drive up to visit him and read to the school literary society, The Popinjay, whose punning name was based on the common slang term 'J' for Jesuit. Meanwhile he agreed, with a reluctance perhaps born of academic shame, to attend a degree day at Oxford. He would have preferred (he wrote) to receive his degree from Dom and Julian, and to dine with Trypanis, Fraenkel and other teachers he respected rather than among his fellow-Jesuits at Campion Hall.[8]

During his first few empty weeks at Stonyhurst he thought the place a grim mausoleum. Bored with the retreat, he longed for the boys to arrive and fill that front vista with its enormous, bleakly glinting duck ponds, that frowning quadrangle and those violently coloured Puginesque interior spaces. 'Anything less inspiring than 2.45 P.M. at Stonyhurst with a blizzard howling past the window, & lunch a nasty taste & tea a grim prospect, & one's pot-pourri having temporarily dried up (made from Botanic Gdn in Oxford, very good, lavender, rosemary, roses & cloves) & work stretching grimly ahead... I can't at present imagine,' he complained early in September to Bertie. To his dismay the new Rector was the former Provincial, Desmond Boyle, who had aborted his study of Greats. The Jesuit masters seemed too hearty or neurotic to be any use as friends. He disliked the dead atmosphere of the empty school, with its petrological museum and galleries lined with dusty heads of beasts, and imagined that life in a state grammar school would be more rewarding.

Then the boys came, with their adolescent scruffiness and miasmic smell. Trying to establish common ground with his young pupils, he name-dropped Christopher Logue and the *New Statesman*, read them an unpublished preview of Logue's colourful interpretation of the first book of the *Iliad*, and told them real life was like that. Only one boy had heard of the *New Statesman*, and none of them grasped that Peter was one of its poets. But he quite soon established a complicity with his classes, glaring and calling them horrible boys, then laughing to show he didn't mean it. He also volunteered to lead the senior scouts, an anarchic bunch whose main idea was to bunk off work and smoke.

Surprised by how easily he got on with the boys, most of whom came from well-off Catholic backgrounds, he felt a spurt of enthusiasm for the job. Early in his first term he talked to the art society, The Palate, about ruins, passing round an illustrated copy of Bewick's *Fables* and praising the beauty of bombed sites. To The Popinjay, on or near November 2, he read Yeats's great elegiac poem 'All Souls' Night', mentioning monkey-gland injections and Platonism and explaining what Symbolism meant.[9] From an intellectually advanced sixth-former he picked up the idea of teaching Taoism, not Confucianism, hoping to fill his boys with untamed energies, an understanding of wild landscapes and fluent Latin.

His most rewarding sessions were with the Oxford entrance candidates. Treating them like adults he let them smoke in his tutorials, probably matching them cigarette for cigarette.[10] After howls of Jesuit protest, the papal diktat of the previous year against smokers had been quietly relaxed. In February Leonard Ingrams and four other boys performed a 'dadada masque' he had written, called *Orpheus' Head, or Dialogue on an Ash-Heap*.[11] It features a powerful god, a questioning young man and sad old one, with a formal Prologue, surreal contributions from a Beckettian rag-man, music from the blues and *Jailhouse Rock*, a move from the ash-heap to a vaguely Homeric rowing-boat at sea, and a closing Pythagorean hymn to Orpheus, the eternal voice of poetry:

> *Harsh face among the pure planets*
> *whose music-making intellect*
> *drops deeply, deeply drops, drops*

from a sheer abstract
which night never forgets, never forgets...[12]

When Dom and Julian visited in March, they were impressed by Ingrams and another talkative sixth-former. As well as their own poetry, they read and discussed poems by Auden, Spender and John Crowe Ransom.[13] 'Your boys! Revolutionaries to a man!' Julian wrote afterwards. He urged Peter to go on corrupting them with Dom's poems and a forthcoming first novel about colonialism in West Africa by David Caute. 'Sir, were they real poets? Sir, is he unhappy? I mean about the bomb and all that,' Peter quoted them back to him.[14]

When Ingrams left school at Easter, he wrote him a farewell.

You, smoking on a cold platform at night,
remembering the languages of schoolmasters
will count among them this unpitying verse,
this harsh-eyed landscape and this boring light...[15]

This poem suggests some of the isolation and yearning for friendship that Dom noticed in him that spring. Later, however, Dom contradicted that impression, writing that he had seemed more at peace and more thoughtful about his religion than when at Oxford.[16]

Schoolmaster, young. He felt his phrases stiff,
plucked from an intellectual wilderness,
wearing his bony peaceful face as if
words were transmuting pain to happiness...

begins another mirror-gazing poem, about Peter's tense relationship with a clever classicist in the year below Ingrams. Ian (later Iain) Watson came from a commercial Catholic family in Preston, and had been at Stonyhurst and its prep school since the age of eight. Moody, challenging, sceptical and in revolt against his provincial background, he had developed a sophisticated interest in French art, and found school life intolerable until Peter appeared. 'I was *by far* his most brilliant pupil. He saved me from shooting myself. We used to drink neat gin on the roof.'

> *Sharp-eyed, ink-grained, a pupil facing him,*
> *grim as a ghost, physical sense and shock,*
> *his jazz was cool and his room-light was dim,*
> *inchoate words, half-truth, a need to mock;*
> *he wore his face as if it were a rock...* [17]

No wonder the reviewers of Peter's next collection, *Water, Rock and Sand,* found it narrower in its focus than *The Gravel Ponds.* Even when the poems were not overtly about masters and pupils at Stonyhurst, the weather and landscape leached into them

> *as if into ridges of a pure and thin green*
> *receding into rain.* [18]

The Christmas holidays were 'a sort of skeleton life' for young Jesuits trapped at the school, Peter wrote to Julian. The repressed homosexual English master, to whom he had been able to talk, had been packed off to Italy to recover from his breakdown. [19] When the boys were away the place echoed, while in term-time he found the lack of proportion intolerably crazy.

> Vast, superhuman truths & goodnesses & events – communion with the death of Christ and the intentions of God, enormous claims & flames of the Jesuit order, superhuman pressures and exigences of life... and then, tiny in a minute foreground, these clockwork children and nervous adolescents and shouting boys.

For the Easter holidays he escaped completely. After ten days at Eastbourne and St. Ignatius's, Stamford Hill, he caught a train to Glasgow, then another to Mallaig, where he stayed in a small hotel by the harbour, facing out towards the southern tip of Skye. He was prospecting for a summer campsite for his scouts, a short boat-ride away from the roadless Knoydart peninsula and from the island of Rum, where they would help ring the colony of Manx shearwaters which landed there regularly to breed.

Then came glimmerings of a more important escape. Realizing that it would be cheaper to teach their scholastics on the premises than farm them out to college tutors, the Jesuits were increasing the tutorial staff of Campion Hall. They had recently recruited a classicist, who stayed for only a couple of years. On a giant postcard of Trafalgar Square, postmarked three days after his twenty-eighth birthday, Peter told Julian that he was going to be a don at Campion Hall in six years' time. ('This is true.') To Willie he wrote that that nothing was certain yet, but he had been tentatively promised a tutorship in classics after he had taught for a further year or two at Stonyhurst, completed the three-year theology course at Heythrop, then spent the largely contemplative tertian year that, for Jesuits, followed ordination.

As a scoutmaster he cut an unusually glamorous figure. Gaunt, dark and bony in his beret and battledress top, he looked like a Republican fighter in the Spanish Civil War. Enjoying the sight of the boys let loose in wild surroundings, he was careful to give them only faint hints of his opinion of the snobbish ethos of the school. His imaginativeness, control and subversive humour were a difficult act to follow, as Billy Hewett found when he arrived for his stint of teaching and took over the scouts where Peter had left off.

The summer of 1959 was one of golden, hay-smelling warmth. Day after day the sunshine poured down as Harold Macmillan, preparing for the autumn election, reminded voters that they had never had it so good. July, August and part of September stayed fine and dry, although the rivers ran clear and swimmable from copious spring rain. On the west coast of Scotland seals basked in pellucid, lapping water near the shore, and Peter sat on a rock and sang them a Greek chorus in a gentle, high voice.[20] The boys stood round listening or joining in, and the seals raised their noses from the water, barking and shaking the drops from their Macmillan-like moustaches.

After the seals, the group's night on Rum, waiting for the shearwaters, was one of Peter's more magical experiences. From the moonlit night of that expedition came *The Shearwaters*, which he wrote in eight days that October. All of its seventy-seven four-line verses have the regular rhyme-scheme ABBA, although many of them contain half-rhymes with no fixed pattern. The narrative begins calmly:

> *It was nearly dusk when we began to climb,*
> *we passed through a deserted garden*
> *between a few bushes, where now and then*
> *some bird called out his echo of softened time.*
>
> *We passed under a long, kept alley*
> *where branchy trees guarded us like a dream,*
> *outside a dead house by a musing stream,*
> *water subdued whose origin might be*
>
> *far up on the unfriendly hillside,*
> *some powerful cistern no engine can take,*
> *or jangling dribbles out of a black lake*
> *making hollows of evening seem less wide...* [21]

Expectancy mounts, and sometimes sags, through another fifty verses, as he describes how the party climbed on, then waited on a bleakly moonlit mountain-side, hoping that a cloud would come up to create the thick darkness that the shearwaters needed for breeding. When the birds arrived, still in bright moonlight, in small, elusive flights, they scattered all over the mountainside, leading the boys ever higher in pursuit.

> *And still over the heads of the searchers*
> *the wind was full of weightless whistling cries*
> *and (passing too swiftly for surprise)*
> *the uncanny wingbeat of the shearwaters.*

The poem ends with an almost *Ancient Mariner*-like description of the empty, moonlit prospect after the birds had gone:

> *Big Trolleval and Arkeval seemed near,*
> *the remote moon was walking on the sea*
> *paving the waves with bright transparency*
> *terrible as justice, nervous as fear.*
>
> ...
>
> *Far out to sea absolutely nothing*
> *moved but the wasted water,*
> *mile beyond mile there was no shelter,*
> *mountain beyond mountain, nothing...*[22]

To Willie, who had recently married, Peter sent a late wedding present of a handwritten copy of the poem with a Greek inscription. Although invited to preach at the wedding, he had known he would not be allowed to do so until ordained. He sent warm congratulations instead, perhaps suppressing mild feelings of resentment that Willie had never mentioned an Oxford girlfriend, and of regret that the all-male closeness of the Opimian Club was at an end. He almost longed, he wrote, for Willie's happiness in old age 'as one might for the maturity of a vine, or the efflorescence of some loved flower-head'.[23]

Getting Anthony to type out *The Shearwaters*, since he had no typewriter and never learned to type, he posted the only fair copy to Julian, who was on a two-year Harkness Fellowship in the United States. Julian thought it fine, and agreed with Peter's suggestion that, like many of his landscape poems, it was transparently religious. 'To me the whole poem is more about you, the landscape in your head.'[24] But André Deutsch found it too long and enigmatic to fit in with current poetic fashions. It hung in limbo for five and a half years until published as a pamphlet by the undergraduate Clive Allison in Oxford.

℃〇

The autumn term of 1959 was a dismal anticlimax. The brilliant summer tailed off into damp post-election weather, and Peter thought his new pupils a shifty, unattractive lot. Anthony had been fast-tracked into the theology course at Heythrop, whereas he, who would be its youngest graduate entrant if he joined it the following year, was threatened with a possible third year at Stonyhurst instead. He moaned to Bertie about everything: the disgusting food, the lashing rain, the smoking fire and leaking windows in his room, the idiotic boys and inanely chattering masters, the oafish Rector and imbecile, feudal servants. It horrified him to learn that Anthony had found anything good to say about Stonyhurst.

One means of escape was drink – the gin or vodka he shared on the roof with Ian Watson, the bottle of brandy, labelled Rust Remover, that he kept behind a pile of scouting equipment in his study. His rescuer and supplier was Julian's brother Tony, who had joined the wine trade between leaving Cambridge and finding his vocation with the National Trust. With a fast car, a love of adventure and a fascination with historic buildings and rugged country, he whisked Peter off on expeditions, entertaining him with accounts of hunt balls, romantic conquests and the local popularity of treacly drinks such as brandy and Benedictine (B&B) during the long, hard Lancashire winters.

Still hoping to make something of the *Cyclops*, although he had failed to sell his translation (Roger Lancelyn Green's, in verse, had been published two years earlier), Peter thought of trying to edit the Greek text. In the spring he had told Bertie that he might spend part of the summer collating the manuscript in a library in Rome. In the autumn he still hoped for permission to do so at Christmas. Like his trip to Greece, it was a mirage which receded until, that winter, it dissolved.

After his first elation at the prospect of teaching at Oxford, he plunged into nervous gloom. That autumn he wrote to Fraenkel asking if he might call on him for some practical advice, and met with a crushing snub. While thanking him for his compliments, Fraenkel made it clear that he no longer regarded him as a serious scholar and saw no compromise between the path he had taken and his own. He particularly asked him not to write back, as he was very busy.[25]

This pushed Peter into a depression which lasted for much of the winter. He wrote to Willie, then teaching Latin at the University of Glasgow, that he desperately wanted someone to direct him. 'Can you recommend me anyone or recommend me to anyone?'

From Heythrop, where he spent Christmas with Anthony, he ventured cautiously into Oxford, where kindly Dominique de Grunne cooked him lunch in his flat above the Catholic Chaplaincy. In London he saw David Pryce-Jones, newly employed as a feature-writer on the *Financial Times*, 'who came beaming out of his office & showed me St Paul's just as if he'd that morning invented it.'[26] Incapable of facing life without a project, he continued tinkering with the *Cyclops*. He met Caryl for lunch with Ned Sherrin, and she hoped this had not broken his concentration – 'was it Sophocles?' While delighted that she and Peter were both writers, she rubbed a little salt into the Fraenkel-administered wound by remarking that Anthony struck her as more of a scholar.[27]

∽

After the Soviet invasion of Hungary in 1956, many members of the British Communist Party had resigned in shame and disgust. Some had even joined the Liberals, with their gentle agenda of racial equality and electoral reform. Yet a more theoretical, global form of Marxism was emerging in academic and trade-union circles, encouraged by the

Krushchev thaw in Russia and in revolt against the economic ascendancy of the United States. The favourite writers of the intellectual New Left included the American anti-capitalist social theorist Herbert Marcuse and the Hungarian socialist-realist critic György Lukács.

The most recent prize fellows of All Souls were the radical romantic Alasdair Clayre and the Marxist historian and novelist David Caute. Following the trend they set, Peter had agreed that autumn to write a review essay for Alasdair, who was commissioning work for *Dialogue*, a short-lived Oxford magazine concerned with Eastern Europe and its relations with the West. Because the book by Lukács that Peter requested was out of print, Alasdair sent him Marcuse's *Soviet Marxism: a Critical Analysis*. Four days after promising that the book was on its way, Alasdair wrote acknowledging Peter's splendid review, which he published in the sole, Russian-themed number of the hybrid *Gemini/Dialogue* in January 1960. As well as Peter on 'Herbert Marcuse on Soviet Marxism' and Alasdair on 'Marxism and Existentialism', it included several poems : one by the future Lord Gowrie, a Balliol freshman, one by Pasternak's Oxford-based sister, Lydia Pasternak Slater, and one by Peter, 'For Poets in Prison without Trial'.

> *All day teaching in some classroom*
> *I can hear your maddened pens,*
> *scratch, scratch, where human foreknowledge comes home,*
> *O images of violence,*
>
> *O condemned poets, O dead who write*
> *with iron pens in your unresonant cells...* [28]

Perhaps Eastern Europe would be the answer for an idealistic young Jesuit, he thought. Before writing his article on Marcuse he had come across the July-September issue of *Soviet Survey* and been excited by Michael Futrell's article 'Evgeny Evtushenko'. The Soviet *Wunderkind*

Yevtushenko, two years younger than Peter and the author of four books of verse, had published a long poem, *Stantsiya Zima*, in the October 1956 issue of the literary magazine *Oktyabr*. Later translated as 'Zima Station' or 'Zima Junction', it describes a summer visit he paid as a student from Moscow to his childhood home in the Siberian town of Zima (literally, 'winter'). Even Futrell's prose versions of parts of the poem breathed its raw, dramatic energy and moral judgments, and the smell of black earth, vegetation, clammy warmth and river water. On the basis of these, Peter claimed in his *Dialogue* article to think more highly of 'the promise of Evgeny Evtushenko, a writer palpably formed by criticisms, difficulties, and the questioning of his loyalties... than of the promise of any comparable English or American writer'.[29]

In February 1960 he told Julian that he would like to spend a month in an East European city, perhaps Budapest. Accepting that his poems were decadent, he blamed this on the limitations of the West. He craved new stimuli, and perhaps the chance of working on a translation.[30] The next month he mentioned Yevtushenko in a fan-letter to the left-wing painter, novelist and art critic John Berger, who wondered where he could have found the poems and whether they had been translated.[31]

Julian, emotionally isolated on his travels round the United States, did not take Peter's East European craze seriously. What he needed, he wrote from Texas, was to fall in love. He should give up religion, do the high-jump, play jazz records, slash bad pictures, but above all live, and root out the destructive force that prevented him from finding love. Otherwise his poems would continue to be sad and negative – brilliant in themselves, full of light and landscape, but too full of the solitude that Julian, unsure of his own future, feared for himself.[32]

Peter rose delightedly to the bait. Of course he fell in love all the time, with 'boys, women, contemporaries, anyone'. He had briefly wondered if he might be homosexual, but that was only because there were no women at Stonyhurst. The idea of going to bed with a boy made him feel sick. Moreover, his vow of chastity forbade physical relationships. He was resigned to being continually, unromantically and unrequitedly in love, and to turning out short, soft-centred lyrical poems, accepting John Berger's pronouncement that failure did artists good. As he wrote, he was invigilating a classroom full of boys with tousled hair, sharp, bored expressions, horrible end-of-term clothes and inefficient fountain pens. *Maddened pens,/scratch, scratch...* But he was not in a Soviet labour camp, only in the prison of a Catholic public school, from which the Jesuit machinery would shortly move him on.

By Easter 1960 he was recovering from his long depression. André Deutsch brought out his collection *The Gravel Ponds* in March, attracting letters of praise and good reviews. The Poetry Book Society named the book as its spring choice. This was excellent for morale, and, after posting seventeen advance copies to friends and family members he asked Mollie to buy further copies for Stephen Spender and others he hoped to impress. 'A stray friend or two,' he thought, might be relied upon to buy the book for themselves.

The *TLS* for March 18 included his elegy for Richard Selig, a four-part seasonal poem which made no direct mention of Selig among a glittering wealth of images from nature.[33] This may have baffled readers who did not understand Peter's growing habit of projecting his emotions into landscape. Already, he told Julian, he was being faulted for his absurd elegiac sadness. But a Jesuit English master at Wimbledon College praised the 'pure, delicate and *hopeful*' tranquillity of the third part of the poem, and told him his scholarship class had been enchanted by it.[34]

In May, he was allowed out from Stonyhurst to give a reading at Foyles with Dom, who had returned from visiting India and was writing a travelogue, *Gone Away*. Before leaving, he had dumped

Henrietta in favour of Dorothy Tutin, an actress with the Royal Shakespeare Company. Peter had sent Henrietta a consoling Samuel Palmer postcard, and received a breathless account of how she had accidentally bumped into Dom in thick fog in the King's Road before laughing hysterically and running away.[35]

Then Dominique de Grunne brought Alasdair on a visit. Restlessly seeking the ideal life, Alasdair had arranged to study architecture on a Leverhulme studentship in London while keeping his All Souls fellowship. Realizing that the marriage with *Dialogue* had effectively killed *Gemini*, he had hoped to keep *Dialogue* going by persuading a graduate student of Russian, Robin Milner-Gulland, to take it on. But Robin was about to spend a year in Moscow, leaving Alasdair stuck with the magazine. Noticing Peter's interest in Yevtushenko, Alasdair told Robin about it in the hope that he might be able to help. Robin offered to make English prose translations of *Stantsiya Zima* and a few other poems so that Peter could transform them into verse, and suggested 'the long shot of writing to the man himself'.[36] At first they thought only of publishing their translations in *Dialogue*, assuming that Alasdair would keep it going. A different prospect emerged, however, while Robin was away.

Once certain that he would be free of Stonyhurst that summer, Peter began to feel fonder of his pupils again. He had absorbed some of Julian's lecture about love and affirmed his own, would-be selfless version of it. He vicariously enjoyed his friends' love-lives and did his best, like Christopher Devlin, to love the boys. Religion would be impossible, he thought, without a 'bias to love'.[37] He sent regrets to John Fuller, who was about to marry his Oxford girlfriend Prue Martin straight after Schools, that he could not attend their July wedding because of playing schoolmasters and scoutmasters. From time to time (he wrote) he found himself imagining their happiness with great delight. All the same, he admitted to Julian that he was starved of love, since his friends were all far away and his pupils were *in statu pupillari*. 'And I'm not, frankly, very heartily in love with the assistant masters.'

That summer he took the senior scouts to camp at Artites, near Dominique de Grunne's family château at Retournac in the Haute Loire, a remote part of the eastern Massif Central. It was only his second trip abroad, and he described the area as extraordinary and wonderful, full of lunar landscapes, impalpable distances, grey volcanic rock and yellow-eyed goats.[38] The peasants were using oxen to pull the combine harvesters because (he believed) they had never learnt how tractors worked. Although shocked by French agricultural monopolies, he felt it necessary to stress that he was not a Marxist, since he did not believe in the 'internal necessity of temporal things'. In a forest he met a French abstract painter, Saby, a pupil of Picasso and Pignon, who promised to send him one of his pictures and introduced him to the Surrealist-Romantic poetry of René Guy Cadou, who had died young in 1951. For general French left-wing atmosphere he enjoyed Simone de Beauvoir's *The Mandarins*, which he found 'very solid and munchable on trains'.[39]

One story about that summer camp gained currency among Peter's friends. As the party prepared to board a train from Retournac to Lyon, the station master made difficulties for them. Prompted by Peter, the scouts lined up at the open windows and, as the train pulled out, they chanted in unison *Le chef de gare est cocu*.

9
ZHENYA

I AM WORKING DAY AND NIGHT AT EVTUSHENKO to finish
20 shorter poems in 3 weeks for a Penguin of him.
> To John Fuller, 13 February 1962

From France Peter went straight to Eastbourne. In spite of complaining
to friends about the opulence of Mollie's flat, he enjoyed sinking into
its comfort and basking in her love. A timid hypochondriac in her late
fifties, who saw little of Gillian since she had entered the convent and
had no prospect of grandchildren, she concentrated her affection on
her sons. Peter depended on her childishly for treats, and in a crisis at
Stonyhurst had even cadged cigarettes ('Yours or Piccadilly') by post.
From Heythrop he often requested permission to spend the odd night
at Eastbourne, asking Mollie to send him the train-fare by post in cash.
She bought him Christmas, birthday and in-between presents of little
luxuries, clothes or books, and would travel up to Jermyn Street or
the Burlington Arcade to buy him some precisely detailed present
for a friend. When *The Gravel Ponds* came out, he told her he could
not write much in her copy because they were too close. The letters
he wrote her during theology lectures were brief and vague, but they
sometimes ended, after the usual 'God bless', with an exuberantly
scrawled 'Love, love, love'.

Knowing she would wish to believe that he was doing well at
theology, he reassured her that it was a satisfying new challenge. To
Julian, however, he complained that he was finding it a 'frantic, sweat-
slippery struggle' with entangled ramifications of history and dead
languages. If still struggling in two years' time he would give up all
thought of ordination and resign. He told Willie that he was appalled
by the antiquated rigidity of the anti-modernist oath, and by the Jesuits'
heavy-handed definitions of Catholic doctrine and the arguments for

belief. Yet, despite admitting to 'a creeping nausea about oneself, chewing ratlike at the corpses of dead books', he made no direct threat of opting out. Willie, as a serious Catholic, represented the good angel, pulling him in one direction by force of moral example while Julian pulled in the other.

His first distraction was a debt he had been asked to repay to Beaumont by writing its centenary history, only a few years before the school closed down in 1967. That August and September he had spent an intensive few weeks at Beaumont, cramming himself with information from the archives and talking to elderly masters. He had read through bills, journals, letters, books, minutes of meetings and piles of school magazines, finding out far more than he wanted to know about sporting results, the introduction of lawnmowers and the history of public school football. School histories can be stodgy, but he won a succession of arguments about the content of the book and wrote it with a light, idiosyncratic touch in spare moments during his first Heythrop term. Stressing the beauty of Beaumont's setting on the edge of Windsor Great Park, he dwelt on the more eccentric details of its late nineteenth-century history while ignoring much of the dull period since the end of the First World War.

Beaumont is a pleasant read, only 76 pages long, and it attracted some journalistic notice when it came out. *The Daily Telegraph* columnist 'Peterborough' wrote that any author of a public school history who could make it interesting to outsiders, as Peter did in *Beaumont*, had his goodwill. A *Times Literary Supplement* reviewer thought it 'rare to find a school historian at once so devoted and so detached'.[1] So relaxed was the publishing business in those days that André Deutsch, to Peter's mild embarrassment, agreed to add the book to their list, and, far from asking the Jesuits for a subvention, offered him a £50 advance on completion, 'twice the price of a book of poems'.[2]

At Stonyhurst Peter had been replaced by Billy Hewett, one of several pairs of brothers in their generation of young Jesuits. Billy's elder brother Mick, in the year above Peter, had gone out to a mission in the Rupununi district of British Guiana. In a fit of Stonyhurst gloom, Peter had wondered if all scholastics ought to 'make off up the Rupununi. Or all retire to Oxford. Or all go & work in factories. But not be such disjointed creatures as I am.'[3]

Billy, reading history at Campion Hall, had been one of the pupils Peter put in Denis's way. Always short of money and keen to teach, Denis had eagerly taken on undergraduates whose normal tutors were on leave or too busy, and within a few months of starting research had six pupils from New College and three from Campion Hall. Later he acquired a fee-paid lectureship at his own college, Lincoln, which brought in further payments by the hour. He took his pupils on walking-tours and seemed the ideal tutor, friendly, enthusiastic, emotionally detached and clearly in love with his subject. No college had a fellowship for him, however, and there was no immediate opening at any of the redbrick universities in which many Oxford dons-in-waiting served their time. He was about to leave unwillingly for a job in Canada when Billy arrived at Stonyhurst in August. Finding the history department short of staff, he had a word with the authorities and arranged for Denis to be hired as his senior colleague.

Even with few friends left in Oxford, Peter gravitated there from Heythrop whenever he was free and had the bus-fare or could hitch a lift. He made peace with Fraenkel and went regularly to classical seminars and lectures, sometimes with former Stonyhurst pupils such as Leonard Ingrams or Iain Watson. Alasdair was sometimes there, having kept his room in All Souls and the nominal editorship of *Dialogue*. The previous Christmas, when Peter had looked up friends in Oxford, Alasdair's bizarre, quick-fire conversation had gone to his head like whisky on an empty stomach. But when Alasdair came out to Heythrop and did a Russian dance at night in the Chipping Norton market-place, he thought him forlorn rather than released.[4]

His favourites were John and Prue Fuller, newly married and renting a North Oxford flat while John began research work on a scholarly edition of the plays of John Gay. His first collection of poems, *Fairground Music*, was due out the following autumn. Calm, happy and absorbed in one another, the Fullers gave Peter occasional twinges of envy and regret. But he and John kept up a long, light-hearted poetical correspondence which included exchanging riddles in verse, a form of gamesmanship which was satisfying because the results, like a haiku, were spare but often beautiful.

His second collection was due out in 1962 from André Deutsch. He had wanted to call it *Sulla's Ghost* in allusion to the ghost's dark predictions in the prologue to Ben Jonson's *Catiline*, but it ended as the blandly unsuitable *Water, Rock and Sand*. Meanwhile he was desperate to continue sharing his poems. Early in 1961 he sent John a strange, ecstatic, lonely outpouring which harked back to the influence of Gregory Corso, as well as distantly echoing the opening of Hopkins's 'Starlight Night'.

Look at the light at the upward beat of light of blue light
where no hawk flies O thin air and no buzzard
but Venus winks and glitters and goes on winking
through showers of dust O thin dust dropping from the moon
I believe no atmosphere is everlasting
my brains are burning out my senses
my senses are burning out my brains
I smell of burning
O thin unbodily light you shine and never burn
I knew a man once who was a philosopher
he wore out five philosophies in one experimental human body
he chewed up air blood light and planetary systems like a breakfast

and built them all into the systems of his bones with ungodly
glue
> *that is with ossein*
> *like thin limestone but bones can bleed the universe was ossified*
in his bones
> *I wish he were a poet he could speak about bones and light.*

In a note he asked John to show it to 'Alasdair or anyone' if he saw them, adding that he would like to share it with Corso but never saw him now. 'Did you know that clouds of dust now in the atmosphere were knocked off the moon by meteors? or that on Venus it constantly rains (hence that vaporous glitter)? Or about calcium phosphate? See you I hope.'[5]

Oxford's fashionable philosophy dons had revived his longing to be part of that scene. Bored with theology, but pursuing the orthodox Catholic idea that religious belief must be based on reason, he told David Pryce-Jones that he had written to Stuart Hampshire, by then Grote Professor of Mind and Logic at University College London, arguing that reason was not 'like' anything, and that he expected 'either an avalanche of ice or a silence de glace'.

Only silence seems to have resulted from this, but David was keeping him busy as a book-reviewer. Having graduated to his second job, as literary editor of *Time and Tide*, he kept up a generous supply of new books for several years. Although Peter had written kind, intelligent reviews for *Isis*, he started brashly with a condescending piece on Cecily Mackworth's *Guillaume Apollinaire*: 'It would be hard to write a boring book about Apollinaire... This book... is a respectable piece of work, at a banausic level.'[6] But when given Rex Warner's translation of the *Poems* of George Seferis, Trypanis's friend and the most eminent modern poet in Greece, he felt too daunted to do it justice. In the end David carried the review forward to include a translation of Cavafy's *Complete Poems* by Auden and Rae Dalven. Cavafy and Seferis had never met, but Peter linked them imaginatively: 'This pair of sensual, dry and economical poets are like a pair of lizards, moving very fast, depending on the sun and on rocks.'[7]

David, like Willie and John Fuller, had married straight after Oxford. Ferdinand Mount, ignoring the wider complexities of the question, identified this pattern as peculiar to the National Service generation of the 1950s, who were mature enough to settle down, impatient to have regular sex-lives but still obedient to parental expectations that they would marry and reproduce.[8] David's bride was Clarissa Caccia, daughter of the British ambassador in Washington Sir Harold Caccia, who later became head of the diplomatic service. Like the Fullers, the Pryce-Joneses now had a baby daughter on the way. David's first novel, *Owls and Satyrs*, came out in the spring of 1961, as did Julian's first novel *Imaginary Toys* and Alasdair's only novel *The Window*. Everyone, it seemed, was being productive except Peter, stranded on his hilltop ingesting wads of theology along with German, Hebrew and Greek.

That spring, however, he was settling back into the company of the brethren. 'Religion for me was like a flock of birds moving across the winter fields and among the stony villages,' he wrote whimsically about that period of his life.[9] Bertie would be ordained that summer, and Anthony in another year. Julian continued to prod him in letters about atheism and sex, but cold water, physical exertion and the company of fellow-theologians helped him sublimate. Sexual stirrings affected him as much as they would any thirty-year-old, but he had resigned himself to the struggles of celibacy, still believing it to be a force for good. March 1961 was warm and sunny, and he swam in the open-air pond every day and worked bare-chested in the grounds in the afternoons. One night he slept out on the long, damp grass of the lawn in a wind that made the stars tremble, and was nuzzled by a passing badger. Woken by rooks before dawn, he trailed back to his room as he heard the first tractor starting up.[10]

While rhapsodizing about the Mediterranean and the Aegean in a review of Lawrence Durrell's *Alexandria Quartet*, he no longer expected that the Jesuits would allow him to go there. He spent winter and spring holidays at Eastbourne or St. Ignatius's, Stamford Hill, with occasional diversions to Beaumont. One senior boy found him exotic and unconventional, daringly recommending the sixth form to read the novels of Graham Greene.

High summer brought the compulsory Barmouth villa, for which he felt less eager than he had ten years earlier. Participants were allowed to take bicycles provided that they rode them all or part of the way there. Paul Haddon, a philosophy scholastic in the early 1960s, remembered cycling as far as Birmingham, leaving his bicycle there and dutifully hitchhiking back to spend the night at Heythrop before beginning the next lap of the journey. Peter preferred to start late in the day and keep going. In those days, he wrote, you could bicycle safely at night all the way from Chipping Norton to the Welsh coast.[11] To make the holiday bearable he had arranged to spend much of it with Tony Mitchell, who was friendly with the white-bearded, sea-loving novelist Richard (Dickon) Hughes, his artist wife Frances and their five children.

The Hughes family lived at Môr Edrin, a square white house on the Dwyryd estuary near Talsarnau. Peter fell in love with the confidently eccentric, rustic style of the household, in which the children had grown up barefooted, sailing, riding and mountain-climbing, and 'even the tables looked wind-scoured and sea-scoured'. He liked Frances's down-to-earth unpretentiousness, her dedication to landscape painting and the way in which she had supported the family with her own money while Dickon worked on the novel he had taken since the end of the war to write. It excited him to learn that, when invited to parties at Portmeirion, girls with ball-dresses tucked round their waists would wade across the estuary from sand-bar to sand-bar at low tide. When he and Tony tried to do the same, led by a girl who had been sent to point out the way, they ended up swimming through deep water fully clothed, Peter with a clerical umbrella gripped like a dog's stick between his teeth.[12]

1961 was Hughes's year. His novel *The Fox in the Attic*, set partly at Laugharne in Carmarthenshire and partly in Bavaria at the time of Hitler's *Putsch*, was published that October. As soon as it came out, Peter wrote excitedly to David asking if it was any good. He enthused about Môr Edrin, 'that big, uncarpeted, luminous, sea-pounded, estuarine house', and his gossipy, friendly chats with Frances as she tramped the mud-flats in an old overcoat and galoshes. Once he got hold of the novel (which John Bowen reviewed coolly in *Time and Tide*), he loved its intimate, conversational tone and its insights into the damage that the First World War had inflicted on all classes on both sides. Keeping in touch with the Hugheses, who regularly visited their children at Oxford, he provided Dickon with details of convent life for *The Wooden Shepherdess*, which followed twelve years later.[13] In June 1976 he gave the eulogy at Dickon's memorial service at St. Martin in the Fields. Later still one of Frances's paintings of Rhaeadr Ddu, the great waterfall near Dolgellau, 'so austere as to be almost Chinese, profoundly exhilarating and light-spirited', hung over his work-table as he struggled to earn a living.[14]

ॐ

Translating Yevtushenko, from Robin's plain prose versions into poems, lasted him from Stonyhurst into his second year at Heythrop. He had told Julian that *Zima Junction* was 'a sort of Winterreise by a Soviet writer with an individual conscience: a less passionate and meditated but informative but cleverer and more committed sort of Pasternak'. The Cyrillic alphabet confused him by its similarity to Greek, but he picked up the basic feeling for the language that was all he needed for the work.

At first Robin had suggested that he might try to reproduce the original rhyme-scheme of *Stantsiya Zima*, in the way that translators of Pushkin have done with the galloping rhythm of *Evgeny Onegin*. Only a fluent knowledge of Russian would have made that possible, so he aimed to convey the spirit of the poem in free verse. The longer he worked on it, the more vividly he imagined that earth-smelling, sawdust-smelling, petrol-smelling corner of Siberia: those wild night swims in brackish rivers, those heroically difficult journeys and iron-hard memories of the war, those sottish relatives and overheard confidences about wretched marriages, and the twenty-year-old poet's mixed excitement and disgust at what he found there after years away in Moscow.

Alasdair had told Robin and Peter that he expected to publish their translations of four-fifths of *Stantsiya Zima* and several of Yevtushenko's shorter poems in a special number of *Dialogue*. Robin sent prose versions of the shorter poems from Moscow, and Peter finished working on them early in 1961, before they realised that *Dialogue* was no more. After a year as an architecture student, Alasdair packed it in and went to Israel to experiment with living on a kibbutz.

In Russia during the Krushchev thaw, Robin had discovered that Yevtushenko was as popular as any rock-singer in the West. He gave vigorous public performances of his poems, attended by crowds of young fans who crammed the halls and broke windows to get in. Although his poems had not yet been translated into English he visited the United States early in 1961, returning home as a symbol of cultural rapprochement with crew-cut hair and drainpipe-trousered suits. In September, while Westerners were absorbing the Holocaust evidence that had emerged during Eichmann's trial in Jerusalem, he secretly circulated his accusing poem *Babiy Yar*. A lament for the Nazi massacre of tens of thousands of Kievan Jews in 1941, it was also a reproach to his fellow-Russians for the anti-Semitism that persisted to that day.

Unlike Yevtushenko, who always loyally returned home to Moscow, the glamorous, twenty-three-year-old ballet star Rudolf Nureyev made a bolt for freedom when he visited the West that June. Perhaps encouraged by the publicity about Nureyev's escape, Peter's agent John Johnson, who handled his output of poetry, saw similar potential in an attractive, well-travelled young Russian poet. By the end of 1961 he had secured a contract for Yevtushenko's *Selected Poems* to come out in the Penguin Poets series, which, with ranks of other Penguin publications, filled the paperback shelves of almost every bookshop in England.

That summer Peter was still obsessed with Eastern Europe. Later, Iris Murdoch would flatter him by suggesting that he was really a Central European poet in spirit. In a lull between spells of work on Yevtushenko he told Willie that he and Dominique de Grunne were translating the poems of Czeslaw Milosz 'if it ever gets done'. He began a novel about the 1956 Hungarian uprising, for which he asked Julian to find him the best book on the subject. ('I want a *chronicle* of some sort.') He was also fascinated by the radical middle-class element in the nuclear disarmament movement, although he came no closer to it than reading newspaper accounts of the Aldermaston marches and the mass sit-down in Trafalgar Square that Bertrand Russell's Committee of One Hundred staged one wet Saturday in September 1961. Like a teenager banned by his parents from joining the duffle-coated throng, he longed to plunge in and mingle with strangers, some of whom *must* be interesting. Planning a long poem about a march on which people would tell one another stories, he defended the idea as 'socially meaningful... and beautiful in quite new ways', and agreed only to 'stop buggering about with Chaucer' after Julian told him to stop prevaricating and write openly about Aldermaston. But the things that seemed most serious to him as he sat in his room, he added sadly, were those his friends took least seriously.[15]

Back from the United States, Julian had embraced the New Left and begun to write socially critical novels about the comfortably-off, smug middle classes and their young. Turning his back on academic life, he took a temporary job as deputy literary editor of the *Spectator*. Single young men could survive quite adequately in London on odd jobs, small advances for novels and reviewing. David Pryce-Jones took a break from journalism to live in France with his wife and baby daughter, writing a critical study of Graham Greene. Willie Charlton moved south with his wife Anne and their twins to take an Oxford B.Phil in philosophy and so qualify himself for a proper university job. The countrified Charltons settled in the mill house at North Aston in the Cherwell valley, a dozen miles east of Heythrop as the crow flies. Peter was delighted to see Willie again and invited him over to shoot pheasants with his dog Milo, who sprayed mud all over his bed. He told him that, once ordained, he might be his curate-in-charge for a year, 'arriving & departing in magnificent noises, dust and possibly fire on a motorcycle', since Jesuits who stayed on at Heythrop for the year after ordination were given motorbikes to help them do duty in the country round about.

In London after Christmas he began a stimulating new friendship with John Berger. An artist by training and a radical novelist and critic, Berger had settled near Geneva and came to England only on brief visits. Warm and informal, with an intensely direct gaze, he was international in his sympathies and firm in his Marxist convictions. He had adopted Walter Benjamin's deconstructional theory of representative art, on which he would base a television series and collection of essays, *Ways of Seeing*. Excited by his conversation, Peter impressed him as passionate about ideas. After reading his novel *A Painter of Our Time*, about an exiled Hungarian artist in London, he told Julian that he longed to write something with a similar flavour (although 'he has no more idea of narrative technique & all that jazz than I have'). Before long, however, his own Hungarian novel sank quietly out of sight.

In the New Year he buckled down to translating *Babiy Yar* and other poems by Yevtushenko. Dominique de Grunne had introduced him to the local landowner Michael Astor and his wife Pandora, who liked him and often invited him to Bruern Abbey, near Burford. The Spenders had a cottage there, and Spender and Donald Davie were planning an encyclopaedia of English and American poetry, 'a peeing, squalling baby I've at present been left holding,' he told Julian early in February, having been pressed into contributing and soliciting work from friends.

John Fuller was seeking contributions for the opening number of *The Review*, Ian Hamilton's Oxford-based precursor of the London-based *New Review*. Peter sent in a critique of a long poem by his friend John Holloway, and was deeply offended when Hamilton turned it down. It did not help that Hamilton was barely out of university, whereas Peter was an established poet of thirty. Predictably, he thought the first number 'contrived, horribly provincial', especially in a discussion between Donald Davie and Al Alvarez about the kinds of writing that could be permitted in view of the Holocaust.[16] From Heythrop, the English poetry scene looked depressing. Critics who still expected poetry to have something important to say were looking out for a new Yeats, Eliot, Frost, even Ezra Pound. In the United States they saw a spectrum of talent that ranged from William Carlos Williams and Robert Lowell to the Beats; in England, a crowd of laid-back, timid ironists. Peter longed for some big, politically relevant movement, some poetic form suitable for the new society which he imagined (probably after reading a hopeful article about the wonders of comprehensive education) 'coming out of the secondary modern schools and the other real growing points of now. (I like now.)'[17]

Then, in May 1962, Yevtushenko arrived in England. *The Selected Poems* were not yet out, but the British Council had seized a good opportunity to arrange a pre-publication tour for him and his second wife Galina. His first marriage to the teenage poet Bella Akhmadulina had been very brief.

Zhenya, as the twenty-eight-year-old poet asked everyone to call him, charmed everyone with his dynamic friendliness. 'It took two *minutes*,' Peter told Julian. When the couple came to Oxford with their interpreters to meet him, they enchanted him with their blend of innocence and mysterious knowingness. Fascinated by Zhenya's energy, he had also felt attracted to the beautiful Galya, as often happened when he met friends' wives ('and lovers of either sex', he added tactfully).[18]

Tall, blond, blue-eyed and open-faced, Zhenya had a simple, outgoing air which concealed a survivor's knowledge of the world. His endearingly shaggy, Russian English, full of heavily rolled r's and nouns shorn of an article, gave the impression of someone eager to communicate at all costs, even when his interpreters floundered. Tactfully steering the conversation between politics and religion, he pronounced sententiously that poetry was a difficult path between the two. When Peter asked his opinion of Pasternak's poetry, he received a quick run-down of the major Russian poets of the past hundred and thirty years. Pushkin was incomparable and sublime. Pasternak, Blok, Mayakovsky and Yesenin were in the second rank, Nekrasov, Tyutchev and Lermontov the third, while Mandelstam and 'all the others' made up the fourth. Peter noted his remarks about 'the soaring inspiration of Blok, the earthiness of Yesenin, the political seriousness of Mayakovsky, and the power over images of Pasternak' and his admiration 'for those who soar, but also those who have earth on their boots.' Pasternak, they agreed, shared the best qualities of all the rest.[19]

While Peter returned to Heythrop, the caravan moved on. Sir

Fitzroy Maclean, the Russianist and former ambassador to Moscow, whisked the couple off to Scotland to meet the Duke of Argyll at Inverary. Having seen traditional dancers in West Africa, they were charmed to be welcomed by the duke in his tribal skirt. Back in London, Zhenya 'went down like a bomb' (a British Council minder remarked) at a crowded meeting of the Great Britain-USSR Association at a Kensington hotel, sharply dressed in an Italian-style suit, striped shirt, silk tie and winkle-picker shoes. Taken to meet T.S. Eliot, he was disappointed to find him tired and old. Journalists interviewed him, and photographers stalked him and Galya as they shopped in the West End. Rival hostesses fought to entertain them. The British Council arranged lunches and tea-parties with lists of approved literary guests. In Cambridge he lunched with Kingsley Amis and spent a family afternoon at his home before Peter arrived for a reading at the Union. An elderly Russian in the audience wept because Zhenya reminded him of Mayakovsky, leaping on to café tables in his yellow shirt to recite his poems in the months before November 1917.[20]

The big London reading took place at the Royal Court Theatre on Sunday, May 13. Literary London was there in force, armed in some cases with awkward questions about Krushchev's treatment of Pasternak. Zhenya strode on to the stage in casual dress, stretched out his arms to his audience and proclaimed that, in Russia, poetry was an art for the people. Then he recited as vigorously as if he had been in a Russian theatre, uninhibited (wrote the *Times* reporter) by the more sedate translated versions.[21] Zhenya's histrionic swagger entranced some members of the audience while disconcerting others. Kingsley Amis had imagined his performance must be like a Russian Shakespearean actor's, while Peter Porter, at the Royal Court, compared it with Dickens's at one of his novel-readings as he hammed up his rhythms, dropped his voice from a roar to a whisper and dramatized everything in direct speech. A few of the poems came without translations, 'for the music'. Peter's versions, read by Ian McKellen, were 'interesting, sane and rather cool' in Porter's opinion, and at times seemed to be saying something quite different from the original.[22] Not attempting the eclectically varied rhythms of the Russian, they had given Amis the impression of 'admirably un-poetical' prose. Yet the elegance of their simple, authoritative rhythm makes them memorable in themselves.[*]

At the end of the reading Zhenya bear-hugged Peter on stage and joked that, if he did not become a Jesuit, Peter would become a Communist. After a merry meal with Robin and McKellen Peter slipped away, while the rest of the party ended up at the Establishment Club in Soho. Zhenya had learnt the Twist in America and showed off uproariously. Stephen Spender, who chaired the reading, had met him at a dinner party the evening before, and had evidently hoped for a more spiritual, Dostoevskian kind of Russian. In his diary he noted someone else's opinion that Zhenya was hard and insincere, and complained that his dancing that evening showed the 'jitterbug night-club side of him'. When Peter and Robin called on him the next morning, he asked if they thought that Zhenya really liked anybody. 'He is his own best friend,' one of them replied.[23]

In Oxford there was a farewell reading at the Taylor Institution on May 22, attended by modern languages students, local Russians and university grandees. Peter wrote anxiously afterwards to Sir Isaiah Berlin of All Souls, a native Russian speaker known for his strong views, excusing himself for having been too shy to speak to him in case he had disliked the poems or found fault with the translations. Berlin replied that he thought Yevtushenko 'small-scale but a genuine poet...

---

[*] Take, for example, the opening lines of Peter's rhyming version of 'Birthday' (p.71): 'Mother, let me congratulate you on/the birthday of your son./You worry so much about him. Here he lies,/he earns little, his marriage was unwise.' For a different approach, see George Reavey's non-rhyming version in *The Poetry of Yevgeny Yevtushenko, 1953 to 1965* (1966) 57: 'I congratulate you, mamma/on your son's birthday./You worry about him/and your worry is strong,/Here he lies,/so gaunt,/large and untidy,/married unwisely,/unprofitable for the house.

vulgar and sincere', and admired him for wanting more honesty, truth and personal freedom of expression within the Communist system. He compared him with Herwegh, a German hero of the 1848 revolution whose fame had been short-lived.[24]

Immediately after returning to Moscow, Yevtushenko published some impressions of his tour in *Literaturnaya Gazeta*. Much of the extract reproduced in the next day's *Observer* was devoted to interpreting the ideological messages of the Establishment Club's dance-floor. He declared himself generally in favour of the West but opposed to decadence. While he had enjoyed seeing a graceful black couple doing the Twist, he had been less impressed by 'bearded youths and girls in narrow black trousers' wriggling and gyrating unnaturally in a smoky fug. He also disliked seeing couples rock'n'rolling 'hysterically and with irony', rather than in the simple, beautiful style of a Soviet workers' club.[25]

At Heythrop, Peter was soon caught up in arrangements for the annual Whitsun diocesan scout camp. The Penguin *Selected Poems* of Yevtushenko, with its striking cover design of a spiny, blood-red plant on a white background, became the book of the moment that autumn for switched-on sixth-formers, university students and poetry enthusiasts. But the Penguin Poets connection held out no further promises for him. In April he had told Julian: 'The latest and greatest disaster is that I'm going to have to write probably a Penguin called "The Jesuits". Ha bloody ha.'

10
NANCY

The celestial globe has dust on it.
No other rose is as simple as this.
Moths in the open might never be hit:
ochre and charcoal as this building is.

'For Nancy and Betty Sandars', *Collected Poems* (1976) 106.

Even the newest young philosophy scholastics in the autumn of 1962 knew Peter, the third-year theologian, by reputation. They saw him striding around, tall and handsome, with his unbuttoned gown over a thick sweater flowing untidily out behind him. They heard what Julian called his grackle laugh at coffee-time, and his dramatic fits of bronchial coughing on the way into early Mass. Cutting down on Jesuit roll-ups to quell the cough, he was cultivating a taste for snuff from Fribourg and Treyer's cigar-shop in Oxford High Street near Carfax. Ignoring most of the regular set work, he relied on last-minute cramming for exams, and was notorious for always bagging a seat at the back of the lecture hall so that he could read *The Times* or write letters or poems instead of paying attention and taking notes. His name on the title-page of Yevtushenko's *Selected Poems* ensured a certain impunity. Like the KGB in its relations with Zhenya, his superiors allowed him extra rope, although, like Zhenya, he would soon find himself smartly yanked back.

As usual, Peter's friends saw more of the world than he did. Willie remained at North Aston, half-way through his B.Phil. course, but Denis had left Stonyhurst for a lectureship in medieval history at Reading. The Pryce-Joneses spent several months in Israel, where David finished his second novel and developed a lifelong interest in Middle Eastern politics. Alasdair, after taking a break from his kibbutz to visit India, decided that life in Israel was not the answer and took refuge with the Hugheses in North Wales.[1] In Oxford again he glimpsed a beautiful, flame-haired Welsh girl standing with her luggage on the far side of the station, waiting for a northbound train. Dashing through the subway, he ran up to her and implored 'Please don't go.' Before long this Zuleika Dobson figure had joined a London art school and was living with him on a houseboat in Chelsea Reach.

The Fullers, like many academic young couples, spent a year in the United States, where John taught English Literature at the State University of New York at Buffalo while waiting for a suitable job to come up at home. On the point of leaving for America the couple had introduced Peter to a pair of sisters, family friends who lived near Heythrop, in an encounter that was to change his life.

'Think of a new subject, as clear and fresh as grass...Consider archaeology.'[2] Nancy Sandars was a private scholar of deep integrity, adventurousness and courage. Her elder sister Betty had been at Oxford with Prue Fuller's mother. After war service in the WRNS, in which she had used her German to intercept radio traffic from naval listening posts on the south coast, Nancy had studied archaeology in London and become an expert on European prehistoric art and culture. The two country-loving, church-going sisters had inherited the Manor House at Little Tew, where Nancy had been born and where they had both grown up. Looking down from the Fullers' flat as their guests approached the front door, Peter was asked to guess which one of them was a famous archaeologist and which

one made jam. As he later wrote, he could not immediately tell; the two were in some ways so alike that 'they seemed one flame from two candles or one fruit from two branches, like sisters in Shakespeare'.[3]

Nancy was in her late forties, with a direct gaze and a luminously intelligent face. While Betty was a jolly domestic and parish organiser, Nancy loved reading, thinking and discussing any subject, from mythology and prehistoric cookery to modern poetry and growing old-fashioned roses. A fearless traveller to archaeological sites in Europe and the Middle East, she responded sensitively to landscapes, describing them with a mystical touch in the poems she wrote at Little Tew. After publishing her first scholarly work, on Bronze Age art in France, she had translated the ancient Babylonian *Epic of Gilgamesh* for Penguin Classics. Admiring her independence and the range of her interests, Peter was touched by her straightforward readiness to accept him as a friend. She respected his vocation, keeping her thoughts about 'all that Jesuit stuff' to herself.

Little Tew is a short cross-country walk from Heythrop. At the foot of the road that winds down from the Heythrop plateau, behind the giant wellingtonia that serves as the village noticeboard, the stone-built, stone-slated, gabled Manor House stands at right-angles to the road with as remote an air as William Morris's Kelmscott. Peter came to love the formal topiary of the front garden and the scrambling roses and fruit trees on the sloping lawn behind, with a kitchen garden hidden round a corner and a final wilderness of tunnels and tangles of overhanging plants. He loved the drawing-room with its clutter of porcelain, books and paintings, its nobly uncomfortable sofa and dusty electric fire. He liked the fact that the upstairs book-room had been the schoolroom in which the sisters, like their friends the Mitford girls, had been taught by a governess when young. Little Tew, in its microclimate of peacefulness, fitted into its setting in a way that Heythrop never could. 'Nancy Sandars has gone to Persia and left North Oxfordshire looking empty,' he wrote to John Fuller that autumn, in a letter otherwise full of cheerful speculation about the poems he imagined John writing about American food.

He had begun to fret a little about his own dignity as a poet. Kenneth Allott had chosen one of his poems for a new edition of the *Penguin Book of Contemporary Verse*, requesting a potted biography which Peter had duly sent in. Perhaps only a frustrated, lonely person would then have written to the *TLS*, complaining that notes on the contributors distracted attention from the poems. 'Who wants to know that I went to Beaumont and Jon Silkin taught English to foreigners and which Building Society employs Roy Fuller?' he grumbled. 'Rooting around for poems in these books is like fumbling for tomatoes in a garbage can.'[4] He had already felt self-conscious about submitting his details to *Light Blue, Dark Blue*, wondering if Julian could explain that he was teaching at a 'snob school' under obedience.[5] His real complaint, however, was against Allott's editorial comment that he was immature as a poet and still trying on various masks for a fit.

Ignoring the biographical issue, T.S. Eliot wrote supportively to the *TLS*, suggesting that Allott had overstepped the mark in criticizing the work of a poet he had represented so minimally. But the Movement poet Anthony Thwaite defended Allott and thought most readers found the biographical notes interesting. He also wondered why Peter had told Allott he believed in the class war if he wanted to keep the fact to himself.[6] Allott's letter of self-defence, accusing Peter of making an unprecedented, bad-tempered fuss, was not the best kind of publicity for him just before André Deutsch published his second collection that November.

Water, Rock and Sand consisted mainly of the poems he had written at Stonyhurst, and its glum mood attracted negative reviews. After his eager mask-trying-on at Oxford, the Lancashire damp and loneliness had coloured his poems a sombre monochrome, full of vague imagery, sad descriptions of landscape, fierce revulsion against schoolmastering and nostalgia for his friends. Ian Hamilton, in the *New Statesman*, compounded Peter's resentment of him by calling the poems 'fluently obscure', 'thinly textured and elusive' and too private to be generally understood. Derwent May in the *TLS* compared him cruelly with a stylish conductor waving his baton at a non-existent orchestra. He had been more impressed (he wrote) with the imagery and quality of Richard Selig's *Poems*, which Peter had edited for the Dolmen Press.[7]

Peter, however, was still convinced that his dearest friends understood and appreciated his poems. Perhaps future, unknown friends might feel the same if given a chance to do so. That winter he sat down at Heythrop and wrote a fan-letter to his long-time literary hero Cyril Connolly, enclosing a gift of his '*quantulumcumque libellum*' ('trifling little book') and telling Connolly how much his writing had meant to him. 'For God's sake don't think you have an obligation to reply if you don't feel like it,' he ended half-diffidently, half-challengingly.

To his delight Connolly sent a friendly answer, suggesting that he was perhaps too happy to write good poetry. Peter wrote back at once ('Heavens what a pleasant letter to get'), defending himself and thinking that his poems were unlikely to change. 'What cure is there for happiness?' he asked, with a Connollyesque rhetorical shrug.[8]

After the success of Yevtushenko's *Selected Poems*, Harvill Press, the scholarly imprint of Collins, had commissioned Peter and Robin to produce translations of his more recent poems, this time to be read with the originals. Peter worked cheerfully away at Robin's prose renderings, happy with Julian's praise for the openness of his earlier versions. Riding on the back of that boisterous poetry, he felt freed from the 'treadmill of the Larkinesque'.[9] His window on the East had been opened. Instead of fantasizing about moving to Hungary or writing a novel set in Budapest, he was able to live vicariously through Yevtushenko, sending his imagination into areas it would never have penetrated alone.

Now so near, it seemed, to leaving Heythrop, he told Bertie that he longed for his 'ordination ticket' and the certainties about his future it would bring. Anthony, who had been ordained that summer, was back at Heythrop for his tertian year, helping out with administration and coaching scholastics in German. Peter wrote to Willie that he preached 'very chastely' on Sundays. 'Bees swarm around the pulpit, and honey runs in rivers from the font.'[10] Perhaps envying Anthony his new authority, he told Julian that the more he wished to be quit of the Jesuits, the more firmly his religion pulled him back. No longer tempted to leave, he now trusted his instinctive faith.[11] Craving sun, he arranged to spend the year after his ordination at a Jesuit house in Naples.

The Jesuits were due to announce his ordination date in February 1963. Meanwhile, there was a long, snowy, icy winter to get through. Everywhere in Britain, blizzards and north winds raged from Boxing Day into the New Year, burying lorries and country buses in deep snowdrifts, filling lanes to hedge-top level, making sudden igloos of parked cars and leaving grey, compacted mounds of shovelled snow along pavement-edges and gutters. The cold and disruption continued into January and February. Cattle, sheep and new-born lambs died in the fields. Rivers froze and pipes and water mains burst. Because few houses had central heating, shoppers queued for solid fuel and paraffin. Heythrop, like its bracing hilltop neighbour Chipping Norton, was one of the coldest, most snowed-up places in England. When the Chipperfield's Circus elephants arrived at their winter quarters at the north end of the Heythrop estate, they came in a procession on foot, trunk-to-tail, along the white, banked-up roads from Chipping Norton station. Peter saw a line of them with glittering frost on their backs, waving their trunks and 'oomphing along' as they passed the house.[12]

For the first three days of blizzards, just after Christmas, he had been enjoyably stranded at the Pryce-Joneses' in London. He had met Dom, 'happy & peaceful' in a new relationship, and Gregory Corso, 'cheerful, full of ape-like energy', but half-wrecked by what he innocently interpreted as 'too much smoking or something'.[13] David's study of Graham Greene's novels was about to come out in a critical series from Oliver & Boyd, and Peter thought of offering a similar study of Cyril Connolly's writings. Two things deterred him: the fact that Connolly's style seemed inseparable from his life, so that the book would have to be a portrait of a man he had never met, and his ordination, which was due the following summer.[14]

Back at Heythrop for the New Year, he told Bertie that he had hardly ever been as happy as he had during those few days in London. He had eighty letters to answer, a New Year greetings telegram from Yevtushenko, a pair of 'bootsmelling new boots', probably from Mollie, and a brilliant water-colour from Saby, the artist he had met in the Auvergne. The Heythrop plateau was transformed by 'bitter blue winds & deep loose snow-drifts'. Struggling to and from Hook Norton, the village several miles away where he helped to run the local scout troop, he had to wade through waist-high drifts past abandoned, half-buried vans. The disused railway-cutting west of Hook Norton glittered sheer and pure in cold moonlight, and he found its tunnel crammed with icicles like chandeliers.[15] By February he had forgotten what the country looked like when not under snow. 'It has at present such gravidity of line & at the same time such economy, & a brilliant madid glitter at the sun's eye,' he wrote to David in their private language, begging him to come on a visit as soon as it thawed.

One day early in March Paul Haddon was with Anthony in his office when Peter stormed in, outraged. He had just been told that his ordination had been postponed for a year. At first he assumed that the reason was his constant failure to appear at prayers in the chapel at half-past six every morning. 'I'm certified sick,' he protested. 'I've got a medical certificate to say I have this bronchitis!' But that turned out to be only one in a number of faults which added up to 'a huge and mildly funny crime-sheet,' he wrote to Nancy, repeating the defensive adjective 'funny' to other friends. Instead of spending a year in the sun he would be trapped at Heythrop, where the damp and cold had already brought on his cough so badly that he had been X-rayed on suspicion of a serious chest condition. 'I say my coughs like saying an office before daybreak & after nightfall,' he told Willie the following spring.[16]

Some of his friends suspected that the Jesuits were edging him towards the door. While they might find it difficult to expel him outright after condoning his literary activities for so long, the postponement could be taken as a hint that he should resign. Six months later Julian compared him in his diary with a wall-of-death motorcyclist, defiantly whizzing round the rim of religious discipline.[17] Why couldn't he simply chuck it? some people asked.

As always, however, he bounced back, insisting that the Jesuits did not wish to break his spirit or change his character but only to correct certain faults. 'If there were to be changes of deep-level personality & any of that jazz,' he wrote to David, 'I should be off my ecclesiastical launching-pad before they could count down to zero.' Dominique de Grunne had persuaded him that they were simply jealous of his literary success and the number of his friends in the outside world. What he had (Peter claimed) was what many of the senior Jesuits would have liked for themselves. His main problem was a failure to conform, since he was neither a predictable scholarly type nor a 'licensed eccentric' like Hopkins. 'If one's intelligent or handsome or whatever, but not an academic, one meets the world rather too late, & far too naively. These late encounters are often semi-disastrous...'[18] Yet the prospect of teaching at Oxford was one he longed for so much, and was still so uncertain of, that he barely mentioned it even to his closest friends.

That spring and early summer he consoled himself by spending more time with Nancy. With the Fullers away he could cultivate her on his own, inviting her to tea at Heythrop with Denis as chaperon, and then to go punting up the Cherwell from Magdalen Bridge with him and Denis in early June. The meeting-point he arranged was his favourite spot by the actinidia in the Oxford Botanic Garden. At Little Tew he shared Nancy's love of the evening magic of the place, with its wallflower scent, diffuse lilac light and tree-surrounded quiet. In a poem about the house and its ancestral clutter, the cuckoos and nightingales he imagined in the surrounding trees and the moths and roses paling into the twilight, he ended with an affectionate tribute to the neighbourliness of their friendship:

> But humanity should have been silent,
> is gravel-tongued, its voice is not true,
> or else lived in one long drawn out present
> talking as friends and as old neighbours do.[19]

Of all Nancy's stories of travel and excavation, he was most enthralled by the ones about Greece. She had gone there first in the early 1950s, when her friend Clarissa Sherrard's brother Philip was spending a year as assistant director of the British School of Archaeology at Athens. On post-war military duty in Greece he had married his first, Greek wife Anna and experienced one of those overwhelming cultural conversions that sometimes happen to English people abroad. Back in England a few years later he was received into the Orthodox Church and published his doctoral thesis as *The Marble Threshing-Floor*, a ground-breaking critique of the poets Solomos, Palamas, Cavafy, Sikelianos and Seferis. Although unhappy as an administrator, he returned to the British School for a further spell and made a home for his wife and two daughters in the abandoned cottage settlement of a former manganesite mine at Katounia, near the port of Limni on Evia (Euboea). Once retired there from academic life he wrote interpretations of Byzantine spirituality and translated modern Greek poets, while combining traditional Orthodox religious observance with a passionate concern for ecology and the natural world.

Not long after her first visit to Greece, Nancy had returned to dig on Naxos with Sinclair Hood, the future director of the British School, who became her lifelong friend. Later she took in Turkey, Armenia and the sites of ancient Persian and Mesopotamian civilizations, but at that stage she was intent on exploring Greece, even to the extent of penetrating the closed military zone in the north. Ignoring the need for an official permit, she attached herself to the anthropologists John and Sheila Campbell in their study of transhumant Sarakatsani families in the Zagorochoria, a remote area of the Pindus mountains near the Albanian frontier. Fifty years later she still sometimes wore a striped shawl or carried a woven Sarakatsani bag from that trip.

Between them, she and Peter made up their minds that he must visit Greece. Although the Jesuits had frustrated all his attempts to go there during Oxford vacations, he might be able to persuade them that first-hand knowledge of the country would be useful when he was teaching Greek, and also that it would be less disruptive to that year's ordinands if, having been refused ordination, he stayed well clear of Heythrop and England until the summer was at an end.

11
GREECE

Parthenon in dark misty moonlight of an eclipse, huge lemon & black
butterflies, an owl toowhitting across the Plaka, rich, rich costume
dances (I was so drunk with it I fell asleep & had to have ouzo to get
sober) and Oh the sky.

To David Pryce-Jones, Athens, July 1963

Amazingly, his arguments worked. Six weeks after his thirty-second
birthday he was as free as any gap-year student. He could abandon his
clerical collar, black suit and tatty gown for a pair of thin trousers, a
shirt with rolled-up sleeves and a rucksack. Nancy had invited Philip
Sherrard, now teaching at King's College, London, to meet him, and
Sherrard, with his sensitive, bearded face and gently dignified manner,
was friendly and helpful. As well as an open invitation to spend a week
or more at Katounia, he gave Peter a letter of introduction to George
Seferis, the most recent of the poets he had featured in *The Marble
Threshing-Floor* and the most distinguished poet alive in Greece. Full
of energy, inoculated against typhoid and equipped with a basic living
allowance, Peter was determined to see as much and to meet as many
people as he could. It seemed an unrepeatable freak of fate that the
Jesuits should have given him these two months of pure freedom.

After a farewell oyster lunch with David Pryce-Jones, who was still
commissioning reviews from him for *Time & Tide* and the *Spectator*,
he left Heythrop at the beginning of July 1963. Persuading someone to
drive him the fourteen miles to Banbury station was the hardest part
of the journey, he claimed; senior Jesuits were notoriously mean about
offering lifts.[1] After a night in a Wimbledon convent he spent hours
wandering round Heathrow, gazing out of windows and marvelling
at the unfamiliar sight of parked planes, until his long-delayed flight
to Milan was announced. Feeling that it would be sacrilegious to fly

straight to Athens he had chosen to approach the city by sea, on a Lloyd Triestino steamer from Genoa which called at Naples, Messina and Piraeus.

His below-decks cabin contained a friendly young sailor from Chios and a pair of Greek hairdressers from London, who went wild with homecoming excitement as the ship glided close to the banks of the Corinth Canal with their smells of sun-warmed pine resin and thyme. Peter, who had been on deck since dawn, was too fascinated by the advancing and receding outlines of mountains, rocks and islands to write much in his notebook. As yet, he could only vaguely grasp the shape of that coast. 'Barren hillsides enmeshed with story-telling. Attica even more bare. Dusty and smoky Piraeus. The yellow akropolis marbles look as if they would crumble' (seen, he added later, through the heat-haze of the city, which was not yet opaque with late twentieth-century smog).[2]

He had arranged to base his stay at the British School, a large, extended, nineteenth-century villa on Odos Souidias in the respectable central district of Kolonaki. With its austere rooms, formidable archaeological library, outdated airmail copies of the The Times and urns of dishwater tea, it was an institution for serious scholars, like a secular version of some of the religious houses he knew well. Among the English residents he found a friend in Canon Francis Bartlett, a Westminster Cathedral priest and uncle of the future Fat Lady television cook Jennifer Paterson, whose sister was an administrator at the School. But most of the regular members were off on excavations and were replaced by casual travellers, popping in to collect their post.

Kolonaki is unexciting, but on his first evening Peter made his way past the Parliament building in Syntagma Square, down past Hadrian's Arch and the Temple of Olympian Zeus and across the main road into the Plaka. By the light of a full moon he gazed up at the Acropolis, surmounted by the faint shape of the Parthenon with its broken portico and wounded central gash. Alerted by the sound of guards' whistles he found that the gates were open, and climbed up towards the glimmering hulk. It was silent and empty and felt to him like a holy place.[3]

After that he spent many evenings in the Plaka, then a wholly intimate, shabby neighbourhood of hilly streets and steps, abandoned fig-tree gardens, feral cats, tavernas and bars. At a café table on one of those first soft, warm nights, relaxed by ouzo and the scents of smoke, shrubs and meat stewing with wine and herbs, he scrawled an exuberant note to David Pryce-Jones, enclosing his review of Allen Ginsberg's *Reality Sandwiches* for the *Spectator* of August 9. Apart from a few breathless letters to Mollie he wrote to hardly anyone else during that trip; he was too busy travelling, meeting people, sleeping rough and breathing clean air under cloudless skies, while scribbling torrential impressions in his notebooks.

Athenian air-pollution in the early 1960s was not as bad as it is now, but July was, as always, very hot. Peter loved the heat. That winter he told John Fuller that he had never, since childhood, been properly warm before, let alone lived in a place that had been properly warm for centuries. 'I am as drunk as the sky every day just with the heat,' he wrote on a postcard to Julian. 'Let alone rocks, dust, peaches, & statues.' (Another child of his generation, Ted Hughes, tasted his first fresh peach from a London stall when he was twenty-five.)[4]

Some mornings he trudged north-westwards to the National Archaeological Museum, with its vast rooms of sculptures and funeral steles in Pentelic, Parian and Boeotian marble. Carved palmettes and akroteria amused him, but his real fascination was with the textures of different kinds of stone. Away from traffic, he breathed in the smell of crushed thyme and oregano on the way up Hymettos to the twelfth-century monastery of Kaisarianí. From the winding paths of Philopappos, with its rocks, wild flowers and scrub, he could see the

Parthenon at eye-level, seeming to float above the heat of the tiled-roofed city. On the Acropolis he could lean out over the ancient defensive walls, marvel at the crumbling caryatids which still supported the Erechtheum, and perch on scattered blocks of marble above the ruins of the Theatre of Dionysus. In the brilliant, reflected light of the Acropolis Museum the statues, reliefs and copies seemed more alive, if more battered, than their Bloomsbury equivalents. But he later noticed the careering gallop of some of the horses on the British Museum reliefs, and asked Nancy if she had ever thought that 'in two or three places on the Parthenon frieze the procession has got *out of control*, as near as dammit?'⁵

Afternoons in Athens could be empty when the museums were shut. At first Peter did not understand the siesta. Having made confused contact with Seferis, he turned up at his house on the wrong day at English afternoon tea-time. Emerging on to a balcony in a large pair of khaki shorts, the great poet waved him away. But when he went back at the proper time, Seferis welcomed him to a session of warm, rapid-fire conversation. Tall, elegant and bald at sixty-three, he had the cosmopolitan ease and languor of a native of Smyrna in the old Ottoman Empire. He had just retired from his final diplomatic post as ambassador in London, and would be awarded the Nobel Prize for Literature that autumn. Deeply serious and learned, he could break into smiling flippancy with a direct, sometimes crude sense of humour. He enjoyed inventing Greek limericks, some of the more printable of which Peter would translate.

Impressed by the tragic strength of his poetry, Peter was touched that Seferis spoke to him as a near-equal. His kindness, appearance and Turkish background may also have reminded him of Bert. He began to see him as a towering literary father-figure, more benevolently approachable than his counterpart in England, T.S. Eliot. That Christmas, when Seferis sent him a copy of his new translation of

Murder in the Cathedral, he naturally thought it '*much better* in Greek!'[6]

Not expecting to take up much more of Seferis's time, Peter asked if he could think of any younger Greek poets he might go and see. Seferis named just one, whom he had met for the first time that year. George Pavlopoulos lived quietly with his wife and small son in Pyrgos, on the west coast of the Peloponnese, where he worked as an accountant in the offices of the KTEL bus company. It would be another eight years before he published his first collection of poems. Seferis thought he led a lonely life for a poet and would be pleased if Peter went to see him.[7]

But he had not exhausted literary Athens. One afternoon he made his way to the large, ornate, now vanished Café Floca, on the corner of Panepistimiou and Voukourestiou streets just north-west of Syntagma Square. As Athens's version of the Café de Flore, it housed its own group of poets: chief among them the song-writer Nikos Gatsos, who had written his famous, six-part poem *Amorgos* during a single night of the German occupation of Greece, before claiming to have given up poetry for good. Named after a Cycladic island that Gatsos never visited, the poem was a disjointed succession of timeless, surreal images, encapsulating all the moods of the traditional Greek spirit from the earthily erotic to the defiantly patriotic. Dom and Henrietta had enthused about it, and Sherrard had told Peter to seek out Gatsos, whom he would find at his table in the depths of Floca's air-conditioned interior, usually surrounded by hangers-on. The procedure was to send a waiter with a message to introduce oneself. Peter did this, and the massive, fiftyish figure of Gatsos, with his Shakespearean domed white forehead and insomniac bags under his eyes, lumbered over with a Cheshire Cat smile of greeting to shake his hand.

Meeting Gatsos and reading *Amorgos* struck Peter like a faceful of fresh spring water. His own surrealistic ten-part poem *Pancakes for the*

Queen of Babylon, which he wrote during the next two years, was an act of homage to Gatsos's bright images and intense mood, although he called it merely 'an experiment... not an adequate equivalent of the Amorgos of Gatsos, which is an incomparable poem'.[8]

One of Gatsos's disciples that summer was Charles Haldeman, a homosexual American writer of Peter's age, who had settled in Crete but often drifted back to see friends in Athens. He attached himself fondly to Peter, and after dinner in the Plaka one evening Gatsos introduced the pair of them to a version of Consequences which he and the poet Odysseus Elytis had played during the war. Each player wrote a question at the top of a piece of paper, then folded the paper to hide it and passed it on. On the next blank piece he wrote the answer and on the piece after that a comment, with sometimes profound-seeming results. Exhilarated by the zany logic of the game, Peter read hints of liberating meaningfulness into its random, dreamlike progression. The limericks of Seferis and Gatsos also seemed to hint at concealed depths in their tight form and quiet wit. He began to feel a bond with the expatriate bachelor Edward Lear, marvelling at his sensitive water-colours of Greek, Italian and Near Eastern landscapes and enjoying the anarchic writings and drawings which had stood so many Victorian assumptions on their heads. Talent was nothing, said Gatsos. 'What we need is something else.'[9]

છ

Once away from Athens, he was on his own. Lorry-drivers gave him lifts, village people offered him beds, and he even hitched an illegal ride in a fishing-boat along the coast of the Gulf of Corinth one night. Although he could chat casually to the people he met, there was nobody he could talk to on the same level as Seferis and Gatsos. When not marvelling at cloud-shadows racing across mountain peaks, he was attacked by mosquito-bites of worry and loneliness. Would ordination mean that he would have to give up writing poetry? And if the Jesuits finally showed him the door, how would he survive? He had been institutionalized for so long that, like certain ex-prisoners, he might find it impossible to adapt. 'Paradise is how to live happily in a sunny climate, and this can be achieved,' he scribbled hopefully in his notebook. But even in the museum at Delphi, anxieties lurked between him and the precious objects in their glass cases and confused his impressions of the sculptures as he tried to memorize their gracefulness by heart.[10]

Like many first-time visitors to Greece he went straight from Athens to Delphi, near the southern mainland coast. Then he crossed the Gulf of Corinth by ferry to Aigion in the northern Peloponnese. After catching an overnight, westbound train to Pyrgos he zigzagged between the sites of Olympia, Pylos, Bassae, Sparta and Mistra, then travelled down to the Veneto-Byzantine port of Monemvasia on a craggy tip of the southern Peloponnese. His progress was a patchwork of bus, train and taxi journeys and long hikes along stony roads and across rough country. At night he often lay among sun-warmed, lizard-swarmed stones in some classical ruin. Many sites were still unguarded in 1963, and even at Delphi, under the shoulder of Mount Parnassus, the security was lax.

In spite of his raw mood, he found Delphi extreme and thrilling. Between the early-morning shadows and the long evening ones he wandered repeatedly round the sloping site with its museum, amphitheatre and temple ruins. After chatting up one of the older guards, he slunk off into the Temple of Apollo to bed down for the night. At one point he woke in the soft blackness to see a large, bright star shining above him. Then he slept again, not realizing that a huge poisonous snake had also curled up in the temple. At dawn a guard clubbed it to death as it slithered out of the ruins to drink. Hearing about it at the barber's when he went there to be shaved, he felt too shaken to join the crowd who were marvelling at the corpse's deadly markings and length.[11]

Once in the Peloponnese, whose agricultural north gives way to mountains, gorges and hill villages towards the centre and south, he began to feel more relaxed. In his layman's disguise nobody could guess he was a clergyman. To villagers he was simply one of those eccentric, foreign, schoolmasterly figures who sat at cafés scribbling notes in the margins of their copies of Pausanias's region-by-region description of Greece in the second century AD. On a bus to Sparta a cheeky National Serviceman, bored with his sleepy companion, tried to talk him into an evening on the town. 'Mr Professor, let us go to the women... The cost for two together is not much.'[12]

Drinking from springs, eating sparingly, and thinking, dreaming and writing poems in Greek, he was blissfully remote from world affairs. The earthquake at Skopje in late July may have caused faint rumblings farther south, but, away from *The Times*, he escaped the squalid English news of early August: Cliveden, John Profumo, Christine Keeler, the sudden death of Stephen Ward and the 'great' mail-train robbery in Buckinghamshire five days later. Crushed by the daytime heat but exhilarated with freedom, he filled his notebooks with impressions of birds, flowers, mountains, shrubs, the blue-green or indigo stained colour of the sea, and 'the wild thick glittering olive groves, the damp, deep tresses of the vines.'[13] His notes did not come with the right rhythms to turn into English poems, but he felt that his head was full of unwritten ones, like a box of butterflies (he told John Fuller) alive but trapped.[14]

From Aigion he sat up overnight on a cramped train to Pyrgos, then caught a bus to Olympia. The quiet there was blissful after the non-stop inquisitiveness of his fellow-passengers on the train. For several days he wandered alone among the fallen columns of the Temple of Zeus, sleeping out on the dusty, pine-clad Hill of Kronos and swimming in the Alpheios in the afternoons. Then it was time to meet George Pavlopoulos, the poet Seferis had recommended to him.

Tired out from a day at Olympia, Peter turned up at the KTEL office in Pyrgos to meet him after work. George had planned the evening carefully, and took him by bus to the nearby seaside village of Agios Andreas, where he had a family beach-hut and spent much of his free time. As they sat under the vine-canopy of a taverna, watching the sun sink over the western islands, Peter felt drawn to this serious, passionate man of thirty-nine who spoke the 'purest, strongest and most beautiful Greek'. They discussed their admiration for Seferis, whose language, George said, reminded him of the immense, nobly shattered pillars of the temple of Olympian Zeus in Athens. They talked about the English respect for antiquity, and the ruins at Olympia. 'Who made those?' George asked as they walked on the beach in the dark, watching dry lightning flashing over the by now invisible islands. 'We do not know what men our fathers were. We have lost our fathers.'[15]

After a night in George and Mitsa's small house, Peter set off down the west coast of the Peloponnese. With a month left in Greece, he was in a hurry to fit in as many places as he could. 'Sandy Pylos', with the Mycenaean ruin and museum known as Nestor's Palace, was an obvious choice because it comes into the *Odyssey*. Then he turned inland through rocky, forested Arcadia towards the temple of Apollo Epikourios at Bassae, hiring a stroppy donkey and its owner for the last part of the rough cross-country journey in the dark. It would have been a dull foot-slog by road, and others had made their way there by mule before the road existed. In 1811 Charles Robert Cockerell, one of Byron's dilettante friends in Athens, had organized the excavation of the site after stumbling on a claw-damaged fragment of the temple frieze in a fox's lair. Years later he had copied the Bassae order of ionic columns for the street front of the Taylorian in St. Giles, Oxford. Peter, in politically correct mode, condemned him as a pillager for having bought the temple frieze at auction for the British Museum, the year before Lord Elgin's surviving boatload of Parthenon marbles and other inscriptions and sculptures was installed in a special gallery there.[16]

Near Bassae, in a remote spot above the gorges and waterfalls of the River Neda, lay the site of the ancient city of Phigalia. Pausanias had recorded the presence there of a horse-headed statue of the local goddess, Black Demeter, a mistress of Poseidon. The village priest showed Peter the finds he had dug up and told him how much he longed to read a certain rare description of ancient Greece. Peter, carrying his own three volumes of Pausanias in the original Hellenistic Greek, had been reading them closely since Delphi, when he first discovered their 'thrilling relevance' to what survived. A year later he found another set in Oxford, bought it and sent it to the priest, but received no acknowledgement that it had arrived.[17]

Nearly half of his memoir *The Hill of Kronos* tells the story of that summer of 1963. It follows him back to Athens, then on to Aegina and Euboea, Mount Pelion and the Meteora in Thessaly, and Patmos in the Dodecanese. It describes many of the Greek people he met, from Seferis, Gatsos and George Pavlopoulos to comic figures like the donkey-man at Bassae who vanished into the dark with the scoutmaster's rope Peter had lent him when his bridle broke.[18] It relives his nights sleeping rough, on hillsides, in ruined temples, on the decks of boats at sea, and like a stork nesting on a tower at Andritsaina in the Peloponnese. Yet it pointedly conceals the identities of any English people he met. The 'friends' who entertained him at Monemvasia in the south-eastern Peloponnese were the Cambridge English don and poet John Holloway and his family, at the end of John's two years as Byron Professor in Athens.[19] And 'What pleasure, and what friends' was his single, evasive comment about his week as a guest of the Sherrards at Katounia on Euboea.[20]

That summer, the Sherrards were in daily contact with English neighbours nearby. One was Sir Maurice Bowra, the classical scholar and Warden of Wadham College, whom Peter revered for his knowledge, wit and vast enjoyment of European literature. He had seen him only at a distance during the past six years, since Bowra had asked Julian to bring poets to help entertain Robert Frost. Now, however, he had a chance to talk to him properly in the country he most loved. Fruity-voiced and noisily ebullient, with a private taste for composing obscene and scatological verses that he probably hid from the Sherrards, the chunky sixty-five-year-old would emerge after a morning reading Euripides, ready for a long, conversational, vinous lunch.

Although blatantly homosexual, Bowra was devoted to Joan Rayner, his intellectual equal in conversation and the 'greatest single love of his life, of either sex' according to Sir Isaiah Berlin.[21] He spent many of his summer vacations, when not lecturing on Swan Hellenic cruises, staying with her and her future husband Patrick Leigh Fermor in Greece. Born Joan Eyres Monsell, she was the daughter of the first Viscount Monsell and his heiress wife Sybil, née Eyres, who had brought her husband an industrial fortune and a Victorian mansion, Dumbleton Hall near Evesham. With a childless marriage behind her, she had first met Paddy in Cairo soon after his dashing wartime military exploits in Crete.

Tall, quiet, self-possessed and beautiful, with a part-time London life of her own, Joan had achieved an almost ideal partnership with Paddy, sharing most of his post-war wanderings in the Caribbean, France, Italy, Cyprus and parts of Greece. A talented photographer, she had illustrated his exuberant travelogue *Mani*, about a primitive part of the extreme southern Peloponnese. Paddy had often borrowed a luxurious villa on Hydra from the artist Nikos Hadjikyriacou-Ghika, until the caretaker, resenting the end of Nikos's first marriage, burned it down. Bowra had stayed with the couple there, and also at a villa on Poros. Now the three of them were occupying a house that belonged to

Sir Aymer Maxwell, the Sherrards' near neighbour at Katounia.[22] With the prospect of spending an inheritance of Joan's, she and Paddy had begun negotiating to buy their own piece of building land, sheltered to the north and east by the Taÿgetos mountains and facing west into the gentlest of sea breezes, on an undeveloped headland at Kalamitsi Bay, just south of the fishing village of Kardamyli, which Paddy had described in *Mani* as the perfect place in which to live.[23]

Half-way through his charmed life at forty-eight, Paddy was gregarious and fun. He had a hero's swagger, a love of the Greek and Latin classics, a dabbler's knowledge of curiosities and historical details, and a dazzling film-star smile which could blacken into a Cretan scowl. Peter may have seen Dirk Bogarde's improbably willowy depiction of him in *Ill met by Moonlight*, the film about his Cretan kidnapping adventure. He may have read Paddy's *Mani*, or his Caribbean novel *The Violins of Saint-Jacques*, or his translation of George Psychoundakis's memoir *The Cretan Runner*. None of that can have prepared him for the bounce and fizz of his conversation, his rapid associative fantasies and multilingual repertoire of poems and songs. The group met for lunch outdoors in the Sherrards' courtyard at Katounia, and again at the tiny local taverna for dinner. Paddy's supercharged *joie de vivre*, Joan's cool sophistication and Bowra's varied moods must have kept Peter fascinated, yet made him feel very innocent and young. Years later Paddy thought he had not been much over twenty, remembering him in jeans and a blue jersey with all his luggage in a book-laden rucksack.[24] The gentle, spiritual Sherrard was keen to divert his mind upwards, pointing out one day how closely the lines of the mountains they could see from Katounia resembled certain forms of Greek sculpture.[25]

After a week Peter said goodbye. He was on his own once more, walking northwards along beaches and cliff tops, through olive-groves, orchards and gorges, and chatting to anyone he met along the way.

'Knowing the language has been a great help I found,' he wrote to Mollie. On a daily level he did well enough, although he later admitted to almost weeping with frustration after trying to keep up with the fast, allusive conversation of poets in an Athenian café.[26]

From the port of Aedipsos on Euboea he took a ferry to the mainland at Volos with its fine archaeological museum. At Portaria on the slopes of Mount Pelion he had arranged to meet Dominique de Grunne (an episode he did not touch on in The Hill of Kronos). After a short trip with Dominique into Thessaly and a stay in one of the monasteries high on the rocks of the Meteora, he returned alone to Athens on the usual dreadful night train.

His last, planned visit was to Patmos, an island he had chosen for its spiritual association with John, the author of the Book of Revelation. Late in August he had a blissful time there, staying in a back street near the harbour, swimming, chatting to the regulars in tavernas and browsing among the manuscripts in the monastic library. To his excitement he thought he had made an important scholarly discovery, although, when he announced it in Oxford, it provoked a snub even more crushing than Fraenkel's four years earlier.[27]

From Patmos he was due to catch the last boat of the season back to Piraeus. News of his interest in the manuscripts had spread to the police, who assumed he must have been buying them illicitly and pulled him away to search him just as he was about to go on board. The gangplank went up, while a grandmother, watched respectfully by her family, howled and thrashed on the quayside because her grandson had been called up for National Service. As the boat headed out to sea, Peter was dumped on board from a police launch and found both decks already solid with people bedding down for the night. Scrambling into a slot between a lifeboat and the rail-less edge of the deck, he lashed his sleeping-bag to the uprights with a rope at one end and his shirt at the other and crawled into it as the boat began to pitch and roll.[28]

It was almost time for him to report back to Heythrop, but he had managed to secure an extra week of freedom by accepting Dominique's invitation to stay at Ribes on his way back to England early in September. A group of Oxford friends would be at the château: Julian, Alasdair, his flame-haired artist girlfriend Ann Griffith, and Angus Macintyre, a newly elected history fellow of Magdalen, whom everyone liked for his dry humour and affable, upper-class niceness. Although his wife was expecting a baby, he joined the house-party on his own.

When Peter arrived by train from Naples, bright-eyed, thin, burnt dark by the sun and bursting with excitement about Greece, his friends were amazed at how much that summer had changed him. Although he still wrangled amicably with Julian, he had gained a new air of certainty. The returning gap-year student was no longer a late adolescent but very nearly a confident, cosmopolitan adult.

Dodo, as some of them called Dominique, was an expert host. His cook, Marie, produced wonderful meals of simple country food, served by a tattooed Algerian girl who had been hired specially from Le Puy. After lunch, coffee and liqueurs the party rested, then went for long walks in the wild country round about. Once they went as far as the Gorges du Tarn in the Lozère, and another time visited the château of Valprivas, a centre for musicological research. One afternoon they stayed at home to pick mushrooms in wreathing Auvergne mist. Dominique knew all the varieties ('half edible, a quarter doubtful, a quarter deadly', Julian noted), and his guests hallooed 'Dodo, Dodo!' in ringing Oxford voices up and down the slope opposite the château, shouting descriptions of what they had found.

At dinner one evening the party decided it was time to settle Peter's future. Saying nothing, he slumped in his chair like a child, then slid forward under the table until he disappeared. Embarrassed, the others made silly remarks in funny voices before continuing the discussion over his head. Julian wondered how he would cope with being ordained when he was clearly so ambivalent about Jesuitism. Yet, while convinced that religious discipline could only suppress the creative impulse, he realized that Peter needed a framework and might find life difficult if left without one. Angus, who barely knew him, tactfully said very little. Alasdair offered unhelpful comments on both sides, finally deciding that Peter ought to go ahead and be ordained. The ex-monk Dominique, however, cited himself as a disastrous example of somebody who should never have joined the priesthood. You could get out of everything except ordination, he said, and that was the final argument for not entering into it unless you were absolutely set on it.

Peter, emerging from under the table, said that of course he was set on it. It was what he had always wanted; nothing had changed. But in the train to Lyon with Julian a day or two later he admitted that the conversation had shaken him. In Greece he had failed to come up with alternative plans for his future by banishing the problem from his mind. Now he felt more uncertain than ever. He needed to make a definite decision, and would try to do so during the next week or two.[29]

12
A PRIEST FOR EVER

All that business of Ribes (quite apart from the marvellous holiday
aspect) was very good for me & I feel much better for it. It has the
result that I can't forecast anything & can only half & hardly decide
(what I already so much wanted to decide) to go on... If they threw
me out it would be death from the blow of a feather: I should be
very happy I think (because I should then *know*, in a way I can't now
know... that this is not for me. Like being divorced. But I intend to
survive it if I can)... All I really badly miss is sex and equality, but
attempts to think myself away from wanting what Jesuits want have
been in a way attempts to be another person.

To Julian Mitchell [23 October 1963]

Back at Heythrop for a fourth year of theology, Peter soon banished the
question of ordination from his mind. He collected the poems he had
written before going to Greece, cautiously assuming André Deutsch
would publish them. He made new friends. One day Dominique turned
up and carried him off to meet Iris Murdoch and John Bayley at Cedar
Lodge, Steeple Aston. Dominique had begun to lecture on African,
Polynesian and Chinese art in the General Studies Department of the
Royal College of Art, where Iris also taught, having been persuaded by
John to resign her philosophy fellowship at St. Anne's College, Oxford
after falling in love with a woman colleague. When their guests arrived
for tea, John was digging up a bamboo-clump in the jungly garden and
Iris was immersed in her writing. Enjoying their brilliance and casual
style of entertaining, Peter became their devoted fan.[1] In the spring he
invited Iris to meet Nancy at tea at Heythrop, and he soon joined the
circle of the couple's friends, winning kind opinions from John about
his poems, fascinating Iris with his enigmatic version of the religious
life and securing their important support when he stood for election
as Oxford Professor of Poetry.

Before Peter left for Greece, David Pryce-Jones had introduced him to the Catholic convert, artist, poet and calligrapher David Jones. Soon afterwards Nancy met Jones, delighting him with her knowledge of prehistory, and from then onwards she and Peter shared their friendship with the reclusive, agoraphobic bachelor. Scarred by trench warfare and a broken engagement to Eric Gill's daughter Petra, he had lived for the past sixteen years in a Harrow boarding-house after being treated for a nervous breakdown in a nearby clinic. With his shaggy fringe and innocent, worn face, his simple, devout lifestyle, pedantry and dated slang, Jones might have been an elderly prep-school master with no home but the school and a lifelong history of emotional repression. In fact he was a delicate, visionary painter and poet whom some critics compared with Blake. His long, experimental epic poems, *In Parenthesis* and *Anathemata*, embraced prehistory, the ancient Mediterranean, Celtic legend, medieval Wales, London and Rome, interspersed with classical and liturgical Latin and English prose, and with voices of legionaries on Hadrian's Wall and of Welsh and cockney infantrymen in the trenches. His stormy watercolour *Trystan ac Essyllt*, with its tilting deck, minutely detailed ship's tackle and wildly flapping, furled sails, suggests both doomed love and the transcendent holiness of Yseult, a toweringly untouchable, Virgin Mary-like figure who appears in visionary form in other pictures to console the dead in battle. Victimhood in Jones's work is always close to martyrdom, perpetrated by soldiers who are themselves innocent victims of an impersonal war-machine. 'What they do is as terrible as what is done to them,' Peter remarked about the Roman garrison in North Wales in *Anathemata*. Contrasting Jones's intimate portrayal of the occupiers of that suffering country with Cavafy's heroic depiction of Roman Alexandria, he added, to Jones's approval, that the difference between the two was 'not one of merit'.[2]

Confined to his bedsitter, Jones remained publicity-shy despite praise from Eliot, Auden and Kenneth Clark. He had long been associated with William Cookson's poetry magazine *Agenda*, and Peter, thrilled by his originality and moved by his compassion, reviewed a new paperback edition of *In Parenthesis* in the winter 1963/4 issue. Knowing that Jones treated the idea of the priesthood with absolute seriousness and did not question its rightness for him must have helped him overcome some of the confusion in which he had travelled back from Ribes.

It was the good angel/bad angel scenario again, for his most exciting meeting that autumn was with the sybaritic agnostic Cyril Connolly. On the evening of All Souls' Night, Saturday, November 2, he arrived in Oxford for a party given by Alasdair at All Souls. One guest was the novelist Elizabeth Bowen, who rented a house in Headington from Lady Berlin, the wife of the fast-talking Sir Isaiah. With her were her weekend visitors, Cyril and his slim, blonde, high-cheekboned, much younger third wife Deirdre.

Years later Peter described his first sight of Deirdre. There (he wrote with hindsight) was the woman he realized he should have married.[3] Glamorous, creamy-voiced and friendly, she was almost exactly his age, with two children from an earlier marriage and three-year-old Cressida by Cyril. Still tanned, rake-thin and alive with enthusiasm for Greece, Peter brought out the nurturing kindness behind her social manner. She had never been to Greece and made him describe his summer's adventures, prodding the well-travelled Cyril into an amused response.

It was Cyril, however, whom he had longed to meet for years. At sixty he had mellowed from the gross 'baboon' who had so antagonized Virginia Woolf into a tranquilly Silenus-like figure.[4] At a time when the quality newspapers still encouraged intellectual display, his stately *Sunday Times* reviews and essays fizzed with epigrams, sharp judgments and obscure quotations in Latin and French. His deepest appeal was to the young, whether in *Enemies of Promise*, with its celebration of Eton friendships, praise for epigrammatic, cliché-less writing and *bon-mot* about the pram in the hall, or *The Unquiet Grave*, a wartime wallow in nostalgia and poignant insights about love and loss.

To Peter, meeting the creator of so much indulgent prose was like finding a tree laden with golden quinces outside his window. A fortnight after the party he sent Cyril an antique postcard of the Gorges du Loup in the Alpes Maritimes, hoping to see him again ('In the Gorges du Loup, perhaps') and telling him that his journalism helped to reconcile him to Sundays. As the Connollys lived near Mollie's home at Eastbourne, in a farmhouse on Lord Gage's estate at Firle, he added that it might perhaps be possible for them to meet.[5]

Cyril's *Previous Convictions*, a collection of ten years' worth of essays and reviews, was one of that year's Christmas books. Three weeks after Kennedy's assassination, Peter puffed the book extravagantly in the *Spectator's* lead review, opening with a portentous reference to recent deaths, the ominous floods and winds of late autumn and his anxiety for the safety of the 'few good writers'. He objected only to Cyril's attitude towards the natives when abroad, 'perhaps because the visible world is to him a sort of treasure-hunt, as it was to Berenson.' In compensation, his vast range of interests included 'the dreams of dogs, the introduction of *Rhododendron sinogrande*, the behaviour patterns of young eagles, and the black magnolia at Lanarth'. Despite a 'necromantic' style, his outlook was that of a lover of classical civilization, full of humanity and light.[6]

After Christmas Cyril called at Eastbourne with an armful of books as presents. Among them were Firbank's novel *Vainglory* and the obscure Louise Guiney's *Recusant Poets*. He must have given an impression of interest in that subject, since Peter promised to find him a copy of Christopher Devlin's life of Robert Southwell. He urged Cyril to finish *Shade Those Laurels*, if only to give future undergraduates the chance to read the whole novel.[7] Still in awe of him, he kept his first few letters to him diffident and brief, with a formal signature and best wishes to Deirdre. Exuberantly affectionate in letters to friends of his own age, he tried out various parting salutations to Cyril and Nancy before settling on the ambivalent 'love & all' to both.

Greece had not transformed him as a poet. His surrealistic homage to *Amorgos* was proving heavy going. That winter, his only complete poem inspired by memories of Greece was 'Thirty Ways of Drowning in the Sea', an idea copied from Wallace Stevens's 'Thirteen Ways of Looking at a Blackbird':

> *Long columns of a green and salty light*
> *Trail downwards, finger for a floor,*
> *disappear in the sand-coloured water.*
> *I am below them in that deep current*
> *a trailing hand of light will never reach.*
> *Among whose grooves and wards the heavy sea*
> *shifts without turning, like a rusted key...*[8]

Fine though this was, it did not fit into his backlog of earlier, unpublished Heythrop poems. Many of them were simply meditations about writing a poem or gazing out of his window thinking about an absent friend. The emotional stasis which had set in at Stonyhurst had become more rigid. 'It was what I felt at the time,' he would protest. But both Julian and David, to whom he sent the poems, condemned them as too feeble to print. He agreed to weed them and submit 'Thirty Ways' to André Deutsch with a handful of others, assuming they would still accept anything he offered them. A year earlier, elated by his correspondence with Cyril, he had been complacently identifying himself with the eighteenth-century poet and landscape gardener William Shenstone. Now, lonely and depressed, he wished he had spent the past few years in London, where Julian had become domesticated in Chelsea, instead of mouldering in isolation on 'this rustic-philosophizing sort of thing'.[9]

As winter rime coated hedges and fields on the foggy, frosty, viewless Heythrop plateau, he lay awake with insomnia and catarrh. An Oxford doctor told him that his nose contained a crooked septum, which often causes painful sinus infections. The chest-trouble was a reaction to English damp and cold, and could be avoided only by spending winters abroad. To Peter, facing a future in chilly Jesuit institutions, that seemed unattainable. Worry about his poems also kept him awake, coughing, shivering and writing compulsively to friends.

Then Nancy, to whom he kept shooting off letters about archaeology, etymology and myth, produced a new project for him. The editors of Penguin Classics had invited Philip Sherrard to make an edited, two-volume translation of Pausanias's topographical and cultural description of Greece. This should be more popular with travellers and students who simply wanted an English translation than the five-volume Loeb Classics edition in English and Greek. Sherrard, immersed in Greek poetry and the history of the Orthodox Church, did not want to take on the job, so Nancy persuaded the editors to consider Peter. Like a dog after a stick he dashed joyfully into the business of producing sample copy, sending Nancy a postcard of the ruins of Ypres in late January with the message that, once started on this work, he could not stop.

After the uncertainty of the previous winter, the details of his future at last began to pan out. In February 1964 the Jesuits confirmed that he would be ordained in July. By Easter, he had an almost firm assurance that from October of the following year he would be teaching Greek and Latin literature at Campion Hall. As Anthony was about to become French tutor there, he and Peter between them would constitute one-third of the tutorial body. Unlike a college fellow, however, Peter would not be expected to teach for all three terms of the academic year. Because the Jesuits accepted that his health was too frail to stand the Oxford winter damp, he would be free to go abroad in early December and stay away until the week before Easter. If Pausanias came off, that would mean that, for at least the first year or two, he would have a sound reason for spending entire winters in Greece.

He could hardly believe his luck. Doing almost exactly as he liked seemed once again to have paid off. Excused from attending further theology lectures, he concentrated on having fun. Pausanias remained on one side until a contract arrived from Penguin, while he wrote a long, spontaneous article about the modern Greek literary scene. Dom came to visit, bringing the manuscript of a scurrilous novel that he claimed would be published that summer, and Peter announced that they planned to write a musical comedy round it. Nothing came of either the novel or the musical, but at some point he dashed off a comic opera libretto, probably for Caryl Brahms, who treated him to the Moscow Art Theatre's performance of *The Cherry Orchard* in London.[10] Billy Hewett, as blasé as Peter about the Jesuit prohibition of theatre-going, hitchhiked down from Heythrop to see the play from the gallery and ended up sitting in comfort next to Peter and Caryl. Practical Billy, who knew a girl who worked for the Heythrop Hunt, took Peter riding with him on free afternoons that winter, having arranged for them to exercise a couple of hunters on the gallops near Chipping Norton.

To the more susceptible scholastics, the air of mystery around Peter intensified as his ordination drew closer. Ignoring the coffee-break apartheid, when theologians huddled at one end of the long gallery and philosophers at the other, he would sit ostentatiously on a window-sill with a large Latin volume on his lap. He seemed detached from the daily business of plodding through theological textbooks, baptizing dolls and hearing pretend confessions, which Julian thought particularly camp when he saw it practised by pairs of half-naked theologians beside the swimming-pool. But when younger scholastics wanted to talk to him about books or confide in him about their shaky vocations, he was approachable, funny and kind.

Brendan McLaughlin, a first-year scholastic from the west of Scotland, had been one of Peter's distant admirers until a *Brideshead* moment one night when the window of his ground-floor room in the philosophers' wing creaked open and Peter, who had arrived back after locking-up time, scrambled in clasping a bottle of brandy. Finding that Brendan loved poetry and the classics, he adopted him as a disciple and friend. He took him to see Nancy at Little Tew, and they walked back along twilit field-paths on a spring evening murmuring snatches of Greek to one another. Like so many of Peter's relationships, said Brendan, it was intensely romantic but chaste.

Easter that year was in late March. As always in Holy Week, Peter was worn out with grief by three o'clock on Good Friday afternoon. At his ordination he would be the same age as Christ had been at the crucifixion. Once Easter was over he spent a few days with Mollie, seeing London friends. David Jones's boarding-house was closing down, forcing him to leave his Harrow hilltop for a viewless ground-floor room in a small private hotel below. Depression was to imprison him there for years, but he was cheerful with Peter and offered to design him one of his famous inscriptions for an ordination card. These calligraphic art-works were a form of visual poetry, mixing Latin, Welsh, English, Anglo-Saxon and Greek phrases with a mysteriously numinous effect. Peter was amazed by the result and had copies printed for distribution, telling Nancy it was '*magnificent*, containing Melchisedech in Greek letters in pink & the Naiades in green & himself [Jones] in Welsh in pencil'.[11]

In May, once his theology exams were over, he was told to spend the next few months in Oxford, living in the St. Aloysius clergy house until the end of term, when there would be room for him at Campion Hall. Because Mollie could not travel to his ordination, it would not be at Heythrop after all. Instead he would join a group of diocesan clergy being ordained at Eastbourne by the Bishop of Southwark. Given the choice he would have been happy to stay at Heythrop, dropping in on Nancy to chat about ancient Greek bread-making methods, Brillat-Savarin's *Physiologie du goût* and the limitations of Oxford linguistic philosophers ('except that Ayer is quite brisk, isn't he? with the ginny quality of Scottish water.') The Jesuits, however, seemed intent on banishing him until the other final-year theologians had been ordained.

That Easter he had persuaded Mollie to buy him a copy of Brillat-Savarin so that he could share a foodie craze with John Fuller, who was back from the United States and teaching at Manchester. His friendship with John had always bubbled along in a froth of poetical riddles and mutual reassurance, with no need for self-justification on his part. With David Pryce-Jones, on the other hand, he probed his own intentions more deeply. Early that summer he felt it necessary to explain what moved him:

> something which seems to me religious for which the appropriate words are the consecrated ones, to do with darkness, hermits, rocks, springs of water, God, the just man. Well, this isn't the only thing I want or the place I inhabit but it is in a sense what I live by in the way that the submerged words & feelings of an underground religion ran so strongly in Wyatt and flowered so fantastically in Shakespeare (the knot in whom all ropes end).

Perhaps the priesthood would help him write better poetry than he had managed during those years of treading water at Stonyhurst and Heythrop, and if he failed he could at least die in the attempt.

☙

Atheists and agnostics, as well as Anglicans and Catholics, flocked to the Catholic church in Eastbourne on the evening of Monday, August 10. A few arrived by train, having travelled with opera-goers who were heading for Glyndebourne in evening dress. The Connollys, Nancy and Tony Mitchell came, as did Julian, Willie, Robin Milner-Gulland and other Oxford friends.

Once the bishop had asked the ritual questions and the ordinands had replied, Julian was appalled to see Peter lying spread-eagled on the chancel floor in a white robe that resembled a shroud. After long Latin prayers had been recited, he and the other ordinands received the silent laying-on of hands, were dressed in chasuble and stole, had their hands anointed with holy oil and were given a chalice and paten to hold, while being formally declared priests for ever according to the order of Melchisedech.

The rites were as baroque as magenta-coloured sugar sticks, Peter told John Fuller, who was away. To Bertie, who had sent a telegram from Scotland, he wrote that the ceremony had been a riot, that Cyril (who gave him a present of Yeats's letters) had flattered his mother at the hotel dinner afterwards, and that he had had to bless eight hundred people the next morning. To Willie, months later, he sent special thanks for having stayed overnight in Eastbourne to attend his first Mass. His being there (he wrote) was 'one of those uncovenanted things one realises one couldn't have done without'.[12]

There would be no chance now of his paying parochial visits to the Charltons at North Aston. Willie had achieved his B.Phil. and accepted a philosophy lectureship at Trinity College, Dublin. And Peter, unlike Anthony, had already spent too long at Heythrop to be invited back for his tertian year. For the rest of August he relaxed at the seaside, helping out at the Jesuits' Corpus Christi church at Boscombe, Bournemouth. (Confessions got odder and odder, he wrote to Mollie.) Then, like Hopkins ninety years earlier, he was packed off to St. Beuno's College in Flintshire, a Victorian Gothic institution perched high up in a precipitous garden on the east side of the Vale of Clwyd, Hopkins's 'pastoral forehead of Wales'.[13]

St. Beuno's had been one of three seminaries for nineteenth-century Jesuit ordinands. After the novitiate at Manresa, they had done their three years of philosophy at St. Mary's Hall, Stonyhurst (which later became the College's prep school), then taught in schools for a year or two before studying theology at St. Beuno's. Hopkins had been enchanted by the valley of the Elwy with its woods and limestone crags. He had loved the gentle sweep of the Vale, with the Clwydian Hills to the east and the Conwy Mountains reaching, fold upon fold, towards Snowdonia in the distant west. He had taken Welsh lessons, hoping to infuse his poems with the spirit of the place, until the Jesuits told him he should use the language only for preaching.

Now St. Beuno's was a Jesuit retreat house, where newly ordained priests were expected to pray and contemplate between pastoral spells elsewhere. To Peter the most amazing thing about it was the food. The tall, draughty seminary building, as grimly Gothic as the plainest 1850s vicarage, had an unspoilt Victorian kitchen garden which produced perfect vegetables and fruit. After being barred from writing letters during the month-long October retreat, he burst out into descriptions of the wonderfulness of it all. The mutton tasted deliciously of a local mountain herb, the carrots (he told Willie) were like the torch that lighted Orpheus, the parsley (he told Nancy) was so green as to be pubic. There were also hothouse grapes. The cook, reputedly the only Catholic convert in the village, had been trained by Jesuit lay-brothers before the war, and Peter fantasized that his bacon and cabbage and his finely sliced raw onion salad were 'degenerate versions of things described by Brillat-Savarin as the poor but honest delicacies of Liège', where the English Jesuits had taken refuge from the French Revolution.[14]

179

He loved the scenery, too: the naked, snow-daubed distant mountains in October; the glimpses of sea on clear days, beyond Rhyl. The Vale of Clwyd, he told Nancy, was 'a place of fantasy like a nursery wallpaper', and Denbigh on its hill 'exactly like a children's story town, everything... of exactly human proportions (Corbusier would shoot himself).' In the valley of the Elwy, under 'hills in full sail of leaf', he saw hedges of ancient woodland oaks. 'When a squirrel could go from Snowdon to Chester without touching the ground, this was its route.'

The retreat left him, like others, feeling drained. Future autumn and Lenten retreats, adapted to a working Jesuit's life, would at least be shorter. He moaned to Willie that the boot-camp regime, based on the *Spiritual Exercises* of St. Ignatius, had been like 'a long grotto overhung with ivy and sprouting improbable fossils', and to Bertie that it had simply been exhausting. He would have been happier with *The Garden of the Soul*, an anodyne, old-fashioned Catholic prayer-book in a soft leather binding. 'Ours used to smell of gloves. It was kept in the glove drawer in the hall.'[15]

In September 1874, Hopkins and his fellow-theologians at St. Beuno's had debated the motion that diary-keeping was a good idea.[16] Perhaps because he had no other outlet, Peter kept a diary during the retreat, but he told David Pryce-Jones he dared not read it and would probably destroy it within a year. Introspection had led him only to think about literary failure and acknowledge the state of 'dreamlike schizophrenia' in which he had existed so far.[17]

Praising Nancy for her letters, which were full of intellectual speculation and radiantly precise descriptions, he told her that they were better than any poetry he was likely to produce at St. Beuno's. While Hopkins had soared into exultant productivity there with 'The Wreck of the Deutschland', 'The Windhover' and 'Hurrahing in Harvest', his own trajectory seemed to be plunging downwards. André Deutsch had rejected his third collection, and his agent, John Johnson, got gloomy verdicts from both Cape and Eyre & Spottiswoode that his early promise had not been fulfilled.

Early in October he had succumbed to the usual coughs and catarrh, and there was talk of sending him abroad to recover. X-rays at the hospital at St. Asaph failed to detect anything wrong with his lungs, but showed a possible sinus infection under one eye. Later tests found an allergy to dry rot, which may have flourished in the Flintshire damp. He decided to sit out the winter there, however, since it would be no colder than the 'terrible ecclesiastical icehouse' at Settignano. At least his Oxford future seemed full of promise, while a kindly new Provincial was encouraging him to write whatever he liked.

By November 5 he was considered well enough to lecture to some nuns at Rhyl, and marvelled on the journey back, in a bus full of excited children, at the bonfires in every farmyard, the fizzing of rockets going off and the 'soft red flowers of flame in the mist across the valley'.[18] Then he moved to another Jesuit retreat house at Harborne, Birmingham, to see if his health would improve. His defiantly secular reading matter included *War and Peace*, all of Shakespeare's comedies and David Caute's 'wonderful' *Communism and the French Intellectuals, 1914-1958*, which he thought he 'needed to read even more than he needed to write'.[19] He pored over the classical antiquities in the city museum and prepared to start translating Pausanias, since his contract had reached him after being forwarded several times.

At a poetry reading at the Guildhall School of Music and Drama he introduced himself to the Connollys' close friend Sonia Orwell. A long-lapsed cradle Catholic, wounded by the failure of her second marriage, she recoiled and spat drunkenly at him that she loathed priests and above all Jesuits. But after he wrote her a sweetly placating letter she apologized, promising to be sober next time.[20]

He had been visiting the Cautes in Oxford in early January and was about to catch a train back to North Wales, not yet having seen a newspaper, when a message came through to him at Campion Hall to ring the office of *The Month* at Mount Street. T.S. Eliot had died the day before, and the editor wanted an appreciation from him for the February issue.

Eliot's death threw him into full elegiac mode. He felt '*absolutely black*' about it, he told Cyril. 'It was like a Greek shepherd boy losing his grandfather,' he lamented to David Pryce-Jones. His article 'The Death of Poets' mourned not only Eliot but Edith Sitwell, who had died on December 9, and a selection of other dead poets from Yeats to Richard Selig and Sylvia Plath. He recalled hearing a record of Edith Sitwell reading her poems in the dusky parlour of a house in a remote village where the garden seemed to drift in at the windows. ('Little Tew comes into it,' he told Nancy.)[21] Praising Eliot's innovative force, he explained the layers of literary allusion in his poems as evidence of his continuous meditation on poetry and the possibilities of language: a point he would later make about both David Jones and Robert Lowell.[22]

When Eliot died it made him seem human,

begins the dark 'New Year's Eve Poem 1965' he wrote for radio.

> *When he died I went into real mourning,*
> *poems are wrecked, this one is the sea-bottom:*
> *the anchor-chains of reason drag and swing*
> *backwards and forwards with a squeak like doom.*

In that elegy he made Eliot and Dante represent the austere 'angel of language': *No one has spoken as clearly as they did.* Yet, while imagining them enjoying a shared afterlife, he could see no place for himself there, wondering gloomily

> *...when the inferno like a complete dream*
> *will eat my poems and swallow my ghost.*[23]

Surviving heroes provided some comfort. Cyril was still in good shape and would live for another decade, while Fraenkel, despite his brush-off, still represented pure scholarly gold. A two-volume collection of his articles, *Kleine Beiträge zur klassischen Philologie*, had recently been published in Rome. Peter arranged to write a centre-page appreciation of him for the *TLS*, and was happy again with his classical hat on, 'wanting just to write a long gasp at his overwhelming victory,' he told Nancy. He especially praised an early article of Fraenkel's of 'about 65 pages on the gender of the Latin word *dies*... fascinating'.[24]

Real life caught up with him in late January. For practical experience he was sent off for three weeks to the Morning Star Hostel in Manchester, a homeless men's refuge in the area known as Little Ireland, attached to the big Jesuit-run church in Oxford Road. 'I'm the cook & the chaplain & the crew of the bosun's gig,' he wrote to Nancy, cramming a volume of French poetry John Berger had given him into his 'tiny tramp-suitcase'. He was a working priest at last, making grimy train journeys into grim cities like other grown-up Jesuits, with their anonymous black suits, neat luggage and deep knowledge of human fallibility and sin.

> We yearned for cities and big towns, we ate sausages that tasted of railway soot, we were at home on the train. By our mid-thirties we knew more different areas of the British class-system...than other citizens, and once we were ordained we began to accumulate a confidential insight into other people's lives that few people are permitted. We knew where in England to expect incest, and where to be unsurprised by murder.[25]

Confronted with the Manchester homeless, he responded impulsively. He had never seen such wretchedness, nor met so many meths drinkers, illiterate travellers, men destroyed by industrial accidents or psychotic misfits, 'a world like the seeds of our own world come true, nearly everyone alcoholic, destitute, ragged, all marriages broken, all jobs lost'.[26] One night he was taken north of the city centre, to Nightingale Street, off Queen's Road in Cheetham Hill, near Strangeways Prison. Here the meths addicts who preferred to live rough occupied an area of derelict waste land called Barney's Brick Croft, a former brickworks containing a rubbish tip on to which sludge from the street drains was dumped. That night, in thickening snow, a few drunks huddled round the remains of a burnt-out grand piano. Peter felt an awed sense of mission at the scene, and even thought for an hour or so that ministering to the destitute might be his vocation.[27] He burned to tell people about them, and promised to revisit the hostel and take an Advent retreat in December. Two years later he took a young BBC television producer, Mischa Scorer, to see the Croft, and wrote the script for his documentary about the lives of the meths-drinkers there.

During the next few years, news trickled through to him of dying inmates in the hostel and deaths on the Croft. Much of it came from a young man from Salford who had decided to dedicate his life to helping the homeless, first in Manchester, then in a grimmer hostel in Dublin. The young man's mother wrote several desperate letters to Peter, begging him to use his influence on her over-idealistic, drop-out son. It was not the last time he received this kind of appeal from a Catholic mother who saw him as a reliable authority-figure, not a rebel in priestly disguise.

His next mission, at the church of Our Most Holy Redeemer and St. Thomas More in Cheyne Row, Chelsea, could not have been more different. The priest, Father Alfonso de Zulueta, an upper-class Jesuit known familiarly as Father Zulu, welcomed him for a stint of parish visiting during the first ten days in Lent, suggesting he should round up some of the many lapsed Catholics in the area. Peter got on well with Father Zulu, an old Beaumont boy and former Catholic chaplain at Oxford. Then he moved on to Mount Street, helping out with hearing

Lenten confessions at Westminster Cathedral. Cyril gave him lunch, probably at the Beefsteak Club, and he took notes at a lecture at the Society of Antiquaries for Nancy, who was abroad.

Back at St. Beuno's from mid-April, he shut himself away with Pausanias, writing his translation on sheets of elephant folio like the ones David Jones used for his letters, and telling Nancy he was rolling in the work like a horse in hay. He had discovered the pleasure of writing explanatory footnotes, and a feast of them lay ahead. For ten days in May he acted as supply priest at the little half-timbered church of the Sacred Heart at Chirk, between Oswestry and Wrexham, living in a convent bungalow where he quietly got on with the work.

Mollie was in hospital that spring. Realizing she was afraid of dying, he comforted her in the simple language of faith he had used to his parents when Gillian became a nun, promising them rewards in heaven for their unselfishness in letting all three of their children go. 'There's only one heaven, & only one earth, & we're all on the one & going to the other, & there's *really* no need to be frightened.' God loved her (he said) not only for what she had achieved but simply because he loved her, as he had shown in his own life, in hers and in the reflections of one in the other.

The final summer retreat at St. Beuno's was more bearable than the October one. He enjoyed the unusual silence at meals and the garden roses, ridges of flowering potatoes and richly coloured hills. After a brief trip to Oxford in late June, he finished drafting the first part of his translation before going abroad in July.

For the Jesuits had given him permission to join an archaeological dig at Tocra in Libya, in the ancient Greek and Roman province of Cyrenaica, that September. Correspondence in English and Latin had flown back and forth between St. Beuno's, Jesuit officials in London and the Italian Vicar Apostolic at Benghazi about the whereabouts of the nearest Catholic church to the dig (seventy kilometres away in

Benghazi), and whether he might say his own Masses with a portable altar and kit. Cautiously assenting to this, the Vicar warned him that he must do so very discreetly and privately, *quia sumus in mahometana terra.*[28]

With the Libyan trip as the thin end of the wedge, he also managed to secure six weeks in Greece from mid-July until the end of August. No grant was forthcoming for this, but Canon Francis Bartlett, the kindly priest he had met at the British School in Athens, offered to pay his air-fare out there to save time. A Jesuit friend at Heythrop advised him not to say private Masses in Greece; in view of the Catholic Church's relaxation of its formerly stringent rules, he would be able to attend the Orthodox liturgy provided he was not known to be a priest and did not take communion.[29] He planned to look at ruins for a week or two, visit George Pavlopoulos in Pyrgos and Philip Sherrard on Euboea, and sort out his visa and immunizations with the Libyan embassy and a doctor in Athens. Then all would be clear for a trouble-free month in North Africa, or so he thought.

13
FRINGE

The fringe of Oxford in which I hop about.

To Willie Charlton [early autumn 1965]

In Greece once more, he felt at home. Although taller than most Greeks he blended in with his straight, dark hair, Byzantine nose, olive skin, and gesticulating responsiveness and fluency in conversation. 'He was much more oriental, more Byzantine, in Greece,' said the philosopher Anthony O'Hear. 'He looked Jewish and Greek,' said John Berger. 'He was an oriental gentleman scholar,' said his former Stonyhurst pupil Iain Watson.

Greek poets and intellectuals saw nothing odd about a man having several different occupations at once. The stuffier members of the British School at Athens may have questioned the soundness of his scholarship and the consistency of his aims, but free-spirited expatriates like Philip Sherrard and Paddy Leigh Fermor welcomed him as a knowledgeable, interested and amusing companion. Greece lit him up with eagerness, and friends gathered round him on every visit.

One of these networks of friendships began in Pyrgos, which Peter told Willie was like pre-war Banbury, with a 'funny band playing on Sundays in blue & white uniforms'. When there, he shared George Pavlopoulos's evenings and his simple, serious domestic life. During the daytime, when George was at the KTEL office, he was free to amuse himself, but in the evenings, while George's wife Mitsa put their small son Charis to bed, George would drive him out to Agios Andreas. Facing the sunset across the near islands and the distant outline of Zakynthos, which they planned to explore together one day, they talked far into the night.

George's whole youth had coincided with the Second World War and the Greek civil war. He told Peter how, as a schoolboy during the occupation, he and his friends in Pyrgos had kept up their morale by producing a literary magazine which the bishop had let them print on the diocesan press, and by putting on cunningly subversive plays. Peter thought they had all been translations of European classics, but at least one, *Freedom or Death*, although passed off as a translation from Victor Hugo, was George's own.[1] The tease had annoyed the Germans, but not enough for them to take revenge on the young men.

Stuck in a humble book-keeping job after failing to finish a law degree in Athens, George was still an unknown poet. Although he had impressed Seferis, he did not push himself into literary life. Dignified and a little lonely, he responded warmly to Peter's visits and keenness to translate his poems. Years later he wrote that Peter had been his 'only true friend until the end, the only person in the world that [he] felt nearest to', in spite of the distance that had separated them for so long.[2]

Through George, Peter met two of his oldest friends. They were the poet Takis Sinopoulos, a doctor in his late forties who practised in a slummy area of Athens, and Takis Loumiotis, 'a lawyer with a Dionysiac laugh', who worked from Pyrgos. Peter spent days being driven around the western Peloponnese by Loumiotis, slipping away to see ancient sites while he dealt with clients, then meeting him to drink rare local wines over lunch. Once or twice they had mad adventures, like an evening of wild dancing in a mountain taverna near the ruins of Sicyon, followed by a perilous descent to a coastal night-club with nine people, including a local policeman, piled into one small car.[3]

In Athens Peter looked up Sinopoulos, but struggled to keep up with the conversation at his literary evenings and was embarrassed when Takis, as one poet to another, offered to find him a woman for the night. Then he moved on to the Sherrards', where, despite a heavy English cold, he worked away at Pausanias and an article about Ezra Pound. On Sunday they stood for two and three-quarter hours during the Orthodox liturgy in church. Afterwards, Peter wondered at Philip's stamina as the harsh cantors' voices and dustbin-like church bell continued to ring in his head. He told Willie that his cottage at Katounia was

almost too beautiful to work in: a small house with a big balcony & a black & white stone floor, looking down over olives, cypresses & vines at that long broad arm of sea, with the opposite coast always rebuilding itself in different combinations of mountains & of blue light.[4]

In early September it was time for him to join the dig at Tocra. With an arm aching from his inoculation in Athens he landed at Benghazi, staying for long enough to explore the gleaming, Fascist-period buildings in the former Italian colonial city centre. As he wandered confusedly out of the Catholic cathedral after meeting, or searching for, the Vicar Apostolic, he found himself half-blinded by the building's whiteness and the sun. Perhaps, in that alcohol-free city, a policeman hoped to gain credit by running in a drunk, and arrested him on the spot. He eventually talked himself free, although some friends later gained the impression that he had been thrown into a Libyan jail.

Travelling east along the coast towards Tocra, he noticed through the headache-inducing dazzle of light the 'sympathetic ugliness' of the villages on the desert plain. At the dig he discovered several familiar, or soon to be familiar, scholarly faces, since John Boardman, Reader in Classical Archaeology at Oxford, was in charge. At night the archaeologists huddled together in one room in the Italian-built fort, reading or writing in the circle of light from the single lamp. By that third and final season of the dig huge quantities of archaic Greek pottery had turned up at the lowest levels, and Boardman and a colleague were already writing them up for publication, with unusual promptness for an excavation report.

Through a blur of queasiness and unease Peter took in the daunting size of the ruins, which he thought much bleaker than any site in Greece. In a vast, flattish setting he saw 'a few handfuls of pillars like blasted groves, mounds, dips, quarries, masonry, Justinian's great wall still half standing, & vast crumbled empty gateways'.[5] The days were blindingly hot and the nights dew-drenched and cold. One night when the moon was full, the whole party went swimming in the flashing surf. But before long Peter discovered that he had a swollen arm from the botched injections and began to feel seriously feverish and ill. Somehow he made his way back to Athens and the train home, writing that he 'nearly died on the railway near Tito Veles'.[6] Back in England, he had several weeks to get through before the beginning of term.

೮๑

Oxford in the mid-1960s was busier than it had been within most people's memories. Scaffolding, duckboards, hammering and drilling were everywhere as the soot-blackened, peeling Headington stone of the older buildings was power-washed, scraped or replaced. Colleges, newly awash with money, sprouted glass, stone and concrete-faced additions. The atmosphere of the expanding university was becoming swaggeringly egalitarian. Young men's voices rarely rang out in the streets in the fruity public-school tones of the 1950s. Subdued, middle-class uniforms of twin-sets, tweeds and grey flannels had been ousted by jeans, plastic raincoats, donkey jackets, mini-dresses and Carnaby Street ties. Heavy rock music and drugs were edging their way into student life, while anti-Vietnam War graffiti appeared overnight on new concrete walls. It was the Oxford of the contraceptive pill, theatrical success and radical chic. Colleges were still single-sex, and a few still made room for the kind of ex-public schoolboys who took fourths, but more drastic changes were being discussed. The contrasts between the generations were very sharp, Peter told Willie. Everyone had changed more than he expected, although 'our time remains unique, once & for all'.[7]

Still depressed by his recent illness, he brooded on his strange position as an academic who was not a real don. He told Willie that he felt closer to him in Dublin than to their former Opimian Club colleague Maurice Keen, who was now medieval history fellow at Balliol. ('I was always close to Denis and Willie, but never to Peter,' Maurice confirmed.) Some young dons of Peter's generation felt humiliated at being talked down to by their seniors, wondering when they would be allowed the full dignity and responsibility that was supposed to come with the job. One or two carried chips on their shoulders for years. But Peter's problem was that, much though he loved Oxford, he would never feel as secure as an established college fellow. 'I wish you would see I'm an imaginary don not a real one,' he snapped, seven years into the job, when Julian accused him of pedantry in *The Light Garden of the Angel King*.[8]

Officially he was a member of the faculty of Literae Humaniores, politely welcomed by fellow-classicists with their double firsts and research degrees. A sense that he had ducked under the rope into the academic enclosure may have been one reason why, in *The Flutes of Autumn*, he did his best to disguise his eleven and a half years as a tutor at Campion Hall. Salaried fellows of Oxford colleges could teach and lecture until they were sixty-seven. They had housing allowances, free meals, generous pension provisions and regular sabbatical leaves. Some married couples were lucky enough to land a fellowship each, with a large North Oxford house and garden and children at the best academic schools. If death, divorce or a career move caused one such family to disappear, another would replace it. Confirmed bachelor dons could shelter inside their college walls until retirement and take advantage of lunching, dining and common-room rights for as long as they continued to turn up.

Few such privileges came with Peter's tutorship at Campion Hall. Fellows of colleges were mutually self-governing and, in most cases, protected by statutes, whereas Jesuits relied on luck, charm and reasonableness to keep occupations they enjoyed. One slip and their superiors could demote them or even send them overseas. Peter's former teacher Christopher Devlin had been happily in charge of pedagogy at Manresa until he made a rash, unmeant offer to the Provincial and was dispatched to a Rhodesian mission school for the last three years of his life. And Philip Caraman, the former editor of *The Month* and chief advocate for the canonization of the Elizabethan Catholic martyrs, had been banished from the Mount Street clergy house for being too obviously fond of his assistant, Evelyn Waugh's favourite, recently married daughter Margaret Fitzherbert. Rather than face a clerical outcast's life in a London bedsitter, he had opted for a remote Catholic ministry in Norway.[9]

Finding himself part of the Jesuit establishment did not cure Peter's feelings of strangeness. Upbeat as always when writing to Mollie, he told her that he was taking a class on St. Paul's Epistle to the Romans, that Denis served his daily Masses, and that he particularly liked Ted Yarnold, the new Master of Campion Hall. But he complained to Willic about the endless 'parabusiness and pseudopleasure (& worse, pseudoduty)' that absorbed his energies. He had only two pupils to begin with, and would give his first lectures, on the development of Greek prose style, to a tiny group in Campion Hall the following summer. Philip Sherrard wondered if his illness could be psychosomatic, thinking it might be defining or pointing him in some particular direction. He urged Peter to get in touch with God's will for him and not 'be in service to nobodaddy'.[10] In the light of his own experience at the British School at Athens, he must have felt that Peter's hopes of achieving a scholarly career were doing violence to his true nature as a lyric poet.

At least he was a welcome arrival on the Oxford poetry scene. With his romantic, un-priestly looks and mysterious, monkish existence, he was everything undergraduates could have hoped for in the translator of Yevtushenko's poems. Some members of the Poetry Society believed that he had special Jesuit privileges which allowed him to shut himself away for weeks on end to write. Craig Raine, in his third year at Exeter College, accosted him chummily in Cornmarket Street to tell him he looked like Degas, with his large dark eyes, dark hair, long nose, full lips and mildly melancholy air. It was an Oxford game to see resemblances between living people and famous dead ones, and Raine, a seasoned Poetry Society member on easy terms with older poets, found Peter a 'wonderful unguarded figure, full of zest'.[11]

Even non-poetical undergraduates were keen to cultivate him. Marina Warner, a sophisticated second-year student at Lady Margaret Hall, wrote that she had just missed him in Athens that summer, and invited him to succeed J.I.M. Stewart of Christ

Church as senior member of the Anonymous Society of Writers.[12] And Martin Haddon, a former Beaumont pupil reading Greats, whose Jesuit elder brother Paul was a student of Anthony's at Campion Hall, invited him out to lunch one day to impress a girlfriend. In the restaurant, Peter made a self-conscious Catholic joke that the waitress's style of taking orders reminded him of hearing confessions. He livened up after lunch while the three of them toured the Ashmolean Museum, exclaiming with un-donnish fervour 'I hate Croton!' when they reached a display of coins from the city-state in Magna Graecia whose bullying military leader Milo had smashed the Sybarites in the early sixth century BC.[13]

He had already given readings to the Poetry Society during his last couple of years at Heythrop, and through it had found a new outlet for his work. Early in 1965 the undergraduate Clive Allison, soon to emerge as co-founder of the publishing house Allison & Busby, had brought out *The Shearwaters* as one of a series of poetry pamphlets he called the Harlequin Poets. Subscriptions had come from Diana Athill at André Deutsch and from members of the University Poetry Society and other well-wishers. Peter sent a copy to John Berger, hoping for praise from him, and was disappointed when Berger replied that, while he liked some individual lines, he could not see the point of the poem and thought it a work of transition.[14]

Now Peter Jay, in his third year at Lincoln College, was beginning his half-century or more as a poetry editor with an ambitious little magazine, *New Measure*. Its opening number had a guest poem by Auden and a mission statement about encouraging poetry 'which enables us to see objects, ideas and actions more clearly'. The second number, on poetry in translation, included Peter's versions of poems by George Seferis, Takis Sinopoulos, Odysseus Elytis and the eminent nineteenth-century poet Kostas Palamas. The magazine ran to ten numbers in three years, publishing emergent international figures such as Gary Snyder and Anselm Hollo as well as Oxford graduates like Gavin Bantock, the medievalist Nicolas Jacobs and the eccentric modern linguist Sally Purcell, who stayed on in the city as a translator and poet for the rest of her life.

Freed from the drab influence of the Movement, Oxford poetry had become more eclectic and experimental. Romanticism was back in fashion, encouraged by freer travel, freer sex and the first stirrings of the cultural upheaval that came to be labelled 'the Sixties'. The Professor of Poetry was the seventy-year-old Robert Graves, a living legend with his craggy satyr's profile and broad-brimmed hat, who commuted from Majorca to deliver rambling lectures about White and Black Goddesses and his personal search for a romantically and sexually satisfying muse.

Oxford Poetry, the organ of the Poetry Society, was in abeyance, but there were literary magazines like *Carcanet*, a successor to *Gemini*, which Michael Schmidt took over as editor before developing it into the Carcanet Press. On the edge of university life and the city, the forty-year-old novelist, former academic and poet John Wain had settled with his wife and family in a grey stone farmhouse on Wolvercote Green. He, Trypanis and sometimes Peter held end-of-term Poetry Society workshops to criticize members' work. Outgoing and compulsively hospitable, Wain held a literary salon to which he repeatedly invited Peter. Sally Purcell was one of his protégées, along with the intensely religious Elizabeth Jennings, who turned against Peter, after years as his admiring friend, when Wain clumsily persuaded him to do his priestly duty and try to talk her out of one of her depressions.

Wain and Trypanis, as the Poetry Society's most dependable local guest readers, took the platform at the first and second meetings that autumn term. Then Peter, as the guest at the third meeting, offered something entirely new. This was the ten-part, surrealistic poem he later published as *Pancakes for the Queen of Babylon.** He had gone to Greece (he said) feeling disillusioned with the state of poetry in England, and Gatsos's *Amorgos* had encouraged him to try a different approach. The poem he read contained a dazzling pattern of visual and mythic images: a white boat rocking on black water, a black wind on white water, a white stone in a black river, desert flowers, birdsong, thunder, mountains cracking open into caverns and the ocean flying apart.

Amorgos was a poem of passionate protest against the German occupation, affirming a timeless, secular, earthily sensual Greek spirit. Peter's poem, on the other hand, has a clear religious theme, which moves through descriptions of a blossoming desert and references to the soul and the law into images that suggest the Resurrection.

> *In the early morning*
> *you see women walking to the sanctuaries:*
> *a light touch of sun on the whitewash:*
> *a light touch of fire burning the oil.*

The earliest part of the poem is almost random, containing (as he later explained) some serendipitous images which had emerged from his word-games with Charles Haldeman and Gatsos. Part of it sprang from a conversation with John Holloway about whether variations on the image of a white boat on black water, which worked so easily in foreign languages, were also possible in English. And much of it owed a debt to Eliot, with phrases and measured cadences reminiscent of *The Waste Land and East Coker*. Later, he acknowledged the obvious 'submerged influence' on the poem's structure of St. John

---

* He explained this as a quotation from the Rev. Ian Paisley, who had allegedly told the Oxford Union Society that the Catholic Church was 'still the scarlet woman offering up pancakes to the Queen of Babylon'. The reference was to the Whore of Babylon in Revelation 17.5, used as an aggressive Protestant metaphor for the Catholic Church. Peter later said he chose the title because he 'wanted to have some secret tinge of the sacred about this poem, which is a religious poem.' (*Paris Review*, Fall 1979, 19.)

Perse's *Anabase*, a long poem about exile, deserts, the building of a city, sensual pleasure and the law, which Eliot had translated into rhythms reminiscent of the King James Bible. In retrospect he thought *Pancakes* was 'really about how to have a new civilization', a theme later expanded in the visionary 'Canticum', which he dedicated to John and Anya Berger.[15]

For Poetry Society members, the fresh, anarchic images of Greece were exciting enough. Roger Garfitt, the secretary of the Society, had spent his gap-year summer of 1963, like Peter, in Greece. A classicist turned English student, on the edge of freaking out on drugs, he was entranced by Peter's freedom with language, and especially by an image of the Greek night sky:

> *And one hoof of a star printing the dark*
> *is ringing like a nail of a new metal.*

After that evening he wrote home to a friend and mentor, whose daughter had travelled with him in Greece, bursting with excitement about this wonderful poet he had discovered.[16] His Cambridge contemporary Richard Holmes was equally enthusiastic about the published *Pancakes*, calling it 'a pamphlet of vivid, meditative poetry, where horse, bird and tree are fixed in jewelled images of mystical radiance'.[17] And twelve years later Sally Purcell's translation of *Amorgos* came out in a style close to that of *Pancakes*, dedicated to Peter.

New Measure ceased publication soon after Peter Jay launched his dedicated poetry imprint, Anvil Press Poetry, in 1968. *Pancakes* was among his first six titles, with a print-run of a thousand in paperback and several dozen presentation copies in hardback. *Ruined Abbeys*, Peter's television script in verse, followed almost at once as an Anvil pamphlet.[18] The penultimate number of *New Measure* had showcased work by several Anvil Press poets, including Peter's biting 'Letter on the Art of Satire' in Pope-like rhyming couplets. Ignoring the Provincial's warning to avoid publicity, he had already read it in an unscheduled appearance on *That Was The Week That Was*, the satirical television show for which Caryl Brahms and Ned Sherrin wrote sketches and topical songs.

He was lucky to have been taken up by Anvil Press, since his prospects in mainstream poetry publishing were dwindling. André Deutsch had agreed to market his third collection *Fresh Water, Sea Water*, but declined to publish it. This was done by a friend of Alasdair's, the thirty-year-old Lord Dynevor, who had set himself up as an entrepreneur after losing most of the family estate to death duties. When he published the book in 1966 he did so in association with André Deutsch, as the first (and for many years only) imprint of his Black Raven Press. Although happy with the Heythrop poems, he refused to include 'Pancakes' or 'Thirty Ways of Drowning in the Sea', since they might have given too much of a jolt to the otherwise sombre mood of the collection.[19]

In Athens Peter had become a friend of Gustavo Durán, who had earned his living as a composer in Spain before the Civil War, become a comrade and friend of Hemingway while fighting in the Republican army, then taken refuge and citizenship in the United States after its final defeat. Sent, eventually, to administer United Nations aid to rural Greece, he had fallen in love with Crete, adopted a remote mountain village, Alones, given it a supply of fresh water and asked to be buried there when his heart gave out. Peter went with him on some of his outings from Athens, and stood in for his American wife Bontë, who was on crutches, to keep him company on noisy evenings of folk-music and dancing in Plaka bars.[20]

When Peter sent him a copy of his collection *Water, Rock and Sand*, Durán was disappointed. The soft, drizzly landscape poems of the Stonyhurst period, their emotional reticence and sad resentment of school life, seemed out of character with his lively, intense companion.

He searched hard for lines with some political resonance, picking out the last verse of 'Humanism' as those he responded to best:

> *But I pray most to those*
> *whose act of suffering*
> *claims no tears or praise*
> *but is voluntary and strong*
> *in a long triumph of peace.*[21]

Then Cyril Connolly, who Peter had hoped would go at least half-way towards reciprocating his admiration, gave *Fresh Water, Sea Water* a damping review in his *Sunday Times* poetry round-up a week before Christmas 1966. While acknowledging Father Levi's 'distinguished mind...warm heart [and] sensuous enjoyment of nature', he criticised the poems in terms similar to Ian Hamilton's dismissal of *Water, Rock and Sand*, calling them 'elusive', 'disembodied' and 'faintly traced'. They made him think of himself as an old roué watching a crocodile of virginal finishing-school girls passing his window and feeling they were not quite ready for him yet. The message was clear: what Peter needed, as a writer, was a sex-life.

'Goodness knows what I can do next,' he wrote to Cyril in a confusion of thanks and reproach, heading his letter with a Lear-like doodle of the Athenian owl next to the address in Greek of the British School at Athens. With an evident effort he conceded that Cyril's criticisms were 'kind as well as strange', concluding whimsically that 'so much of life is an endless tangle of buildings and traffic and telephones...that perhaps one is what one is by reaction.'[22] He did not bother to point out that the poems in *Fresh Water, Sea Water* belonged to a period in his life that was over, and that Dynevor had rejected the ones inspired by Greece. Nor did he tell Cyril that for the past year he been heterosexually, if chastely, in love.

14
A Ballet of Love

At one moment, I even thought or pretended to myself that I had fallen in love, but it was only a ballet of love.

The Hill of Kronos (1980), 11

While waiting for his ordination date, early in 1963, Peter told Julian that he wished he knew more about people's marriages. He was in the celibate cleric's usual predicament of having a purely theoretical view of sex and marriage.

'It's in a way too private isn't it? and this is what is wrong?... I sometimes imagine marrying & I think if I did now (or you did) it would go much better than it might have ten years ago. One would see exactly what one was having to pay & why one was prepared to pay it. But I think what one actually means by marriage has to be more formal & explicit than most people's private relationships apparently admit.'[1]

None of the pastoral teaching at Heythrop had helped him to understand the sexual and emotional dynamics of close friends like the Charltons, Pryce-Joneses and Fullers, who had married in their early twenties, had children and seemed blissfully content. As he became more curious about how other people lived, he could not help wondering what kind of wife would have suited him if he had not chosen to be a priest.

On three Sundays in November 1965 he kept his promise to Father de Zulueta and preached at the church of Our Most Holy Redeemer and St. Thomas More, Cheyne Row, Chelsea. The Catholic convert and mystical poet Kathleen Raine, who had taken a fancy to him, introduced him after Mass one morning to her friend David Gascoyne, who seemed polite and charming, although pale and trembling from the nervous breakdown that had brought him back to England after ten years in France. During the next few months Peter was pursued by frantic letters from Raine, begging him to help her cope with Gascoyne, for whom she felt a panicked sense of responsibility, thinking he had gone mad.

On one of those Sundays he also met Henrietta Moraes. Having ditched her for Dorothy Tutin while he was still at Oxford, Dom had found that Dorothy had dropped him while he was in India gathering material for his travelogue *Gone Away*, and had married Henrietta on the rebound at the Chelsea Registry Office late in 1960. For several years they had cohabited in drunken, smoke-ridden, fractious squalor in her slip of a house in Apollo Place. Then he had walked out one day to buy cigarettes and moved in with a new girlfriend, Judith St. John, whom he had met in a King's Road pub. Henrietta's noisy neighbourhood harassment drove the couple to Islington, where Judith gave birth to a son and Dom wrote feature articles for the new, progressive, glossy women's magazine, *Nova*. (One was a snidely mock-compassionate interview with his former publisher David Archer, who had been reduced to selling wallpaper at Selfridges after bankrupting himself supporting poets.)[2] Henrietta became hooked on amphetamines and began to steal, claiming that she did so for the thrill it gave her, but also evidently needing the money it brought in.

None of this bothered Peter, innocent and fresh from Mass, when she greeted him with her familiar sexy warmth. Older, sadder and more eccentrically dressed than the King's Road girls with their straightened hair, raccoon eye-makeup, white lipstick and miniskirts, she seemed vulnerable, friendly, and the more desirable for having been Dom's. Peter had often visited the couple while Dom was living at Apollo Place, although his dutiful prothalamium,

> *Rain-threaded, gull-wheeling, bell-clamorous air,*
> *by wind shifted, by smoke lightly weighted...,*

perhaps spoke more of his excitement at heading west along a blustery, rain-flung Chelsea Embankment, past the site of the lost Adam and Eve pub, than of a sense of the archetypal moment when Adam *woke…, and bent suddenly over Eve, and spoke*.[3]

In her state of abandoned misery, unwilling even to look after her own children, Henrietta had become convinced that her house was haunted, perhaps by John Minton's suicidal ghost. She begged Peter to come and exorcise it and was chagrined when he refused. After leaving her, however, he felt elated. That breath of loneliness, frustration, thwarted motherliness and sex made him long to step into Dom's vacated place. 'How she does contrive to make the deserts of London look inhabited,' he wrote to Julian, enjoying a fantasy that, if he were in a position to marry, Henrietta would be his *'flamme fatale'*.[4]

That December he left England before the end of term. From the Blessed Edmund Campion's day, a Jesuit holiday at the beginning of December, he had permission to stay away until Holy Week. Equipped with a sheepskin coat from Mollie and a Greek *propemptikon* or farewell poem from Maurice Bowra, he stopped off in Geneva to stay with John and Anya Berger in the modernistic new town of Meyrin. John drove him up into the Jura to see the peaks and breathe mountain air. Then, after catching an overnight train to Venice, he took an Adriatic ferry to Piraeus. A Sarajevo ballet company came on board at Dubrovnik and did wild, exhilarating Slavonic dances. In Athens he took up residence for the winter as a regular member of the British School.

Before leaving he had kept his promise to the Manchester hostel and spent a few days there giving an Advent retreat. Still appalled by the night-time existence of the derelicts on the Croft, he had suggested them as a subject to Mischa Scorer, a recent Oxford graduate working on religious documentaries for BBC television, when he dropped in at Campion Hall to discuss ideas. First, however, over glass after glass of red wine ('Oh good, my case has just arrived from Berry Brothers'), he had proposed a filmed tour of monastic ruins with his own commentary in verse. Forty years on, this would only have seemed more preposterous if the poem had been in Latin, but *Bare Ruin'd Choirs*, a meditation on ruined Cistercian abbeys in North Yorkshire, went out as a *Viewpoint* programme in the autumn of 1966 with the actor Alan Dobie reciting Peter's poetic script in a soft, respectful voice.

Poetry might be struggling for publication, but the BBC maintained its traditional highbrow commitments, with clear cultural divisions between the various broadcasting channels. That winter, when Peter was in Greece, Sir Michael Redgrave recited his lament for Eliot, 'New Year's Eve Poem 1965', on the Third Programme. Two years later, invited to write a 'kind of soliloquy' for the evening of Christmas Day on Radio 4, Peter recorded his anguished 'Christmas Sermon', a poem about human suffering and struggling religious belief, which reflected his despair not only about poverty and bleakness in the English winter but about conditions under the military dictatorship in Greece.

By the early to mid-1960s Greece had begun to be a popular, still mainly cultural, holiday destination. Students arrived there by boat, on cheap charter flights or slow, dirty trains through the Balkans with bath-plugs and lavatory paper in their rucksacks. They slept out on flat roofs or in caves and sold their blood when they ran out of drachmas. The 1964 film of Kazantzakis's *Zorba the Greek*, with Anthony Quinn as the wily Cretan Zorba and Alan Bates as his succulent young English employer, was the film of the year for sentimental lovers of the exotic, whose imitations of Zorba's dance, to a record of Theodorakis's bouzouki music, became one of the more excruciating ways of making a party go.

Recovering during the 1950s from the losses of the civil war, Greeks had started to build hotels, open tourist restaurants and transform fishing villages into resorts. Growing numbers of the yacht-owning and cruising classes filled the islands and Aegean ports. Even Germans, although still hated, had begun to spread their money around. But the recently propped-up monarchy was unstable and the parties split by internal disagreements. The right-wing Prime Minister Constantine Karamanlis, who had promoted Greek membership of the Common Market and the establishment of Cyprus as a republic, exiled himself to Paris after quarrelling with King Paul in 1963. Early the next year Paul died and was succeeded by the twenty-three-year-old Constantine II. Fighting had broken out between Greeks and Turks in Cyprus, and the elderly liberal Prime Minister, Georgios Papandreou, who supported *enosis* or the union of Cyprus with Greece, had sent a division there to help keep the peace. In July 1965 Constantine was pressured by a right-wing military clique to force Papandreou's resignation after he had tried to take control of the army by combining his office with the Ministry of Defence. From then onwards, a succession of short-term governments represented factions of Papandreou's Centre Union party. Constantine, although weak, promised elections for late May 1967, when the more optimistic liberals assumed that Papandreou would return to power.

So far, all this meant little to Peter. He planned to work hard on Pausanias that winter, although he had almost finished translating the text. Writing the footnotes had been so fascinating that he wanted to expand them into a separate, full-scale scholarly work. An exhaustive, region-by-region commentary on the archaeological history and mythological associations of the places mentioned by Pausanias should keep him busy for satisfyingly long periods in Greece. Having failed to secure a British Academy grant, he knew that he would have to subsidize the research work with his allowance from the Jesuits until he could persuade a new publisher to commission his commentary. That winter he planned some expeditions to ancient sites, a visit to the Leigh Fermors in the Mani and (he hoped) several weeks at an archaeological dig on Naxos, where Dominique de Grunne was clamouring to join him.

Athens in December can be a magical escape from English greyness and pre-Christmas commercial tat. The evenings can be balmy enough for walking or even sitting outside, and oranges glow among clusters of dark, pointed leaves on pavement-edge trees. Peter called on George Seferis, and at Nikos Gatsos's table at Floca met the beautiful young novelist Yaël Dayan, the daughter of the one-eyed Israeli politician and general who would soon become a hero of the Six Day War.[5] He bought himself a red bicycle and rode it round the city centre, tethering it to a tree outside Floca and grinding along to the Catholic Cathedral of St. Dionysius the Areopagite, where he had volunteered to hear confessions in English and do duty at the seven o'clock morning Mass. After trying that painful dawn cycle ride once or twice, he decided it would be better to clear his head by walking and enjoy the reflections of sunrise on the Parthenon.[6] On the fine afternoon of Christmas Day he saw its clear, pillared bulk glittering in the sun above an empty Acropolis, which was closed to the public for the day. He described to Nancy how a gang of American sailors tried to storm it, armed with beer-bottles and cheered on by the crowd.

> The silver-tinsel in the sunshine of the Christmas eve market, & the smell everywhere of incense & narcissus & orange trees in fruit, & the kind of clear dank darkness in the National Gardens – well, what can one say? And today I scrambled up some rocks on Philopappou in a storm, and saw the Parthenon with a lilac & dark-grey storm shrapnelling just behind it.[7]

Dominique, under the impression that Peter was having an enchanting time in Athens, longed to share it. The Naxos arrangement had fallen through by early January, but Dominique suggested a string of alternatives for February: trekking in the Argolid, helping the Leigh Fermors to build their new house in the Mani, or visiting Delos.[8] In the end, however, he had to cancel his trip, leaving Peter free to travel on his own.

Paddy and Joan Leigh Fermor had bought their piece of cliff-top land on its olive-growing headland just south of Kardamyli. They had spent most of their first winter in a flat over a waterfront taverna in the village, while Paddy, an enthusiastic architectural amateur, added his own touches to the plans drawn up by an architect from Athens, dealt with builders and oversaw the beginnings of a very detailed, protracted work. In the spring and summer they had lived in tents on the site or stayed with guests in a small hotel on the pebbly edge of Kalamitsi Bay, which they took over entirely the following winter.

Here Peter arrived after wandering in the Peloponnese, enjoying 'the cold, the freshness, the smell of olive-harvest & its smoke, the oranges in the trees & the sparks in the forges', proclaiming that he was able for the first time ever to write poems 'out of times of pleasure and excitement', and concluding that rural Greece in winter was 'a kind of gold & silver age' which needed five different notebooks to do it justice.[9]

There is nothing in providence but leaves,
there is nothing in my heaven but stone,
no one in mountain villages believes
what I believe when I am alone;
the hammer strikes again and again,
it is the gold and silver age again. [10]

After crippling a knee on a rock he had limped back to Athens for treatment, then flown down to the little airport at Kalamata. The hotel, he told Mollie, was delightful, looking up towards the snowy peaks of Taÿgetos above villages strung out along ledges. The kind landlady, Eleftheria, looked after him and the '3 or 4 friends' who were in residence. Lying in his sleeping-bag on a crimson and cobalt blue bedspread, he could hear Paddy through the wall singing 'The Road to Mandalay' after an orgy of reciting all the Kipling poems they could remember. His letters and notebook entries filled up with embryonic poems, while those he completed described journeys from the grim, cold north to a region of *girls in their fresh white stinking of jasmine*, and from the devastation of war to the regenerate green shoots of peace.

Yet they were also ambivalent. It was as if his journey south had tunnelled into his subconscious, filling it with nightmarish evocations of other, dreadful journeys – '*A long, bellowing train*', '*The Rome express goes screaming through the wood*', '*They burnt it down in nineteen forty one*'.[11] The poem 'For Joan and Paddy' begins

Fifty years ago I might have died.
Nothing is growing in the villages
but scraggy wheat, ploutos [wealth] *repurified.*
The children are in leaf darker than trees.
I think there are bare voices in the stars.
The mutterings of those cold fires are wars.

> *Something died and has come alive in us,*
> *it withers cobble stones and old railings;*
> *beautiful poverty was victorious,*
> *I am fighting the coherence of things.*
> *All my true-seeming words will shake to pieces*
> *when my lamp dies and the dawn cold increases.*

Dismissing his own past achievements (*I have built nothing in thirty-five years/except five wooden gates into a wood*), he had acquired a raw awareness of the darker side of history which undermined many of the certainties that had held his life together before.

Encouraged by Paddy's love of Latin, he was reading the comedies of Plautus, the earliest known complete Latin literary works, between gulps of borrowed John Buchan. Plautus (he wrote) made him understand how much the Greeks must have influenced the Romans.[12] Paddy's darting, adventurous mind, as eclectic as a seventeenth-century gentleman's library, suited him. They could talk for hours, jumping sideways from one subject to another as if on rocks in a mountain stream. He responded to Paddy's dash and sense of fun and to Joan's quietly confident manner. And Paddy missed nothing of his attraction to their other guest, Miranda, the twenty-five-year-old widowed mother of a half-Algerian daughter, Da'ad. An ardent, impulsive rebel, she had been cut off by her father, Lord Rothschild, for marrying Boudjemaa Boumaza, a political dissident living in exile in Tunis. When he was assassinated, less than three years into their marriage, she had searched through piles of abandoned corpses to retrieve his body for burial, then fled with Da'ad to Greece.

She and Peter had met briefly that summer when she had been staying in an Athens hotel. Recognizing him in Floca on his way to Katounia or Libya, and having known about him since her brother was at Oxford, she had approached him and introduced herself as Jacob's sister. ('I loved his face and his poetry,' she explained.) Among the friends they found they had in common were Joan and Paddy, with whom Miranda and Da'ad stayed that summer at the little Kalamitsi hotel. Other visitors there included Miranda's mother Barbara and her third husband, the artist Nikos Ghika, whose remarriage had provoked the caretaker into burning down the villa on Hydra. But it was to Joan, rather than to Barbara, that Miranda turned for comfort and support. Back at the hotel in the winter, she fitted happily into the household and enjoyed the admiration of Paddy, who thought her intelligent, tremendous fun and a promising painter and poet. 'You had coins on your forehead,' he said later, praising the Greek-style beauty in which she had bloomed as a Muslim bride.

Peter kept quiet about Miranda in his letters to Julian, Willie and Mollie, but could not resist telling David Pryce-Jones about this exciting new friendship. He, Miranda and Paddy (he wrote) formed a 'Balkan trio in the nonexistent palm court' round the wood-stove at the hotel in the evenings, chatting, reciting and singing after one of Eleftheria's meals of herb-infused rabbit stew. On those evenings Paddy noticed, or thought he remembered, Miranda twining her arms round Peter's shoulders while he stroked her absent-mindedly like a pet.[13]

'We adored one another,' said Miranda, adding that they had exchanged no more than 'spiritual hugs'. But Peter, despite his later, ungallant dismissal of their relationship as 'only a ballet of love', clearly saw it as the real thing. While remaining technically celibate, he told Miranda that he now knew for certain that he was not homosexual. Under Paddy's twinkling eye, in the tolerant atmosphere of the hotel, he let his instincts take him as far as he dared go.

If his leg got better, he wrote to Willie, he would like to cross the Taÿgetos range under snow. The more he saw of Greece, the more awe-inspiring and unknowable it seemed, making him feel he had been absurdly ambitious in thinking he could comment on the whole of Pausanias. He was writing poems to distract himself, although (he added piously) the best poetry seemed to him to be silence, or the voice of God saying something very simple on a mountain-top.[14] He was not, however, about to search for God alone in high places, but to go with Miranda to Crete, where she planned to paint throughout the spring.

For the first time he was part of a couple. After reading some of the poems in *Fresh Water, Sea Water*, Deirdre Connolly had remarked sympathetically on the loneliness they expressed.[15] That 'I' now became a companionable, sometimes passionate-seeming 'we'. The neat little poem *The sky cleared and we came to an island* is about a pair who are absorbed in one another and the weather of their relationship.[16] The atmospheric 'For Miranda', about a thunderstorm on the Cretan Sea

> *(... you were awake*
> *banging the iron blanket, one free hand*
> *like fire burning without wires in the air),*[17]

may have led some people to assume that they had been lovers, although its praise of the subject's purity and airily rhetorical conclusion (*I tell you in that storm nothing can live/but what is without life, and true, and free*) suggest the eventual triumph of restraint.

Back in Oxford after Easter, Peter told Julian that he had not yet prepared his first course of lectures, the first of which was due in two days. Years later he shocked Elizabeth Chatwin by dashing unprepared from one speaking engagement to the next, relying on the familiarity of the subject and on asides, jokes and emphatic repetition. Not mentioning Kardamyli or Crete to Julian, he said only that Naxos had not come off, and that he had 'spent the whole time working like a mad creature, & just finished 24 hours before coming home'.[18]

From Crete, and then from Athens, Miranda wrote to him affectionately. Gregory Corso was lurking in Athens, a shaggy wreck from his heroin addiction. She nursed him, offered to find him a psychiatrist, tracked down a doctor who was willing to prescribe him morphine and was appalled when his dealer resurfaced to undermine her work. She was getting up at dawn to paint huge, symbolic pictures. In a letter of mid-July thanking Peter for a review of his travel book *Roumeli*, Paddy mentioned that she had visited Kardamyli a few weeks earlier, telling horrifying stories about life in Athens and impressing him with her painting talent.

That summer Peter was mobile. To get out of Oxford he bought a tiny, feeble Yamaha motorcycle which could reach fifty miles an hour but normally wobbled along at nearer twenty. In those miserable, wet summer months he skidded about with L-plates, laboriously riding the bike as far as Ottery St. Mary to be best man at Robin Milner-Gulland's wedding, then crashing it on the steep slope down to Dyrham Park, near Bristol, where Tony Mitchell was working for the National Trust. John Berger offered to send him a more powerful motorcycle that a friend had left with him. This terrifying machine, which Peter called the Thunderbolt, took until the next spring to arrive, with many changes of plan as it got delayed and misdirected on the way.

There were *longueurs* in the Long Vacation, prompting him to write bored letters about grass growing between the cobbles of the nineteenth-century High Street. He and Mischa Scorer spent a few days together in North Yorkshire, 'with everything scarfed in mist & sunshine', inspecting the remains of Cistercian monasteries for the film *Bare Ruin'd Choirs*.[19] During the next week or two he wrote his long, regularly rhyming script, celebrating the innocence of the religious life and the moral significance of stony, weed-choked monastic ruins. Kathleen Raine remarked on its flexible, plain style, which she thought sometimes reached great heights, while Anthony conceded that bits of it were very effective, although, as a cynical career priest, he found its piety about medieval monasticism over-simplified and cloying.[20]

In September Peter spent nine days on Jura with Michael Astor's family, who thought him a calming influence on their troubled daughter Jane. He wrote to Nancy about the eagles, ravens and wild goats, the stags roaring on the precipices, the salmon, sea trout and sea-birds, and a colony of Atlantic grey seals 'with heads popping up like magic men & enormous lollopping bodies'. He described how the party watched them

> on the beach where the newly born young were trying to hide in the rocks – small bundles of white fur with charming black currant eyes. The parents knew we were there so we didn't stay as long as we'd have liked; but I shall never forget them or forget that place (rocks, seashells, a whale's skeleton in a bothie garden, a great glen below the Paps of Jura, which is a purely surrealist grey lunar cone in the mist, the healthy cheeks of the heather & the children, blazing red ash-berries).[21]

His autumn teaching duties must have been exceptionally light that year. He told Betty Radice, his editor at Penguin, that the early damp had brought on his catarrh and made him useless in the mornings in England, whereas in Greece he would be able to work. He would certainly be away until January, but possibly until March. On November 18 he flew to Geneva to spend a week with John Berger and inspect the Thunderbolt on his way to Greece. The day before he left, the Connollys arrived in Oxford to hear Bowra give the Romanes Lecture. As a favour, Cyril had arranged for him to review Bowra's autobiography for the *Sunday Times*. The style of *Memories* is deadpan, but Peter claimed loyally that he had not kicked the ground from laughing so much at a book since he was eighteen. To be condemned by Bowra's magisterial figure, he added with relish, was to be 'damned backwards by dead generations of Chinese administrators'.[22] Knowing that Bowra was Miranda's godfather, having been the tutor and friend of her mother's second husband Rex Warner, may have made his connection with him seem almost a family one.

എ

In Athens Miranda was waiting for him, having settled in a neighbourhood he would later come to know well. He told Cyril that she had got much better and was painting unexpected and very good pictures. Athens was overcrowded before Christmas, and Paddy and Joan passed through like whooping swans, winging their way south.

For eight days he escaped from the British School to wander on 'tea-smelling' mountains in the Argolid, chatting to shepherds and olive-grove farmers in the cafés of Ligourio in the evenings, and enjoying the fresh wind and hot sun and the scent of olive-wood smoke.[23] One day, sated with official sites and following a mountain mule-path, he stopped to rest for a minute and take off his sweater, and discovered that he was sitting on a buried mosaic pavement. Scrabbling further, he found part of an elaborate terracotta lamp. He reburied everything and reported it to the local archaeological service, but never heard whether they had followed it up.[24]

Then, in January 1967, he and Miranda followed the Leigh Fermors for another stay in the Kalamitsi hotel. He enthused on a postcard to Cyril about lemon and olive trees under the 'icy snowhatted mass of Taygetos', and told him that he had found an akropolis scattered with fifth- or fourth-century potsherds, but left no space to mention his fellow-guest.[25]

For much of that winter, however, he was in Athens and depressed. The year-old pain in his knee had come back. The last stage of writing footnotes on Pausanias had dwindled into a chore. He continued to plan an exhaustive, illustrated commentary, which he hoped would attract a commission once the Penguin translation appeared.

Many of his Athenian friends had begun to fear that it would only be a matter of time before tanks rolled in to resolve the political situation by force. He told Cyril that there was more unhappiness in the city than could be measured, and that American writers there were 'much more shot up than the akropolis but with less dignity in the dark'. That probably referred to Gregory Corso, in spite of a postcard he had sent from Crete in September, claiming that he was healthy and spiritually ('or musely') on the mend.[26]

Early in March, to his friends' relief, Peter was back in England, followed a month later by Miranda. On one of her visits to Oxford he smuggled her into Campion Hall in a laundry basket out of childish bravado and a desire to show her his room. Joan Leigh Fermor, also back in London, told him how much she had enjoyed having him and Miranda at Kardamyli, thanked them for a cornucopia of presents and suggested inviting them to dinner with Barbara and Nikos. Another member of her set, Mougouch (or Magouche) Phillips, wrote from Athens that she was in 'an indigestion of questions' about Peter and about 'darling quail'.[27] That second 'about' was tactful, although by then their more worldly friends, while puzzled by their relationship, had begun to treat them as a couple. Caryl Brahms entertained the pair of them with the Pryce-Joneses and told Peter that Miranda would be a very good painter one day.[28] Maurice Bowra, meeting Miranda at lunch with the Ghikas at their house in Blomfield Road, Little Venice, had discovered that she was spending a day a week in Oxford and suggested that Peter should bring her to a meal in Wadham, perhaps to meet Iain Watson, whom he knew she liked.[29]

From Stonyhurst Iain had gone up to Wadham to read classics. His time there had been brilliant but emotionally fraught, and he had taken a third class in Mods as clever, highly strung people sometimes do. Frances Partridge, meeting him in Tuscany in 1969, recorded doubtfully in her diary his story that five out of ten of his friends at Wadham had committed suicide and he had been the person who discovered his best friend's dead body.[30] Bowra, who liked him, had suggested ('Dear boy') that he should move into the country near Oxford to sort himself out. He had taken a flat in Yarnton Manor, a few miles to the north, and used to fetch Peter from Heythrop by car so that they could go to Fraenkel's or Dodds's seminars together. Instead of Greats he had taken the second part of his degree in Modern Greek, after which he had stayed on at Yarnton to do research on Byzantine wall-paintings. He was nervy, black-bearded, soft-voiced and thin, with strong feelings about people, a fierce loathing of his Catholic upbringing, deep loyalty to Peter, a streak of fantasy and considerable eccentric charm.

In Iain's version of events, Peter had taken Miranda out on the pillion of the newly arrived Thunderbolt to show her the scenes of his past at Heythrop. On the way back he decided that they would call in at Yarnton for tea. He rang the bell of Iain's flat ('but I was in the garden, so he didn't need to'), and introduced him to Miranda. During the next couple of months he was too busy catching up with life in England to notice where that had led. In common with everyone else the couple knew, he was not invited to a hasty ceremony at the Marylebone Registry Office early in July. To Miranda this seemed to be the answer to a problem that had worried her for some time; her lawyer had told her that unless she married a British subject who was prepared to join her in adopting Da'ad, the child would not qualify for a British passport and would remain effectively stateless. But Peter was not to know that when he burst into a dinner-party at the Pryce-Joneses' with the appalled cry, 'Did you know, Miranda is married!'[31]

15
JUNTA

> As a government they [the junta] were like the Marx brothers without the talent, and there was something venomous about them that recalled Hitler, and had its roots in the Nazi period in Greece. Their police were a poor man's Gestapo. They lasted seven years.
>
> *The Hill of Kronos* (1980) 136

Recovering almost at once from the shock, Peter joined the Watsons on their honeymoon in Athens. Miranda felt that, as their joint best friend, he had begun to assume a benign responsibility for having brought them together. To justify the trip to the Jesuits, he told them that he needed to take slide photographs for a series of lectures on Athenian antiquities which he had put off from the spring term until the autumn. Meanwhile Penguin had scheduled his two-volume translation of Pausanias to appear both as a paperback Penguin Classic and as an illustrated hardback, with air-photographs by Jean Mohr of Geneva, whom John Berger had recommended and Penguin had agreed to pay. Mohr had arranged to spend the whole of that April in Greece, but could hardly have chosen a worse time. Caught out by the military coup of April 21, he had managed with great difficulty to take all the necessary photographs and leave the country with his films intact.[1] Meanwhile Peter hoped to build up his own photographic collection, as 'another move in the crab-like progress of a commentary on Pausanias'. Later, he wrote that he had photographed every surviving stone of the steadily vanishing ancient walls of Piraeus.[2]

Miranda's flat was in Mets, a hilly, informal neighbourhood at the south end of central Athens, between the First National Cemetery on the slope up towards Hymettos and the wooded hill next to the Panathenaic Stadium, above Ardittou. Peter liked to believe it was a former red light district. The switchback streets look down over the

Temple of Athenian Zeus and across to the Parthenon, which he saw every morning through his curtainless bedroom window, reflected in an old Venetian mirror.

The Watsons had a car, and Peter was soon organizing them on trips to ancient sites in the rocky Boeotian country north-west of Athens. One day they managed to talk their way into a village storehouse near Tanagra which was kept locked against the public, being crammed with priceless archaeological finds. Iain was a resourceful explorer and fearless driver, and Peter relaxed in the rush of sunlit air through the car windows and the couple's closeness to him and each other. While they chose to ignore the existence of the junta, he was able to suppress his feelings about it. Being in the midst of things in Greece, where they personally had nothing to fear, was perhaps better than hearing distant rumours of mass imprisonment, tortures and executions. It was August 1967, four months after the military coup, when archaeologists, classical scholars and tourists had begun to face up to a choice between supporting Greek shopkeepers, hoteliers and restaurant-owners with their custom or showing their disapproval of the regime by staying away.

That spring and early summer Peter had barely noticed that Miranda had less time for him than before. He gave an Easter retreat at the Morning Star hostel in Manchester, whose inmates would see *Foxes Have Holes,*[*] his and Mischa's documentary about the homeless drunks, on television the following August. With permission from the Catholic Archbishop of Birmingham he preached at an Evensong in Christ Church Cathedral, followed by dinner and a glacial Senior Common Room evening. He gave lunch-parties in a small private room at Campion Hall. One was for the Connollys, after which Deirdre, touched by Lenten solemnity, asked him to pray for them as

---

[*] 'and the birds of the air have nests, but the Son of man hath not where to lay his head' (Matt. 8:20, Luke 9:58).

Easter approached.[3] Another was for Nancy, who was about to finish an archaeological dig on Naxos. She had struggled with the decision about whether she ought to go, and, once there, was oppressed by most people's frightened silence. But one evening Philip Sherrard's wife Anna smuggled her into a crowded room over a café, where she found herself at a clandestine recital of Seferis's protest poems and Theodorakis's banned songs.

Peter ricocheted up and down between Oxford and London, sometimes losing a night's sleep in the process. 'My message to the churches today is, never travel by the milk-train,' he quipped blearily one breakfast-time at Campion Hall. Henrietta, now a liability rather than a temptress, had been kicking up a fuss in Holloway while awaiting trial for burglary. Her probation officer told Peter in some puzzlement that she had named him as her closest friend, and asked him to try to sort her out once she was free. He must have felt relieved when George and Diana Melly stepped in and took her off to their tower house on the Usk. Even then, however, she begged him to become involved with another prisoner, Clancy, whom she had visited in Wandsworth with a couple of Chelsea friends, the boutique-owner Michael Rainey and the fashionable antique dealer Christopher Gibbs.[4]

Prison imagery pervades 'Christmas Sermon', the poem Peter recorded for broadcasting that December. The fates of political prisoners in Greece had haunted him for much of that year. Even before mid-April he had believed the predictions of Athenian friends that the army was about to stage a coup. One of the most outspoken was Vanna Hadjimichalis, an archaeologist attached to the French School at Athens, whose clever, amusing, left-wing architect husband Nikos had drawn up the plans for the Leigh Fermors' house on which Paddy elaborated. Early in April Vanna had written to Peter that the 'political mic-mac' was very bad, although she hoped the forthcoming elections would calm things down.

Then the tanks rolled into Syntagma Square at dawn, and the accounts that emerged from Greece were more appalling than he could have imagined. The police raided Nikos and Vanna's flat in search of incriminating papers, and Nikos had to go into hiding for several days.[5] Peter was enraged that the British Embassy and the British School at Athens remained firmly neutral. He told a journalist acquaintance that during the three weeks after the coup some hundred thousand Greeks had been taken as political prisoners, and people had been shot dead in the streets.[6] Stories leaked out from the prisons about tortures, beatings and executions, although he knew that many people kept quiet for fear of reprisals. Silenced by his membership of the British School, he was intent on urging others to condemn the junta. The former Conservative MP for Oxford, Montague Woodhouse, who had served heroically with SOE and commanded the Allied military mission to Greece when still in his twenties, was one of the first English politicians to speak out, and Peter wrote to congratulate him.[7]

Not long before the troubles broke out he had begun to explore a new sideline as a general writer about Greece. An unsolicited copy of *Pancakes* he sent Lawrence Durrell brought him praise for an article about the Acropolis in the American magazine *Greek Heritage*. More ambitiously, he had a contract from Collins for a 70,000-word history of the 'rape' of the Parthenon. Several years earlier friends had brought Adrian House, a young Collins editor, to meet him at Heythrop. Peter had insisted that they drove to the Rollright Stones, where, standing in the megalithic stone circle and looking down over the shimmering Warwickshire plain, Adrian had sensed his feeling for ancient landscapes and hoped he would one day be able to express it in prose. In the autumn of 1966 Peter's agent John Johnson began negotiations with Collins about the Parthenon book. Adrian promised an advance of £250 up front, with a further £50 to follow, and suggested that Peter might like to broaden the account to include the whole of the Acropolis.

Confident that he could dash off the book at any time, Peter blandly told Betty Radice that he planned to use the 'big money' from Collins that winter to finish his Pausanias fieldwork in central and southern Greece. In the end, however, he found that he was not allowed to take more than £50 out of England, so the advance remained largely unspent. Meanwhile he was sounding out publishers about a commentary on Pausanias, depending on their ability to make a deal with Penguin Classics.[8]

Early in April 1967 Diana Athill, his former editor at André Deutsch, invited him to contribute to a collection of essays by various writers about different aspects of Greek life, history and culture. Edited by the Greek novelist and translator Kay Cicellis, it would be the second in a celebrity-linked travel series from Deutsch, following *Ian Fleming Introduces Jamaica* in 1965.[9] Peter sent off his essay, about foreign travellers in Greece, a day or two before the military coup.

The first casualty of the Greek situation was the Parthenon book. At the end of May Peter returned his advance to Collins, telling Adrian that for political reasons he could not go on with the book.[10] He also suggested to Penguin that they should delay the publication of Pausanias, but was told that nobody would understand the reason why. At least, he replied, he would like to dedicate both volumes to the freedom of Greece, an idea the editors surprisingly accepted. The first news about the intended book of essays came in October, when Diana Athill told him it was in cold storage because of the junta, and that if the publishers decided to abandon it (as they did) he would be paid half his promised fee in another six months.[11]

'Peter did *go on* so about Greece,' said Deirdre. On his visits to the Connollys at Firle while staying with Mollie in Eastbourne, he described in indignant detail the atrocities that were taking place in Greek prisons. Deirdre began to wish he would change the subject only when it seemed that his obsession with the junta would never end. In the autumn of 1967, writing on Cyril's behalf to acknowledge a typed batch of the poems Peter had written in Greece, she told him that Cyril was about to spend three weeks in Kenya and Uganda. But 'I am here, & so is the stock-pot, & apple logs & music, plus Cressida dog & cat.' Had there been any developments about his magazine? she asked encouragingly.[12]

He had been discussing the possibility of starting a magazine with John Fuller, who was back in Oxford with a fellowship at Magdalen College. John had wanted to edit a magazine of his own since his involvement with Ian Hamilton's *Review*, while Peter was desperate for a political weapon to brandish in print. Impressed with the extreme left-wing principles of John Berger and David Caute, he attempted to bring them into his project as trustee and editor. In a letter offering Caute the prospective editorship, he told him he hoped the magazine would fill a gap in English journalism by commenting on the news 'on the intellectual level of Temps Modernes or Novy Mir'.[13]

Peter knew that he could not be publicly involved in running the kind of magazine he wanted. It would not be like *The Month*, which Father Caraman had edited from Mount Street with contributions from Catholic writers such as Graham Greene, Muriel Spark and Evelyn Waugh, or the more eclectically literary *Aylesford Review*, which the Carmelite Brocard Sewell had edited from his monastery in Kent. What he had in mind was a magazine with political punch – a rival to the discredited *Encounter*, which Stephen Spender had co-edited with Melvin Lasky until the spring of 1967. As political attitudes became polarized over the Vietnam War, the partnership of a hawkish American with a soft English liberal intellectual had aroused ill-feeling and suspicion on the Left. Seizing on a widespread rumour that *Encounter* was in the pay of the CIA, Conor Cruise O'Brien, a new, visiting recruit to the American anti-war party, had proclaimed it as a fact in an article in the *New York Times*. Documentary confirmation in the journal *Ramparts* had pushed Spender into resigning from the editorship, although neither he nor Lasky admitted that they knew anything about the tainted source of the funds.

Spender had always been kind to Peter, in spite of rejecting many of his submissions. Like Bowra, he had praised *Fresh Water, Sea Water* as the achievement of a true poetic voice.[14] James Fenton remembered that, on his desk at Campion Hall, Peter kept a Greek silver box with a figure of a lion on the lid that Spender had given him. Immediately after leaving Oxford, Spender's son Matthew had married the artist Maro Gorky, whose mother Mougouch Phillips belonged to the Ghikas' smart set in Greece. After Spender replied in friendly terms to his letter of commiseration about *Encounter*, Peter felt confident about trying to involve him once he was back for the summer after lecturing in Illinois.[15]

His mistake lay in imagining that he could talk a magazine into existence without consulting the interests of its future backers. After a lunch-party full of misunderstandings, Spender wrote sternly disabusing him of his ideas about procedure. He could not simply nominate an editor, then hope that his sponsors would approve. The right person would have to be chosen carefully by a committee. If Peter and his friends could assemble one quickly (he added), they should be able to cash in on the liberal sympathy for him that the *Encounter* affair had stirred up.

Within a few days, however, Spender had assembled a magazine committee of his own, consisting of W.H. Auden, Sir Isaiah Berlin, Stuart Hampshire and Karl Miller, a Cambridge man of Peter's age who had recently become editor of *The Listener*. Cold-shouldering Peter, he suggested that he should plan a different magazine altogether, since he would undoubtedly find it frustrating to have to co-operate with members of the older generation.[16]

Peter had already offered his editorship to David Caute. Having publicly resigned from All Souls in protest against its refusal to modernize, Caute thought he might seem too extreme for most people's tastes. At John Berger's suggestion Peter then wrote to Victor Anant, a left-winger who was temporarily teaching in Kuala Lumpur, offering a co-editorship with Caute, which Anant accepted.[17] By the autumn Peter thought he would try to attract a rich patron like George Weidenfeld, who had made his firm's fortune by publishing Nabokov's *Lolita*. Ignoring a friend's warning that Weidenfeld was more likely to be impressed by important trustees than by a clique of young writers and academics, Peter decided to try approaching him through John Berger's former editor at Penguin, Tony Godwin. The financially savvy Godwin, who was working for Weidenfeld in New York, agreed to discuss the project in London after Christmas. By then, however, Peter was in Greece, and before long he had abandoned the magazine idea altogether.[18]

❧

Teaching must have been a positive rest from all these distractions. As an Oxford tutor he was sympathetic, imaginative, discursive and funny. Most of his handful of students were Jesuit classicists in their twenties who had just finished their stint of philosophy and the fined-down pedagogy course. Sometimes a fellow of a college would send a group of freshmen to him for a term, promising a reciprocal arrangement some other time. Very occasionally he taught a non-classicist such as the eighteen-year-old poet James Fenton, who went up to Magdalen in October 1967 with John Fuller as his tutor. In those days undergraduates taking English Prelims at the end of their second term were examined on passages from either the *Æneid* or the *Odyssey*. Everyone who read English had at least Latin 'O' level, and most of them chose Virgil as the easier or only possible option. James, however, who had already done the set books of the *Æneid* at school, chose the Nausicaa episode from the *Odyssey*. By late October John had arranged that Peter would take him for Homer for the rest of that term before departing for Greece.

James remembered that his tutorials were at midday, and began with enormous glasses of sherry. Life as a don allowed Peter to be lavishly generous with drink. He had also taken to smoking cigars from Fribourg and Treyer, but eventually cut down on them in favour of snuff, an affectation which became part of his personality as he broadened into snuff-sprinkled, waistcoated middle age.

Tutorials with Peter were adventures, ranging from the *Odyssey* to modern Greek poetry, Russian writers, social and literary gossip, and a survey of oral traditions of poetry in other European languages. Sometimes he uttered impossible paradoxes and had to argue his way out them of in self-mockery. He was impressed that James had met Auden and acquired some of his toughness, and lent him the book he was currently keenest on, a collection of Mandelstam's prose. After the tutorials he usually took him for a modest lunch at the Sorbonne, which was then the fashionable Oxford restaurant, in an alleyway south of the High Street. It was a benevolent relationship on Peter's part, based on love of his subject, a conviction that all humane interests were connected and enjoyment in teaching a brilliant literary adolescent. For James it was an extraordinary time, which did not last beyond the remaining few weeks of that term.

Brendan McLaughlin, Peter's young friend from Heythrop, was another new pupil of his that autumn. Visiting Campion Hall to make arrangements, he, too, had been given lunch at the Sorbonne. Not understanding Peter's privileged arrangement with the Jesuits, who let him keep his literary earnings to cover expenses, he assumed that Campion Hall must pay his restaurant bills like college battels. After lunch, during a stroll in Christ Church Meadow, Peter dropped to his knees to examine something in the grass and began to murmur a poem about a bee. Even crossing a road with him was romantic, said Brendan; yet, like James, he stressed that their relationship had been utterly chaste.

Different people saw different versions of Peter. He was the library-haunting scholar and poet, the cigar-smoking *bon viveur*, the name-dropping friend of Rothschilds and Astors and the wistful radical who wished he had been a worker priest. Because of his attractiveness to both men and women, some people assumed he must be either a homosexual or a womaniser in priest's clothing. Relishing extreme contrasts, like those dons who claimed to value only a first- or fourth-class degree, he enjoyed smart restaurants, grand hotels, luxurious shops, austere living and squalid back-street pubs. Anthony O'Hear, a young Jesuit who lived at Campion Hall in the late 1960s, described how Peter liked to take him into the grimmest pubs in St. Ebbes, the working-class neighbourhood between Campion Hall and the river. A Balliol undergraduate remembered being taken for the walk that had also been Auden's favourite, round the gasworks and canal.[19]

That kind of bleak urban setting was the scene of 'Christmas Sermon', an intense personal and political confession in which hope barely struggles through suffering to survive. Its expressions of fear and sleepless grief recall '*L'Aurore Grelottante*' of ten years earlier, but this time the voice is more intimate, urgent and real.

> *... Somewhere it is all starting again,*
> *worse than a dream. Christmas starting again,*
> *lamplight choking to twilight on my table.*
> *I am colder than Christ was in his stable.*
> *The house-walls shiver and sweat in the back-street,*
> *grimy town-halls repeat and repeat*
> *what my mouth drops, what the English cannot say,*
> *pink motor-tyres of roses, Christmas day.*
> *I am terrified of what is beginning.*

Everywhere it is snowing on the dead:
look how the glittering cover has been spread
over the blackened complicated dead
where the mist and the winter sun waded;
and it is snowing, it muffles the air,
the sun disappears in a blast of fire,
Where are you God? in the rustic desert,
I am freezing, these animals are hurt,
I do not comprehend my religion.
I think it is a matter of cities,
as if I did not know what this street is
but was in love with its stone and darkness,
and have been wandering with no address
and am diminished. Christmas is mute.
Christ is reason and I am destitute...

Peter told Nancy that he read it for the recording and was weeping at the end. They said 'That's marvellous but just a fraction slow at the beginning & now would you read it again. So I did, with grim & cynical thoughts I dare say, smoking a cigar both times.'[20]

ജ

Returning in September from his stay in Athens, Peter had sent the sweet-toothed Bowra, who was in isolation with mumps, a present of his favourite *loukoumi*, Turkish delight. Bowra had missed going to Greece but was glad, in a way, that things there were so appalling; he had decided to stay away until the junta fell, and did not want 'these blackguards', the Colonels, to be loved.[21]

There would have been plenty to keep him occupied if he had decided to follow Bowra's example. The market for Greek travel books was dead, and Thames & Hudson turned down his proposal for an illustrated commentary on Pausanias, thinking it would clash with the Penguin hardback. He could have knuckled down to learning Russian, since Robin Milner-Gulland was keen to collaborate with him on a translation of poems by Nikolai Zabolotsky.[22] He made co-operative noises about this but went no further, and in the end Robin found another co-translator for a different work of Zabolotsky's.

A Jesuit at Boston College, Massachusetts had been urging him to visit for several years, even tempting him to spend his tertian year in a New England Jesuit house with the offer of a lecture that would have covered the cost of his passage. He conceded that he could spare a single weekend early in December 1967 ('WILLING LECTURE READ TWICE EXPENSE 150 POUNDS LETS GO PETER'), but refused to compromise on dates and let the opportunity slip. He did minor pieces of journalism, such as an article commissioned by *Nova* for the series 'God & I', which was spiked when the series ended at Christmas. *Nova* paid him a generous £70, whereas the BBC paid only forty guineas for 'Christmas Sermon', which later appeared in the Catholic weekly *The Tablet*.[23]

Early in December he left for Geneva to stay with John Berger and Anya in their flat in the industrial suburb of Meyrin. He enjoyed the warmth and sleek, impersonal modernity of the place and the steady writing routine he and John followed every morning. The invigorating mountain air of John's conversation, taking in Marx, God and Hölderlin, would inspire his apocalyptic poem 'Canticum', with its evocation of a kind of visionary madness

> *(Mountains awestricken like alchemists.*
> *The torn books have fermented.*
> *Then rivers and branches run down to me.*
> *And God has become young, has become just,*
> *the Holy Ghost is locked up in a book,*
> *and God is spitting natural fire),*[24]

and its final depiction of an antiseptically dystopian state in which children ran riot in museums, poets' minds remained blank and all memories of the past were obliterated. Then he left Geneva by sleeper for Venice and caught the Adriatic ferry to Piraeus.

'The regime is UNUTTERABLY bloody awful, but all right if you keep your eyes on sun, sea, squids and bronze statues,' he scribbled at the top of a letter to Cyril, whom he hoped to meet at the Leigh Fermors' in March. He made a token attempt to ignore the political situation, but was infuriated by the bland neutrality of Peter Fraser, the new director of the British School, whom he would caricature as a leaden academic in his archaeological thriller *The Head in the Soup*. There was an incident when he left a card on the British ambassador in Athens, provoking a telegram of complaint from a minor Embassy official to Fraser, who was in England at the time. Back at home, he was summoned to Whitehall and lectured by a 'highly stupefactious foreign office spy', who issued the kind of warning that such officials do to British subjects who threaten to cause embarrassments abroad.[25]

Knowing that nearly all Greek intellectuals from Seferis downwards loathed the military government, and that colleagues such as Vanna lived in permanent fear of raids and imprisonment, he could not help retailing atrocity stories to sympathetic English friends. When the military governor of northern Greece strode into Saloniki Cathedral in the middle of the Epiphany liturgy, the archbishop stopped officiating and walked out. He was immediately sacked and placed under house arrest. A priest in Piraeus was imprisoned for three weeks for succouring the children of communists who were in prison. Peter despaired for the opposition, since all young men were conscripted for National Service unless they went into exile abroad, and the horrors of the civil war were still too recent for many people to want to risk their lives by protesting openly.[26] Although the United States ambassador in Athens had disapproved of the military coup, the CIA, being closely linked with the anti-communist special forces behind the junta, had more effective influence. And Western liberals, appalled in 1968 by assassinations, conscription and race riots in the United States, napalming of children in Vietnam, Soviet bullying of Czechs, Israeli bullying of Arabs and the heavy-handedness of the French police towards student protesters in Paris, had little energy to spare for Greece apart from deciding to spend their holidays elsewhere.

Peter, however, could not leave the question of the prisoners and their families alone. His attachment to the Roman Catholic Cathedral in Athens put him in touch with some priests who privately told stories against the regime, although he gave up going to the cathedral and started saying Mass in his room after hearing a sermon in defence of the junta.[27] Naively, he hoped to be able to operate as a clergyman in a way that he was forbidden to act as a member of the British School. His idea was to appeal to all the Church authorities in Athens to ask the Minister of the Interior, the tough Cretan Stylianos Pattakos, one of the three senior army officers behind the April coup, for permission to provide food and clothing for the prisoners' families. All of them, including the Anglican, whom Peter thought the most despicable, refused. 'But we must do something, mustn't we?' he appealed to Mollie. In frustration he joined Amnesty International, and secured a commission from *The Tablet* to report on the Stockholm conference in August 1968 at which the seven-year-old organization met to redefine its purposes.[28]

On top of everything, he had disappointing news about Pausanias. A new managing editor at Penguin had decided to cut production costs, and plans for the hardback had been scrapped, in spite of the money already spent on its illustrations.[29] The editor of Penguin Classics, the scholarly Betty Radice, remained largely in control of her list and brought out the two-volume paperback in 1971. But John Johnson's attempts to find other publishers for a de-luxe, illustrated version came to nothing.

Full of fight, Peter bounced back the following spring, announcing that he expected to be spending longer in Greece in future working on a 'huge new edition' of Pausanias.[30] He had found two Greek archaeologists to collaborate with him on a commentary on Book One, with its survey of Attica and full description of second-century Athens and its cults. It would have a bilingual text in modern Greek and English, and would be aimed at scholarly publishers in both England and Greece.

A special, translated Greek poetry issue of *Agenda*, edited and with contributions by Peter, came out early in 1969. Ranging from Homeric hymns to poems by Seferis and Odysseus Elytis, its content was a valiant, if not particularly useful, gesture of solidarity with Greece. Peter's mercifully brief editorial did little to clarify its message, rambling on about the classical backgrounds of certain English and American poets and the possible influence of ancient or modern Greek poetry on others; claiming that Milton, who had merely considered extending his Italian journey to Sicily and Greece, was almost 'the father of Greek archaeology' and 'the first systematic English traveller to the classical sites'; and asserting gnomically that the Austrian Georg Trakl was 'the only modern German poet who could possibly have been a Greek'.

In Athens, he had become convinced that he was being followed. Soon after his approaches to the Church authorities, a policeman turned up at the British School and asked to see him. He was out at the time and nothing further happened, except that he believed, probably rightly, that his movements were being watched. Were his followers from the Greek police, or had they been put on to him by the British Foreign Office?

Increasingly, he began to believe that the British or Americans were after him. He raged about this to David Pryce-Jones, whose father-in-law Lord Caccia had recently retired from the diplomatic service.

David passed back a message that the British ambassador in Athens had never heard of Peter. He made him promise not to telephone the Embassy and swear at the person who answered (although Peter said he reserved the right to continue swearing about them). Disagreeing fiercely with David's advice to keep his head down, he pointed out that, as an unattached priest in a foreign country, he had no institutional affiliations and none of a married person's obligations to keep quiet for his family's sake. With a churchman's humane interest and credibility as a witness of injustice, he was determined to continue his crusade. 'I am too old to be morally annihilated in that way.'[31]

Few people took Peter's sense of mission as seriously as he did. It was time he took a break from Greece to immerse himself in a country so remote and culturally alien that the lives of its inhabitants did not involve him, leaving him free to enjoy a sublimely wild landscape on its own. That possibility had been at the back of his mind since the first summer of the junta, and two years later it took shape.

16
AFGHAN ROSES

All my life I have wanted to travel in Central Asia; the discovery of a Greek city at Ay Khanoum, on the banks of the Oxus, just inside Afghanistan on the Russian border, was the final straw

The Light Garden of the Angel King (Preface to 1984 ed.) 12

Bruce Chatwin was a gauche but ambitious young Sotheby's employee, recently promoted from a porter to a junior antiquities expert, when Peter first met him in the autumn of 1961. Tony Mitchell had arranged for Bruce, his dealer friend Robert Erskine and the millionaire collector George Ortiz to fetch Peter from Heythrop on their way to visit George Spencer-Churchill at Northwick Park, near Moreton-in-Marsh. Their purpose was to inspect Spencer-Churchill's collections of pictures and Greek and Etruscan bronzes and try to persuade him to sell them through Sotheby's.

Peter, who had never seen such treasures in a private house before, was enraptured by their quality. He wrote to Mollie that he thought they beat even the Thyssen collection in grandeur. But he did not mention his new friend Bruce, with his sharp, angelic face, blond hair and laser-bright blue eyes. Intellectually curious, amusing and socially and professionally on the make, Bruce had charmed him with his naive eagerness and bitchy sense of humour. Peter, in turn, became a new person for Bruce to name-drop – a 'great friend', he told his Catholic future mother-in-law, when assuring her he would do everything in the religious line her family hoped for short of actually becoming a Catholic himself.[1]

In the summer of 1965 Bruce married Elizabeth Chanler, the American secretary of Sotheby's Bond Street chairman, in the private chapel of her family's home in upper New York State. He and several other promising young employees had just been made junior directors of the firm. A year later, however, aged twenty-six, he resigned from his job, telling friends he was fed up with being sent to act as bait to rich, elderly, homosexual collectors. He wanted a proper knowledge of antiquities instead of the conveyor-belt superficiality of auction-house scholarship. Frustration at being only a junior director increased his bitterness. Perhaps hoping to become a version of the young T.E. Lawrence, bargaining in *souks* for Hittite seals and digging in areas never previously mapped by white men, he applied to the University of Edinburgh to take a degree in archaeology.

Here Peter came into the picture as the kind of scholar Bruce most wanted to know. To please Elizabeth, who liked a country life, he had agreed to spend money from her mother on a farmhouse in the steep, almost sunless Ozleworth valley near Wotton-under-Edge. Peter found the setting fascinating.

> You more often meet a fox or a badger than a human being down there. It leads nowhere, it comes from nowhere. The valley floor is grass, but its walls are hanging woods dripping with dew and resounding with the voices of birds. The valley runs a long way, like a cleft in the rocks; no road leads into it, only a track. Near the valley head grows the remnant of a natural boxwood forest, more strange than beautiful. The trunks of the trees twist like ropes. Crawling through it is like dodging among greenish silver ropes entangled everywhere, behind the scenes of some petrified theatre.[2]

But while Elizabeth loved the wild animals, birds and solitude of the valley, Bruce felt trapped there in vacations and liked to drive over to Oxford to use the libraries and talk to Peter, whom he found more stimulating than his Edinburgh professor, the mild-mannered but emotionally possessive historian of the Neolithic period, Stuart Piggott. Elizabeth sometimes went with him and walked her cat in the

Botanic Garden while Bruce closeted himself in Campion Hall with his tame Oxford don.

At first he deferred to Peter, enjoying his eclectic knowledge and red-hot literary enthusiasms. Peter introduced him, as he did James Fenton, to the writings of Osip Mandelstam, which Bruce later acknowledged as a major influence on his taut and vibrant style.[3] In return he told stories about his holidays in Afghanistan: one summer combing the bazaars of Kabul for antiquities with Robert Erskine, the next on a failed botanical errand to the mountains of Nuristan. Romantically drawn to the wild spaces of Central Asia, he yearned to blend into them, Kim-like, and describe them with the casual wit of Robert Byron's pre-war travelogue *The Road to Oxiana*. Archaeology, he soon discovered, was a static discipline, boringly reliant on teamwork and unsuited to someone who was always restlessly on the move. Fascinated by the idea of nomads, he decided after a couple of years at Edinburgh that he would rather study wandering herdsmen than stay in one place picking over burial mounds for potsherds, stones and bones.

Bruce was all boylike charm while his quasi-tutorial relationship with Peter lasted. At Campion Hall one day, James Fenton sensed a faint sexual frisson as Peter emerged from his room with Brendan and Bruce. That charm must have been particularly powerful during Bruce's first summer vacation, when, probably from boredom on his side and unhappiness on Peter's about Greece, they began to discuss the possibility of an Afghan trip together.

Without Bruce, Peter would never have considered venturing so far. The idea emerged as they discussed Alexander the Great's march from Persia into India in 327-326 BC. As he went, he had established a Greco-Bactrian kingdom south of the Oxus and left fortified cities along his route. Some of these had been clearly identified, like the remains of the city of Ai Khanum in the far north-east, where a major French-led excavation and reconstruction was taking place. Others, including some named by Strabo, might still be waiting under layers of dust for questing amateurs to find them. Peter thought an Afghan archaeological exploration would make a good subject for a book, although the idea made Nancy anxious in case it distracted him from finishing Pausanias.[4]

Bruce dropped out of Edinburgh before Christmas 1968, eager to become a writer like Peter and impatient with Piggott's insistence that he should take the full four-year course. Ignoring Sotheby's protocol about transferring loyalties to rival firms, he arranged to earn fees in strict secrecy as an occasional consultant for Christie's. He also charmed Tom Maschler, the editorial director of Jonathan Cape, into offering him a beginner's advance of £200 for a short, general book about nomads, to be based on researches in Afghanistan. Peter's intended travelogue, for which Bruce agreed to take photographs, raised only a £250 advance from Collins after Adrian quashed his suggestion of writing it in the rhythm of *Don Juan* or Wordsworthian blank verse.[5]

He and Bruce left England separately in June 1969. Bruce had an appointment on Christie's business in Cairo, so they agreed to meet in Tehran and spend a week becoming acclimatized to the heat in Persia (as Peter, like Nancy, called Iran). This was Peter's chance to visit his ancestral city of Istanbul. Staying in the old part of the city, Sultanahmet, he may have half-hoped to see someone with his own face, or the face of one of the Levi relatives he had seen in photographs. He did fantasize about a grandparental carpet shop, but those thoughts faded to nothing as he took in the dazzling water and sky-piercing minarets, the massive, ancient city walls, which he thought finer than those of Rome, the soaring interior of the dome of Hagia Sophia, 'a kind of transfiguration in architecture', and the collections of Greek sculpture from all over the Byzantine Empire in the archaeological museum.[6]

His world-view was beginning to shift. Until then Greece and

Rome had shaped it, but 'one can't visit Central Asia without being smitten by it,' he told Willie after getting back, adding that he had been converted to a new sort of history, not just a different landscape. Flying from Istanbul to Ankara, then Tehran and finally Kabul, he noticed the growing intensity of the light. The darkness was equally intense, even in Tehran, where he slept on the roof of the British School of Archaeology under a thick black sky full of unfamiliar constellations. Then there was the thrilling clarity of empty country, in which he could look down from thousands of feet on wrinkled mountains, shifting sand-dunes, a pipeline, a dried-out river bed, a cluster of yurts. He felt that the kind of history which had happened against such backgrounds moved not in a steady progression but in sweeps and loops like the uncoiling of a river across a plain.

His relationship with Bruce was also shifting. From Tehran Bruce took charge, although occasionally thwarted by Peter, who refused to agree to a bus-journey of over five hundred miles to Persepolis once they found the flights to Shiraz all booked up. Instead they flew to Isfahan, where he fell in love with the plain lines of the clay-brick mosques and their flower-spangled, cobalt-glazed tiles. Then, barely stopping back in Tehran, they were airborne again, flying eastwards over a baked desert which he saw as 'the metamorphosis of the skins of dead lions'.[7]

Almost the first thing that happened to them in hot, stuffy Kabul was a beating. Military security was tight in the fenced-off area below the towering ruined fortress of Bala Hisar. Peter subscribed to the nineteenth-century idea that the fortress, which had never been properly excavated, must represent the vanished city of Ortospana, which Strabo placed on a road running south from the ancient Zoroastrian city of Bactra (Balkh in northern Afghanistan, beyond the western Hindu Kush), through a mountain pass towards the Indus.[8]

Blithely assuming, in spite of Bruce's warning, that Afghan soldiers need not be taken seriously, he insisted they should investigate the potsherds they could see littering the ground inside the fence. At once an angry guard rushed up shouting and thrashed them both off the premises with his belt. Bruce felt particularly sore about that incident, blaming Peter's wrong-headedness and congratulating himself for having been triumphantly in the right. Every subsequent mention of Peter in his notebooks was condescending or irritable, complaining about his moans of discomfort, his conviction that every ruin they saw must be Hellenistic, or some fatuous passing utterance.[9] Peter's learning and seniority had begun to count for little once Bruce, supercharged with energy and know-how, was intent on catching him up.

They agreed in despising hippies, of whom there were large numbers in Kabul in a more or less permanently hashed-out state. One, however, a lonely homosexual named Nigel, attached himself to them on the strength of being fluent in Pashto and having been at Marlborough like Bruce.[10] In their shared room one night, Bruce complained furiously into his notebook that he could not sleep because Peter and Nigel were scribbling so intensely in their own notebooks that he, too, was forced to sit up and write, venting his irritation about Peter's tendency to draw a moral from every situation they discussed. The quarrel continued in secret, entirely on Bruce's side, in the cheap, red, cardboard-covered notebooks he crammed full of his tiny writing in ink. On most evenings Peter read out his own entries as he wrote them, urging Bruce to let him know if he had described something inaccurately or left something important out.

Occasional squabbles apart, they were still friends on a cultural level, with the solid bolster of literature between them. Bruce introduced Peter to the travel journal of the Japanese haiku master Bashō, a book Peter treasured for the rest of his life and had by his bedside when he died. With Bruce he shared Andrew Marvell's poems, to which

John Fuller had introduced him. Several weeks into their journey, they soothed their homesickness with Marvell's ode 'Upon Appleton House', with its praise for simple, seventeenth-century English vernacular architecture and gardens. They took turns to read from a volume of Lorca's poems. In a neglected, almost unspoilt garden of the sixteenth-century Mughal emperor Babur at Istalif, eighteen miles from Kabul, they read extracts to each other from a translation of Babur's memoirs, the *Baburnāma*.[11] In his tomb garden, the Bagh-e-Babur, a public park on a hill outside Kabul which was already half-wrecked by design rather than bombardment, they saw the mosque that Shah Jahan had erected in the seventeenth century to celebrate a victory at Balkh. A translation of the inscription over the entrance calls the mosque's setting, the Bagh-e-Babur, 'the light garden of the godforgiven angel king', from which Peter took the title of his book.[12]

In 1980, a year after the Russians began to tear the country apart, Bruce published a moving 'Lament for Afghanistan' as a foreword to a new edition of Robert Byron's *The Road to Oxiana*.[13] Readers may have wondered why, as he evidently knew the country so well and had visited it so often for pleasure, he had never written a book about it. His notebooks from the trip are full of sharp observations of buildings, landscapes, plants, people, and amusing or banal incidents and conversations. Some of the notes are finely written; a few are accompanied by sketches. Old Testament extracts and other references to religion suggest that he was intermittently pondering some profound scheme. He also drew up an outline of a narrative of their travels as if planning a book in direct competition with Peter's, although this did not go very far.[14]

While Bruce was too fascinated by everything around him to concentrate on thinking about nomads, Peter's mind hovered high above archaeology. He had told Willie that he wanted to see both Greek and Parthian ruins and try to work out what kind of relationship had existed between the last Greeks and first Buddhists. Before leaving England he had immersed himself in Buddhist scriptures and studied Buddhist art in museums. He may have felt some kinship with the American Trappist Thomas Merton, who had gone east the previous year to study Buddhist spirituality and died of an electric shock in Bangkok. In the Afghan mountains he was in a Buddhist dream, inspired by clear blue skies and ice-caps, the lines of shimmering poplars along the river-banks and the giant stupas, small shrines and domed hermitages at Bamiyan. 'The pure teachings of Gautama Buddha are like snow-water,' he wrote.[15]

Drunk on landscape, he and Bruce visited the Buddhas of Bamiyan on one of their first trips out of Kabul. From Charikar, north of Kabul, they followed the Gorband valley westwards in a beat-up Russian taxi. Peter noticed how the wind brought the smell of distant clover and balsam poplars into the closed car and intensified the 'snowglitter' and 'snakeglitter' of the higher and lower peaks. At Chardeh he saw his first Afghan bus, a gaudily decorated open lorry covered in old-fashioned, sentimental landscape scenes which Bruce thought were like coloured postcards from British India in the 1920s and 1930s.[16]

Thirty-two years before the Taliban blew them up, the two huge images towered in their niches as if only a nuclear war could destroy them. Their features, carved from perishable material, had worn or been cut away, but their bodies, hewn out of the mountain, were rock-solid. Peter and Bruce climbed through cavernous, stepped galleries to stand on a Buddha's head as tourists did, then on through carved grottoes where Peter claimed he saw Hellenistic elements in the Buddhist clay statues that lined them. They explored the valleys round Bamiyan, climbing one day over a thousand feet towards the summit of Koh-i-Baba, where they found a ruined, seventh-century clay-brick castle unknown to the French archaeologists who were studying fortifications in the area. Peter was scared by the 'jackhammering' of his heart and nearly paralysed with exhaustion from the climb, but relaxed as they came down through rocky fields, where meadowsweet, orchids, sorrel, cranesbill, fennel and vetch flourished wildly among the crops of lucerne, flowering bean-plants and grain. Below these they found bushes of wild single roses, whose scent wafted up to meet them in advance.[17]

After a wind-battered flight in a tiny plane over the mountains to Kabul, they rested for several days in a garden in the diplomatic compound. The friendly Oriental Secretary at the British Embassy, Christopher Rundle, had opened his house to them. Peter loved the vast Embassy gardens and the visiting hoopoes, birds associated with Greek legend which he thought confirmed a Greco-Afghan link, although by then they were almost extinct in Greece.[18] Human interest was provided by taxi-drivers high on opium, singing loudly as they drove into the city in the morning; hippies, on whom Bruce later blamed the political ruin of the country; even a group of supposed ex-Nazis, who, turning up at a ball in full, swaggering SS uniform, were said to have picked a fight and been ducked *en masse* in the club swimming-pool.[19]

They had meant to fly west to Herat, then swing south and east to Kandahar and back north to Kabul on the usual tourist track. Having Nigel to interpret for them, however, they decided to seek out some nomads at a large fair at Chagcheran, a desert town with a tiny airfield half-way to Herat. Disappointingly, the fair was over when they arrived, and most of the nomads they spotted from the plane had been moving away. At a camp of the Pashtun tribe of Kuchi, whose men travelled north every year to trade artefacts for sheep, only forty tents were left out of the thousand that had been there the week before. A disillusioned Bruce noted tribesmen with hernia, goitre, catarrh, fever and bloodshot eyes. His nomad research was clearly going to be less fun than he had hoped, and he felt nervous of catching fleas. Peter enjoyed the men's sly humour, which he only half-understood, their flourishing of chintz-covered rifles, their beautiful horses and ferocious dogs. He made a joke of having to retire into the sand-dunes, repeating the saying 'Desert is toilet, all Chagcheran is desert, all Chagcheran is toilet.'[20]

More rewarding was the minaret of Jam, a soaring, diminishing

column of intricately patterned brickwork at the apex of a gorge of sheer cliffs where the Jam river meets the deeper, faster Hari Rud. To reach Jam, among saw-toothed mountain peaks, they caught a lorry from Chagcheran to Shahrak, then made a fourteen-hour trek on horseback with a boy and a soldier to guide them. Peter was cross and feverish with dysentery and had to stop at least once to throw up. It must have been on the return journey that he sat smiling under a turban on his skewbald pony, between the soldier and a cheerfully squinting, turbaned Bruce, while Nigel took the photograph with Bruce's camera that appears on page 96 of *The Light Garden of the Angel King* and on the cover of the paperback edition.

At Herat they loved the faded, grandiose comfort of the Park Hotel, where Robert Byron had stayed in the 1930s. They would have spent longer enjoying the bazaar and the glittering colours of the minarets and mausoleum, but for the sudden realization that there was cholera in the city. Packing up at the hotel, they fled by taxi along the hippy route to Kandahar, more than three hundred miles to the south-east.

The desert city founded by Alexander was stiflingly hot and squalid, under a permanent cloud of brown dust. They both noted the hair-oil taste of the Coca-Cola and the stupefaction of half the population by hashish. Bruce was scornful when Peter insisted that the city walls must be the surviving ancient Greek fortifications. He was exasperated on the bus back north, when Peter complained that his neighbour was expectorating all over him and that this was the last bus-journey he would ever take.[21] Having assumed that Elizabeth would dislike Asia, Bruce now felt desperate for her company. He urged her to fly to Kabul and join them in the north-east of the country, before travelling back with them (as they hoped) across the Anjuman Pass in the northern Hindu Kush.

'This is not a book about people,' Peter stated clumsily in a footnote, before remarking on Elizabeth's 'unusual qualities'.[22] His book was supposed to be about archaeological discoveries, and on the rich northern plain between the Hindu Kush and the Pamirs he tried hard to concentrate on his subject. They visited Balkh, an important but depressing ruin where archaeologists had failed to find Greek levels below the mud-brick late Islamic ones. Then, following up a Russian description, they found a decorated ninth-century mosque which electrified Peter as 'a lost meeting-point of Sassanian and Islamic art'.[23] Once, near Baghlan, he thought he had stumbled on an ancient settlement mound full of fragments of Kushan pottery from the first to the third century AD, until Bruce pointed out that you could find modern pottery like it in the bazaar in Kunduz.[24] At Surkh Kotal, a recently excavated royal Kushan site, he was impressed to find a 'big Hellenistic agora, lavishly marbled and pillared', but conceded that its scale was Iranian rather than Greek. At Tashkurgan he had himself driven to inspect yet another group of pottery-littered mounds, leaving Bruce to read Marvell in the green shade of a garden whose owner fed him slice after slice of different kinds of melon.[25]

From Kunduz, a town owned by the Spinzar industrial firm, Bruce left by taxi to fetch Elizabeth from Kabul. Peter was left alone in the slow-moving, chenar-shaded city, with its traffic of pony-carriages and bicycles, its laden camels and Uzbek boys on barebacked horses, its convoys of departing melon-lorries, and its main-street conjuror who swallowed needles and pebbles, made obscene gestures with a wooden phallus and waved handfuls of snakes in the faces of passers-by.

Forty years later, the brutalized city of Kunduz was in the centre of a war-zone. On September 4, 2009, allied forces mounted a retaliatory air-strike which killed over a hundred civilians a few kilometres to the south. But to Peter, that August, the city was a place of deep, melon-scented calm. After inspecting the taxi bazaar, he announced to the local museum officials that it contained several half-buried classical pillar-bases and remnants of Kushan stone carving, obviously from 'some big public building in a pure Greco-Roman style,' he told Mollie. He made friends with the youngish patron of the local theatre, Tawab, and a poet, accountant and comic actor, Wazir Mohammed, and spent afternoons with them potting at coins with Tawab's rifle in a garden full of purple flowers.

> *Wooroo of wild birds in a ragged garden.*
> *A gunshot hardly motions them at all*
> *banging away at sixpence in the wall.*
> *I choose peace, and the dumbness of this season.*[26]

Then Bruce and Elizabeth arrived. Elizabeth noticed that Peter had lost weight and no longer limped. ('I am... of an Indian complexion & a sylph-like thinness and beauty,' he wrote to Mollie a few weeks later.) In Kunduz they ate rice, lamb, vegetables, salad and fruit, and in the mountains they sometimes survived on brandy and biscuits. Bruce had obtained a *firman* which allowed them to cross the Anjuman Pass, 15,000 feet above sea-level between the high peaks of the Hindu Kush. This should take them down into the Panjshir valley near the border with Pakistan, from which it would be easy to get back by road to Kabul.

Banged around in the back of a Russian-built jeep, they were driven for thirteen hours along pebbly drovers' tracks and up dry river-beds to Faizabad, in the north-eastern corner of the country on the rocky River Kokcha. 'This road is *kharob* [fucked], all Afghanistan is *kharob*,' said their driver.[27] At the police-station in Faizabad they were told that, because of a technical error when the original *firman* had been written out in Kabul, they could not, after all, cross the pass. For several days they hung around by the noisy Kokcha, while Elizabeth mended Peter's torn jeans and he, amazed by the river, marvelled at the height of the wild rose-bushes above the gorge.

> *Tree of roses. The water crashed headlong*

tearing the darkness out of the stone face,

he began a poem which ends on a characteristic note of gloomy uplift:

whatever lives has inward boundaries.
God has none, he is natured like a stone
frosteaten and sunbitten and alone.[28]

Echoing these lines, he ended an elegy for a friend thirteen years later by comparing him with *an old stone/upright, raineaten, mooneaten, alone.*[29] By then his impression of the limestone rocks of the Kokcha valley may have blended with an older, Heythrop memory of the ancient, wind-eaten Hawk Stone, fretted on one side and with a single, round hole at the top, in an arable field on a south-facing hillside between Spelsbury and Chipping Norton.

Allowed only as far as the pass, they took a crammed public lorry as far as Jurm. Elizabeth had adopted a quail that some Faizabad children had been teasing and took it home with her in a covered birdcage. Wearing his turban in an orchard outside Jurm, Peter surprised the Frantzes, an American doctor, and his wife and three young daughters, who had crossed the pass on foot from the south and were heading for Faizabad. Their practicality, health and good nature humbled Peter and Bruce, who had assumed until then that they must be the best-informed and most enterprising western travellers in the whole of Afghanistan.

Their last stop on the journey was Bahrak, a small town just below the frontier area of the Wakhan where Tajikistan begins. There were mulberry and apple trees, tall white hollyhocks and vines coiling up into poplars. The Warduj river roared down with great force under its cantilevered bridge, feeding irrigation canals on the hillsides. They slept in the Club, a grim, kitchenless building with a doorless lavatory which opened straight into the bedroom. In the teahouse with its Russian samovar and portrait of Mao, nobody could tell them how close they were to China. Many of the people they chatted to had been as far as Faizabad, but none to Kabul.[30]

By mid-August they were back in the monsoon heat of the Embassy garden, after flying with the Frantzes to Kunduz, then taking a diversion through Herat. They had planned a last trip to Nuristan, on the southeastern slopes of the Hindu Kush, where Bruce had fallen ill on his abortive botanical quest five years earlier. This time Christopher Rundle went with them. He arranged for an Embassy Land Rover to take them the ninety-odd miles east to Jalalabad, where the British had holed up in flight from Kabul in 1841-42, and then a similar distance into the mountains to the north-east. At Kamdeh, the highest navigable point on a stony track, they stopped, bargained in the village for porters and camped. They were to be picked up many days later at Kamdesh, at the head of another track beyond a mountain pass at fifteen thousand feet.

Close to the Pakistan border, and high above the Pech valley, they entered an area which, forty years later, was torn apart by fighting between the Americans and the Taliban. At that time, however, the people of Kamdeh were chiefly afraid of the next villagers up the mountain. To protect them the porters brought the local policeman, who helped to carry the sleeping-bags, waterproofs, medicines, guns, the Chatwins' tent, a small stove for baking chappatis and some tinned food from the Embassy which they may have dumped or sent back uneaten. Meals were sketchy and occasionally consisted of no more than swigs of brandy. At night Bruce, Elizabeth and sometimes Christopher burrowed into the tent, while the others lay round a smoky fire in whatever shelter they could find. The porters kept their guns at the ready in case of wolves, which were only a distant threat, and snow leopards, which once or twice they saw streaking away through the woods. Peter was particularly proud of himself for having identified snow leopard's dung.

Exhilarated by the high, thin air, and by the layers of walnut and birch woods, deodars, junipers and wild roses above the snow-line, he felt strong and confident, and coaxed Elizabeth when she was nervous of heights. ('Peter was so brave,' she remembered.) Once, having left the porters behind, the three or four of them were crossing a plank over a mountain torrent when they noticed a group of hunters on the far side pointing rifles at their heads. Bruce screamed at Elizabeth to stop. Peter urged her on, and they wobbled across the stream and sat down, silent and nervous, under a tree. Then Peter pacified the men with cigarettes, followed by helpings of Fribourg and Treyer's most powerful snuff. At Jurm he had already made friends with an old man who took a giant pinch of it, sneezed, wept, laughed and then begged for more to ease his gummed-up eyes. Afghans carried coarse, green snuff for chewing, in little mirrored boxes; it had 'the same smell of herbs and donkey-dung as a hillpath on a hot day'.[31]

Still climbing, they passed through villages of former Kafir or pagan tribes, whose inhabitants had been forcibly converted to Islam in the late nineteenth century, after which their country became Nuristan instead of Kafiristan. They had hoped to cross the mountain by the Kungani Pass, but a villager misled them into traversing a snowy col which brought them out high above the Anjuman, before following the Nichingul river down towards Kamdesh. 'The whole walk was thrilling from beginning to end,' Peter wrote to Mollie: '– waterfalls lashing & streaking down hundreds of feet, & high valleys where nothing will grow but juniper, & the air smells of sun, snow & gin.'

Back in Kabul at the beginning of September, the party broke up. Bruce and Elizabeth left for Pakistan, but Peter did not go too because his visa would not have allowed him back into the country to visit a politically sensitive area in the far north. While waiting for permission do this he made contact with Maurizio Tosi, a young Italian archaeological director based in Iran, who took him to the excavation of an early Buddhist monastery at Ghazni in the south. He might go farther south (he wrote to Mollie) to see the 'classical or medieval elephant stables' at Lashkar Ghar, since he knew the proprietors of a cotton factory there.

Then it was time to visit the excavation of Ai Khanum, at the confluence of the Kokcha and the Amu Darya (Oxus), near the border between Russia and Afghanistan. Hiring a Land Rover and driver, he sped north through the Salang tunnel, stopped overnight in Kunduz to look up Tawab, then headed on towards the northern plain.

'The most exciting thing was the steppe,' he told Willie that autumn,

> a desert of rough pasture extending for what appear to be endless infinities towards the forbidden area of the Oxus & the Russian border. I did in the end get to the Oxus, & within a stone's throw of Russia: there was not one sentry, not one soldier or policeman, but once I heard a shepherd's flute playing on the Russian side. Otherwise Russia as far as I can see is uninhabited, although there were beautiful woods higher up the river (I was at Ay Khanum) & once the very distant lights of a car.

'Central Asia is the place for us, isn't it?' he wrote to David Pryce-Jones, adding that he could not live there but had been thrilled by the spiritually energising effect of its clear air and huge horizons. As on the Taÿgetos mountains, he had felt an immanence in the landscape. 'Babur & Babel speak the same language & about the same people... Is it silly, but I think it may be the only language in which to talk about God.'

He was struggling to write the second chapter of his book, and hating himself for brushing the dust off the butterfly's wing of his notebook entries. Should he write a straight, structured account, like those of the great Victorian travellers he admired, or something more experimental? Rejecting the old-fashioned approach, he produced a narrative that was closely based on his notebook entries, but with archaeological passages and footnotes to give it ballast. He had reckoned, however, without Bruce's sensitivities about the impressions and descriptions they had shared.

'Most of our best observations and all the best jokes were his,' Peter wrote disarmingly in a preface to the 1984 Penguin edition.[32] By then, however, the damage had been done. Despite the inclusion of his impressive photographs of bearded tribesmen, loaded pack-animals and the Jam minaret, Bruce was both scornful and resentful when *The Light Garden of the Angel King: Journeys in Afghanistan* came out in 1972. Passages he had improved on during the notebook-reading sessions had been used without acknowledging his input, and felt to him like plagiarism. Twenty-eight years later, when both Peter and he were dead, a travelogue reprint firm packaged the book with a new subtitle that might have appeased him: *Travels in Afghanistan with Bruce Chatwin.*

17
MY POOR LOST BROTHER

Say what it was, what were you looking for
in the darkness, in the trees, in the cold?
My brother who has for so long understood
the fruit on the fruit trees and is lost now.

Life is a Platform (1971) 23

Between touching down from Kabul and beginning the Oxford
autumn term, Peter made a quick dash to the United States. George
Seferis had spent the previous autumn at the Institute of Advanced
Study in Princeton, preparing the lacerating attack on the junta that
he would deliver in Greece in the spring. At a conference of Modern
Greek specialists at Princeton that September, Peter read a paper
about Seferis's poetical language, which he called 'Mr Seferis's Tone of
Voice'. He was nervous about the prospect and uncertain, afterwards,
how his paper had been received, but hoped he had 'illuminated some
fragments'. When David Pryce-Jones left for Athens to write an article
about the opposition to the junta, Peter asked him to tell Seferis he had
been lecturing on him, and take him some Sobranie Smoking Mixture
with his love.[1]

Keyed up for his own return to Greece, he found Oxford expensive,
dim and flat. He felt bored with classical scholarship and archaeology,
and after the summer's travels was in a mood in which only language
mattered. He enthused to Nancy about his discovery of the medieval
Shetland ballad 'King Orfeo', with its two-line refrain about the spring
migration of deer into the greenwood,

> *Scowan ürla grün*
> *Whar giorten han grün oarlac,*

the kind of mysteriously unattributed quotation he would scatter through his memoir *The Flutes of Autumn* or insert into a didactic poem.

There were other, more complicated reasons for his unease. By the end of the 1960s Catholic churches in England, as everywhere else, had been affected by the Second Vatican Council's recommendations for change, which meant diluting the centuries-old, universal ritual as well as relaxing some of the more oppressive rules. The sonorous Tridentine Mass, previously celebrated in Latin, gave way to flat vernacular translations. Jingly, kindergarten-style hymns, sometimes with guitar accompaniments, ousted fire-breathing Victorian favourites. Catholics were still theoretically forbidden artificial birth-control, and abortion was still condemned as a mortal sin, but the faithful were no longer expected to make weekly confessions or to fast from midnight before taking communion. Instead of devoutly ignoring one another throughout Mass, they were encouraged to share the sign of peace by exchanging smiling handshakes with as many other participants as they could reach.

The changes affected Jesuits, too. Scholastics left off their clerical dress and went round like ordinary students in open-necked shirts and jeans. Nobody knew where they were any more, complained Brendan McLaughlin, who left the Jesuits when part-way towards a postgraduate philosophy degree. Grim old Heythrop College closed in 1970, after struggling for five years to establish itself as a Pontifical Academy offering degree courses in philosophy and theology to lay students and religious scholastics. When it reopened in a former Mayfair convent, with the Jesuit historian of philosophy Frederick Copleston as Principal, it did so as a specialist college of London University. The curriculum in the remaining seminaries became more liberal, and Latin was no longer required. It was a shame, said Kevin Donovan, who still taught at the college in his seventies after it had moved to Kensington, that the reforms had come too late to prevent large numbers of disgruntled Jesuits from leaving, and benefited only the tiny handful of new recruits.

Anthony had gone with the flow, which included encouraging more Jesuits into academic jobs. Disciplined, efficient and focused, he had been a major asset to Campion Hall. Even before becoming a tutor in 1964, he had used his spare time at Heythrop to begin an Oxford D.Phil. thesis on the theory of the passions among seventeenth-century French moralists. Peter had wondered if he, too, ought to acquire a doctorate while teaching at Campion Hall, but was soon persuaded that it would be a waste of time.

Two years into his Campion Hall post, Anthony began to crave more varied teaching experience and took an additional job as a college lecturer in French at Christ Church, earning £500 a year for six hours' tutoring a week during term-time. Always happy abroad, especially in Italy (when he dropped into the Harvard study centre at I Tatti from Settignano, the director considered him 'very mondain' for a Jesuit),[2] he nurtured a short-lived ambition to become professor of canon law at the Gregorian University in Rome. In 1966 he took an intensive summer course in canon law at Bellarmine College in upstate New York; but by the following summer Bellarmine had closed down and he had given up the idea. Curious to find out more about American universities, he spent an enjoyable summer in New York, giving lectures and taking classes at the Jesuit-run Fordham University in the Bronx and spending his dollars on bottles of Scotch and cab-rides in and out of Manhattan.[3]

That autumn he joined the academic mainstream as Reader in French at the University of Warwick. Still nominally attached to Campion Hall, he reduced his commitment to Christ Church and spent a night or two in Oxford every week to meet his teaching obligations, paying a proportion of his earnings to the Jesuits. Before long he had both a car and a flat, arguing that he could not be expected to live like a student in the Catholic chaplaincy at Warwick. The car was a rakish Triumph Vitesse, which he drove very fast between Coventry and Oxford. Striding up and down the campus in brightly coloured clothes, puffing at a foul-smelling pipe, he cut an extroverted, aggressively energetic figure. University life with proper status suited him, and he crammed in as much intellectual and cultural activity as he could. Women students were intrigued by the argumentative, forty-year-old bachelor Dr. Levi, who responded with frankly sexual interest. What had he been missing all these years? Like other celibates of his generation, he began to wonder if it was time to find out.[4]

Anthony's new lifestyle offended Peter. His own wayward version of Jesuitism was one thing, but Anthony's seemed grossly materialistic. Its chief benefit to him was that he inherited Anthony's room at Campion Hall. Instead of a standard bedsitter on a corridor in the main building, he now had the first-floor back room of the old house next door, Micklem Hall. It had been a student lodging-house when the Jesuits bought it to develop their site, and before that a private house with a backyard brewery, the last owners of which, in the early nineteenth century, had been Micklems. Brewer Street's earlier name had been Slaying Lane or Slaughter Lane, and the Trill Mill Stream, which passed the ends of the gardens on the south side of the street, had carried butchers' offal and sewage from domestic privies as well as powering a water-wheel connected with the brewery equipment. Long before Peter's day the stream had been placed in a culvert, which thrill-seeking young men (including Peter himself, someone thought) liked to navigate by torchlight and canoe from a gurgling black hole near the Castle to an opening on the far side of St. Aldates, before the ends were closed up with gratings. Micklem Hall now had a neat, characterless back garden overlooked by the Georgian sash window of Peter's room.

Visitors pushed open the street door under a little pediment, climbed the stairs and turned the corner of a passage past a rocking-horse left over from some previous phase in the house's history. In the centre of the room stood Bert's old leather armchair, and on every wall were shelves filled with books; Deirdre saw the room as a shrine to books. Visitors for whom there were not enough chairs would perch on the edge of the book-laden bed. On a pile of books by the door Peter kept his dusty, inverted mortar-board with a supply of stamps in the crown. The electric fire was usually switched on, with a sleeping-bag dangerously close to it on the floor. Quiet classical music played on the radio, which was permanently tuned to Radio Three.

Back in Athens he also moved house. Already fearing expulsion from the British School for his entanglements with the Embassy and the police, he had told Mollie at the beginning of the year that he was thinking of taking a flat. In December, finding that his membership of the School had been revoked, he moved temporarily to an address nearby, then found a refuge in Miranda's neighbourhood, Mets.

It was not a conventional living-space, although he called it a *retiré* or penthouse flat. Most apartment buildings of a certain age in that part of Athens have a small, square hovel, originally built as a drying-room or maid's room, on the roof. Peter's, above a modest 1930s block of flats on a hilly corner, 1 Odos Miniati, had windows on three sides. It was reached from outside by a rickety fire-escape, and was next to the communal laundry which served him as a bathroom.[5] The landlord, keen to exploit every inch of the building, had equipped it with a single bed and a tiny hotplate or gas-ring on which he could boil a kettle. 'It has an awful lot of blazing blue light in the morning, like a hermitage, which I like,' he wrote to David Pryce-Jones,

> and a huge old Turkish carpet from before the Smyrna disaster, & one can write in it, [and] if necessary which it never is cook in it, & I have a record of Monteverdi & one of Dowland, & a gramophone. Bought in gallon jars very good wine is 10/- a

gallon.

Best of all, he told Willie, was the view, 'looking across at the Parthenon on equal terms & down to the sea through a biochemical mist'.[6]

The Watsons had gone away, leaving a tenant who gave Peter the carpet, but Vanna and her husband lived nearby and offered him a standing invitation to dinner. Usually, however, he ate out with friends in tavernas. He told Mollie that he paid the equivalent of about £11 a month for the room, plus ten shillings for water, electricity and telephone calls. For an extra twenty-five shillings a maid, Pagona, came in once a week to wash his clothes and clean the room, and would cook for him on the hotplate if he liked. He planned to have his own telephone installed, and was having writing-paper printed.

Seferis's seventieth birthday fell on February 28, 1970, according to the Julian calendar which had been in use among Christians in the Ottoman Empire in 1900.[7] Athenian poets and intellectuals celebrated that day in recognition of his status as the nation's most famous poet and champion of freedom in defiance of the junta. Then on March 13, Seferis's birthday according to the Gregorian calendar, Peter delivered his Princeton lecture to an enthusiastic audience in Athens. The British Embassy and the British Council in Athens, backed up by various American officials, almost managed to prevent the lecture until Seferis intervened. Peter was told to lecture in English but was allowed to answer questions in Greek, and circulated printed copies of a Greek translation of his text. Seferis thought it tactful to stay away, but his wife Maro represented him and the hall was packed.[8]

At Kardamyli, a week or two earlier, Peter had met Cyril Connolly. After the lecture he sent him an exultant postcard from Patras, telling him that it had gone off peacefully and well 'with a funny aftermath until 3 in the morning, & full page reports in the next day's papers'. The papers were, of course, those not directly controlled by the junta. Spring had arrived, with judas trees in mauve flower, and he was on a 'drunken happy journey through the provinces'.[9] With Takis Sinopoulos he was touring north-western Greece and Corfu before catching a ferry to Brindisi to arrive home in time for the Jesuit Easter retreat. Only his last few hours in Corfu, after Takis had said goodbye, gave a frightening twist to the trip.

The Athenian police had found out his address in Mets, but the landlord had covered up for him whenever they came round without bothering to tell him they had been. As he waited on the Corfu quayside, however, uniformed men closed in on him and hauled him off to the police station in the town. This was evidently a more serious arrest than the business about manuscripts on Patmos. Although realizing that he must be on a blacklist, he told himself that a well-connected foreigner was the least likely person to be tortured or made to disappear. Even so, the policemen's impassive faces and the brutal reek of sweaty uniforms and stale cigarette smoke alarmed him. The Corfu prison was notoriously vile, and once he was handcuffed anything might happen. He waited for nearly an hour while telephone calls were made to one office after another, until permission came through for his release.[10] After that he felt uncertain what to do in future. Should he return to Greece in the summer as he had planned, or would it be more prudent to stay away?

Early that summer he did go back briefly with Bruce, who hoped to combine work on his nomad book with holidaying in a rich, chattering crowd on Patmos. Now openly homosexual, he had begun to drift away from Elizabeth, although he still wrote her affectionately gossipy letters. In Athens, he told her, he and 'the Father' spent two nights with friends of Peter's – possibly Iain and Miranda, who were on the point of leaving for Istanbul. He loved the room in Mets for its view, and Peter told him he could stay there whenever he did not need it himself. But he also charmed Miranda and her mother, and from Patmos he and Mougouch Phillips went to Kardamyli, where he became Paddy and Joan's new best friend. Peter, with work to do in England, took the consolation prize of a quiet August in the Watsons' exotically draped Yarnton flat.[11]

He expected his Pausanias translation to be published in January 1971, and hoped that Collins would bring out *The Light Garden of the Angel King* that Easter, although they delayed publication for more than another year. Meanwhile Betty Radice had commissioned him to make a prose translation of the Psalms for Penguin Classics, perhaps hoping it would share the popularity of the *New English Bible* and its spin-offs. He had begun the work in February at Kardamyli and continued with it at Yarnton, when not exploring the neighbourhood or entertaining guests to lunch on whole poached salmon from the fishmongers in Oxford's Covered Market.

Always enthusiastic about new places, even in the flat land north of Oxford, he raved about the 'dreamlike' Jacobean house, down a dead-end lane next to the church, remote from the suburban ribbon development along the main road but close to the main Oxford to Worcester railway line. He became an expert on the intricate conjunctions of the railway, the Evenlode, the Thames and the canal, telling Willie that he had been exploring abandoned tracks, probably on the old Witney and Fairford line, and that one could 'climb up signals or get lost between loops and branches, particularly at night'. He guessed that the line in Belloc's poem 'The Evenlode' about 'Yarnton's tiny docks of stone' must refer to Duke's Cut, a channel with a lock which links the canal with the Thames between Yarnton and Wolvercote.[12]

Translating the Psalms was heavy going. He worked hard, finishing the first fifty at Yarnton, with a hundred still to go. As well as reading the Hebrew, Greek and Latin versions he consulted several German ones, including Martin Buber's, which he loved. True to the predominant Hebrew term he used the word 'God' throughout (even in the disconcerting 'God is my shepherd' in Psalm 23), rather than 'the Lord' as in the Hebrew *Adonai*, Greek *Kyrios* or Latin *Dominus*. Some Hebrew scholars criticised his scholarship fiercely, although at least one reviewer praised his version for its colourfulness. He dedicated the translation to the memory of Fraenkel, who had killed himself in February 1970, soon after his wife's death.

Toiling at a Biblical translation was not the only way in which he fell into line as a Jesuit. During the six years since his ordination he had functioned only minimally as a priest, saying Masses alone or with small Jesuit congregations, preaching the occasional public sermon and baptizing babies of Catholic friends. Now it was suggested that he might spend at least part of the summer vacations experiencing a working priest's daily grind. In September he admitted to 'occasional gaieties like saying special Masses for the I.R.A. prisoners in the top security wing at Brixton'.[13] This was evidently a gradual introduction; in 1972 he told Bertie that he would be 'incarcerated in Brixton' to relieve Tony Lawn for eight days or so in September, although a long trip abroad that summer may have cancelled the arrangement. He certainly did duty in Brixton in August 1973, and again during subsequent summers.

After finishing up at Yarnton he had tensions to cope with at Eastbourne. Several years earlier Mollie had moved to a house in Saffrons Road, which she shared with a lady companion in an intermittent state of emotional stress. Earlier that year, at sixty-seven, she had suffered her first stroke, and in spite of making a good recovery she was upset. Apart from a natural fear of dying she felt deserted by her one-time model son, since Anthony felt stifled by the atmosphere of the house and her constant demands for help. When he stayed with her that summer he took a favourite Warwick graduate student, Honor Riley, for company. Surprising them in the sitting-room when she was supposed to be lying down, Mollie was scandalized to find Honor, in tennis shorts, sitting on Anthony's knee. All her illusions about her chaste, priestly elder son fell apart, and Peter, visiting her in September, was almost equally shocked. Anthony had always been the hard-line Jesuit against whose position he could rebel; now, worryingly, their positions seemed to be reversed.

&

Two slim hardback collections of Peter's poems were published by Anvil in the autumn of 1971. Their titles, *Life is a Platform* and *Death is a Pulpit* (perhaps reversing the original meaning), came from Cesar Vallejo's 'Sermon on Death',

> *¡Pupitre, sí, toda la vida; púlpito,*
> *también, toda la muerte!*[14]

Life is a Platform included his lyrical poems from Kardamyli, Crete and Afghanistan. After appending the Afghan poems to *The Light Garden of the Angel King*, he maintained that they were 'the nut of the book'.[15] *Death is a Pulpit* contained more formal, public poems: his lament for Eliot, 'New Year's Eve 1965', the shudderingly gloomy 'Christmas Sermon 1967', and two further sermons in verse, 'Sermon on St Thomas More', for the Catholic church in Cheyne Walk on More's feast-day in July 1968, and 'Whitsunday Sermon', for the Catholic Chaplaincy in Cambridge in 1969. All three of these were in his favourite didactic form of pentametric rhyming couplets.

The same bafflingly indistinct photograph appears on the dust jackets of both volumes, one on grey paper, the other on dusty pink, although irrelevant to the content of either book. Its subject is a massive, scrub-clad Cretan mountainside with a small, remote village at the foot. Alones, a former centre of resistance to the German occupation, was the village to which Peter's friend in Athens, Gustavo Durán, had given a piped water-supply. Early in 1969 he had been struck down with heart disease, and Peter, although desperate to leave Athens and join the Watsons at Kardamyli, had sat by his bed every afternoon, knowing that Bontë liked having him there. Gustavo had died in late March and been buried, as he wished, in the cemetery at Alones. Two years later the local people arranged a ceremony in his honour, adding a bust and memorial tablet to the public tap in the centre of the village. Bontë was unable to travel, so Peter, tender-hearted towards friends' widows, agreed to go in her place.

This time he took Brendan with him. That Easter vacation was the one in which Brendan should have been revising for Schools, but Peter persuaded him that a walk through Crete would be just the thing to clear his mind for the philosophy papers. Early in March the two of them left Oxford on an early-morning train. They lunched with Dominique de Grunne at Overton's ('I had *sole au diable*,' remembered Brendan), then crossed St. James's Park to Swaine, Adeney & Brigg, where Peter bought them walking-sticks, and to Fox's, where he bought them large, luxurious cigars. The two smartly dressed, well-equipped Jesuits arrived by train in Venice and stayed at the Europa Hotel on the Grand Canal. (*'Due gentlemani inglesi*,' an elderly dandy murmured as they passed.) From Piraeus they took the overnight ferry to Souda, near Chania on the north-western coast of Crete.

Peter was discreet, even in retrospect, about identifying Brendan. He referred to him as 'an undergraduate' in a letter to Willie and an 'Oxford friend' in *The Hill of Kronos*. [16] Perhaps there was something not quite right about an older Jesuit leading a younger one on such a wild adventure. He had assumed they could walk the entire width of Crete, about two hundred miles of fierce terrain, in three weeks, at a time of year when icy rain can blot out the snow-capped mountains and lashing seas can flood the harbour edges, coating everything nearby in salt.

In the end they walked mainly round the west end of the island, and were lucky with the weather. From Falassarna near the north-western tip of Crete they walked to Palaeochora on the south coast, took a boat-ride as far as Sougia, then walked inland to Omalos, avoiding the famous Samarian Gorge in which walkers can be swept away by spring floods. From Omalos they caught a bus back to Chania, then another along the coast road to Rethymno, sixty kilometres to the east.

Although shaggy-haired Brendan wore a kilt (so as not to be mistaken for a German, he explained) Peter's fluent Greek made up for their lack of Orthodoxy, and they managed to stay several times in monastery and convent guest-rooms. It was Lent, which involved fasting as well as abstinence. Brendan carried a large bar of Cadbury's Dairy Milk in his sporran, and the nuns allowed them a square each after their supper of plain pasta. At the monastery of Preveli, near Plakias on the south coast, supper consisted of theological conversation, salad and *paximadia*, the ubiquitous Greek hard rusks. They ate better in shepherds' huts, and were fed generously once or twice by Cretans for whom the British still counted as their allies in war.

Alones, where Peter was expected, lies roughly two-thirds of the way between the north and south coasts at the narrowest point of central Crete, where the distance between the two coasts is about eleven miles as the crow flies. The tiny, isolated village lies under the frowning precipice of Mount Krioneritis to the north. From Rethymno they caught a bus as far as the turning to Argyroupoli (which Peter misnamed in *The Hill of Kronos* as 'Argyrokastro'), a village above a valley full of plane trees and piped springs. The next day they took a short cut on foot round the huge, shaly mountain between Argyroupoli and Alones, leaving at dawn and tottering, hungry and blistered, into the village in the evening. Doors flew open and they were offered wine in every house, before sitting up for most of the night as guests of an old lady who cracked walnut after walnut for them. Peter wrote that the village tap, surmounted by the bust, 'projects from the tablet just about where his [Gustavo's] private parts would be. It is a curiously moving monument; Gustavo would have liked it greatly.'[17]

Alones, he told Willie, was 'all eagles & snow, & wild lilies, & epic poems sung by old men weeping over their wine'. He was proud of having been moved to tears when he heard a shepherd reciting the seventeenth-century Veneto-Cretan epic poem *Erotokritos*, and again during the ceremony for Gustavo.[18] Spring had come early, and the mountain slopes near the coast were covered in wild flowers, a revelation to Brendan, as were the expanses of the Cretan Sea, blue, cloud-shadowed, and wine-dark under purplish-red cliffs.

In Athens for a last few days, they squeezed themselves into Peter's rooftop retreat. Peter slept on the roof terrace or the floor, letting Brendan have his bed. At Floca they met Nikos Gatsos, Takis Sinopoulos and George Pavlopoulos, who was about to publish his first collection of poems that autumn. George Seferis had been ill and was still weak, but Peter and Brendan met him lunching in a taverna at Sounion on the feast of the Panagia or Annunciation, March 25, a national holiday and celebration of spring even during the junta. With him were his wife Maro, George Pavlopoulos and Takis. Peter and Seferis swapped limericks in English and Greek, and Peter described his visit to Edward Lear's favourite places in Corfu. Seferis questioned him about his oddly dressed young friend and warned him not to let him make a shipwreck of his life. Then after lunch he announced that he would like to go up the hill behind the town. Takis drove him part of the way, after which he and the others struggled to the top of a slope covered in flowering gorse or broom. There was some discussion about its name, and Seferis mentioned an old word, *aspalathos*, for a flowering, aromatic, thorny shrub. (Also the name of an ancient Greek colony on the Adriatic, it gave its name to Spalatro or Split.) That evening he tracked down the word in Plato's *Republic*, 10:616, and six days later he finished his last poem, '*Epi Aspalathon*', about the beauty of the wild shrubs that day at Sounion, and how the tyrant

Aridaios of Pamphylia had been punished by being flayed and having his skinless flesh shredded by impalement on *aspalathos* thorns.[19]

ᏬᏬ

Leaving Greece unhindered by the police, Peter went home to a difficult summer. A few weeks after his fortieth birthday Mollie had another stroke. He spent most of that summer at Eastbourne, and eventually had to find her a nursing-home and put her house on the market. Maurice Bowra's death in July left him feeling bereft. Too soon people would begin talking about 'Bowra's Oxford' as an era of the vanished past. 'I wish I could resurrect him,' he wrote to Nancy. 'In Siberia they sweep the graves with flowers every spring to clear the eyes of the dead; but I can't believe his eyes will ever need clearing.'

One advantage of staying with Mollie had been the amount of time he could spend with the Connollys. After Lord Gage refused to renew their lease of Bushey Lodge on his estate at Firle, Cyril had bought a large Victorian suburban house in St. John's Road, Eastbourne, within walking distance of Mollie. Some fifteen months after the move Deirdre had fallen pregnant, giving birth to Matthew, whom they named after Cyril's father, on April 14, 1970. She had travelled freely with Cyril when Cressida was small, but with a baby and a daughter of ten, and holiday visits from her two older children, she found herself more tied to 48 St. John's Road than she had been to Bushey Lodge. Although an elderly, affectionate father, Cyril was away a lot, either on the *Sunday Times* assignments that he needed to keep up his income or on secret trips abroad with his mistress, Shelagh Levita. At home, worn out by visits to London (which, as well as assignations with Shelagh, included purchases of expensive first editions and lunches at White's or the Beefsteak Club, to which he introduced Peter as a member), he often went early to bed. Deirdre and Peter would sit up chatting, sometimes making him wonder jealously what they could find to talk about. Once they heard a strange noise above them and saw Cyril hanging over the banisters 'like a bat, straining to listen in'.[20]

Peter had never been certain about Deirdre's feelings for him. From quite early in his friendship with the couple, Cyril had palmed him off on Deirdre from time to time. If too busy to reply to one of Peter's letters he would ask Deirdre to answer it. Once Peter began to realize that Deirdre was interested in him for himself, he felt curious to know more. 'Deirdre Connolly sends me postcards of Eastbourne bandstand in a storm but not saying anything,' he complained to David-Pryce Jones from St. Beuno's. Tenderly motherly since Matthew's birth, and patient as always with Cyril, she remained a calm, consoling, mildly enigmatic friend. Yet, witty and attractive as she was, he may sometimes have wondered how things might have turned out but for her marriage and his vows.

Consolation was what he most needed that summer, since, apart from coping with Mollie's illness, he had to deal with Anthony's announcement that he intended to leave the priesthood and marry. He had seen enough scholastics leaving the Jesuits to accept the inevitability of that kind of wastage, but he agreed with Dominique that one could never give up the priesthood. Echoing his own melancholy line about *my brother who... is lost now*, he began to talk mournfully about 'my poor lost brother'.

From his readership at Warwick Anthony had successfully applied for the chair of French at St. Andrews, then begun the long process of having himself officially released from his vows. Intent on remaining a Catholic, he began the full formalities of laicization, which meant that he was still officially a Jesuit priest when he started his new job. 'If it had been a matter of merit it would have been me, but I stick on & corrupt slowly,' Peter wrote to Willie. A new worldliness in Anthony from the time of his American visits may have alerted him to a crack in that impenetrable Jesuit orthodoxy, but he had been used to relying on him as his counter-self, and without him as a fellow-Jesuit he felt as if a sheltering wall around him had collapsed.

By the time Seferis died in Athens, on September 20, Mollie was settled in a nursing-home in Dundee. She would be within easy reach of St. Andrews, where Anthony planned to install her in a flat if she recovered. Once released from his vows he stood to inherit Mollie's money, since both Peter and Gillian had renounced all claim on it. The nursing-home turned out to be unsatisfactory, Mollie had to be moved to another, and Peter went up and down by train that autumn, visiting her and sorting things out. At the end of that year, on the day Anthony received his formal discharge from the priesthood, Mollie died.

The next event was a wedding early in 1972. Although Honor was a Scottish Presbyterian, Anthony chose the full Catholic ritual, with a Latin nuptial Mass celebrated by Peter in the neo-Byzantine glory of Westminster Cathedral. Into the promises the bridegroom had to repeat after him Peter slyly inserted an extra one, that Anthony would bring his wife *jentaculum in lectulo* (breakfast in bed) every morning – a promise he devotedly kept for the rest of their joint lives.[21]

18
A FLOWER OF THE AGE TO COME

> The fruit-shadows on metal are to come,
> the bone-structure of time in midwinter
> foretells a flower of the age to come.
>
> 'Canticum', *Critical Quarterly*, June 1971

From soon after his ordination Peter had been intent on conveying a moral message in his poems. Confused and sometimes apocalyptic, it linked his sermonizing impulse with his hatred of political injustice, his longing for reciprocated love, his preoccupation with what poems could achieve and his sense of the immanence in nature of a remote, powerful and terrible God.

> *Listen: it is the Word with scything wings*
> *purging the sky of his imaginings,*

he urged in a poem addressed to Miranda and Iain. The Leigh Fermors, the Watsons and the Bergers became dedicatees of intense, often obscurely worded declarations, full of coinages such as 'batlight' and 'owlfire', of his belief in the redeeming power of revolution and love.

His commitment to a generalized, celibate, spiritually based benevolence gave an air of doomed hopelessness to his evident yearnings for *eros* as well as *agape*. These emerged most clearly in the poems he wrote during and after the first winter at Kardamyli. In some moods he portrayed himself as a *mad hermit* or *bible hermit*, confined in a bare autumn wood, becoming impassively *wooden-breasted like the trees* while concluding that *life is a coarse language, it shall be love.*[1] Elsewhere he suggested that love must inevitably be accompanied by silence. But he also made vicarious attempts at sensuality, as in an image of a warm offshore wind carrying the musky smell of girls to their sailor lovers out at sea, and odd, startlingly clunky affirmations such as *I wear love on my chest like a horse-brass*.[2]

In the elaborate, metaphysical 'Canticum', dedicated to John and Anya Berger, he described an ideal state, achieved fearlessly through a form of romantic madness, in which

> *God has become young, has become just,*
> *the Holy Ghost is locked up in a book,*
> *and God is spitting natural fire.*[3]

Its main theme is an elemental struggle to break away from the past and arrive at a transcendent future, not at all like the brainwashed state of terror in *Nineteen Eighty-Four*, yet one which involves forgetfulness and is *dense and bewildering, like snow*. Clear images of a timeless, Utopian lakeside city, suggesting aspects of Meyrin or Geneva, in which old people have forged a simple, new language, children run wild through museums and *no one will remember history*, are interspersed with images of ice, fire, rocks and wild terrain like that of the poppy-growing country in which *God being so old... The future... is hardly beginning to be born*. Hölderlin's 'wonderful' late poems (Peter told John Haffenden in an interview), together with discussions with John Berger about the failure of Marxism, had made him think, longingly but self-denyingly, of an existence in which new forms of popular culture might transcend a poet's private need *to speak in language, to be instructed*.[4]

That was altogether more complicated than the rhetoric of his 'Sermon on St Thomas More', preached at the Catholic church in Cheyne Row on More's feast-day, a few weeks after the Parisian events of May 1968:

> *Liberty is mankind's oldest friend,*
> *it is the knowledge of God in the end.*
> *The inheritance of God's children shall be*

liberty: equality: fraternity.[5]

༄

As an exception to his usual rule, he spent the winter of Mollie's death and Anthony's marriage in England. In the gloom and damp of Oxford, early in 1972, he was cheered by an encounter with the rationalist poet and critic William Empson, who was giving the Waynflete Lectures at Magdalen College. He had long admired Empson's book *Milton's God*, but challenged him over dinner at Magdalen for portraying God the Father as a vengeful tyrant who had forced his son to die in reparation for the sins of mankind. Peter described himself, like Auden, as a patripassionist, who believed that Christ's sufferings had caused God the Father himself to suffer.[6] Empson argued that, as he understood it, the Father's willing sacrifice of his son was a fundamental tenet of Christian belief, explained by the eleventh-century philosopher Anselm in *Cur Deus Homo* ('Why Was God Made Man?'). Peter cited Aquinas and Duns Scotus in defence of the gentler opinion that Christ came to earth as a manifestation of divine love, and that his death had been an inevitable outcome of conditions in the Roman Empire at the time.

Back in Hampstead, Empson resumed his argument in a letter, quoting the *Catholic Encyclopaedia* on 'Sacrifice (Christian)', and citing a passage in Aquinas about God the Father's satisfaction at the sacrifice of his son. He signed off with a friendly but unnecessary jibe about the Pope and birth control – a sensitive subject with him since his early twenties, when his Cambridge college had dismissed him from a fellowship for keeping contraceptives in a bedside drawer. Peter never finished his reply and later regretted having let the conversation lapse. Empson's clear insights were more important to him than any amount of pious waffle about faith, and he admired a lecture about Donne's manuscripts that he gave in near-darkness during a power cut. Later he felt that Empson had crossed his path like 'some heaven-sent ghost... or some sort of hero or saint of reason'.[7]

Two years had passed since he had entered Greece on his own. After his brush with the police in Corfu, he had felt frightened at the thought of being arrested again without a companion to bear witness and bring help. He told Bruce Chatwin something of his involvement with the Greek resistance, which by that time included an abortive plan to spring one of its members from prison. ('Harum-scarum Scarlet Pimpernelery,' Bruce jeered to Elizabeth, in his mood of disgust at *The Light Garden of the Angel King.*)[8] Athens seemed fraught with dangers, since he suspected he would be picked up by the police if he arrived there alone, and he could no longer rely on the neighbourliness of the Watsons, who had left the city and were now divorced.

As Pausanias devoted two full books of his history to Olympia and its cults, Peter talked a friend into driving him to the western Peloponnese in the summer of 1972. Anthony O'Hear was a thirty-year-old university lecturer who had spent ten years as a Jesuit novice and scholastic after leaving St. Ignatius's, Stamford Hill. He had met Peter through the scouts at Heythrop and again at Campion Hall, where he had lived for much of the time while studying for a doctorate in philosophy at Warwick. Anthony Levi had encouraged him to learn to drive and let him practise in his Triumph Vitesse. In 1970, newly qualified, he had left the Jesuits for his first academic job, teaching philosophy at the University of Hull. Two years later, still single, he was the owner of a brand-new white Ford Escort. He had not yet tried driving abroad, and until then had felt no particular interest in visiting Greece.

In *The Hill of Kronos*, Peter maintained that he had set out in all innocence with Anthony ('another Oxford friend'), intending to visit George Pavlopoulos and Takis Loumiotis at Pyrgos and spend time relaxing with George at Agios Andreas.[9] Anthony thought he must already have known or suspected that the junta had banned him from Greece, and believed that his only hope of sneaking into the country would be in a crowd of summer visitors on the Brindisi to Patras ferry. As a passenger in a car whose driver spoke no Greek and was not on the unwanted list, he might automatically be waved through. It is hard to know exactly what went through his mind.

Like Brendan in Crete, Anthony found himself whirled off on a cultural adventure. Peter insisted that they should stick to minor roads to see as many places on the way as they could. Since neither of them had much money, they agreed to eat well and sleep out in fields or on beaches. It did not seem to occur to them to stay at campsites or take more equipment than a sleeping-bag each.

After a farewell meal with Cyril and Deirdre at Eastbourne they took the Newhaven ferry and headed south. Peter had heard from Nancy and John Berger about the Iron-Age burial treasures from Vix, on Mont Lassois in Burgundy, and they stopped at the archaeological museum in Châtillon-sur-Seine for his first view of the famous Vix krater, a sculpturally ornamented Greek bronze vessel over five feet tall, of the kind that had been used for mixing wine at Homeric feasts. That, and the exotic jewellery and Greek wine-cups, all apparently of the sixth century BC, sent him off on an excited tangent. A book about archaic Greek cultural influence on France joined his ever-lengthening 'to do' list, and his fascination with the treasure surfaced later in his archaeological thrillers.

Crossing expensive Switzerland in a hurry, they swam in Lake Leman and picnicked on wine and cheese bought in France. From Verona they drove south to cross the Po, and, after a comfortless night on an Adriatic beach, where Anthony was bitten on the nose by a crab, they took in the Byzantine mosaics in Ravenna and the fifteenth-century, neo-classical Malatesta Temple at Rimini. Zigzagging across the Apennines, they searched for Roman remains near Tivoli, then continued past Naples and Salerno to the high point of the Italian trip, the Greek temple at Paestum. Anthony had never seen a Greek classical building before, and it was Peter's first visit to Paestum. He talked non-stop, darting about, marvelling at the massed ranks of solid, standing pillars and admiring the fresco on the Tomb of the Diver in the museum, with its erotic, all-male symposium scene and its swooping figure of a naked, deep-sea diving boy.

'It is very south & hot... Anthony looks like a radish & I like unsuccessfully clarified butter,' Peter scribbled on a postcard to Julian and his partner Richard. South of Naples, modern civilization seemed to have come to an end; no wonder Carlo Levi had called his Mezzogiorno novel *Christ Stopped at Eboli*. But they were in the ancient Greek colonial territory of Magna Græcia, and he kept up a steady historical commentary as Anthony drove from Salerno to Bari. There were no classical features in the housing stock of concrete cubes and conical-roofed *trulli*, but they were following the road the defeated consul Regulus was thought to have taken on his way back from Rome to North Africa to be executed by the Carthaginians. Peter recited the ode about Regulus from the volume of Horace he carried in his pocket.

After a long, hot drive down the Puglian coast they arrived at the ferry port of Brindisi. The Greek immigration authorities checked their passports. They put the car on board and settled down on deck with their sleeping-bags and a picnic of grapes, wine and bread. Then Peter, who had already drawn attention to himself by talking plummy, educated Italian in a lorry-drivers' café in Verona, started a conversation in loud demotic Greek. Soon after that, the ship's loudspeaker crackled into action. Would Mr LENI please report to the Captain? Would Mr LANI kindly come below at once?

Corfu was the official point of entry into Greece, and Peter was told that his deportation order required him to disembark there and take the next boat back to Italy. The car could not be unloaded until the ferry reached Igoumenitsa, a small port in the far north of mainland Greece. Anthony was stranded there, out of touch, for several days until able to return to Brindisi, where he found Peter walking up and down the quayside reading Horace.

So they turned back to the Calabrian coast, spending a first hot night at Palinuro, a small, crowded seaside resort village south of Salerno. Cyril's literary persona in his wartime meditation *The Unquiet Grave* had been Aeneas's helmsman Palinurus, the mythical ancestor of the Romans, who was said to have been washed up alive from the sea and later buried on the headland at Palinuro. Peter could not resist sending Cyril a postcard, quoting *Nudus in ignota Palinure jacebis harena* ('You shall sleep naked on a strange beach, Palinurus') from the *Æneid*, and adding that, but for mosquitoes, they would have done the same.

From Rome they drove north to Genoa and up into Haute Savoie, since Peter had decided they could not pass that way without calling on the Bergers. He was proud of 'Canticum' and longed for more of John's bracingly radical conversation. That autumn, when awarded the £5,000 Booker Prize for his novel *G*, Berger made a revolutionary acceptance speech, attacking Booker McConnell, the industrial sponsors of the prize, for exploiting plantation labourers in the West Indies and promising half his prize money to the Black Panthers. Anthony, who was shy and tired, found the talk at the Bergers' heavy going and longed to head for home. A much happier period began for him two years later in Pyrgos, when Peter introduced him to George Pavlopoulos and they became close friends. After that he went back every summer with his wife and children to spend seaside holidays with George and his family at Agios Andreas.

≈

Eager to see more of the ancient Greek world, Peter had been hoping for some time to visit Egypt. In the spring of 1972 he wondered, not very seriously, if the Charltons could leave their children behind and come too.

> I've found a tribe who look like zulus & dye their hair blonde with cow-piss. I would have to write a book to pay for going, proving that the Greeks never got there or alternatively that the cow-piss imitates the gold coinage of Alexander as Helios. What do you think?[10]

At the end of that year he spent ten days in Egypt, managing, with his talent for attracting police attention, to be arrested while poking round the ruins of the ancient capital Fustat in the oldest part of Cairo.[11] He would probably have stayed longer, and even visited the Upper Nile, if the ban on his entry to Greece had remained in force. Finding that it had been withdrawn, however, he plunged back into resistance politics, only to be banned again before long.

In Greece he was ill, perhaps from nervous exhaustion. At Kardamyli he went down with a chill and fever in the midst of fierce winter storms. Hearing about the first large-scale gesture of defiance against the junta as he recovered in February, he wrote a ten-line poem about his feelings as he contemplated mountains, rocks and sunlit sea. Its title, 'The Law School Riots, Athens, 1973', appears in italics and parenthesis in the *Collected Poems* as if to confirm the vagueness of its connection with actual happenings in Athens. Its ending, like its beginning, is symbolic:

> *Everything fresh is breathing in one stream:*
> *the breath of rock when we are free in dreams*
> *cracks a bone open, courage is this shock,*
> *scatter of white snow on a screen of rock.*[12]

Joan and Paddy Leigh Fermor had succeeded in ignoring the existence of the junta, except when it particularly distressed someone they knew. A Kardamyli neighbour was being harassed by officials, and Paddy and Peter decided to try to help him. After Peter returned to Athens they corresponded about this in Latin, partly to fox the censors but probably also for the fun of the thing, 'in polished elegiac couplets on his side' (Paddy wrote inventively) '& rather plodding prose on mine'.[13]

Friends of friends in Athens then begged Peter to help smuggle out a student who was being hunted by the police for his part in the Law School riots. Dismayed that he did not have a spare room in which to hide the young man, Peter hastily kitted him out to match the photograph in his fake British passport and put him on a flight to London. Although instructed not to tell anyone about the plan for his escape the student did so, and word inevitably leaked back to the police. Peter, by then in England, took the blame for arranging it, as he had agreed to if the young man talked. This time his room in Mets was sealed and he was banned from Greece without hope of reprieve.[14]

His 'Good Friday Sermon', broadcast on the BBC Third Programme on the evening of April 20, 1973, was the last religious poem he recorded for radio. Lacking the intense personal anguish and gloom of the 'Christmas Sermon' of 1967, it carried a simpler message. Christ was the supreme figure of reason and justice whose mercy would save a wicked, unfree world. Meanwhile, certain radical causes cried out for immediate support.

> *The prison is the street: the lonely farm*
> *will not be broken open without harm:*
> *the dirty flag degrades the uniform.*
> *And all this suffering will increase*
> *until the anger of reason makes it cease.*
> Vox populi ira Dei,
> *voice of the people wrath of God, say I.*[15]

ೋ

In the autumn of 1972 John Fuller's father, Roy, neared the end of his
five-year term as Oxford Professor of Poetry. Several of Peter's friends
suggested that he should stand in the next election, but he urged John
Wain to do so instead. Describing their conversation as they walked
up New College Lane in the dark after Fuller's November lecture,
Wain professed himself amazed. While he saw himself as a pedestrian
author of novels, biography and criticism, Peter was a coruscatingly
original poet and brilliant multilingual scholar, 'admired by the young,
respected by the old'. Only the fact that he was a Jesuit, which Wain
did not specifically mention, might have been against him. Wain was
also five years older than Peter, which he concluded was reason enough
to stand, hoping Peter would do so next time.

Half a dozen friends and supporters, including Philip Larkin,
Anthony Thwaite and Christopher Ricks, gathered in the Wains' back
garden off Wolvercote Green on the afternoon of Saturday, 26 May
1973. The noises of the Whitsun funfair on Port Meadow reached
them on a westerly breeze. Peter, more interested in amusing a small
boy than in speculating about the election result, had taken Toby
Wain, whose seventh birthday it was, across the high bridge over the
canal and the railway to the fair. Thinking Toby could never win at
the coconut shy he did a secret deal with the showman, offering to
pay him for a coconut and let Toby believe he had won it, but Toby
scored a direct hit. As the two of them arrived back, the telephone
rang inside the house and the eldest boy rushed triumphantly into the
garden shouting.[16]

That summer, priestly duties caught up with Peter. After several
weeks helping a yacht-owner sail in rough seas round the British coast
to Cowes, he spent a fortnight acting as holiday relief for the Jesuit
parish priest at Charlbury, where the tiny, simple Catholic chapel

had been endowed as a dependency of Heythrop. An ex-Jesuit friend came to keep him company, and Deirdre, learning that the priest's housekeeper had gone on holiday, invited herself to look after them at the presbytery, bringing three-year-old Matthew and staying at the Bull Inn just down the road. Cressida was away, and Cyril, whose seventieth birthday celebrations were to take place in September, had taken Shelagh to visit his ex-wife Barbara in the south of France.

Deirdre relaxed with the two men, singing duets with Peter's guest in the kitchen, driving them on trips into the Cotswolds while they sang along with her in the car, and cooking for them in the evenings. Peter enjoyed the easy domesticity of the life, the friendly, small-scale town, the Evenlode flowing calmly under its bridges, *so old and green/there might be no upstream*,[17] the cloud-shadowed hills towards Chipping Norton and the long, dark line of Wychwood in the west. Then, too soon, he had to spend several weeks in London, commuting daily from Mount Street to the Brixton chaplaincy.

Blocking out all thoughts of Greece, he had fallen in love with rivers

that summer, concentrating on them in an almost mystical way. Before the sailing trip came up he had planned to spend his free time pottering in small boats on the Thames as John Wain sometimes invited him to do, and perhaps beginning a history of the river. A sequence of short river-poems begins with Charlbury-like images of harvest brightness and country rain. In fine weather he imagines himself merging into a small river, to *grow a sort of river-skin/and glitter and die like a sun-fragment.* Later he watches

> *this curdled river under sparks of rain*
> *lucid as a bream ignite himself,*
> *ruffle his bank and run black under it.*

A 'blighted summer' in London makes him dream of solitary riverside walks, then remember what it was like to wake at dawn as a child at Ruislip when the street-lights threw out *long rays like crocodiles.* He visits the source of the Thames at Lechlade, probably on one of Deirdre's expeditions, and hopes it will help him to fathom the confusion of his life. *A limestone statue in a meadow/cut off by railings is father Thames,... Shall be my father and my grandfather.* Early winter brings wet fields, black ditches and silent mist. River water *is moral but obscure*; he can feel its timelessness, but not explain its deep mystical attraction for people who lean contemplatively over bridges or follow a river downstream through fields on foot.[18]

Exhausted after Brixton, he spent a few days with the Charltons in Northumberland in late October. Willie had left Dublin for a philosophy lectureship at the University of Newcastle and settled in his ancestral homeland of the North Tyne valley. Peter loved the large, plain house, Lee Hall, and apologized for his feeble state on arriving; but, much though family life and the stark beauty of the country cheered him, he clumsily cut short his stay. Auden had died in Vienna at the end of September, on the way back from Kirchstetten to spend another winter in Oxford, and a memorial service was held for him in Christ Church Cathedral on Saturday, October 27. Having already arranged to meet Cyril and Deirdre for lunch before the service, Peter made a hasty dash back. Playing down the social aspect of the occasion, he told Willie that he had found the service even more of a 'lunatic mess of shadows' than he had expected. Stephen Spender gave the address, and Auden's two brothers, who were said not to have spoken to him or one another for the past forty years, sat in front among an ominous phalanx of poets' widows.[19]

That winter, visiting Sicily instead of Greece, he found the island primitive and slightly menacing. There were moments of interest as he toured Greek sites and enjoyed the baroque architecture of Palermo, but he felt jarred by the nasal intonation of the vernacular Mass in churches decorated with bloody altarpieces and stuffed with spangled kitsch. Did he really belong to the same Church as these inscrutable peasant priests? Newman had written 'Lead, kindly Light' on the voyage home from Sicily after an illness which pushed him into extremes of piety, first as a proselytizing high churchman, then as the nineteenth century's most famous convert to Rome. Sicily had the opposite effect on Peter, unsettling his already shaky certainties about the calling to which he had given himself for life.

Greek politics, meanwhile, were in meltdown. Four months after the Law School riot the leader of the junta, Georgios Papadopoulos, had announced the abolition of the monarchy and declared himself President of the Republic. To legitimize his regime he had suspended martial law and proposed various minor reforms. That did not satisfy the students, who on November 14 occupied the Athens Polytechnic and organized a massive popular demonstration for full democratic rights. Panic-stricken, the provisional government ordered the army to crush the uprising. A tank smashed into the Polytechnic gates and soldiers fired at random into the crowd, wounding hundreds of people and causing several deaths. Papadopoulos was forced to step down, and the junta reconstituted itself under an even more ruthless officer, Dimitrios Ioannidis.

Friends in Athens kept Peter informed of news which did not appear in the papers. In late May 1974 he wrote a letter of protest to *The Times* about the junta's arrest and ill-treatment of the distinguished Athena Kalianessi, the owner of the bookshop and poetry publishing house Kedros. Just over a fortnight later a letter signed by eight senior London publishers confirmed that Mrs. Kalianessi had suffered hallucinations after being tortured with sleep deprivation in prison. Her husband was dying of lung cancer alone at home. 'When will these horrors end?' Peter had exclaimed in his letter, little guessing that the end would come in only two months' time.[20]

In the end, Cyprus brought the junta down as it had brought down Papandreou nine years earlier. The Cypriot Greeks who still hoped for *enosis* with Greece had felt trapped in their independent, ethnically mixed republic under a constitution presided over by Archbishop Makarios. On July 15, with the encouragement of Ioannidis, a gang of officers from the peacekeeping detachment of the Greek National Guard in Cyprus, supported by the violent pro-*enosis* movement EOKA B, deposed Makarios and replaced him with a puppet president, Nikos Sampson. The normally sporadic hostilities between Greek and Turkish Cypriots flared up into civil war, and Turkey sent an invasion force to occupy the north-eastern part of Cyprus. When the junta responded by declaring a general mobilization, panic broke out in Greece. Ioannidis was forced to resign, followed by the rest of his colleagues. To jubilant popular demonstrations, the ex-dictators announced that they had invited Karamanlis to return from exile and head a provisional government until elections could be held in the autumn.

Peter had arranged to give a paper at an archaeological conference in Cyprus, and had invited Anthony O'Hear to go too. When they heard the Cypriot news they cancelled their plan, and Peter went to Fifeshire to stay with Anthony and Honor, where he baptized their new baby Claudia in a fruit-bowl. Lapped in family life and sweet-smelling country air, he felt reluctant to go back to the piles of work that were waiting for him in Oxford. Now that Greece was free (he wrote to Willie in August) he had an urge to abandon the makeshift alternatives to Pausanias he had set up. He felt like behaving wildly and cancelling the next term's lectures on Horace in case his opinions of the poems should become too fixed.[21] But the real reason was that he could not face another autumn in Oxford when he longed to go straight back to Greece.

The junta might have resigned, but its hired thugs were still at large in the streets and hanging out in their well-known bars and cafés. The tortures, beatings and disappearances, the playing of taped screams in the prisons, and above all the Polytechnic massacre, seemed too terrible to Peter to be forgotten or covered up. Determined to encourage witnesses to speak, he knew that he could count on highly articulate ones in Athens and would find more ordinary ones with stories to tell in towns and villages in the Peloponnese and Crete. He suggested to Mischa Scorer, by then in the documentary department of BBC Television, that they should make a film recording the atrocities of the junta, based on interviews he would conduct with a cross-section of Greeks. In mid-August, once he had obtained permission to enter the country, he and Anthony O'Hear flew to Athens, where George Seferis's widow Maro put them up.

Floca was still there, and Nikos Gatsos loomed joyfully out of his corner to greet them. Peter discussed the film idea with the novelist Stathis Tzirkas, the composer Manos Hadjidakis and Gatsos, who promised to write a tragic poem to be set to music. Seferis was dead, and so was the polemical novelist and diplomat Rodis Roufos, who had died young from the stress of the regime. But Roufos's widow

Arietta and the novelist and translator Kay Cicellis were both calmly understated English speakers who would balance the vehemence or inarticulateness of other witnesses in the film. And in the neighbourhood of Pyrgos, where he and Anthony went to reconnoitre, Peter found a network of local people, many of them friends of George Pavlopoulos, who were eager to speak their minds.

'There was still fear and division in the villages, just as there had been when I first went to Greece,' he wrote. Yet, although many of the dictators' local placemen remained in power, there was little sympathy anywhere for the junta. Unlike the opposing sides in the civil war, it had operated from too narrow and secret a power-base to inspire much loyalty. Its tactics of intimidation and murder had deeply offended Greek instincts of self-respect. Peter was unwilling to let victims describe their experiences of torture; that would be too intimate a subject, he said, like sex. But once, at Ligourio in the Argolid, he found himself confronting a former torturer, who told the crowd how, as part of his training, he had been systematically tortured for six months before being sent out to do the same to others, on pain of dire punishment if he failed.[22]

Mischa, whose boss had urged him to go ahead with the film at once, arrived on the October evening of the first concert Mikis Theodorakis gave after his return from exile in Paris. Peter met him at Athens airport and took him straight to Syntagma Square, where a huge, emotional celebration was taking place. Speeches were made from a platform in the middle of the square, and Maria Farandouri sang Theodorakis's heart-wrenching songs. 'It was an overwhelming and thrilling evening with the square packed with tens of thousands of people (maybe hundreds of thousands),' Mischa wrote. 'Somehow Peter managed to get us both close to the action.'[23]

Soon after that Mischa's young assistant June Henman arrived, followed by the camera crew. Their headquarters was the elegant (and, like Floca, now non-existent) Athenée Palace Hotel, a block or two north-west of Syntagma Square on the corner of Kolokotronis Square and Stadiou. Like the Randolph in Oxford, it was the kind of old-fashioned, cigar-smelling hotel Peter loved. Floca, where they usually ate dinner, was nearby, and when the crew was driving back into the city in the evening Peter would say 'Point towards Floca and drive like hell.'

June was sensitive, eager and admiring. Impressed by Peter's knowledge and familiarity with Greece, she spent evenings chatting to him in the hotel bar and came to realise how passionate about the film he had become. Like nearly all his enterprises, it was a labour of pure love. Touched by a similar spirit, she slipped down from her room on her first day in the city to get close to a crowd of demonstrators who were marching towards Syntagma Square, and was moved by their quiet excitement. The atmosphere before the election was tense but joyful. In the following weeks she was almost as affected as Peter by the stories of recent horrors that emerged.[24]

Most of the places they visited were those Peter already knew. From Athens they went to Ligourio, then on to the western Peloponnese. At Pyrgos, Peter's questioning brought a solemn and detailed account of local indignities from George Pavlopoulos and cruder, more impassioned testimonies from other people. He planned to finish the filming at Alones, whose villagers would remember his visit with Brendan in the spring of 1971. First, however, he slipped back to England for a week, leaving the team to manage without him. During his absence he asked them to film a barracks in the centre of Athens where some of the most horrifying tortures had taken place. They had obtained government permission to film there, and a civil servant was sent along to make sure that things went smoothly. But the guards marched out, surrounded the producers and crew and seized a blank film the cameraman had slipped in just in time. Peter was disappointed to have missed the confrontation and the chance to harangue the guards in his best bloody-minded demotic.

Early in December he was back, telling nobody why he had gone away. On the night ferry from Piraeus June came up on deck and saw him gazing over the rail with his raincoat slung over one shoulder. She approached him timidly, thinking he might prefer to be left alone, but spent the rest of the voyage chatting to him until the boat docked in Souda harbour, with the sun just touching the White Mountains' snowy peaks. She drew closer to him between Chania and Alones, catching his enthusiasm for the Cretan people as he strode along with his dark blue trousers tucked into a pair of high Cretan leather boots. Everyone they met fell into easy conversation with him. He would stop by the road to talk to an old man minding goats or clearing a vegetable patch, and suggested to Mischa that it would be a wonderful project to film the life of a Cretan shepherd, as if already planning his next trip.

Because he knew that there would be very little food in Alones he insisted on buying a whole slaughtered goat from the market in Rethymno and taking it as an offering. This time, instead of walking across country, they took the more circuitous route on steep, winding mountain roads. Once they had parked on the edge of the village Peter marched into the centre carrying the goat, followed by the crew with their equipment. June was allowed to help the women prepare the feast, chopping vegetables and stirring pots over a charcoal fire while the goat turned on a spit. Then, as a guest, she was invited to sit with the men at table while the women waited on them. Hands were shaken and noisy toasts drunk. Peter leaned forward opposite her, tensely gripping the bench, as someone took a photograph. Around them sat generations of villagers, their lined, bony, moustached Cretan faces steeped in memories of shared hardship, siege, occupation and civil war.[25]

19
A THREAD

I was hanging on by a thread to my old vocation and my complicated way of life.

The Flutes of Autumn (1983) 154

Two deaths had shaken Peter that autumn. David Jones died on October 28, a few days before his seventy-ninth birthday. Too frail to live alone after a fall, he had spent the past four years in a nursing-home run by nuns. Long before that he had been housebound with agoraphobic depression in his narrow ground-floor room in a residential hotel in one of the more leafless parts of Harrow. In his *DNB* article on Jones, Peter slyly remarked on his habit of conducting '*amitiés amoureuses*' on the telephone in old age, holding the mouthpiece at arm's length so that Nancy, increasingly deaf as she was, said that she had to jam the receiver against her ear until it almost drew blood.

As an admirer of his work, Peter had contributed to two special David Jones issues of *Agenda*, with Nancy, Stuart Piggott, René Hague, Sir Kenneth Clark, Saunders Lewis, Nicolete Gray and others. These specialists in their fields had praised Jones's knowledge of antiquity, his artistic and calligraphic genius, his love of Latin and medieval Welsh, his historical empathy and intense compassion for anonymous, representative figures from the past. In the 1973/74 issue Peter had considered 'History and Reality in David Jones', dwelling especially on his disregard for chronology and his habit of making a tapestry or palimpsest out of different episodes, from imagined moments in prehistory to the life of Jesus, the Roman occupation of Britain, the heroic backgrounds of medieval legends and his own experience of the Flanders trenches. 'He uses the whole backward and abyss of time.'[1]

He had seen little of Jones since his ordination, keeping up with him by letter and through Nancy, who saw him regularly. Other things had absorbed his time, while Jones's simple, ardent piety may have made him more aware of the different quality of his own. Straight off the plane from Athens after filming in Crete, he gave a highly wrought address at Jones's Requiem Mass in Westminster Cathedral on December 13. The congregation included Nancy, Valerie Eliot, Father D'Arcy, the sculptor Henry Moore, the engraver Reynolds Stone, the poet Keidrich Rhys, the publisher and former radio producer Douglas Cleverdon, Jones's close friend, literary executor and fellow-Catholic Harman Grisewood, and Lady Antonia Fraser with her husband and eldest daughter.[2]

Peter commended Jones's innocent, sweet nature, his devotion to religion, myth, history and the spirit of place, and his sorrow at people's loss of contact with these sources. As a visionary painter and poet, he had acknowledged the inexorable flow of history but had also been sensitive to the points at which it 'runs backward into its origins, the point at which the whole world suffers its metamorphosis not into fire, not into ice, but otherwise in an unbloody manner at this stone, at this church, on this black battlefield.' Interspersing the sermon with repetitions of his Latin text, a sentence from Exodus 12.5 in the Vulgate, *Erit autem agnus absque macula, masculus anniculus* ('Your lamb shall be without blemish, a male of the first year'), Peter argued that religion was more powerful than poetry or language; it was about the renewal of innocence and the recognition of Christ in all things. The 'whole Welsh thing', for Jones, had been inspired by a Christ-like passion, in the 'Spirit of God calling out to his Father', to retrieve the dying language and lost culture of a marginalized people. Echoing a passage in Jones's late poem 'The Kensington Mass',[3] he ended with a declamatory flourish:

We are creatures, our service and our remembrance are creaturely. We kiss the cloth on the altar. We shall all die. The

Christ who is in this church is the Christ of Stonehenge and of the earliest centuries of mankind, the Christ of every star in the sky, and of every nameless, ignorant soldier dying in a wet ditch... Let us transform ourselves at last, let us enter that mystery, whatever our measure is our calling is to become Christ. Let us pray for one another, recalling David Jones to the mind of Christ and to our own minds. We must become Christ.[4]

The rhetoric was clearly heartfelt, although not all the emotion behind it may have been due to Jones's death. A week after the Requiem he was back in London for a literary memorial service at the church of St. Mary Le Strand. Stephen Spender gave the address, John Betjeman read the lesson and Peter read an extract from Cyril Connolly's *The Unquiet Grave*. Among the smart crowd, which included the philosopher Freddie Ayer, the publisher George Weidenfeld, the archivist and author Noel Blakiston representing the Beefsteak Club, and Deirdre Connolly with her four children, there was one obvious absentee.

Cyril had had a major heart attack in the south of France on his seventy-first birthday, September 10. With him had been his mistress Shelagh and his ex-wife Barbara Skelton, who had got on well with Shelagh the previous year and invited the pair of them to stay again at her house at Grimaud, near St. Tropez. Flown to England in a frail but fighting state, he had hung on through the autumn in one London hospital bed after another. Abandoning the BBC crew in Athens, Peter had joined Deirdre at Cyril's bedside before he died on November 26. Six days later, before catching a plane back, he had attended the funeral at the medieval flint church at Berwick, in the Cuckmere valley between Firle and Eastbourne, with its Bloomsburyesque murals by Duncan Grant and the Bells. He told nobody, not even Mischa, the reason for his dash to England, and even Deirdre thought later that he must have been there for some cultural event connected with the fall of the junta.

Peter's and Mischa's hour-long documentary, *Greece: The Seven Black Years,* was shown on BBC1 on the evening of Tuesday, April 29, 1975. Nine months after the fall of the junta it might have stirred emotions in Greece, but it provoked little outrage in England. Television reviewers ignored it in favour of a documentary about the Arab world, while Peter's more critical friends were inclined to dismiss it for re-hashing old atrocity stories. He wrote a partial description of the autumn's filming in *The Hill of Kronos,* including lively, verbatim accounts of conversations with villagers in the Peloponnese and Crete.

Glad that the whole political show was over, he was keen to get back to scholarship. The following winter he returned to Athens, hoping to find it peaceful and welcoming with no secret police on his tail. In fact it was noisier, more competitive and more polluted than before. He had lost his rooftop shack in Mets and could find nowhere else cheap to live. Among all his friends in the city, from café-dwelling poets like Gatsos to cultured women like Maro Seferis, Arietta Roufos, Vanna Hadjimichalis and Kay Cicellis, there was no-one on whom he felt he could impose himself as a guest. Constantine Trypanis, as a distinguished Greek intellectual, had been invited to join the new government as Minister for Culture and Sciences, but Peter, who had not seen him since he left Oxford to take up a professorship of classics in Chicago, was shy of presuming on their past friendship. The archaeologists who had agreed to his suggestion of a joint, dual-language commentary on the first book of Pausanias had quietly abandoned the project, taking with them the prospect of a Greek publisher for the work. Feeling more at home with George Pavlopoulos in Pyrgos, he decided to start again in the middle of the commentary and work on the descriptions of Olympia in Books Five and Six.

At Katakolo, a port town near Agios Andreas, an elderly couple named Pylarinos owned a fish restaurant near the beach, which was open all the year round and had the best cooking on that stretch of coast. Mr. Pylarinos, a small, wise man with yellowish skin and hooded eyes, was one of the father-figures with whom Peter loved to talk. Aware of his loathing of the junta for the harm it had done his business, he had interviewed him for the film. Now he joyfully looked up the couple, and even thought of renting a wooden beach-house at Katakolo for the winter. Finding, however, that no trains to Pyrgos ran at that time of year, he took a room in a hotel at Olympia rather than enduring long, dark, lonely evenings of blowing sand and crashing waves.

Rural Greece was, as usual, bracingly cold, with a tang of wood smoke. 'The sun melted like honey in the pine forests... The air smelt of snow.'[5] He chatted harmlessly to the local policemen over lunch in the only restaurant that produced a hot meal, and in the evenings ate a chop or an egg among elderly single men who had nobody to cook for them at home. Maro and Arietta drove down from Athens in the early spring, when wild flowers were out on the sheltered slopes of Olympia. On an impulse they decided to take him on a trip to Bassae, driving up snow-clogged mountain roads through a black and white, rocky landscape he found frighteningly harsh.

Urged on by Seferis, he had translated George Pavlopoulos's collection of poems *To Katogi (The Cellar)*, which had been published several months before Seferis died. Grave, dreamlike narratives of fighting and destruction, the poems reflect the private, individual traumas of the German occupation and the civil war. Peter's simple, unrhymed stanzas made them readable and clear.

> *Don't forget, he said, don't forget. But everything blackened*
> *like the wall they demolished where the fireside was.*
> *And suddenly you see where your house used to be,*
> *you see the place lit up*
> *as if someone turned up the wick in a lamp*
> *and there were the women bent over knitting,*

mouths tied up in black kerchiefs,
eyes like flowers weary on their stalks...[6]

More ambitiously, because the American scholar Edmund Keeley had got there first, he had translated several poems by Yannis Ritsos, a poet of great intensity and radical political commitment, whom the junta had imprisoned for several years on the wretched island of Gyaros. ('Ritsos,' said John Berger, 'is what Peter was all about.') The *TLS* of 14 November 1975 included Peter's translations of several poems by Pavlopoulos and one of 'Greekness' by Ritsos.

Translation can sometimes improve on the original, he said later in a lecture on Seferis, adding that he resented the fact that his own poems sounded better in German.[7] Seferis's own vast and consistently serious *œuvre* of translations had ranged from the Song of Songs and the Book of Revelation to Eliot's *Waste Land and Murder in the Cathedral*, dialogues of Plato, poems by Paul Valéry and limericks by Edward Lear. It was his inwardness with his own language, said Peter, his ability to tell true expression from false, that gave a quality of absolute soundness to everything he wrote. He sensed something of the same sincerity and purity of language in Pavlopoulos and did his best to replicate it.

George was fifty-one, with a single modest collection of poems to his name. He seemed in no hurry for recognition, and would be in his seventies before his *Poiimata 1943-1997* appeared. Peter, however, energized by the oxygen of translation and exalted by the achievement of long poems such as 'Canticum', 'In Memory of George Seferis' and 'Rivers', felt by 1975 that he had reached the point in life that demanded a *Collected Poems*. A succession of recent, shorter poems contained his favourite images from the natural world – wild animals, trees, stone, ragged gardens and the moon, which he had celebrated with panache in his lamentation for Seferis as *the moon stone-footed in the sun's eclipse*.[8] He had pondered philosophical questions (*Nothing is free in nature. Freedom lies in the inward of nature*)[9] with the paradoxical tendency he later applied to considerations of the soul. He had comforted Miranda after the end of her marriage, recommending *Heaven of sleep on a pillow of time/among the lemon trees and the white chickens*. And he had sympathized with an older woman in 'for Barbara', probably addressed to Miranda's mother.

> *You run down sometimes, you go blind,*
> *cobwebs of yellow paper in the trees,*
> *damp weather, quietness of a kind,*
> *olive, grape, there are no distances:*
> *you fumble the world for touch and sight,*
> *stone underfoot, animals, half-light.*[10]

Answering a questionnaire about rhythm, in the autumn/winter 1972/3 *Agenda*, he had admitted to two conflicting wishes:

> to write a language so fine, strong, supple and good that it would somehow not be everybody's English, and... to write a language so genuine, popular and traditionally musical in its sound, in the sense of a fairground organ or ballads, that it would limit what one ought to say, what people are in fact waiting for and demand.

Carrying disembodied rhythms in his head as he did Beethoven quartets, he found it easy enough to fit words to either kind. His verse sermons and lectures in couplets were full of thumping repetitions and assertive, one-line sound-bites: a kind of writing that was usually aimed at a captive but intelligently receptive audience. In his 1989 Oxford lecture *Goodbye to the Art of Poetry* he played to the audience's knowledge by slipping lines from well-known poems and ballads into the rhythm of his text. At the end of 'Canticum' he had imagined a silent, amnesiac future, resulting from the triumph of populism over intellectual culture:

All these words will have crumbled in the people's speech.
And I have already forgotten my life,
and have forgotten.[11]

But the forgetfulness he later celebrated in poem after poem was the outcome of a previously unimaginable, non-political happiness of his own.

In contrast with Colin Falck's savage treatment of the *Collected Poems* in the *New Review*, he received the usual kindness from *Agenda*. John Bayley, always prepared to boost an Oxford friend, had devoted an entire article to his poetry in the Spring 1968 number, praising his Keats-like innocence and the Hardyesque intimacy of his early poem 'Longwall Street', about loads of hay and autumn timber being driven along a narrow Oxford street. (In the same number, Peter had stood that demure image on its head with five poems written in Greece and a warm review of a collection from the harbinger of ecological Rocky Mountain Zen culture, Gary Snyder.) Cal Clothier, reviewing *Life is a Platform*, had called the repetitiveness of the poems prayer-like, comparing Peter with a player of Patience who hoped his hand would come out right in the end. Now Jeffrey Wainwright represented the *Collected Poems* as a continuous, meditative whole, whose images of snow, woods, rivers, mist, rain and icy ponds showed how Peter's sensibilities responded to the natural world by reflecting and almost melting into it.[12]

> *(It seems to me that the sea and the sky,*
> *the unreasonable, variable sea,*
> *clouds, storms, mist, coloured immensity*
> *make me a mirror of my universe,*
> *and its weather is always growing worse.)*[13]

Peter himself saw a similar tendency in the poems of Martin Robertson, the Lincoln Professor of Greek Art and Archaeology at

Oxford. His introduction to Robertson's 1977 collection ended with a dazzling, if far-fetched, simile:

> It is as if the whole work were a dark tree tufted with snow at the moment when a bright sun melts the snow into a constant shower under the tree like small rain, but without appearing to diminish the snow on the branches; the sun makes the dark tree glitter and the snow glisten and the rainfall of melted snow sparkle in the shadows of the tree. There are many kinds of poetry and many stages of thoughts, but the sun is the same and the natural tree is one tree in all its branches... I am trying to describe a relation not only between the poems but between the poems and their author.[14]

Although this did not become obvious until a year or so after publication, the *Collected Poems* encapsulated Peter's whole period as a Jesuit poet. From eager undergraduate to reluctant schoolmaster, passionate sermonizer and dabbler in ideas of revolution, they reflect the successive influences, affections and frustrations of the first half of his poetry-writing career. The overall mood is far from consistent; among the syntactical experiments, vague imagery, sad landscape poems and strivings to make a moral point comes the sudden bright knife-thrust of a simile, as in 'Thirty Ways of Drowning in the Sea':

> *Here the deep sea is moving between rocks,*
> *fretting itself to marble-paper foam;*
> *deadly as chemistry, and green as tea.*[15]

(Years later, in a similar rhythm, he would call Larkin's poetry *as lively as jazz, as clean as gin.*)[16] A new, mature tenderness suffuses the last few poems, as he ceases to preach about love and begins to express it. The elegy for Seferis is a meditation on life and the spirit in terms of a wild Greek landscape, prefiguring the lamentations he would write for friends nearer to himself in age. And 'Pigs', a long poem for Deirdre Connolly, who was fond of pigs, is a new departure, funny, whimsical, sensuous, observant and beautiful in parts.

> *Pigs are the moon's creatures,*
> *and the small hedgehog moving at night*
> *and the grey and black badger in moonlight*
> *are the English moon's priest and acolyte.*
>
> ...
>
> *Humans make bad pigs,*
> *old silver-backs with rosy faces*
> *clever with truffles, hating each other,*
> *bristlers and tuskers upright in chairs*
> *pleased with possession, liking their smell,*
> *dark hairy snorters in undergrowth,*
> *brushed Foreign Office pigs with swine eyes*
> *and gloating piglets of great families.*
> *They are the poor relations of true pigs,*
> *they never get their snouts in real buckets.*
> *They lack hedges and mist and cabbage-stalks.*[17]

✺

Deirdre spent most of the eighteen months after Cyril's death disentangling herself from his debts. She had not realized that he had managed to squander so much since the move to Eastbourne, as if owning a house for the first time in his mid-sixties had given him unlimited credit. Overdrafts were easy to acquire at that time of loosening financial constraints, and Cyril's had ballooned as wildly as house-prices during those few years. Happily for Deirdre a relief fund organised by Sonia Orwell, a loyal friend of Cyril's since her post-war years as his assistant on *Horizon*, raised tens of thousands of pounds from rich supporters to pay off his debts. His library and papers went to the University of Tulsa, Oklahoma. Many of his possessions were also sold, although Deirdre kept the collection of exotic sea-shells he had inherited from his conchologist father. After finding a buyer for 48 St. John's Road, she was ready, at forty-four, to begin a new life elsewhere.

> *They do not need to believe in you:*
> *our kind of women, with hair untidy,*
> *no money left, and warm, beautiful eyes,*
> *dressed in an old coat from a silent film*
> *and a scent from the Festival du Jazz.*
> *The soul has dregs, a clouded residue,*
> *in them a clarity, a superstyle.*
> *They have given their lives away long ago.*
> *You hear their music on the radio*
> *and the song has something they gave away,*
> *but they have not forgiven anything.*
> *They grow old and grow younger at once.*
> *The courage, the cooking, the excellent legs.*[18]

At first she had thought of moving to Scotland, where she had cousins, but that would have taken her too far from friends and family members in the south. She wanted to be close to her daughter Sarah, who was newly married and living in London, and to Peter, whom she knew she loved.

You could cook for a priest and drive him around in your car, provided you only touched him discreetly. You could even take him away on holiday, provided you slept in separate beds. Deirdre understood some of the subtleties of Catholic practice, since her mother, who had been married five times, had become a Catholic after marrying a convert. 'There! Five Hail Marys and all forgiven,' she had said gaily one day when Deirdre picked her up from confession. And Peter interpreted the rules with fine, idiosyncratic boldness.

After Mass on the Easter Sunday following Cyril's death he arrived at St. John's Road for his and Deirdre's first holiday together, taking Matthew as chaperon.

Deirdre had booked rooms for them in a cottage on the Isle of Wight. They both knew the island well, but the chilly seaside setting and the landlady's presence made them feel restrained and shy, as if acting the parts of a recent widow and a respectable Catholic priest.

When their week was up, however, they crossed straight over to France to give Peter a second look at the Vix treasure, rejoicing in the sheer adventure of being abroad together. Staying at the main town brasserie in Châtillon-sur-Seine, they ate their way happily through the standard French dishes on the menu. For Matthew's fifth birthday Peter made a little Edward Lear-style alphabet book with sophisticated, zany drawings and rhymes. (S is for Sincerity, Sausage and Sand. Two improbable robed and keffiyeh'd figures toast sausages over a fire in the desert, under a crescent-topped flag reading 'We are friendly. Have some sausages.' U is for Unhappiness, 'has it a use?' X is for Xenophobe, with a joke about garlic-haters.) Towards the end he added a secret, wry Latin inscription, then wrote that the blank pages were for Matthew's drawings, which soon filled them up.

After that, said Deirdre, it seemed natural for them to take a summer trip through France. This time she drove them to the Landes and the Pyrenees, stopping for the night wherever they happened to be. The hotels were crowded with French families, and the three of them sometimes had to share a room. 'He's a priest!' Deirdre exclaimed, to which receptionists simply shrugged.

By the following winter she had decided to move to the country near Oxford. She would be able to pop in and out of Brewer Street when Peter was not away in Greece, and he would be able to spend days at her house and be back at Campion Hall for the night. The Dragon School, Oxford's most academically competitive prep school, took day-boys, and was known to coach pupils for Eton scholarships. Until he was old enough for the Dragon, Matthew could attend a small, mixed pre-prep, the Squirrel. A ladylike North Oxford establishment, St. Clare's, part sixth-form college, part finishing school, seemed right for Cressida.

From Eastbourne she made several house-hunting trips in the spring of 1976, staying at the Bell Hotel at Charlbury and searching the country nearby. She told one of the more up-market estate agents her requirements: a detached period house of a certain size with a decent garden, in a pretty setting within easy reach of Oxford, costing only as much as she could afford. Peter, like Cyril, enjoyed house-hunting and joined in eagerly. He took Deirdre to meet Nancy and Betty at Little Tew, and it was they who spotted the right house for her in the property pages of the *Oxford Times*.

Austin's Farmhouse at Stonesfield, twelve miles north-west of Oxford, was a shabby, roomy old house built of silver-grey limestone and roofed with the local limestone slates. It backed on to the main street, with a long, enclosed garden stretching back to the churchyard wall near the tower with its gilded, 'fish-flat' weathercock.[19] There was a cobweb-infested outhouse with disused farm implements lying about, and a pear tree on the front wall of the house with a froth of white blossom in spring. Stonesfield is in high arable country, above a loop in the Evenlode, where the dark, rolling mass of Wychwood fills the skyline to the north-west. Below a field full of overgrown slate-workings a rocky path plunges down between ancient hedge-banks towards a footbridge over a pool in the river, which attracts children and energetic dogs. Every hour or so the rattling of a train in the valley echoes faintly inside the house. Charlbury station, three miles up-river from Stonesfield, is fifteen minutes by rail from Oxford.

Deirdre could not move in at once. The run-down house needed months of work, and the long, hot summer with its ferocious drought kept builders busier than ever. New estates of little houses for commuters were going up everywhere, and some older brick houses had developed subsidence after the clay under their foundations shrank. In August, while Peter was in Brixton, she moved with the children into a rented flat in Cunliffe Close, a modern cul-de-sac off the Banbury Road in North Oxford. From time to time during the autumn she drove out to Stonesfield to find piles of rubble in the garden, bags of sand and cement all over the ground floor, the concrete-mixer at a standstill and the workmen off on the other job. The site supervisor was evasive. October, then November came and went, and she began to reconcile herself to spending the whole winter in Oxford. Peter came to Christmas dinner at Cunliffe Close, unwrapped his presents, played games, told funny stories, let Matthew bury him with cushions as he lay on the floor, then walked back down the empty Banbury Road to Campion Hall.

He had put off going to Greece until the Easter vacation, as he had taken on extra teaching at Pembroke College and was also booked to preach the University Sermon on Sunday, February 20. By Easter itself, early in April, when he got back, Deirdre should have moved house. He planned to spend a day a week at Stonesfield, exploring the surrounding country, keeping Matthew amused, helping to cut back the wilderness at the far end of the garden and doing some writing in a spare room which he hoped to be allowed to use as a study. He loved Austin's Farmhouse from the beginning, and later gave the protagonist of his thrillers, the classical archaeology don Ben Jonson, a humbler version of it as a bachelor retreat.

In the New Year Deirdre decided that she had spent so much on building works that she would have to move into the house before it was finished. The owner of the Cunliffe Close flat had given her notice, telling her he wanted to sell, and she could not afford another short-term lease. The farmhouse kitchen would be transformed with new units, plumbing, electrical fittings and an Aga, but this had not yet been done. In February she moved, creating a makeshift kitchen upstairs where she cooked the family meals on a Baby Belling. Peter saw nothing wrong with that. He had always eaten out in Athens, not bothering to use the basic cooking arrangements in his rooftop room in Mets.

He was thinking about his sermon, one of a pair on the Grace of Humility and the Sin of Pride, which a seventeenth-century clergyman had endowed to be preached annually at the university church of St. Mary the Virgin in the High Street. As ecumenism was fashionable it was not unusual for a Catholic to be invited to preach at St Mary's, but Peter knew that he should observe at least some of the conventions. His sermon, on Humility, must not be too personal, or in verse. On the other hand it must original, or he would see no point in preaching it. For his text he chose an enigmatic sentence from the Book of Job 11.12, 'For vain man would be wise, though man be born like a wild ass's colt'.

The power of sermons fascinated him. He would have liked to be able to preach a long, enthralling prose poem like the sermon of John Donne's he had once read aloud at a university ceremony. What he could not manage was the kind of low-key, congregation-friendly sermon that begins with a relaxing anecdote before introducing a logical theme. High in his rhetorical pulpit he fired off an opening question, 'Why do we say humility is a grace? Is it unnatural?' Man (he asserted) has no innate knowledge of God; God's spirit lures every generation into a wilderness of love and belief; and humility is a rainfall of grace in that wilderness. Then he launched into a confusion of similes ('A human being is a kind of animal... a kind of tree... a kind of walking orchard of trees... a kind of fruit in the end... and the fruit of mankind is Jesus Christ.') Citing Shakespeare's songs and Johnson's and Brillat-Savarin's essays as worldly yet humble creations, like certain houses, he claimed that the grace of humility could penetrate whole human societies and conflicting historical traditions. It was better to be an atheist (he said challengingly) than to worship a tribal or sectarian deity. 'God is the God of this planet and of the whole history of mankind.'

After a torrent of largely metaphorical allusions to wildernesses, deserts, rainfalls, the breath of the Holy Spirit, the dignity of animals and the humility of the saints, he made a final, seemingly paradoxical assertion:

> We love God naturally... as we love one another by connaturality, because we shall share his nature and he has shared our nature. Surely we must confess what God has done, and what Jesus Christ has been, and what he is... In this city, in this university, we ought to pray to be humbled. Through Jesus Christ our Lord. Amen.[20]

Nancy was at the service with her archaeological friend Sinclair Hood. On the way out they exchanged worried glances. 'I don't see him lasting much longer as a Catholic priest,' said Sinclair Hood.

&

Peter did go briefly to Greece in late February. He spent some time dutifully wandering round Olympia, then went to stay with Takis Loumiotis near his vegetable garden and vineyard on the hill above Katakolo. Low and anxious, he caught pneumonia and returned to England early, a little shaken.[21] It was not only illness, however, that shortened his stay.

One day soon after Deirdre moved to Stonesfield he had found her in her makeshift kitchen in tears.

'What's the matter?'

'I can't cook lunch. The Belling's gone stone cold.'

'Has it blown a fuse or something?'

'I've absolutely no idea how it works.'

'Can't we just have bread and cheese, then? Something simple.'

'I can't *live* on bread and cheese. I can't feed Matthew on it. We've got colds. We need decent hot food.'

'Couldn't you get somebody to see to it, then?'

'On a *Sunday*? Do you know how long it takes to get anyone out here? And I've got all this food going off. I should never have tried coming here so soon. It was all a mistake.'

Still sniffing, she drove him to Charlbury station just before dark. Her eyes streamed with cold, which made everything seem worse. Getting out of the car he saw Leonard Ingrams and his wife, on their way back to London from their weekend cottage, and brusquely told Deirdre to stop crying. She drove off leaving them talking on the platform.

A few days later, things were beginning to come right. The Belling had been mended, and the builders turned up unexpectedly to discuss the final details of their job. She made them tea and waited for them to talk. The telephone rang once, went silent, then rang again.

'Peter. Things are rather busy here. The builders have arrived.'

'Please could you come into Oxford?'

'I've only just come back from taking Matthew in. And I've got the men here.'

'Please would you come into Oxford? I need to tell you something quite important.'

'Later, perhaps, when they've gone, so that I can pick Matthew up.'

'As soon as you can manage. Come and find me.'

From Campion Hall you can cross St. Aldates, walk downhill past the corner of Christ Church, turn in through the War Memorial Gardens and cross the bridge over the Trill Mill Stream into Christ Church Meadow. An ancient notice on a wall forbids entrance to hawkers, beggars and persons who are improperly dressed.

Along the walk that leads to the river-bank, a few skeletal poplar leaves were still pasted to the muddy gravel by rain. The seats were too wet to sit on. Distant shouting and games-masters' whistles came from the school playing-fields across the meadow. They stood on the bank looking out at the choppy water below Folly Bridge. Deirdre felt the damp rising through the soles of her shoes. There was a drip on the end of her nose.

'I must start fetching Matthew soon,' she said.

'You haven't asked what I rang up about.'

'What particular thing was it?'

'It was... will you marry me?'

'What? That's impossible.'

'I told the Master this morning. I'm leaving the Jesuits and the priesthood.'

'I don't know what to say,' sniffed Deirdre, searching for a handkerchief.

'Just say yes.'

20
SECOND LIFE

Moonlight, the garden clear and intricate.

...

This island is the grave, our second life;
after the second life there is no other.

Private Ground (1981) 46

After that everything happened very quickly. Peter wrote that he 'left the priesthood... by due process of church law', and that his 'old life washed away nearly at once, with the sour blessing of a Roman court'.[1] But he did not wait to be officially released from holy orders before marrying Deirdre at the Chipping Norton Registry Office on March 31, 1977. Nancy and Betty Sandars were the witnesses. Peter wore a navy-blue suit to which Sonia Orwell had treated him, knowing that he had no formal, non-Jesuit clothes. Her friendships had meant everything to her since the end of her own second marriage, and she had greeted the news of Deirdre's engagement gaily, exclaiming 'Oh no, not *another* one with books!'

Peter would have liked a Catholic wedding even if it had meant waiting to be released from the priesthood, but that was ruled out by Deirdre's first marriage to Jonty Craven, the father of her children Sarah and Simon, who was still alive. As he wanted a religious celebration of some kind, a Christ Church friend, Peter Walker, the Anglican suffragan bishop of Dorchester-on-Thames, blessed the marriage on Easter Monday, April 11. The setting was one of daffodils and lambs, at the remote, little-used church of St. Oswald at Widford, a hamlet in the Windrush valley south of Burford. Usually approached on foot through sheep-nibbled pastures from Burford or Swinbrook, the small, bell-turreted medieval church with its dark wall-paintings and Victorian box pews stands alone inside a stone-walled enclosure. Deirdre had hated the idea of publicity since finding a reporter from a local paper in her kitchen, so her children were the only people at the service and the lunch in a Burford hotel. Leaving Sarah to take care of Matthew, the couple drove off for a honeymoon in Provence.

Sex, and the comfort of a shared bed, changed everything. No longer an insomniac, Peter slept and slept. He loved chatting in bed with Deirdre in the morning, hearing the geese cackling next door, the church clock striking the quarters and distant trains rumbling past in the valley. With a ready-made extended family ('I am suddenly a step-father, -grandfather and -uncle,' he announced to Willie on a postcard of the Arco de Cristo at Cáceres), he felt the bliss of a new kind of belonging. He enjoyed village life and domestic bustle, and would sit writing steadily at the kitchen table or gossiping with Mrs. Parsons, the daily help, while Deirdre slipped upstairs. In his notebook he wrote that love and happiness could consume whole weeks of winter: 'happiness so real it's like a person, with its own habits & rhythms, always in the house'.[2]

Some middle-aged, childless men make the most affectionate stepfathers. Peter had been a stepfatherly figure to Matthew even before Cyril died. He would soon become almost as fond of Sarah's boys: Arthur, a small baby when he and Deirdre were married, and Jack ('the age our child would have been,' said Deirdre), who was born within the next two years. Always ready to amuse a toddler, he would bounce Jack on his knee at the kitchen table with his little red wellingtons dangling in the air. Any regrets he may have felt at having avoided fatherhood emerged glancingly in poems:

> ... *the wild cherries in the end of woods,*
> *my ghostly daughters in the rain and wind.*[3]

On leaving the Jesuits he had stepped into a jobless void, without even a record of contributions towards a state pension. It was a bad time for a middle-aged scholar with an unorthodox background to try competing for academic jobs. Although he mentioned on his April postcard to Willie that he hoped for a fellowship in the next few weeks (a tactless remark, since Willie had been shortlisted at least once for a philosophy fellowship at Oxford), he did not explain that it was a fellowship by special election, which involved no teaching and was unpaid. In return for meals and the use of a room at St. Catherine's College, he would be expected to attend special functions and make intelligent, amusing conversation at lunchtime and in the senior common room.

Other fellows of St. Catherine's by special election were either single young scholars starting out on their careers or retired academics with pensions. As a springboard to something else, it might just succeed. Hugh Lloyd-Jones as Regius Professor of Greek and John Wain as Professor of Poetry both gave him enthusiastic references, and he outlined an impressive programme of work. As well as the commentary on Pausanias, he referred to his planned study of the infiltration of Greek artefacts such as the Vix treasure into Iron Age France, and a book on Greek tragic poetry which he said he had written but needed to re-think. St. Catherine's did not question the viability of those projects, but Peter knew that, having lost his support from the Jesuits, he would find it difficult to spend long enough abroad unless he could secure large travel grants or a salaried teaching fellowship with subsidized free time.

Like Anthony and Denis before him, he had become a part-time college lecturer the previous autumn. These appointments, which involved tutorial duties but no actual lecturing, were usually short-term, although some older members of the academic fringe managed to keep them going for years. Having felt less eager than usual to spend a whole winter in Greece, he had taken over the teaching of the Pembroke College classics don, Godfrey Bond, who was on a year's sabbatical. As Pembroke was just north of Brewer Street it was easy for him to pop round there, and he enjoyed having a change of company and the use of Bond's room, as well as standard tuition fees and the extra £40 retainer. But when he went back to Pembroke after Easter, its nearness to Campion Hall made him feel shy and slightly sick. Driven into Oxford by Deirdre, he persuaded her to wait nearby while he gave tutorials, then walk back with him to the car. Even so, if he recognised a Jesuit in the street he would dodge into the nearest shop doorway to hide. His rift with Campion Hall seemed absolute; after emptying his room, he felt convinced he would never set foot there or speak to any of its members again.

Like most former Jesuits he knew, he still thought of himself as a Catholic. The jovial, pub-loving Jesuit priest at Charlbury, Robert Bulbeck, said Mass every Sunday at Stonesfield, and at first he dutifully went along. Good Friday was always a painful time for him, and the one which fell eight days after his wedding must have twisted the usual knife in his heart. He had scruples about taking communion, however, since his marriage had not received a Catholic blessing and Father Bulbeck knew quite well who he was. The abolition of the rule about fasting from midnight meant that the entire congregation usually filed up to the altar rails, taking children with them to be blessed. Should he wave away the host as it approached, stay alone in his pew or slip out of the church as communion started? Deirdre, a descendant of Ulster Protestants whose paternal grandfather had been Prime Minister of Northern Ireland, would never join him as a Catholic. In the end he gave up going to Mass, telling himself that the two of them were awaiting the union of their churches as others awaited the resurrection of the dead.[4]

'Peter ought to learn to drive,' said Sonia Orwell, who could not understand why Deirdre did not teach him. His claim that his ankles were too weak to control the pedals came oddly from someone who had scrambled for days on end along Afghan and Cretan mountain paths.[5] It was true that polio had affected his ankles, but he had managed to drive a tractor in the grounds at Heythrop as well as riding the Thunderbolt on L-plates while periodically failing the test. Cars, however, like typewriters, baffled him. Once he had finished at Pembroke and felt able to face Oxford alone, he was happy to go there by Worth's bus, which followed a slow, roundabout route from village to village, filling up with garrulous old people and young mothers with pushchairs. He enjoyed the salty backchat between seasoned passengers and drivers, and liked to speculate that certain local faces had characteristics of the Wicci, the ancient British tribe who had once inhabited the area around Wychwood and were still, he imagined, 'the people you meet on the Witney bus'.[6]

Stonesfield is a hilly, straggling village of no particular beauty. Deirdre had been drawn to the house rather than the village, having narrowed down her choice to Austin's Farmhouse and a less attractive house in the prettier village of Wootton, near Woodstock. Peter, however, loved the down-to-earth localness of Stonesfield. He liked to call in at the Black Head pub round the corner with a large cut-glass jug he had bought in Charlbury and carry it home, to the regulars' amusement, slopping up to the brim with draught beer. He learned all the folklore, like the story about the corpse in a coffin whose bearers mislaid it in Wychwood on its way to the churchyard in Charlbury and found it weeks later after the snowdrift that buried it had melted, and jokes that certain villages like Combe and Leafield were populated by inbred half-wits. His first thriller *The Head in the Soup* is partly a love-letter to Stonesfield and Oxford, in which the innocent archaeology don Ben Jonson, in the intervals of a far-fetched antiquarian chase between New York, London, Rome, Greece, Israel and France, returns thankfully to his bachelor country cottage and college room.

Friends from his past turned up to inspect the Stonesfield household. Denis, so absorbed with life at University College Dublin that Peter had been afraid he had dropped him, came to visit soon after the wedding.[7] Brendan came, straight from Athens, and fell asleep with exhaustion behind a sofa while Deirdre was cooking lunch. And Bruce Chatwin, who had failed to publish his nomad book but was about to burst on to the scene with *In Patagonia*, could not resist inspecting Peter in his married state. Footloose with typewriter and rucksack, he had begun his compulsive travels into the more uncomfortable parts of the world, fetching up now and again at friends' houses to write and be cosseted and fed. At Stonesfield he sat preening at the kitchen table and gazing round like a meerkat, sizing the place up (Deirdre thought) as a potential home from home. On her guard against scroungers and unseduced by his glittering charm, she made sure that Peter saw him off.

Although he loved entertaining and was happy to see old friends, Peter no longer yearned for their company or felt much need to communicate with them. Deirdre had to prod him to visit Anthony, Gillian and others with whom she felt he ought to keep up. When

Bertie, in Glasgow, began sending him regular birthday letters, he answered warmly and begged him to come south on a visit but could never remember when his birthday was. Some friendships hung in abeyance, while a few perished from neglect.

The American poet Robert ('Cal' for Caligula) Lowell had been a friend Peter rated highly, in spite of seeing little of him. In 1970, four years after failing to be elected Oxford Professor of Poetry, he had been a visiting fellow at All Souls. Peter had met him at literary parties like John Bayley and Iris Murdoch's Eights Week lunch, in company with Lord David Cecil and Lady Berlin.[8] He admired the grandeur of Lowell's poetry and liked his self-deprecating warmth, thinking later that very few poets could have been so much loved as human beings.[9] An alcoholic and manic depressive, Lowell had been in the process of leaving his second wife Elizabeth Hardwick for the literary *femme fatale* Lady Caroline Blackwood. With Caroline's three daughters and their small son they had led a turbulent life in London and at the large old house, Milgate, Caroline had rescued in Kent. Then, in September 1977, fleeing back to Elizabeth but clasping a portrait of Caroline by her first husband Lucian Freud, Lowell died of a heart attack in a New York cab.

To Peter, the news was enough of a shock to make him start the first notebook of his married life. He reflected on Cal's 'classic line that Roethke can also write', with the depths and complications that lesser imitators failed to achieve.[10] Cal's last collection, *Day by Day*, published only weeks before he died, was full of calm confessional poems about love, madness, hospitalization, enforced loneliness and reconciliation, amazing Peter with 'that intimacy, that entry into privacy and the soul, which great art so often promises and so seldom delivers'.[11]

At Cal's memorial service he found himself in the glowering presence of Ted Hughes. 'I suppose you sucked your experience as a Jesuit dry, used it and moved on,' challenged Hughes. Peter was shocked by this apparent cynicism in a poet he barely knew. Proper poets (he thought) did not treat their vocations like that, although they might be drawn by instinct into poetically nourishing situations. 'A poet's themes are passionate engagements, they are not flirtations to be exploited.'[12]

He and Lowell had worked quite differently. In 1976, while Lowell had been refining his traumas into taut, open-ended poems, Peter had found himself blocked. Lowell's driving force had been the tensions of an emotionally fraught late marriage, whereas Peter had been struggling to remain a passive celibate. Until he left the priesthood, he told the young American journalist Jannika Hurwitt, who interviewed him for the *Paris Review* in the late spring of 1977, he had not understood Seferis when he said that not writing poems amounted to a disorder. Surely, he had thought, poems must spring from an impulsive disordering of the senses. Then he realised that Seferis had been right. Poems were the natural expression of the soul. 'One's got to write poems. Like one has to go to church... One might as well get on with it.'[13]

By that autumn, although still shy of celebrating married happiness, he was writing poetry non-stop. *Five Ages*, published in 1978, is wintry and low-key, full of bare-branched landscapes, early sunsets, and meditations on the struggle of 'reason' (or faith) to survive in a hostile world. But Fram Dinshaw noticed how the 'oracular pronouncements and imperatives' that had sometimes antagonized readers of his earlier poems became more smoothly incorporated into those he wrote after his marriage.[14] No longer in a pulpit or waving a political flag, he was finding a gentler tone of voice, producing what the Anvil Press poet Heather Buck called a 'poetry of integration'.[15] One poem in *Five Ages* seems to have sprung from a need to reconcile his feelings for Deirdre with his long-established religious beliefs.

Often the same conversation,

and the sun setting, winter in the woods,
wind in the air, hill one hard line.
Nobody alters but us.
We are eaten away with love of life.

The confused, bare trees outside his window turn his thoughts to the wintry confusion of the Nativity, and the 'one star' from which 'we can never go backward'; then to Deirdre alone in past winters with violin-music for conversation, and 'the telephone the instrument of love' stringing its 'long wire over the wet field.'

What is time? We alter in it,
love is a process, life is a process,
the flint of a religious heart is so.

Finer, more egocentric, and perhaps influenced by Bruce Chatwin's favourite Bashō, is the title-poem 'Five Ages of a Poet', in which nature composes itself like a Japanese landscape in charcoal or brushwork, and the poet, alone among trees, black water and swans, becomes absorbed into the things that affect him most intensely.

Now the young scholar under a pine tree
with the thin inward meaning of pine trees;
yesterday the plume of the reed,
today the knotted pine, the winter wind,
and a pure smell before it will snow.[16]

Other poems revealed a new talent for imaginative vignettes. '*Crust of a honeycomb is dawn...*' describes a young revolutionary fighter in a hot, arid, mountainous country. The affectionately observed 'North Oxford' suggests lives glimpsed through lighted windows as the Worth's bus trundled up or down the Woodstock Road.

They have accepted houses about which
there was little enough to be said,

they use clear, plain colours,
they are talkative in untidy gardens,
they observe weather through windows.
The dead are familiar to them,
they are aching bones inside history.

...

One morning, it will have snowed outside,
you can see the yellow light of their lamps,
you can hear coughing and the kettle.
The Asian hunter in the ice mountains
and the dark tide of cities and of men
and the great claw of the Australian crab
were slower and more useful than they knew.

☙

St. Catherine's, where he took up his fellowship in October 1977, was not an ancient, stone-built college like the one in which his character Ben Jonson holes up from his pursuers behind the double oak doors of his room. It stands to the east of central Oxford, on the edge of the River Cherwell, in landscaped grounds planned to match the rectangularity of its glass, brick and concrete buildings by Arne Jacobsen. Opened in 1962, it had a progressive, egalitarian atmosphere and had been one of the first five men's colleges to admit undergraduate women. Peter enjoyed the company and the food, hurrying back across town to lunch in college even when entitled to eat elsewhere. Ben ridicules the horrors served up on certain High Tables, while praising his own college's lunchtime food as 'a gentle lyrical poem on most days of the year'.[17]

St. Catherine's had no classicists. Pre-eminent in English studies, it made Peter think dreamily of being in 'a wood near Athens'.[18] The genial John Bayley had moved there three years earlier as Thomas Warton Professor of English Literature, bringing the relaxed, gentlemanly-amateurish attitude to his subject that had characterized his time as a fellow of New College. His former student and friend A.N. Wilson referred waspishly to his 'slapdash brilliance' and wilfully erratic research[19] – qualities, with an Iris-like breadth of interests, that Peter increasingly shared. Chiefly interested in nineteenth-century Russian literature, he had published studies of Pushkin's poetry and Tolstoy's novels and still regularly reviewed serious books on Russian themes. Shortly before Peter joined St. Catherine's the former diplomat Sir Charles Johnston (whom Peter later called 'a life-enhancing writer and friend')[20] had published his verse translation of *Evgeny Onegin*, which Bayley admired for its sophisticated replication of Pushkin's galloping Byronic stanzas. An entry in Peter's notebook, contrasting Pushkin's moral warmth towards the characters in *Onegin* with Byron's indifference towards those in *Don Juan*, suggests that Bayley had welcomed him to the college with conversations about one of his favourite Russian works.[21]

In his college room he taught and wrote. The Botany fellow, Barrie Juniper, with whom he was supposed to share it, gave him almost uninterrupted use of it, since he was nearly always in his departmental office. Classics dons in other colleges farmed pupils out to him and once or twice sent him research students to supervise. A little fee-paid tutoring even came up now and again at St. Catherine's when an undergraduate needed help with a classical paper in English or History. The room was meant for daytime use only, although Brendan caused some awkwardness when discovered to have been camping in it one summer.

Meanwhile, with persistent but dwindling hopes, he applied for any salaried academic post for which he thought he had the faintest chance of success. The Principal of Lady Margaret Hall, Sally Chilver, was due to retire in 1979 when the college began admitting men. Her job was thrown open to men and women, and Peter, ignoring his own complete unsuitability to run a college, was among the failed applicants. In less improbable situations established dons closed ranks, sometimes letting him know that, although intellectually well qualified for the job, he was ruled out by his age. Most academic jobs went to young, recently qualified scholars, who started at the low end of an age-related salary scale. Holding an unpaid fellowship in his late forties also did little for his chances, since it sent out a signal to potential employers that he must be at least partly retired.

He had become too attached to Oxford to think seriously about applying for jobs elsewhere. 'To me it was an old coat I was used to wearing,' he made Ben Jonson remark in his second novel.[22] He liked bright spring mornings when the York stone paving gave off a clear gleam, the south-facing limestone walls turned a melting silver-gold, the almond tree by St. Mary's was in pink flower, and Catte Street filled with the stilt-like shadows of walkers and the flying shadows of bicyclists. He loved working in the Bodleian Library and popping into the classical sculpture and cast galleries in the Ashmolean Museum. And then there was the Stonesfield household, now as much part of his Oxford existence as Deirdre's was intertwined with his own.

So a patchwork living was all he could expect for the time being: a bit of tutoring, bulked out with as much commercial writing as he could fit in. The dynamics of thrillers were not something he understood, but *The Head in the Soup*, which Constable published in 1979, contained the kind of background detail that educated readers often enjoyed. Ben's Oxford life includes vignettes of some of Peter's favourite things: ancient, fortress-like colleges, knowledgeable museum staff and polymathic high table conversations in which 'silver-haired dinosaurs' showed off madly. Ben comes across at first as a rather priggish, withdrawn person, keener on archaeology and Homer than on bedding the girl, who remains as coolly comradely as the heroine of a novel by J.I.M. Stewart or John Buchan. In 1984 Peter told John Haffenden that Ben was not at all like him, implying that he saw him as a plodding meritocrat. 'He has a much bigger chip on his shoulder than I've ever had... and he's a much better scholar.'[23] But in his second attempt, *Grave Witness,* which he was writing at the time, Ben emerges as a sympathetic, cleverly amusing character, more like his creator and more contentedly rooted in the Stonesfield-like village where much of the action takes place.

At home and on weekly trips with Deirdre to London, where they sometimes stayed in a Notting Hill flat, he enjoyed being accepted by her friends. One or two, like the Spenders, had known him for years, but on a different social footing. Other former close friends of the Connollys included the bibliographer Anthony Hobson, whose wife Tanya (née Vinogradov) was a stepsister of Deirdre's; the *London Magazine* editor Alan Ross, a former lover of Deirdre's, and his tolerant wife Jenny; Miranda's mother, the seductive Barbara Ghika, whom Deirdre thought 'so romantic'; and Sonia Orwell until she died of cancer in December 1980. In Oxford Asa Briggs and his wife Susan, who had known Deirdre since their time at the University of Sussex, invited them to parties at the Provost's Lodgings at Worcester College and lent them the house in Lewes they had kept as a retreat. Lunch-parties at the big round kitchen table at Stonesfield went on into the late afternoon while Peter plied the guests with food, wine and cigars. In London he kept up his membership of the Beefsteak Club, enjoying the random lunchtime conversations with strangers and the gossip that sometimes developed. Like other wits of his generation, he perfected a fogeyish imitation of one of its most senior members, Harold Macmillan.

There were still one or two occasions on which he felt shut out. Early in September 1978, at the private view of Rodrigo Moynihan's

Royal Academy retrospective, he felt alienated by the superficiality of the smart crowd he saw hugging and kissing or cutting and avoiding one another. In his notebook he complained that their brittleness reminded him of certain Oxford grandees like Hugh Trevor-Roper and Raymond Carr, airing their snobbish impatience with bores in the review pages of the *Sunday Times*.[24]

There remained one possibility of improving his standing both in Oxford and beyond. The next Professor of Poetry was due to be elected in the first week of November, as John Wain's last lecture was scheduled for that term. Peter now saw no objection to standing, since winning would transform his prospects and bring him a useful, if very modest, five-year stipend. Fifty resident and non-resident Oxford MAs had nominated Wain, but Peter mustered sixty-eight, including Alasdair Clayre, David Pryce-Jones, Constantine Trypanis, Maurice Keen and twenty fellows or other members of St. Catherine's, including Brendan, who had found a foothold in the college.

That election was extraordinarily hard-fought. Wain had been opposed by Stephen Spender, with eleven nominations, and three also-rans. Among Peter's seven competitors was the respected poet Donald Davie, then teaching at an American university, with thirty-eight nominations. The two most powerful candidates, however, were John Jones, a senior English don, and John Sparrow, the controversial dilettante and former Warden of All Souls. Politicking was widespread, with dons and graduates who rarely showed any interest in poetry lending their names to one faction or another. Against Sparrow's 102 nominations, Jones, the safe pair of hands and eventual winner, had 246.[25] Peter stayed well out of the way during the campaign, since he and Deirdre had already decided to spend the whole of that autumn in Greece.

He had no teaching lined up for that term, and was anxious to get on with Pausanias. Adrian House had commissioned him to write a memoir of his Greek adventures which would pay the expenses of the trip. Cressida had left home and taken a job in London, while Matthew, at eight, was thought young enough to miss a term of school. Deirdre helped him with the travel-diary his teachers had demanded, only to find that they showed no interest in it. They took the car through the Balkans rather than down the Brindisi route, and spent much of the autumn in and near Olympia with stops in Athens at either end.

It was an epic journey for Deirdre. She made a detour to Châtillon-sur-Seine to give Peter another look at the Vix treasure, then continued through Switzerland and the Alps as far as Venice, where they rested for a week, marvelling at the buildings, the light-filled, watery spaces and the colours of the stones. It was utterly different from the kind of hotel luxury Cyril had indulged in. 'Gardening stops in the Alps, God stops in Venice, milk stops in Yugoslavia,' Deirdre quipped as they met the forested slopes, gimcrack hotels and grim provisions of the Balkans.

There was mild trouble when they reached the Greek frontier, since Peter's name had not yet been removed from the list of undesirables. Spending a night in a grand hotel in Saloniki, they were shaken in their beds by an earthquake, which felt (Deirdre said) like the beginning of *The Wizard of Oz*. The next day they set off for Mount Pelion, with its chestnut trees and clear streams, and the seaside near Volos, where Matthew collected pebbles and they swam in a warm, buoyant sea.

Everything went well until Peter developed a poisoned tooth and urgently needed a dentist in Athens. After a hot drive on fume-choked main roads, during which Deirdre complained that God had abandoned Greece to lorries ('He's at Florian's, he's just slipped out of St. Mark's for a minute or two'), they spent a lavish couple of nights at the Grande Bretagne. Then, after a cheap, nasty overnight stay in Corinth, they headed west through the Peloponnese to Pyrgos, where George Pavlopoulos was waiting to greet them in his best suit.[26]

For the next few weeks there were reunions, hugs and congratulations to Peter on his beautiful new wife and pretty, blond young stepson. They stayed at first at the old-fashioned railway hotel in Olympia where Peter had wintered three years before, then in cheap farmhouse lodgings at Korakochori ('village of the crows'), with weekends of relative comfort back at the hotel. The Leigh Fermors were away, so they did not try to reach Kardamyli. Together they paced out the site of Olympia, examining everything from the bare rocks and scrub of the Hill of Kronos to the solitary standing column, heaped-up masonry and mosaic fragments of the Temple of Zeus, while Peter made notes for his commentary. Sometimes they had lunch at Katakolo before spending an afternoon at the seaside with Matthew. Mr. and Mrs. Pylarinos were about to close down their restaurant and join their children in Canada. For the last time they ate Mrs. Pylarinos's runner beans with tomatoes and herbs, while Deirdre tried to work out the recipe, which she puzzled over for years.

As the cold came down from the mountains and their money began to run out, they said their farewells at Pyrgos, Olympia and Korakochori and headed back to Athens. For several days they looked up old friends such as Barbara and Nikos Ghika, and went to Floca to find Gatsos, with whom Deirdre struck up an immediate, almost wordless rapport. Then they retraced their journey through Yugoslavia, crossed the Alps, stopped off in Salzburg and Frankfurt, visited Deirdre's favourite Van Eyck altarpiece in Ghent's cathedral, and arrived back at Stonesfield in time for Christmas.

Serious work began for Peter in the New Year, when he started on the memoir for Collins. He would not see Greece again for eleven years, and the commentary on Pausanias would remained unfinished. That winter, however, he discovered a talent for autobiographical narrative. Within a few months he was half-way through the third chapter of *The Hill of Kronos*, describing his first visit to the Peloponnese. Adrian

House, a tactful and supportive editor, admired the clarity and wit of his prose while discouraging him from the fantasies and digressions of Paddy's *Mani* and the casualness of Robert Byron's *Road to Oxiana*. The book falls neatly into two halves, the first of which recounts his adventures in the summer of 1963, while the second, resuming two years later, describes his experiences during and after the junta, with a final chapter on the recent family trip.

Discreetly knowledgeable and lightly allusive, *The Hill of Kronos* gives the impression of saying everything there is to say about Peter's involvement with Greece. While incorporating snatches of conversation and jottings from the notebooks, it avoids the raw edges and didactic passages of *The Light Garden of the Angel King*, in which the poet and archaeological scholar never quite resolved their differences. Its most obvious omission, to those who know the background, is any acknowledgement of his debts to Nancy Sandars, Philip Sherrard and the Leigh Fermors, whether from delicacy about protecting the identities of his English friends or from a belief that a book about Greece ought only to be about Greeks.

'He is the true romantic – but with learning,' Dilys Powell wrote in a *Times* review, barely eighteen months after he had started writing the book. While mildly criticizing his political naivety she praised his narrative verve, his eye for detail and responsiveness to people, and the way in which 'this devoted, splendid... unique book' conveyed 'all the feeling familiar to those of us who care about Greece – who have, one might say, Greece in their blood.'[27]

21
MUTATIONS OF LIGHT

Everything we see is a mutation of light, even the crests of woods.

Notebook, spring 1979

While finishing *The Hill of Kronos*, Peter started a new teaching job in Oxford. 'Christ Church beating its luminous stone wings about my head, day after day,' he wrote in his notebook.[1] His immediate employer was the Christ Church classics don Colin Macleod, who arranged for the college to hire him on a three-year lecturer's contract from April 1979 to relieve his own teaching load. In return for tutoring undergraduates for six hours a week for three eight-week terms a year, he was initially paid £1,152 a year, or £8 per teaching hour, with lunching and dining rights and a proportionate tiny pension – about one-ninth of the salary of a senior fellow of the college of his age. The arrangement lasted until midsummer 1982, six months after Macleod committed suicide at the age of thirty-eight.

A stiffly reticent but brilliant undergraduate, Macleod was the kind of scholar the aged Fraenkel had once thought he saw in Peter. After winning two of the most prestigious university classics prizes he became Fraenkel's favourite and travelled regularly with him to Italy, where he met his future wife. Fragile and intensely hard-working, he developed the kind of cerebral remoteness that certain classicists and mathematicians achieve. As an academic he published important papers on Aeschylus, Catullus, Propertius, Thucydides and Horace, before beginning a detailed commentary on the last book of the *Iliad*, in which Priam reclaims and buries his son Hector's body. His single published volume of poetry, *Beginnings*, was an epic of the Creation.[2]

Peter had no illusions about his own comparative standing among Oxford classics dons. Shortage of money had made him ready to take on anything with an ancient or modern Greek connection that would pay. As a spin-off from Pausanias he compiled an *Atlas of the Greek World* for the Oxford art-book publishers Phaidon, repeatedly popping into their offices in St. Ebbes to make changes in the proofs. He wrote the text for a volume of photographs by Eliot Porter called *The Greek World*, and a travel article for the *New York Times* about the glories of the Cretan spring.[3] For the eightieth anniversary of its original publication in 1903 he translated Alexandros Papadiamantis's novella *The Murderess*, about a Greek island midwife who, from philanthropic motives, relieves poor families of their potentially expensive, unwanted baby daughters. He also undertook a *Pelican History of Greek Literature*, a wittily casual attempt at a 'new classic statement', which he hoped might at least encourage some people to learn Greek.[4]

Later, in regretful moments, he thought about the contribution to classical studies he might have made if he had been as single-minded as Macleod. The year he graduated, Professor Dodds had warned him against the scholarly outsider's twin *malaises* of inertia and despair. Working alone without institutional support, he realised that he had little hope of publication except to satisfy the demands of the market. A few years later he thought of himself ruefully as a barren planet, open to 'the excitement of any passing comet of an idea and any crumb of new fact'. Most classical scholars seemed to him so densely wrapped in knowledge and thoughts about fragments of knowledge that it was hard for any new thought or fact to penetrate them.[5] Macleod, in the end, had been a proud exception to those colleagues, refusing in his *insulted spirit* to accept any *consolation delusion or drug*.[6]

Yet for most of his three years at Christ Church, St. Catherine's and Stonesfield, he was blissfully happy. Undergraduate teaching suited him, and he even put up with students turning up for tutorials in pyjamas. At home, Deirdre's absolute devotion and staunch, unsentimental practicality gave him leisure to read, write and think.

Perhaps remembering Bert's arrivals home from Houndsditch, he would come in from a day's work and formally ask if he might take off his tie, at which Deirdre reminded him that it was his house too.

Early in spring, a troupe of ghost dancers filled the woods across the river when the wild cherry trees came into flower. Every Good Friday (said Deirdre), when he felt vulnerable and especially in need of her company, they made a ritual of scrambling together down to the Evenlode footbridge, following the wooded path upstream on the opposite bank and returning across Stonesfield Common, with its view of the embracing curve of the valley. In May they wandered in a cowslip field above the river. Those walks, with images of the house and garden, became his metaphors for their marriage. *Now we are walking in our own landscape;/our future will become a memory*, begins one of the poems in *Five Ages*. He liked the fact that he and Deirdre were only seven months apart in age and remembered similar things from their childhoods. In his imagination they became *children exploring a small field*, with a wren's song coming from a wild rose-bush and the rumbling of a distant train.[7]

In fine weather Deirdre drove him on cross-country trips, on which every glaciated valley and sweep of downland fascinated him as if he had never seen it before. On his birthday, when the white Triumphator tulips were out and the hedges were full of cow-parsley and cranesbill, he would choose a route for them into the Cotswolds or the country round Stratford-upon-Avon, or to Avebury, Stourhead or Stowe. They took guests of all ages on riverside picnics to favourite spots by the Glyme or Evenlode. Absorbed in poetry in seven or eight languages, he liked to read in the garden ('under the spell of Foscolo' one summer)[8] in the friendly shadow of the church tower. Sometimes he tried to do useful outside jobs, telling himself he enjoyed swinging a scythe like Levin in *Anna Karenina*, but he was out of training for strenuous work and gave up quickly. 'He had such poor, thin arms,' said Deirdre.

Short of money though they were, he and Deirdre entertained generously and celebrated successes with champagne.

I am free to speak of money these days.
The expense of my life horrifies me;
spent on my sweetheart would be trivial,

begins a poem which at once veers away from the subject of finance to celebrate the *white bony full moon*, the glitter of winter sunsets and the generosity of flooded, dark days.[9] Even on catarrhal early mornings at the bus-stop he noted the dawn chorus or the honking of geese across the village, and during the journey gazed out into seas of sunrise light. The power of light streams through his notebooks, sometimes transforming stone buildings or gleaming on green wheat fields crossed by the clear shadow of a telephone pole or tree.

When he did have money, said Deirdre, he carried wads of about it in his wallet, strewing it right and left. In 1980 Bertram Rota negotiated the sale of a first batch of his papers to the Jesuit-run Boston College, Massachusetts, to add to their collections of books and manuscripts of British Catholic authors. He also received a windfall from selling his childhood coin collection, and decided to treat the family to Christmas in Devon. He and Deirdre had chosen a favourite pub, the Masons Arms at Branscombe, near Seaton, but when their booking was cancelled at the last moment he went all out for luxury and took the four of them to the Imperial Hotel in Torquay. He and Deirdre might have been Bert and Mollie as they sank into its insulated comfort, with wind-buffeted seagulls wheeling over the clifftop and deeply carpeted warmth within. Among the guests were another Mr. and Mrs. Levi, with whom they struck up a jolly friendship in the richly convivial atmosphere.

At Stonesfield, early in 1981, they were snowbound. Oxford was said to be colder than Moscow, and even London filled up with piles and patches of dirty slush. Bread and milk came into the village by tractor, and no buses penetrated the drifts. Peter's long poem 'Village Snow' celebrates the communal friendliness, cosy isolation and heightened awareness brought on by a heavy snowfall in the country. He describes the morning *gilt light and the blue light*, the noise of trains rattling through snowy fields, the flaming bleakness of early sunsets and *The fresh stone glittering in country towns/on winter mornings with snow underfoot*.[10] One can almost smell the snow, feel the icicles dripping and see the birds pecking across the garden for crumbs. Then the poem reaches out to Venice, Salzburg, Russia, New York and Crete, ending (*And the snow falling and the snow falling*) with an echo of Pasternak's famous refrain from a poem of 1957, *Sneg idet*.[11]

'Village Snow' came out later that year in *Private Ground*, Peter's happiest collection of poems. Critics noticed its visual tenderness, as well as an almost Greek-inspired celebration of freedom and light.

> *I strayed into a time bluer than air*

and

> *Morning light in the freshly cut flowers:*
> *they are made of light, no one will ever see*
> *even one white narcissus completely*

and

> *the storm-light, the blue light, the lucid gold* .[12]

While a few poems complain of aching bones and the wintry draining away of the light, the general tone is naively ecstatic. Fiction *withers away on the branch* ('of seriousness' he added in his notebook),[13] but

> *Life, unexpected,*
> *has offered the simplest solution,*
> *life is an old unlikely servant.*
> *There is no other place but this place.*[14]

Life, however, had one cruel trick in store. That year, at fifty, he was diagnosed with Type 2 diabetes. Like Anthony, who was found to be diabetic four years later, he had become heavy and sedentary, taking shorter walks, eating and drinking more and sometimes struggling asthmatically for breath. Deirdre read up everything she could find about the condition and tried to reform his diet, but he pooh-poohed her efforts. ('Vitamins? No such thing.') The drugs he was given failed to stabilize his glucose level, and five years later he moved on to insulin treatment.

1981 was also a year of deaths. Peter had known for at least six months that Denis Bethell was dying of cancer. When they had met the previous year Denis, brave but exhausted by his treatment, said he felt as if he had been run over by a bus, '& I must say he looks it,' Peter reported to Willie. When the news came of Denis's death on February 15, he mourned a friendship attenuated by distance. At Oxford they had imagined a continuous, shared future of intellectual adventure, in which 'the notebooks would simmer on our bookshelves and swell in our coat pockets'.[15] Denis had shown him the connections between historical events, chronicles, ballads and myths, the fun side of antiquarianism and the seriousness of medieval ruins. ('The long poem *Ruined Abbeys...* owes everything to him.)[16] All too soon, however, their ways had parted, and Denis's Dublin life had been one in which Peter was only a rare passing guest.

A few months later another forty-six-year-old friend died of cancer. Anne Pennington was a specialist in Serbo-Croat literature, recently elected Professor of Comparative Slavonic Philology at Oxford. Fresh-air-loving, religious and jolly, she had been drawn to Peter in his Campion Hall days and stayed friends with him and Deirdre as a couple. So, too, had her co-translator Andrew Harvey, before resigning his All Souls fellowship to become a spiritual teacher in

India. Peter had joined Anne in translating a collection of songs about a medieval Serbian folk hero, *Marko the Prince*, hoping to find points of comparison with the *Iliad* for a class in heroic poetry he gave in the summer of 1974.[17] *Marko* was published three years after Anne died, and Peter sometimes liked to claim that his share of it was the best piece of work he had ever done.

Steeped in the rhythms of Tennyson and Matthew Arnold, he turned to the outmoded formal elegy to commemorate his dead friends. He and Denis might have been the Arnold and Clough of 'Thyrsis', with night walks down the Thames instead of rambles on Hinksey Hill. Both Anne and Denis had believed in the afterlife, and Peter's poems about them were tranquil, accepting, sunlit and riverine. He remembered Anne, *sleek as a bird*, swimming on riverside picnics, her happiness in *the long snowy discipline of books*, and her collegiate life at elegant, red-brick Lady Margaret Hall.

> *Architecture is the measure of man;*
> *the tall white colleges disrobe themselves*
> *to see their own beauties in floodwater;*
> *they were the decoration of your soul*
> *Anne.*

Because she had once asked him to write her an Easter sermon he included one in the poem, comparing her calm, clear scholar's mind with *The lark ascending when Christ is risen.*[18]

Then, a week before Christmas 1981, Colin Macleod put his head on the railway line just south of Oxford and waited for a train to crush him. He was not the first, or last, Oxford don to choose that method, and he had given clear warning that he planned to kill himself once depression became too much for him. *The god himself will free me when I will*, Peter quoted him in a powerful lament, fitting his tone to the gloomy violence of the act.

One uncontainable deep grieving rage
sweeps through the wood and the last leaves let go:
sky full of death, wind blast, one iron taste,
one fall of snow.[19]

In late January he and Deirdre drove into Oxford for the memorial service in Christ Church Cathedral. The early morning had been as dark and foggy as November, but by nine the towers and walls of Tom Quadrangle were full of blue shadows and gold light. Seeing the crow-like figures of dons flocking together in their black gowns, he thought of the passage in Plutarch's *Lives* about the crows which cawed and pecked at Cicero before his murder.[20] Those flapping figures appeared ominously in his poem as if planning an assassination. As in his earlier lament for Eliot, he extrapolated chaos and decline from Colin's death, uniting landscape, religion, love and despair in a single dynamic:

our world is broken, it lies where it fell,
under the crust earth is an iron bell
heaving its awful weight around the sky:
it is swinging and clanging silently.[21]

On a practical level, it meant the end of his employment at Christ Church. Colin, beginning a sabbatical year in the hope of finishing his work on the *Iliad*, had increased Peter's teaching hours to a normal don's load, raising his annual stipend to £1,821 from October 1, 1981. But when the governing body reviewed his contract in the spring they decided to end it in June, before Colin's successor started. On Midsummer's Day 1982 he sat down with his notebook to contemplate an insecure future as a 'self-employed writer/retired man'.[22]

◈

After the success of *The Hill of Kronos*, with its barely stated personal details, Adrian House had suggested that Peter wrote an autobiography.

As before, however, he had recoiled from the thought of exposing a delicate web of English friendships. Although as keen on gossip as any Jesuit, he drew the line at scurrility ('He was very *pudique*,' said Iain Watson) and could be painstakingly discreet in print. In his notebook he brooded over the fact that he had never bothered to keep a diary and thought very little of his ability to 'register... intimate & fresh feeling' about other people. That applied as much to poets like Cal Lowell and David Jones as to his family and Oxford friends of the 1950s, while he thought he had given 'pitiably little' of Seferis in *The Hill of Kronos*. Even Bowra he could 'recapture only by parody, & Cyril hardly at all even in talk'.[23]

What possibilities remained? After the feebly imagined adventures of *The Head in the Soup*, Constable had not encouraged him to write another thriller. While his translation of the Psalms had not impressed Hebrew scholars, he continued to attract small religious commissions, translating St. John's gospel from Greek for the English Churchman Press and compiling the *Penguin Book of English Christian Verse*, a surprisingly tricky project for which John Wain's wife Eirian did much of the work. He could not afford another research trip abroad, so while his scholarly projects withered he turned his attention to the country near home.

It was already there in his poems: the black, ice-edged streak of the Evenlode making its way through snowy fields, the dark, undulating skyline of Wychwood. On walks he had discovered the irregular, leaf-covered mounds of Grim's Dyke, a late Iron Age earthwork which loops through parts of Blenheim, Cornbury and Ditchley parks and extends as far east as the Glyme, almost linking the Stonesfield country with Heythrop. On drives with Deirdre he had been fascinated by Avebury, whose mounds and ring-ditches reminded him of the antiquarian speculations of John Aubrey and William Stukeley, and by the rounded hills of north Gloucestershire and Herefordshire. Perhaps, he suggested to Adrian, he could write a book about 'humps and tumps' in the spirit of John Moore of Tewkesbury, one of his favourite post-war countryside writers. But Adrian insisted that if he wrote about landscape he should do so in the context of his own life.

The Flutes of Autumn, which he dashed off during the second half of 1982, is a strange, profound mixture of memoir and meditation. The description of his Ruislip childhood is light and charming, only hinting at the intense piety of the household but acknowledging Bert's suppressed Jewishness and Mollie's simple, fierce beliefs. His vigorous accounts of life at school and as a novice and scholastic are consistently reticent about people, identifying Father D'Arcy, Christopher Devlin and a few other senior Jesuits but no friends of his own age. When Bertie congratulated him on his discretion, he admitted that he had still been afraid of causing offence.

After the Oxford chapter, with its memories of Denis, chronology begins to give way to meditations on history. The topographical slant of the narrative, although lyrical in places, suggests an almost exclusive preoccupation with landscapes and their past. Disguising his Campion Hall teaching as archaeological research, Peter portrays himself as a dedicated scholar, with no reference to his other life as a poet. There are brief vignettes of Nancy Sandars and Tony (but not Julian) Mitchell, mainly in connection with archaeology and expeditions into rugged hill country. A passage describes his and Tony's visit to Richard Hughes, but he mentions no Oxford friends apart from Denis, and none of the senior literary figures who were such important influences on his life. Deirdre, although identified by name in *The Hill of Kronos*, appears only as a nameless figure with whom he had been 'more and more in love for something like thirteen years',[24] in a chapter which begins with his final summer in Brixton, skirts delicately round the subject of his marriage and ends with long, involved speculations about the history of Grim's Dyke.

Yet the appeal of the book is not only in its lyricism, or because spare, elusively impressionistic accounts can be more fun than stolidly factual ones. Its allusive leaps and digressions are like the conversation of a delightful, knowledgeable new friend, while its landscape theme has a deeply elegiac undertone. Nancy wrote that Peter's absorption in landscapes meant that he '*becomes* the landscape, its history and its poetry'.[25] Like David Jones (whom he did not mention in this context), he had come to associate certain British landscapes with the annihilation of ancient tribes and peoples and the destruction of the cultures attached to their homes. A repetition of that process, on an unforgettably monstrous scale, was the slaughter, in Georg Trakl's words, of 'generations of the unborn' in the First World War.[26] Peter owned several copies of the poem 'Grodek', Trakl's testimony to his horror at the suffering of the casualties he tended in Poland before taking a fatal cocaine overdose in November 1914. The preface to *The Flutes of Autumn* is a translation of one line from that poem, *And in the reeds the dark flutes of autumn mutter their undertone.*

❧

Shortly before writing *The Flutes of Autumn*, Peter received a literary crumb from Penguin Classics in the form of a contract for a new edition of Johnson's and Boswell's tour of Scotland and the Western Isles. John Wain, who had created something of a Johnson industry for himself, may have arranged the commission for him. A summer holiday in Scotland was just what he needed after losing the Christ Church job, and in August 1982 he, Deirdre and Matthew stayed at the Eriska Hotel on its lonely island north of Oban, Argyllshire. Twelve-year-old Matthew loved the wild setting, and Peter was delighted that Angus Macintyre, whom he had come to know better since Dominique de Grunne's Auvergne house-party in 1963, invited them to stay with his family at their woodland cottage on the Kintyre peninsula. Angus was now a senior history don at Magdalen, and he and his wife Joanna had several children, of whom the oldest, Ben, had reached university age. Peter and Deirdre returned three years later, by which time Angus had moved his family to the big house down below. From their first stay Peter remembered the pure taste the spring water gave to whisky, *the rattling of the climbing car/with children on the bonnet*, and kindly Angus casting for trout

> *like a rock for quietness,*
> *or human heron, born to riversides,*
> *fishing the black pool in your antique hat.*[27]

Those lines come from the long, calm lament he wrote for Angus after a truck-driver fatally ran him down on the M6 on his way to Scotland for Christmas in 1994, a month or two after he had been chosen to be the next Principal of his old Oxford college, Hertford.

That lament, one of Peter's last, was his finest and most controlled. He had written several in the 1980s, mourning not only Denis, Anne and Colin but Caryl Brahms, Alasdair Clayre and even the distant Charles Haldeman, who had died suddenly of an infection in Crete. Those laments, usually written some time after the event, were exercises in love for, and sometimes deep empathy with, the deceased, exploring the ways in which their lives, creativity or culture had touched his own. The lament for Angus was more detached, in keeping with a friendship which had been admiring on Peter's part but always based on a certain gentlemanly reserve.

Caryl Brahms had been a friend for years. To console him for the shock when 'Cousin Miranda' married she had sent him her father's blessing cloth, which had covered the family's ritual bread and salt every Friday evening of her childhood. With it she had sent a length of their grandmother Sultana's cerise-lined velvet as a wedding present for Miranda and Iain, adding that she could not part with her father's silver chalice but meant Peter to have it later. If Jewish solidarity could rescue him from depression, she would make sure that it did.

After his marriage she had taken greatly to Deirdre. Driven to Stonesfield by Ned Sherrin, she had become an affectionate great-aunt figure to the whole household, sending them her favourite joky, antique postcards and giving Deirdre Jewish recipes to try. After she died shortly before her eighty-first birthday in December 1982, in her exotically cluttered flat high up in Cambridge Gate, Peter imagined the Friday evening rituals at the grandparents' house at Croydon and the young Caryl/Doris's piano-playing chiming out into the suburban road. To commemorate her tough, salty humour and ingrained London-ness, he conjured up images of the Blitz and the original Globe Theatre as dawn *breasted Thames water like a swan*. Reaching out to her through religion (*I praise my God in your name and in mine*), he suggested a transcendent religion of love, wonder and scholarship that could sustain close friends whatever their affiliations or beliefs.[28]

Alasdair Clayre's suicide had been a greater shock. Peter and Deirdre had kept in touch with him and his pretty, blonde young wife, the journalist and literary agent Felicity Bryan, until their six-year-long marriage ended, after which Felicity had married her stepbrother and begun a family. Lonely and burnt out by his late forties after a drifting, eccentric career as folk-singer, song-writer and Open University tutor, Alasdair had been on the edge of success with a television series about China. He had taken three years to write, direct and produce *The Heart of the Dragon* with Mischa Scorer, adding a short history of Chinese civilization as a tie-in with the documentary. One sleepless January morning just before the first film went out, unable to face the reviews, he had thrown himself under a Northern Line train at Hampstead station.

Alasdair's funeral took place in Winchester, where his mother lived.

To please her Peter agreed, somewhat nervously, to speak at the memorial service in London in February. He had done nothing of that kind since he was a Jesuit, when funeral orations had gone to his head like wine. He wrote his elegy two months later, finishing it on Easter Monday, which was also Shakespeare's birthday, April 23, 1984. The volume of elegies for Caryl, Alasdair and Charles, *Shakespeare's Birthday*, has a cover photograph of the Stonesfield church tower flying the St. George's flag, taken, probably by Deirdre, that same day. Its significance will have been lost on most readers, but Peter's lamentations were so personal that much about them remained unexplained.

The poem opens in Alasdair's Oxford, the setting of his Utopian ideas and carefree experiments with love.

> *Love is a nowhere country, who builds it?*
> *It is where we should hide and be and build.*
> *The lover unloved is the working class*
> *and more complaining is the more unloved,*
> *starving to death in nineteen forty-four.*
> *The alcohol of folksong is no cure.*[29]

Less harshly, Peter remembers the kitchen radio playing Heine's lyric of rejected love, *Ich grolle nicht*, which Alasdair once sang to him when they were young. The rhythm of the lament becomes more musical as he seeks consolation from the thought of Shakespeare's death, the inevitable slow withering of the spirit and Alasdair's avoidance of this through his plunge into *heaven's fire*. Hoping, as always, for resurrection, he bids Alasdair's unquiet ashes sleep *until... the wasted ash of men shall rise in light*.[30]

ↄ

With *The Flutes of Autumn* out and little teaching to keep him busy, he plugged on with Johnson and Boswell and the history of Greek literature. In the July heatwave of 1983 he, Deirdre and Matthew stayed with the Hobsons in Normandy, where they visited museums and the medieval buildings of Vernon and Les Andelys. Then Deirdre rented a seafront house at Aldeburgh for her children and grandchildren in early September. Matthew was about to start at Eton, a testing moment for them all. Peter was relieved that he seemed to enjoy it, and told Bertie what an exceptionally sweet-natured, shy and funny boy he was. During his Dragon School period they had sat together watching endless episodes of *Doctor Who,* fondling the dachshund Mozart or, later, the West Highland terrier Pip. Entering into Matthew's jokes and crazes, Peter had sometimes embarrassed him with juvenile scatological rhymes. In his notebooks and his letters to Bertie, who taught Glaswegian Catholic under-elevens, he had fondly registered various stages in Matthew's development, from his jumpy playfulness and progress in arithmetic and French at nine to his wry account of the Dragon School leavers' talk at thirteen.

Rooted at home, with no further need to catch the early bus to work, he continued to read foreign poetry, exhilarated by Pasternak, Blok, Huchel, Sabais, Quasimodo, Foscolo, Góngora, Lorca, Baudelaire, Jacottet and Valéry. He enjoyed the primitive energies of Villon and the 'Brother Sun' canticle of St. Francis, which he decided he preferred to Dante.[31] He even tried to insert a prose translation of Villon into the collection of *English Christian Verse,* among which he and Eirian included the atheist Shelley's 'Ode to the West Wind' and the agnostic Clough's snide parody of the Ten Commandments, but none of Clough's deeper meditations about religious doubt and belief.

He needed company as much as solitude and often clattered downstairs from his book room to share literary absurdities or rare descriptions, reading them aloud with laughter or, sometimes, tears. Perhaps affected by the mood of *The Unquiet Grave,* or by notebooks of Cyril's which he and Deirdre had kept to read, he began listing things in his own notebook – favourite artists and landscapes, memorable picnics, dead friends. In such backward-looking moods he brooded, wishing he had enough money to be both a writer and a scholar, and regretting that he had not been more single-minded about scholarship in the past. Only immortality after death seemed certain, since his happiness in marriage prefigured it in a way he had never previously understood.[32]

❧

In the spring of 1984 *The Flutes of Autumn* won the Southern Arts prize of £1,000. Peter did not hasten to spend the money on a research trip to Greece or France, since John Jones's tenure of the Oxford Chair of Poetry was due to end that summer. The campaign for his successor began early in the spring, and this time Peter was the clear favourite. Unlike Jones, a worthy academic at Merton College, many of whose supporters had been intent on keeping Sparrow out, he was a genuine, penurious romantic poet who had recently published an enchanting prose work. There could be no doubt that he would have interesting things to say about poetry. Asked why he had agreed to stand, he amused people by saying that he was in it for the money. The stipend at that time was less than £3,000 a year – 'generous as a price per lecture,' he later commented, but 'it is not a living wage: it is more like an enormous tip.'[33]

Once again he had support from St. Catherine's, where his friend and efficient campaign organiser was the new young English Fellow, Fram Dinshaw. A brilliantly erudite Old Etonian from an eminent Parsee family, Fram was a student of seventeenth-century poetry. They had first met at Eton when Fram was in College and Cyril, accompanied by Peter and Deirdre, had been guest of honour of the College Literary Society. Peter's own turn to address the Society had followed after Fram had left. At the beginning of the evening the organizers had tested his worldliness by priming him with strong drink. Characteristically he had not prepared a talk, and, woozily facing a dozen critical, sharp-eyed boys, dithered about how to begin. Then he launched into readings and a cheerfully improvised account of his life as a poet, telling stories about Yevtushenko that the journalist Charles Moore remembered, and keeping the audience amused until long after the formal meeting was over.[34]

Slightly to Peter's embarrassment, one of his opponents in the election turned out to be his former pupil, the poet and journalist James Fenton. With a house in Bartlemas Road, Cowley, not far from his old college, he had attracted support from literary dons who were his friends and from medical ones he had known as an undergraduate after switching to Psychology, Philosophy and Physiology. In 1984 he won the Geoffrey Faber Memorial Prize for his collection *Children in Exile*, having already broken new ground in *The Memory of War*, his coolly shocking poetical reportage from Cambodia and Vietnam. He was thirty-five and impressively bald with a direct manner. Peter telephoned him to placate him in advance. 'Dear boy, if I'd only known you were going to stand... I think you'd make a marvellous Professor of Poetry, but it's too late for me to pull out.'

As the campaign hotted up through the spring, Peter and James emerged as the main rivals. In his *Spectator* 'Diary' of April 21, A.N. Wilson wrote that he intended to vote for Peter because he was older and had stood the last time, and he thought there should be a 'pecking order' about these things. Besides, he added provocatively, 'in a just world, Peter Levi would in any case be a Professor of Greek, but it so happens that he is not.' He urged all *Spectator* readers who were Oxford MAs to vote for Peter this time, and for James in five years' time.

Two weeks later James Fenton responded in a prickly *Spectator* article 'Poetry and Buggins', arguing that the principle of Buggins's turn was both absurd in that context and insulting to Peter. There were better reasons to vote for him than his age. What the University needed was a real, practising poet who would act as an unofficial writer in residence. Either he or Peter, who happened to be friends as well as rivals, should be able to fill that role. It would still be possible for some scandalously unsuitable candidate to be manoeuvred into a winning position, but the final decision would rest with voters on May 31 and June 2.

A week before the election began, the *Oxford University Gazette* published the names of the candidates and their supporters. All five candidates were poets of varying degrees of seriousness, two of them on the elderly side. F.T. Prince, aged seventy-two, had twenty-seven nominations; Gavin Ewart, aged sixty-eight, had two; Duncan McCann had thirteen and James Fenton twenty-one. Peter's hundred and seventeen supporters included twelve Oxford heads of houses, twelve members of Christ Church and fifteen members of St. Catherine's. They also included five Jesuits: four from Campion Hall and the aged philosopher Frederick Copleston, formerly Principal of Heythrop College, London, as an MA of St. John's. Peter's support from inside Oxford was so overwhelming that it did not seem to matter that he had little from outside, apart from the poets P.J. Kavanagh (Merton) and John Heath-Stubbs (Queen's).

He was at home with Deirdre on the evening of Saturday, June 2 when the telephone rang to announce his success. His first impulse was to rush into Oxford and celebrate at St. Catherine's, but by the time they had got organized and on to the road he began to feel it was too late in the day, and they turned round and drove quietly back to Stonesfield.[35]

22
SUCCESS

The Professor [of Poetry] is not now quite like a writer in residence; the University has grown too big for that to be possible. He sees young poets and corresponds with them, he may go to student societies, and he judges occasional competitions, but he has also to make his living.

Art of Poetry (1991), Introduction, 3

I am hellishly busy as the wolf has his snout in the door. Everything I do seems to attract more & more useless publicity & less & less money. My revenge is to write thrillers.

To Bertie Granger-Banyard S.J. [May 1985]

'So now I have stopped being famous, which is a great relief,' Peter wrote to Matthew soon after the election. There had been interviews and telephone calls, including a jubilant one from Takis Loumiotis in Athens, who said he had stayed up all night after hearing the news on the BBC World Service. A short film made in advance at Stonesfield for BBC2's *Saturday Review* showed Peter ponderously ascending the stairs to his book-room, then fair-copying the beginning of his lament for Alasdair while reciting it in a flat, measured tone. Even moderately successful writers in the 1980s were vulnerable to the grainy close-up photograph and the televised domestic intrusion. 'If only I could stop having flu as well (& if Mum doesn't catch it) then we'd be happy.'

The new publicity boosted interest in his backlist. He told Matthew that he had been invited to a travel writers' party at Blackwell's and met various heroic explorers 'all 8 feet tall & carved out of solid oak; one of them was extremely sweet & old & they got his name wrong & he smiled & said Wilfred, I'm Wilfred.' He enjoyed his talk with Thesiger (in fact a fit and well-preserved seventy-four), who bent down from his great height and said sadly 'There's nowhere I've been that I want to go back to now.'

With months to go until his first lecture on October 25, he did not rush into composing it. His summer job, arranged earlier that year, was to stand in for Alexander Chancellor as television critic of the *Spectator*. As an occasional *Spectator* book-reviewer he had found it easy to assume the wittily opinionated, casually knowledgeable house style. That June he roundly criticized Anthony West's 'badly flawed' biography of his father H.G. Wells and his 'awful' novel about Wells and Rebecca West, while praising Wells for a public career like an energetic Edwardian bicycling tour, 'setting cats among pigeons in every direction'.[1] His television reviews sometimes targeted the dullest programmes, criticizing the impure vowels, nannyish delivery and drab dress of a female Open University philosophy lecturer, and dismissing a certain Lord Morrison, boring on about technology (who was not, as he assumed, the long-dead originator of the eponymous air-raid shelter) as an 'old booby'. But he admitted to a growing affection for the documentary series *Diary of a Maasai Village*, and praised Roy Strong and, especially, Iris Murdoch for their performance in interviews. 'Firm in voice and lovable in appearance, and... so genuinely an individual,' Iris had spoken unpretentiously about Titian's 'Flaying of Marsyas', arguing that great art and religion were both remedies against egotism. He found her 'so clear-headed and precise in one way, and so entangled in another' that he could appreciate the mental richness that came from years of studying Plato, experimenting with Marxism and feeling drawn towards Buddhism, even though he could not agree with her conclusions.[2]

In Iris's company he must sometimes have felt her making mental notes. Her fictional borrowings from reality were well known, and she particularly liked endowing her male characters with physical features of certain men she knew: a densely hairy chest, a bushy moustache like Elias Canetti's, a mouth whose upturned corners in profile reminded her of a canine smile. Some of those characters were based on former lovers or close friends; others were largely invented.[3] In *The Sacred and Profane Love Machine* (1974), she gave Monty Small, a fastidiously withdrawn, prematurely widowed ex-classics master turned successful thriller-writer, a 'Jesuitical face', 'dark Jesuitical eyes' and neat, straight dark hair like Peter's. When a neighbour's wife, Harriet, declares her love to him, she finds him 'jesuitically untouchable'. A grotesquely Bowra-like figure, Edgar (head of an Oxford college, Fellow of the British Academy, eminent classical scholar and homosexual) is also hopelessly in love with Monty, and, like Harriet and Monty himself, thinks he resembles a Jesuit. If Peter read the novel he was probably amused at finding himself caught in Iris's capacious net, which its occupants often took as a compliment, not an affront.

How could he make his poetry lectures worthy of John and Iris? Of James Fenton, who (Gavin Ewart complained) ought to have won as the better poet?[4] Of Auden, in whose steps he said he most feared to tread; of Bowra, another distinguished Professor of Poetry; or Lowell, who had failed to be elected where he, Peter, had 'shamefacedly' succeeded?[5]

Enthusiasm and generosity would be the key. The lectures would not be a platform for displaying himself as a poet, but they would convey half a lifetime's enjoyment of the poetry he valued most. As eulogist, even rhapsodist, quoting freely and at length, he would share his appreciation of Lowell, Larkin, Auden, Fenton, Aeschylus, Horace, Pasternak, Seferis and Edward Lear, with more respectful genuflexions towards Shakespeare, Milton and Dryden. If not brilliantly analytical, he would at least be sincere.

That summer was one of the happiest he ever spent. As soon as Matthew was free of school the three of them spent a week in a cottage in Swaledale, among wild flowers, hay meadows and woolly sheep. The only drawback (he complained) was Tyne Tees Television, with its sinister local news of murder, arson and violence and its low-grade summer entertainment. Later they stayed at Lyme Regis, where he had raced up Golden Cap while recuperating from polio at seventeen. Swimming in a calm evening sea as sunset gilded the cliffs, with Deirdre reading James Lees-Milne on the beach and Matthew searching for fossils, he wondered if there would ever be so perfect a moment again. Two years into his marriage, he had told Bertie he was so happy that he hoped to live to ninety. Now, a shadow of insecurity was beginning to darken his life. After so many deaths of friends, and in the knowledge of his own uncertain health, he felt haunted by a sense of 'this may be the last'.[6]

So his decision to base his first lecture on an obscure Irish keen for the dead may have been less odd than it seemed. John Wain's inaugural lecture had been on a Celtic subject, Macpherson's corruption of ancient legends in *Fingal and The Death of Ossian*, which Wain had used as a stalking-horse to attack young 'alternative' poets for despising traditional forms. Peter's choice was Eilis Dillon's simple, plangent, poetical translation of 'The Lament for Art O'Leary', which he had first heard recited at a literary festival in Dublin and said he could seldom read without tears.[7] A young wife, Dark Eileen or Eibhlin Dhubh O'Connell, was said to have written the poem in Irish after finding her husband murdered in 1773. Moved as he was by the translation, Peter took the original on trust to be the greatest eighteenth-century poem written in the British Isles, and 'a disgrace to us all that so few of us know Irish'.[8] He led up to this with a general survey of lamentations for the dead, from Paul Éluard's patriotic lament for the Resistance fighter Gabriel Péri to the 'praise poem' for the heroic dead in *King Henry V,* Homer, *Lycidas*, the *Edda*, the Book of Samuel, *Marko the Prince* and the mourning rituals of Greek village women as Patrick Leigh Fermor described them in *Mani*. He was lecturing (he announced) on Agincourt day, the feast of Crispinus and Crispianus, and owed the mention of the fact to 'Shakespeare, the genius of our poetry, and in this part of England the genius of the place'.[9]

Such magniloquent flourishes suited the gilded pomp of the Sheldonian Theatre, where the Professor of Poetry was inducted by the Vice-Chancellor after arriving in a procession headed by the Esquire Bedel with his silver mace. It was Peter at his most pulpit-happy, always ready, as in his lamentations for friends, to celebrate the spirits of the dead. The fact that he had made such inflated claims for an Irish poem he knew only from a modern translation provoked Tom Paulin, not yet an Oxford don, to attack the lecture in a hostile review of the reissued *Collected Poems*.[10] But Paulin overreached himself, not only in generalizing about the 'winsome sensitivity' and 'smooth, fake facility' of the poems but in excoriating Peter as one of the 'dwindling, disinterested Arnoldians who [could] still be uncovered in the home of lost causes'. Peter's references to Arnold in the lecture were not genuflections to his memory as Professor of Poetry and poet (in *Tennyson* he dismissed Arnold's 'Rugby murk'),[11] but suggestions of what Arnold owed as elegist to his own favourite Theocritan pastoral tradition.

His remaining lectures took place, without ceremony, in a tall-windowed room high up in the Examination Schools. He read all fifteen lectures straight from the hardback folio notebooks in which he had composed them, with the text on the right-hand pages and tangles of balloon-enclosed afterthoughts and corrections on the left. Every now and again, while deciphering what he had written, he looked up to add jokes, digressions or asides.

Defying an English don's sneer that Milton was 'dodgy' to teach,[12] he decided it was time to honour one of the greatest English poets. Ignoring *Paradise Lost* and *Paradise Regained*, he hoped to reach out to young poets by concentrating on Milton's schoolboy and undergraduate verse. Much of this was in Latin, the international scholarly language of the time, like the poems he had thought about writing as a lonely young Jesuit scholastic. Having reckoned without the educational and cultural shifts of the last thirty years, he realized too late from baffled faces in the audience that many students knew no Latin, and probably would not recognize original quotations from modern European poetry either. After that he took care to translate everything in advance. Teaching seventeenth-century English (he later wrote in his notebook) was like teaching Christianity to savages. You had to make students appreciate that Donne's sermons were better than his quotable, sexy poems like 'The Flea', and that he and George Herbert had been real people with seriously held beliefs.[13] In the autumn of 1985, although hard pressed for writing time, he taught a weekly class on Donne's sermons out of pure love.

Once the Milton lecture was out of the way he sat down at once to write about Lowell, a subject much closer to his heart. When he gave the lecture on May 22, Lowell's widow Lady Caroline Blackwood, a contemporary of Deirdre's during their Ulster girlhood, brought her thirteen-year-old son Sheridan and his older half-sister Ivana and joined the family at a champagne party afterwards at the Petit Blanc. It was Peter's most personally revealing lecture, full of admiration for Lowell and regret that he had not known him better as a friend. Praising the imaginative sympathy of his *Imitations* of Propertius, Juvenal, Dante, Racine, Aeschylus and Pasternak, he also celebrated the monumental quality of *For the Union Dead* and the 'chamber music' of *Life Studies*, 'played to be overheard of course, but... [displaying] a musing privacy, a sadness which is the reverse of depressing'. For Caroline's sake he tactfully attributed reticence even to the late, wry poems about their messy marriage and Lowell's breakdown, insisting that he was not a confessional poet in the fullest sense. In the spirit of Yeats's poem 'All Souls' Night' he declared that he was commemorating Lowell in order 'to summon up his mighty ghost'.[14]

That lecture, and a birthday outing with Deirdre to Stourhead, were bright spots in a cold, wretched spring. The steady rise in the cost of living, with inflation at around ten per cent a year, was making it more difficult for people to survive on small, precarious incomes. Some who had drifted along happily without thinking much about money began to suspect during Mrs. Thatcher's government that they might be poor for the rest of their lives.

'Two straws clutching at one another, that's what we are,' Peter wrote in his notebook. He told Bertie that he was 'hellishly busy' trying to earn a living by writing, since, despite all the publicity, he was making very little money. *Grave Witness*, his second thriller, set in Stonesfield and the Isle of Wight, was published that February by Quartet. *The Pelican History of Greek Literature* also came out that spring, to at least one mildly scathing review.[15] Then Peter Hall invited him to write a play for the National Theatre. ('Peter... says it has all got to be about Greek gods, & have no jokes, so I say I am dreading it!' Deirdre wrote to Matthew). He spent much of the summer on the script, called *The Causes and the Crimes*, but Hall rejected it. Time spent on a 'flawless' translation of Martine de Courcel's *Tolstoy: the Ultimate Reconciliation* also seemed to have been wasted, although the book came out three years later in the United States.[16] In view of his Jesuit past and sympathetic appreciation of monastic ruins, Adrian House invited him to write a historical study of monks and monasteries. He accepted, but dismissed the project in private as 'a trudge in a graveyard of dead ideas'.[17]

From time to time he appeared on television, looking uncannily neat, meditative and priest-like in his dark, high-waistcoated suit. He was funniest talking about himself, as when Frank Delaney interviewed him about *The Flutes of Autumn* in a line-up with Stephen Spender and Peter Porter. ('When did you begin to write poetry?' 'When I was nine. Because it was raining.' 'And when did you start to think of yourself as a poet?' 'I considered myself more of a poet at nine than I do now.') His staccato, timed responses to Delaney, with bent head and impish upward glances from under acutely angled eyebrows, raised more laughter than his later contributions to panel discussions of the arts, in which he seemed both ponderous and lightweight in comparison with more thrusting guests. Invitations to appear on *Bookmark* or *Thinking Aloud* were rare, although he did a few presenting jobs. Once, oddly for a non-gardener, he fronted a short history of gardening programmes. In an excruciating two-part programme called *The Silver Trail* he acted as a kind of disc-jockey for video performances by young poets. Then in 1989 he made an entirely serious, final appearance as presenter of the Channel Four series *Art, Faith and Vision*, an examination of the spiritual element in contemporary arts, with Iris Murdoch, the sculptor Elisabeth Frink, the composer John Tavener and the stained-glass artist Cecil Collins.

Outwardly he seemed the Arnoldian figure Tom Paulin so despised: a snuff-scattered monument to dead poets and old-fashioned education. Yet, lacking the brittle armour of success, he remained an emotionally soft touch. In his notebook he wrote that he sometimes loved Deirdre 'with a despairing love, as if she were unattainable'. To love someone else more than oneself struck him as 'a fault, a dislocation where it is not a paradox'.[18] Reading Frances Partridge's diary *Everything to Lose*, which ended with her husband Ralph's death in 1960, made him feel that he 'had 15 pages not 15 years to live', and would be able to do nothing to save Deirdre from desolation when bereavement came.[19] *Shall we be joined together in one death/as we lie now with one soul and one breath?* he asked in a five-line fragment. And in another poem he declared *I will lie with you for a thousand years.*[20]

Still lovingly supportive of Matthew, even when he showed more interest in maths and science than in literature or the classics, he hid his dismay when Matthew dropped out of Eton to take his 'A' levels at a further education college and chose not to attempt university entrance. Home life resembled the 'perfect trinity of love' that Iris

Murdoch remembered from her childhood,[21] and when Matthew was at school Peter kept him supplied with amusing postcards and letters. Once he asked for some old postcards to decorate his room and Peter gave him a random handful, all of which turned out to be from well-known writers like Iris or Bruce Chatwin.

Cressida, working part-time in an antique-shop after marrying Richard Hudson's son Charles, a gentleman farmer in Worcestershire, was beginning a book-reviewing career. Peter urged her to keep sending her work around until editors acknowledged her existence. He himself had been 'more or less dropped as a reviewer by reputable organs,' he told Bertie early in 1986. His scholarly classical reviews for the *TLS* had tailed off, as had his reviews for the *Spectator*. Always a willing hack, he was writing for Auberon Waugh's *Literary Review* and 'being v. unkind to all'.

Two slim volumes of his lamentations, *The Echoing Green* and *Shakespeare's Birthday*, appeared in 1983 and 1985. By chance, he pointed out, they were symmetrically arranged, the first three being about scholars who died young, the next three about creative writers. The first three, he urged, should be read as a triptych of different moods: one of elegiac affection for an old friend, one of respect for a devout Christian and one of 'unconsoled grief and unreconciled anger' at Colin's death. All the poems use associative or symbolic imagery: Colin's referring to his schooling at Rugby with an opening echo of Matthew Arnold's *Rugby Chapel*, Charles's to their shared friendship with Nikos Gatsos in translated lines from *Amorgos* and the surrealistic image of *Waves like blue tigers... lashing against the rocks with tails of foam*.[22] Liturgical quotations in his poems for Anne and Caryl (*I will go to the temple of my god; I will stand before the altar of my God*) suggest that he never entirely lost a priestly attitude towards women.[23] Sliding delicately between blank verse and rhyme, with clear divisions between stanzas or movements, the lamentations are the most musical and emotionally revealing of any of his writings up to that time. He was right in believing that the poem for Alasdair had taken that kind of intense empathy to its limit. The few that followed fell short of that standard, until in 1995 he wrote his superb lament for Angus Macintyre.

His less confident lyric poems piled up until a collection of eight years' worth, *Shadow and Bone* came out in 1989. The title itself suggests gloomy preoccupations, borne out by many of the poems. Death is never far away, and he seems uncertain about the afterlife despite frequent, optimistic references to the hand of God. The spring-like opening poem 'Note on Twelfth Night' (*A willow cabin is a shepherd-house/woven like sheepcotes in the high pasture...*), written for Shakespeare's birthday in 1981, must have just missed inclusion in *Private Ground*. From then onwards the mood is autumnal, often expressed in rolling, Tennysonian decasyllables (*The woods are sombre, soon the leaf will fall... A gale of wind shakes rooks out of the trees*).[24] It is also uneasily mixed, with one powerfully religious Christmas poem (*God has gone down and heaven is empty...*), much vague speculation about the soul and a couple of shallow squibs about dull Church of England services and torpid vicars.[25] Despite his veneration for the English Bible, of which he had compiled an anthology of translation extracts while still a Jesuit, Peter never lost his feeling of alienation from Protestantism, although he kept Matthew company at church services at Stonesfield while he was being prepared for confirmation at school.

The witty series 'Seven Old Railway Posters', if less memorable than Larkin's 'MCMXIV' or 'Livings', shows a Larkinesque facility with vignettes of the English past. (*Nature is vast. It belongs to a few Dukes.*) And in almost purely Larkinesque language, quite unlike the anarchic modernism of 'Canticum' fifteen years earlier, he imagined a horrible end to nice, ordinary village cottage gardens, *amazing in*

August with their red hot pokers, michaelmas daisies and dahlias.

> *Easy to prefer England to all that:*
> *which is dying, has been dying, will die,*
> *the sliding moment that the clock stopped at,*
> *war after war, then the mature goodbye.*[26]

Larkin died of oesophageal cancer on December 2, 1985, aged sixty-three. During the few days before that Peter had been in a tranquilly receptive state, noticing 'the most beautiful (wild & melting) full moon', and enjoying the changeable weather as he travelled in and out of Oxford by bus. 'Pink & orange suns, seas of sunrise light over Combe (bus) & Pear Tree roundabout. Cold vague shores of coloured cloud at dawn from the village & at dusk over Port Meadow.' The news of Larkin's death crashed into that mood 'like a cricket-ball suddenly shattering a window-pane'. It was his desolation at Eliot's death all over again. 'Now no English poet of undoubted greatness is still alive. Since the death of Tennyson things have never been so bad.'[27]

The memorial service was in Westminster Abbey on February 14. Peter, who had known Larkin only slightly, took no active part. 'It was *icy*,' he wrote to Matthew, 'even the jazz-band shivered as it played & William Rees-Mogg's nose was blue. We sang Abide with Me as if on the Titanic as it sank.' Clive James and Andrew Motion had already written 'quite good' commemorative poems, causing Peter to note 'Philip has done 2 miracles'. Then in March he wrote a Larkin lecture to give in the summer term.

Like his lecture on Lowell the year before, it was one of his most deeply felt. In October he had examined Dryden's translations of Virgil ('not a very popular subject,' he noted afterwards). On Ash Wednesday, February 12, he had spoken about 'Visionary Poets', including Horace (who, Fraenkel had claimed, really *did* see Dionysus), St. John of the Cross, Dante, George Herbert, Traherne, Blake and Hölderlin. His audience may not have emerged with a very clear idea of the difference between experienced and imagined visions, but they had been treated to verses in English, Provençal, Italian and Spanish, including a scrap of love-song that St. John of the Cross overheard from his prison in Toledo:

> *Muérome de amores*
> *Carillo. ¿Qué haré?*
> *Que tu mueras alahé.*

('Of love I die, dear love, what shall I do? Die, alas, die.')[28]

Larkin's poetry, he said, was something entirely new. A vignette such as 'Dockery and Son' read 'like the best chapter in a novel'. In addition to a kind of poetical fiction, with vivid, sharp-edged descriptions of imaginary people or moments from the past, Larkin described real things and places with economy and a genuine emotional range. Unlike his contemporaries in the modern movement, who were overshadowed by Eliot, he created his own tradition, leaving clear principles for later poets to follow. A long, thrilling analysis of the imagery in the tripartite poem 'Livings' (*Chaldean constellations, Lit shelved liners...like mad worlds*) brings out the deep isolation of the travelling salesman, the eighteenth-century fellows of a Cambridge college on a sparklingly cold night and, apparently, a lighthouse-keeper somewhere off the Atlantic coast.[29]

There remained other heroes to worship – among them Pasternak, who fitted the criterion for Peter of being both modern and foreign. Although ignorant of Russia and its archives, he had begun the difficult quest for a publisher who would commission a biography of him. Like Bowra, who, in Pasternak's grateful words, had 'invented him', he had come to regard him, more than Eliot, Yeats or Blok, as a giant among poets, 'a life-giving force, strong enough as it were to make one believe in the resurrection of the dead'.[30]

He had been immersing himself for some time in a grim, imaginary Russia. After finishing *Grave Witness* he had cast round for a new setting for the next Ben Jonson novel. Cold War politics were constantly in the news with the Soviet war in Afghanistan, the women's peace camp at Greenham Common, Brezhnev's mysterious, slow decline and death and the rapid displacement of his successor Andropov by Chernenko. Peter fed all this material into the novel-writing machine that, in 1986, produced his last published thriller, *Knit One, Drop One*. Its plot is fairly far-fetched, combining archaeology and spying, and Ben Jonson is reduced to a characterless pawn with a disagreeable feminist wife who seems quite different from his previous golden girlfriend. Yet, just as readers of *Grave Witness* could enjoy the fruity flourishes of High Table conversation, *Knit One, Drop One* has some agreeable background details. Icebergs on the Neva at the second stage of the thaw can be heard 'clinking and tinkling together for a week of frightening music'. Professional and academic shop-talk has a familiar ring. Senior employees of ministries, museums, universities and archives in Paris, like their similarly entrenched counterparts in Bloomsbury and Oxford, exchange gossip and reciprocal favours over lunch. In Moscow, an almost equally cosy network includes a powerful but innocuous-seeming elderly lady archaeologist, supposedly a professional acquaintance of Nancy Sandars, who lives alone in an apartment with her cats.

The plot turns on the invention of a French machine, similar to ground-penetrating radar, which can read invisible material such as buried artefacts or the writing on decayed papyrus, but could be used for spying if it fell into the wrong hands. Once Ben has revealed an innocent interest in it, a former Cambridge spy who is a double agent in the Ministry of Defence sends him to report on it from Paris. While he is there, a disguised Russian from Soviet military security steals the machine, wrecking it in the process. An American Nato official has the

Russian assassinated, but the remains of the machine are never found.

After failing to reclaim his wife from Greenham Common, Ben travels to London, is debriefed in Downing Street and is sent to Moscow to befriend the archaeologist, who is suspected of knowing about the machine. He is followed, nearly imprisoned in the Lubyanka, then compromised and betrayed to the Americans by the double agent, who claims to have been sent to look for him but in fact hopes to be exchanged for him. The Americans cause a huge explosion at a nuclear submarine yard. After a second, equally violent explosion at a dockyard, the long-time naval enemies of the head of military security conspire to have him sacked. The Brezhnev-like Chairman has died, but is impersonated in the May Day procession by an actor, who is then immediately killed. The double agent escapes to Travemünde, where the British have him shot to prevent the CIA from capturing and debriefing him. The archaeologist lures Ben to her forest dacha and abandons him. He is ambushed and chased but escapes, and returns to England to be awarded the OBE.

ↀ

For Matthew's sixteenth birthday in April 1986 the family spent Easter in the Isle of Wight, where Peter breathed pure Tennysonian air. Then Matthew returned to school and Peter went into the private Acland Hospital in Oxford to have his diabetes regulated. He had reached the point at which he needed insulin injections. 'Strewth it is boring here,' he wrote to Matthew. 'Mum likes the food but is scared of the needles... And if you ever need a blood test I can give you one. Now I am having some whiskey next & I even know how to inject it.'

Deirdre, however, was more upbeat. Visiting hours were generous, Peter's room was civilized, and he was encouraged to take walks with her and the dog in the University Parks. She had filled the room with spring flowers from the garden at Stonesfield, there were books on every surface and 'also a photo of a bust of SHAKESPEARE!!!' For that elusive giant was next on Peter's list, since Macmillan had agreed to commission him to write a *Life and Times*.

23
SHAKESPEARE'S SEEDS

Poetry is a dead horse, it's a mess,
a competition in the weekly press.
Yet Shakespeare's seeds are sleeping in that ground,
fatal and poisonous, and to be found
by who chooses, who searches and who needs,
with resurrection sleeping in his seeds.

Goodbye to the Art of Poetry (1989) 19

It was a commission full of pitfalls, but Peter plunged enthusiastically in. On his fifty-fifth birthday, when the beech-leaves were softly unfurling and cowslips, bluebells and crab-apple blossom fringed the lanes, Deirdre drove him north across country past the Rollright Stones and Edgehill towards Stratford, 'as a route unbetterable,' he wrote. Four days earlier he had recorded the kind of dream that haunts biographers. He had been asked to decide which, if any, of several hundred sonnets were Shakespeare's. In his dream he went through them all twice, realizing that few of them had any connection with Shakespeare and that none of them was actually his. The ones that were closest to Shakespeare's, however, had a 'melting quality'.[1]

His approach was intuitive and personal. The figure who emerges from his narrative is a kind of Levi-Shakespeare, tenderly uxorious, profoundly moral and attached to the clear air, freedom and country values of the Forest of Arden. Travelling to London on foot in early summer, he must have heard a 'deafening dawn chorus' of nightingales like the ones Peter and Denis heard on their overnight walks through the Chilterns at the end of the Oxford summer term. When exhausted from acting and writing, he must always have hastened home to the wife and children whose 'nest he was building' at Stratford. A harder-nosed biographer, Russell A. Fraser in *Young Shakespeare* (1988), put a different interpretation on the marriage; but, as a reviewer of the two books shrugged, 'you pay your money and you take your choice.'[2]

Shakespeare's sonnets, Peter declared, were 'the most thrilling and intimately deep poems in our language', and like 'windows of clear glass that open into his soul'.[3] In his seventh poetry lecture early in 1987, he remarked enticingly that they showed traces of Shakespeare's personal life like 'the silver trail of a snail on a blackcurrant leaf'. While there had been a tendency among 'dry' critics to think of the sonnets as artificial exercises, he sided with the 'wet' ones in seeing them as expressions of real feeling. Their 'deep theme' (as in his own poems) was 'immortality in love... an earthly immortality through the power of verse to transmit beauty, a refusal to die, a defiance of death and age'.[4]

Were the sonnets about consummated or unconsummated love? While accepting the genuine intensity of Shakespeare's feelings for the Earl of Southampton, Peter insisted that a man of such obvious moral integrity would have sublimated his attraction towards the youth he called 'the master-mistress of my passion' (yet conceded to be inconveniently 'prick'd... out for women's pleasure') into a benevolent, if socially unequal, relationship. Anthony Powell raised the point that Shakespeare would felt inhibited about mentioning the earl's private parts, and suggested that Sonnet 20 was addressed to a young man of a quite different class.[5] Peter, however, preferred to see the whole sequence as a private emotional education for Southampton, not only in a social inferior's feelings for a beautiful, well-connected younger man, but also in the kind of shabby adventures an older man might have on the side. Anxious to keep Shakespeare's image clean, Peter thought he had perhaps imagined an affair with the Dark Lady, although the sonnets about sexual jealousy and post-coital depression reek of real, foul-tasting experience. Perhaps (he suggested) those sonnets were meant for Southampton's eyes rather than for a woman's. Writing for a private reader, Shakespeare could afford a certain ambivalence, toying with the entire range of sexuality like an 'infinite nest of Chinese boxes'.[6]

In his introduction to the biography Peter wrote that he had always taken an outsider's view of Elizabethan England, thanks to Christopher Devlin's teachings about recusants. So it was perhaps surprising that, far from seeing Shakespeare as a crypto-Catholic, he decided on his birthday trip to Stratford that both he and Shakespeare were Socinians. Instead of dwelling on the religious question, he preferred to concentrate on Shakespeare's rural roots. John Shakespeare had come from the village of Snitterfield, a few miles north of Stratford, and Peter chose to believe that, in London, William was still a countryman at heart. While admitting that the plays probably revealed little of his character, he believed that Cleopatra's dread of the mob may have reflected his horror at the street crowds who gathered to watch public executions, while his fear of catching the plague in the city could have inspired Hamlet's revulsion against the coarseness and decay of the human body. 'Ghastly Rome', in *Julius Caesar* and *Coriolanus*, must have equalled 'ghastly London'. In *King Lear*, in particular, Peter contrasted small-community and family values with the gross self-interest of Goneril, Regan and Edmund, whom he characterised as rootless city types: 'Snitterfield as opposed to Cripplegate'.[7]

Religion, however, was inseparable from his emotional response to *King Lear*. The sheer intensity of language in the late scenes made the king's passion and death 'almost holy'. They were 'like the passion of an old Irish weather god or the King of Summer, and like Christ's passion in a Mystery Play that moves from taunting to suffering'.[8] Analysis of the sources for the play was something he left to scholars, although he mentioned the well-known case of Cordell Annesley, a young gentlewoman living at home with her widowed ex-courtier father in Kent, who in 1603 (two years before the appearance of the anonymous *King Leir*, and three years before Shakespeare's version)

PETER LEVI: OXFORD ROMANTIC

had stopped her two married sisters having their father declared a lunatic and his will rendered invalid. He found it interesting that Shakespeare wrote the play in a year of miserable weather, ruined harvests and starvation in the Midland counties, and touching that old women in Northamptonshire were still recounting the original Lear folk-tale when the poet John Clare was a boy.

Apart from its poetical language and odd, homely details, *The Life and Times of William Shakespeare* revolves round the idea of the playwright as committed moralist. 'His affronted moral sense had eaten into its edges,' Peter concluded about his near-abandonment of comedy in the early 1600s.[9] After *Hamlet* (a 'rerun' of *As You Like It*, with the prince as a more developed satirical figure than Jaques), the 'moral machinery' of the tragedies broke down further in *Othello*, *King Lear* and *Macbeth*. It was harder, however, to fit the last few plays into a strict pattern, and in calling the defeated Aufidius's passion for the victorious Coriolanus 'innocently homosexual' he merely flicked the lid of a particular Shakespearean can of worms before moving on.

The main text of the book took a little over six months to write. In a whirl of last-minute research he believed he had made an original discovery, which he planned to publish in an appendix and also as a separate work. In spite of Deirdre's cautious scepticism, he was convinced by his own excitement; the verses he had found *must* be genuine, and he looked forward to convincing the scholarly establishment that they were Shakespeare's own.

೧

In June 1986 Cressida had spent her first literary earnings taking Deirdre and Peter for a few days' holiday in south Cornwall. They stayed at George Perry-Smith's small Riverside restaurant with rooms, down a network of precipitous lanes at Helford on the Lizard Peninsula.

356

Above the Helford River, with its weekend scattering of dinghies and speedboats, cows graze gorse-crowned cliff-top fields. The creeks which break up the shoreline fill at high tide, then drain out like baths. It is a secretive landscape of wind-bent trees, deep valleys, one-shop villages, isolated roadside chapels, manor houses hidden down rough, bosky drives, and groups of cottages which share only a postbox and a name on the map.

A few miles beyond the crossroads above Helford, the narrow road plunges down into St. Anthony in Meneage. When Deirdre mentioned Helford to the Dragon School dentist he told her that St. Anthony was his family's favourite sailing place. It consists of a single large house on a knoll below St. Dennis Head, a thatched cottage up a stony, wooded lane, a little harbour for sailing-boats, and next to it a medieval granite church with pinnacled tower and a former farmhouse and buildings converted into holiday lets. Gillan Creek runs a mile inland between steep woods. At high tide it looks as calm as a lake, its brimming green water reflecting the vegetation along the edge, while at low tide a thin stream runs through it with seabirds flocking on the mud.

Peter and Deirdre fell in love with St. Anthony and arranged to rent a place there later that summer. Meanwhile they spent a week at Caervallack farmhouse, higher up the Helford river valley, with Matthew, Deirdre's daughter Sarah and her two boys Arthur and Jack. Sarah's marriage had collapsed and she started to house-hunt nearby. Aware that Austin's Farmhouse was becoming too expensive for them to run, and that that there would be little point in continuing to live near Oxford once the Professorship of Poetry was finished, Peter and Deirdre made an impulsive plan to sell up at Stonesfield and buy the Caervallack farm buildings to be near Sarah and the boys. (But it would never have done for Peter to be so cut off from libraries, said Deirdre.) Later, in a private, sad farewell to the 'rustic muse', he wondered about a town house in Penzance or Truro, or even a flat in Bath.[10] Scholars and poets were thin on the ground in Cornwall, although the bachelor poet Charles Causley lived at Launceston, having taught at the former National School he had attended as a child. Peter wrote him a sonnet about roses, and much later an acrostic poem for his eightieth birthday, mentioning the roses *shyer than children* that still soared inside his garden walls.[11]

That September Fram Dinshaw married the novelist Candia McWilliam from his parents' Tuscan home near Cortona. Peter's prothalamium for the couple was a meditation on Gillan Creek.

> *How fresh and easy came the equinox,*
> *the autumn wedding day of moon and soul*
> *and the sun wading as the cattle wade*
> *in pools of light between the ragged trees.*
> *The sea's dark glitter carries the mind*
> *as lightly as a saint on a dead leaf*
> *to anchorage under hillsides of trees,*
> *rank hedges where the elm is still alive*
> *and the yacht swings and tinkles in the tide.*
> *Clear sun, the heron and the brown curlew*
> *on wet sand in the shadow of the wood:*
> *the wind has withered, the leaf is alive,*
> *and full moon oils the hinges of the year*
> *for homo, luna, sol, their wedding day.*

The echo of George Herbert's 'Vertue' (*Sweet day, so cool, so calm, so bright, The bridall of the earth and skie*) may have been a tribute to Fram's study of Herbert's poems. *I never had a friend so much in love... we have consumed the all-consuming fire* was Peter's six-line concession to romance, before ending on a spiritual note. Once the moon has risen *over the torn clouds and the sea's distress*, and the sun vanished into a mist,

Leaf after leaf will drop away in light:
anima naturae, the soul's course
and seeding-ground of time and of the mind,
to wither only in the hand of God
seeking for resurrection in his hand.[12]

Early in 1988 Candia published her first novel *A Case of Knives*, which she had written between leaving her first husband and marrying Fram. In his notebook Peter acknowledged Mrs. Dinshaw's novel to be a remarkable study of characters without souls, 'or how the novel survives when only the novelist has a soul firing on all cylinders'.[13] Candia's intense, almost visionary nature impressed him while keeping him at a respectful distance. Years later, half-blind, in frail health and having self-confessedly wrecked her marriage, she found the framed wedding poem hanging in the room in Fram's North Oxford house which he and his new partner had given her as a guest.[14]

Peter still clung to Christian terminology, if only to give his poems a consoling sense of resolution. In 1984 he told John Haffenden that he was not a nature mystic; he wrote his poems as reflections on the surrounding world, to convey a sense of being 'at peace with oneself and God'.[15] Three years later, however, he decided in his notebook that God had become a useless word in both poetry and ordinary language, while the 'blatantly' indefinable soul had become more useful than ever.[16]

In his view this palpitating emotional instrument was the romantic rather than the theological soul, and its likelihood of survival after death was uncertain. He decided that immortality in Shakespeare's sonnets was so closely associated with sexual love that it suggested 'an unorthodox, private, poet's and lover's religion', more influenced by the extremes of the Italian Renaissance than by conventional religious beliefs.[17] Meanwhile his own poems revolved round the question of the soul like a dog trying to settle into its basket. Sometimes they seem meshed in paradox (*Immortal by nature, the soul will die*), sometimes confident that *there is natural immortality/and the nature of God is in nature*.[18] The soul could be projected into a vision: *Souls in rivers of butterflies that stream/on ghost-looking bushes, grey white and green*.[19] (The ancient Greeks believed that butterflies carried the souls of the dead, and called both soul and butterfly *psyche*.) The soul was *simple breath, or the truth as you breathe it away, but could be heaved and tumbled as clouds heave at the sea*.[20] It would *melt away* in death, as in his bitter, Larkinesque poem 'Life is failure. Life is failure to live'.[21] Yet the souls of lovers could merge, as in Donne's poem 'The Extasie', when they lay imagining eternal union, *soul on soul and breath on breath*[22] His concept of God flickered on and off like a lightbulb, sometimes eternally present, sometimes replaced by the Platonic life-force eros, as in *We die when eros has abandoned us*.[23]

Paul Valéry's *Le Cimetière Marin* brought a partial escape from these conundrums. Peter became 'obsessed' by the poem, with its powerful rhythm, evocation of Mediterranean sunlight and exhortation to live in defiance of death. At St. Anthony early in May 1988, when the creek water was 'as green as engine-oil', he enjoyed the contrast between Valéry's marble graveyard and the changeable sky, damp lichen and crashing waves of the Cornish Atlantic coast. 'There is no *vide* & no *événement pur*: just cow parsley...'[24] He imitated its length and form in two monumental examples of his tranquil, late mature style: 'Poem for the Time of Year: Homage to Valéry' and 'Poem for the Time of Day (Gillan Creek)'. Several years later, with less success, he made the 'rough... unsatisfactory' translation that he published at the end of the same volume, *Reed Music*.[25]

ൟ

Greece was never far from his mind, perhaps especially when gazing out from the furze-crowned cliff top at St. Anthony towards ships lying off Falmouth Bay as they lay off Souda Bay in Crete. In November 1986 he gave a lecture on Seferis (warm, solid, truthful, funny, a brilliant linguist and passionately Greek), quoting translated chunks of his *Mythistorema* in the hope of inspiring poets in the audience. In February 1987 he lectured on Shakespeare's sonnets, and in May on Auden, whose poems he respected but had never loved. That was one of his least convincing lectures, full of other people's views on Auden and his own barely relevant digressions about the twentieth-century German poets Peter Huchel and Heinz Winfried Sabais, whom he admired a great deal more.

Extra-curricular duties inevitably came with the professorship. As a not-quite-sixty-year-old, smiling public man, he gave talks at literary festivals and in schools – none of them quite as much fun as the amateurish 1984 Steeple Aston festival, at which he read half a dozen of his poems next to a beaming Iris. He unveiled a memorial tablet to the Dorset dialect poet William Barnes, the last of the Bible translators in the anthology he had compiled, just north of the county boundary at Mere. Probably with lucrative travelling expenses in mind, he agreed to join the Kingman Committee, which the Department of Education and Science had set up to recommend a model of the English language to be taught in schools. But when Lorna Sage asked his opinion of the project before the committee's inaugural meeting in February 1987, he dismissed the idea as pointless. Schools (he said) were already teaching parataxis, a disconnected form of expression like Mistress Quickly's account of Falstaff's death, instead of syntax, 'a rhetorical strategy that originated in the law courts in the fourth century BC'. Favouring 'Eton' (or T.S. Eliot) 'for everybody', he came up with the simplistic idea of giving each school a first-class library and leaving it at that.[26]

Deirdre wondered if the meetings would be as amusing as *Yes, Minister*. But Peter, sweltering in his three-piece suit in an overheated government building, found them a predictable waste of time. 'I had to go to London to my terrible committee on the first hot day,' he wrote on a postcard to Matthew on July 1. 'Got v. lost in Hyde Park & bought some cherries & it got hotter & now I am on floor eleven & the sun & noise of Waterloo pin us all down.'

Knit One, Drop One had been published that spring, as had his study of monks and monasteries, *The Frontiers of Paradise*. This received a scathing review from the liberal theologian Don Cupitt, calling it a desultory piece of work, attractively written in Peter's usual flyaway style but with piercing insights marred by an inconsequential jumble of facts.[27] Adrian House remained a loyal friend, but there were no further commissions from Collins, which was shortly to be transformed from an old-fashioned family firm into one of the glitziest world publishing conglomerates, Harper Collins.

The Life and Times of William Shakespeare came out the spring of 1988. Shortly before releasing the book, the publishers marked Shakespeare's birthday (two days late, since April 23 fell on a Saturday that year) with a 27-page booklet by Peter, steeply priced for its modest length at £7.99. *A Private Commission: New Verses by Shakespeare* drew naively hopeful conclusions from a set of early seventeenth-century occasional verses which were long known to have existed on a stray sheet of paper attached to the manuscript of a masque by John Marston. Written in a hand that was clearly not Marston's, the verses were initialled 'W.Sk.' or, by a stretch of the imagination, 'W.Sh.'. The masque had been performed in the summer of 1607 at Lord Huntingdon's house at Ashby-de-la-Zouch, probably to celebrate the engagement of his wife's elder sister Lady Anne Stanley, daughter of Alice, Dowager Countess of Derby, to Grey Brydges, 5th Baron Chandos of Sudeley. The Countess was a famous patroness of poets and playwrights, and the verses, each assigned to a different lady to read out, may have been hung on paper hearts from an artificial tree before being accompanied by gifts.

John Payne Collier, the early nineteenth-century *littérateur* who suggested the conceit of the paper hearts and the tree, had seen the 'poetical relic' among the papers of the Egerton family, descendants of the countess's second husband Thomas Egerton. With 'some hesitation' he attributed the initials to Shakespeare, if only because he could not think of any other writer of the time with a name beginning 'W.Sk.'. To fudge the issue he suggested that the writer of the initials had probably had a shaky hand, giving the h a 'slight indentation in the middle of the last stroke' that made it look like a k. (He ignored the upper loop which definitely made the letter either a k or a distorted R.) Shakespeare, he admitted, did not usually write party pieces, but on balance he preferred to believe that the verses were his.[28]

Supplied with a primitive photocopy of the verses from the Huntington Library, Peter convinced himself that he was the first person to have looked at them properly, and that the initials had been interfered with to turn *W.Sh.* into something resembling *W.ShR*. He consulted Reg Alton, an Oxford English don, who said he thought they were a monogram or rebus, possibly indeed incorporating an R. Not only had Shakespeare been a close friend of Marston, Peter argued, but the initials looked as if Marston had written them to attribute the verses to his friend. Collier, although known for other forgeries, had clearly not tampered with them. Shakespeare was known to have performed for various of the party, including the Countess and her first husband Ferdinando Stanley, 5th Earl of Derby, in the early 1590s.

Macmillan's publicity for the 'discovery' only deepened the resultant layer of egg on Peter's face. Sebastian Faulks, the literary editor of the *Independent* who had sometimes sent him books to review, hesitantly approved the newspaper's publication of the verses. Peter gave a press conference to present his case. Then, four days after the booklet appeared, the *TLS* published a densely reasoned article by

James Knowles, an Oxford graduate student who taught part-time at Leicester University, identifying the author of the verses as Sir William Skipwith of Leicestershire, and pointing out that an acquaintance of Collier's had already made this connection in print in 1845. Peter had discussed the matter with Knowles the previous autumn, but had been too deeply entrenched in conviction to change his mind.

The ensuing correspondence rumbled on into June, while gossip columnists exaggerated the disagreement into a vicious catfight between academics. As Oxford Professor of Poetry, Peter was especially vulnerable to being made to look foolish. Anthony Powell gave *The Life and Times* an intelligent analysis in the *Daily Telegraph*, remarking that it was difficult for anyone to write sanely about Shakespeare but he considered that Peter had kept a level head. Anthony Burgess praised the book generously in the *Observer*. The literary world, however, was more easily pleased than the academic, and in January 1989 Peter groaned at the 'bombshell' of a negative *TLS* review by the doyen of Shakespeare scholars, Samuel Schoenbaum.[29] Awareness of his hollow achievement may still have dogged him the following April, when he, Deirdre and Matthew joined the festival procession through Stratford under a banner inscribed 'Love's Labour's Lost', before he gave the address at the Sunday service at Holy Trinity the next day.

Knowles wrote later that Peter had been 'charming, generous and self-deprecating' when they met, and unfailingly courteous in his public handling of the affair.[30] When challenged, however, Peter maintained that he still believed he had been right about the verses, and that the manuscript required at least a further, searching look.

24
TEXAS, RUSSIA, GREECE

Virgin of the Alamo, the cottonwood tree,
enthroned on leaves in a desert of stones,
circled by noiseless rivers, by the roadless roads,
virgin of hot lead and of the hot wind,
lean quiet-handed over the dead men
make a garden with shadows for our south.

'Austin, Texas' 10, *Shadow & Bone* (1989) 107

'Exmoor, 8th-11th aug. the smell,' Peter noted in the summer of 1988, recalling sun-heated heather, whiffs of animal dung and sweat and the dusty pungency of whortleberry scrub. Thoroughly discomfited by the Shakespeare business (although Deirdre maintained that he had been more upset by losing the Dr Who scarf she had knitted him out of Jacob's sheep's wool), he went on to brood and moralize in his notebook about literary insecurity, concluding that older writers suffered from it less often but more painfully than young ones. He knew (as he would admit in the introduction to *Boris Pasternak*) that he had failed to get as close to Shakespeare as he had hoped. Would he be able to bond more effectively with Pasternak, although he had never set foot in Russia and knew the language only from books?

Two biographies of Pasternak had appeared in England five years earlier. Guy de Mallac's critical and biographical study, originally published in Paris in 1963, had arrived in translation from the University of Oklahoma Press. Then Ronald Hingley, the translator of the Oxford Chekhov and a widely recognized general authority on things Russian, had brought out a popular life with Weidenfeld. Unsurprisingly, Collins had rejected Peter's proposal for a biography. The project had languished for several years, until Hutchinson unexpectedly took it up in December 1987 with the offer of a £4,500 advance.

'A long evening of Pasternak worn to tatters,' he wrote the next spring. Although Pasternak's poetry mattered to him more than the events of his life, he was working hard to understand its background, even to the extent of reading the works of Lenin. In Oxford he spoke to any elderly Russian who might help. Sir Isaiah Berlin, visiting Russia in September 1945, had taken Pasternak a gift of boots from his sisters in England. Shown a draft of part of *Doctor Zhivago*, he had warned Pasternak that publishing it could endanger his life. George Katkov of St. Antony's College had found English translators for the novel after Feltrinelli had published it in Italian in Milan. Sir Dmitri Obolensky of Christ Church, a medieval historian of great modesty and charm, had left Russia as a baby soon after the Revolution, but through his exiled princely family had absorbed much of the cultural atmosphere of Pasternak's youth. And the writer's sisters Josephine Pasternak, the widow of a second cousin, and tough, forceful Lydia Pasternak Slater, a former biochemist whose poetry in several languages included translations of Boris's, had lived in Oxford as refugees from Nazi Germany since before the Second World War.

Peter must also have remembered Maurice Bowra as Pasternak's most energetic promoter in the West. An enthusiastic translator of modern European poetry, he had introduced Pasternak's poems to English readers, boosted his self-confidence as a writer, repeatedly nominated him for the Nobel Prize for Literature and placed him firmly in the European Symbolist tradition of Valéry, Rilke and Blok (although, Peter liked to maintain, he was more 'human' as a poet than any of those).

Easily tired that spring, he found that a *Spectator* party in London left him exhausted the next day. An evening glass of whisky was like 'a pillow between you and the aching bed of your tiredness'. Yet music, birdsong and the clarity of winter light on ashlar limestone still delighted him. Road journeys in and out of Oxford were visual treats.

On the Pasternak evening, soon after the clocks moved forward, he noticed how, for a few moments at twilight, blackbirds cut 'like saws' across the *St. John Passion*, making even Bach seem vapid, although the music had moved him that evening more deeply than before.[1]

He found he needed spectacles to read Cyrillic and had middle-aged memory problems when trying to bring his Russian up to scratch. Iris had once told him that, because she was mortal, she would never learn Chinese, although he understood that she had made a start on it since then. Once so eager for new languages, he realized that he now shied away from things he would once have felt bound to plunge into, such as the synagogue poetry of Byzantine Bulgaria.[2] Any mention of such a recondite subject would once have provoked Bruce Chatwin into instant competition, but Bruce died on January 18, 1989 after wasting away to a near-skeleton from Aids. Peter had visited him in hospital before he left to die in France, and attended his crowded memorial service at the Greek Orthodox cathedral in Bayswater on February 14. Probably unaware of the whispers about a *fatwa* in the group that surrounded Salman Rushdie, and almost as confused as anyone by the sung liturgy, he concentrated on the 'wonderful bee-buzz' the sound made under the dome, and decided in a Bruce-like mood that, because pre-Roman baths were often domed, people must have learnt about acoustics by singing in the bath.[3]

In less than five weeks' time he would fly to Moscow. It was not the first time since his marriage that he ventured abroad without Deirdre, although his stay in the Nuffield Hospital in April 1985 had been the first time they had slept apart in eight years. Recently, however, he had made a couple of short work-trips abroad, leaving her at home. Part of an episode of *Art, Faith and Vision* had been filmed the previous summer in Euboea, where he had taken the composer and Orthodox convert John Tavener to meet Philip Sherrard at Katounia and experience the liturgy in his local church. Then towards the end of

October he had spent a few cathartic days in Austin, Texas, which may have purged some of the Shakespeare anxieties from his mind.

He went officially as a classical scholar to attend a conference on Hellenistic history and culture. One of the more distinguished participants was his friend Martin Robertson, the former Oxford professor of classical archaeology and art. Admiring his aesthetic approach, Peter had written in an introduction to one of his collections of amateur poetry that he was 'more like Ruskin than like Winckelmann' – more interested in the creative spirit that gave rise to ancient art than in its importance to archaeologists or anthropologists. A widower in his late seventies, long since retired to Cambridge, he may have engaged Peter as his companion some time before remarrying that May.[4]

When not drinking with colleagues in an oyster bar, giving the paper on Theocritus's idylls he had dusted off for the occasion or touring the Harry Ransom Center at the university to see *Compton Mackenzie's writing chair/and Belloc Lowndes in oils*,[5] Peter reacted to his surroundings with a torrent of poems. Harsher than his usual gentle musings, they were products of homesickness, insomnia and cultural shock. Austin was utterly different from prim, *faux*-Oxford Princeton, which he had visited nineteen years earlier. Glinting skyscrapers, looming aeroplanes, howling sirens and roaring freeways represented the America he feared most. He disliked the large, impersonal budget hotel on the outskirts and wished they could have afforded a boutique hotel in a nineteenth-century Greek Revival town house. Awake and alone before dawn, he watched the first orange sunbeams and their reflections edging downwards from the tops of tall buildings. A long line of gleaming, white-topped Texan clouds reminded him of 'fabulous cattle'. He could already hear the continuous whiz of commuters' cars and smell the encroaching jungle-smell of humid heat. It would be ninety-two degrees at midday, and the trees which seemed to press into the city centre were still covered in unseasonal green leaves.[6]

His Austin poems portray a city empty of humanity but loud and bright with machine-like energy and incessant light pollution. Exploring downtown streets and museums one humid afternoon, he smelt the brewery smell of the Colorado river, heard the *rat whistles* of birds in magnolias and felt a sinister breath of the old South,

> *where whiskered senators in waggons brewed*
> *their drinks and drank them at their waggon tails,*
> *saw their sons killed in feud after failed feud*
> *and paid dues in tobacco and in nails.*[7]

This was not Larkinesque nostalgia but the product of a gloomy fit of the imagination, in which the nearby wastelands of coarsely grass-grown lots, giant riverside weeds, clumps of cottonwood trees and migrating grackles seemed equivalent to a Central Asian *wider Texas* where Alexander had *stamp[ed] humans like trash*, or even to *the unwatered desert where we die.*[8] With relief he arrived home to an autumnal welcome: 'The Aga, the warm air, the crackling of the fire, the bottle & the bells going.'[9]

In Moscow he was a guest of the Soviet Writers' Union. With no interest in trying to penetrate the archives, he hoped simply to absorb the ambience of the city. Scribbling in his notebook on the way in from the airport on the afternoon of March 19, he did not see the way in which sunset light gilded the Kremlin domes with a rainbow edge, although he noticed it later, adding that in moonlight the domes looked like green silk.[10] His first impression was of the overwhelming bulkiness of post-Revolutionary architecture with its 'extraordinary and triumphant touches of ornament'. The big buildings reminded him of cigar-boxes, while at night, against a glittering sky, the illuminated stars on their façades made him think of cigarette-lighters. He thought that his hotel, unlike any in London, really looked like the kind of old-fashioned hotel his grandfather might have stayed in. The rooms were so noisy, however, that he wondered if anyone ever slept. Against ferocious restaurant background music he ate a £20 dinner of smoked trout, a salad of fish and mushrooms, red caviar and 'some highish sturgeon in a delicious mess', while chatting to a visitor from Padua in Italian.[11]

Two days later Yevtushenko bounded back into his life with a vigorous show of unbroken friendship. 'You are not part of my schedule, you are part of my life... I want to stand first with you at the grave of Pasternak.' The restaurant at the Central House of Writers was officially dry 'because of what might occur', but Yevtushenko commanded a jug of beer for their dinner. Later, as they walked by the Moscow river, Peter mocked his own phrase-book Russian, solemnly proclaiming 'Eto nye Volga, eto kanal'.

From the vast, impressive Kiev Station they took the electric train to Peredelkino and followed the forest path to the writers' colony. Built in the 1930s to salubrious German designs, the fifty-odd wooden dachas were thronged with literary ghosts. Pasternak's house, with its deep, curved bay and horseshoe-shaped, wrap-around windows, had become a State-run museum with cleaning-ladies in every room. One 'huge old thing' was particularly intrusive, and Zhenya, whom she evidently knew well, found it hard to shake her off. After Peter had stood for a time in the large, light, empty room where Pasternak had finished *Doctor Zhivago*, they visited his grave in the forest cemetery, surrounded by echoing birdsong. It was the beginning of spring, and a ceremony was taking place at the grave of Kornei Chukovsky, whose birthday had been in late March.

Before meeting Zhenya, Peter had visited the Scriabin museum, which was arranged to evoke the composer's last years in 1912-15. Scriabin, a friend of the Pasternaks, had encouraged the young Boris to take up music, which he had abandoned in favour of studying philosophy at Marburg, the setting of one of his most heartfelt poems of disappointed love. The house was full of paintings by Leonid Pasternak and a strange assortment of furniture. 'No taste,' Peter reflected, 'but certainly a style.'

On another bright, hot day he was driven the 120 miles south of Moscow to pay homage to Tolstoy's estate at Yasnaya Polyana, near Tula. The Russian Orthodox Easter was still some weeks ahead, but the English Easter was over by the time he arrived home, before the first spring snow flurry of early April. Austin's Farmhouse was on the market, and he, Deirdre and Matthew expected to move out some time after his last poetry lecture in May.

❧

'Life', he was fond of quoting from Pasternak's poem 'Hamlet', 'is not just a walk across a field.' Although retirement of a kind lay ahead, it would not mean idleness. In the autumn of 1987 he had had fun with 'Anon.', quoting foreign jingles as well as ballads, nursery rhymes and rhyming epitaphs in English. (*'Kukuk is de kulengräver, Adebor is de klokkentreder, Kiwitt is de schäuler Mit all sin schwester un bräuder,'* he recited a Low German version of 'Cock Robin' from a late medieval stained-glass window at Buckland Rectory, Gloucestershire.)* The next year's lectures, however, all anticipated planned books, on Edward Lear, Pasternak and Horace. Eighty-six-year-old Lydia Pasternak Slater shared his platform at the Pasternak lecture and declaimed some of the poems in Russian. Partly in deference to her presence, Peter praised Pasternak's personal dignity as well as his spiritually liberating lyric poetry. While claiming Seferis as his favourite modern poet and the one he considered most 'honourable in his lifework', he had acknowledged a vein of granite in his make-up.[12] Pasternak, a true romantic, had put his own emotions at the centre of his writing, unlike the intensely

---

* The cuckoo, the stork and the peewit family are gravedigger, bellringer and choir at the funeral.

political but inscrutably private Greeks.

Pasternak's life story, he wrote, was 'essentially a love story'.[13] Fascinated by Leonid's humble Sephardic background in Odessa and his self-propulsion into the late nineteenth-century Moscow art world, he rattled through the early part of the narrative in short, tense sentences, building up the excitement as he went. Concentrating first on Boris as a poet, he explained the 'exalted state' of sleepless disappointed love in which he had written the first draft of the Marburg poem, before turning his back on philosophy and Germany in 1910. Calling him the 'poet laureate of railway journeys', he praised the fire and dash of his pre-1914 railway poems, whose violently experimental urban imagery was so unlike Edward Thomas's quiet 'Adlestrop'. A later, meditative poem, 'The Waves', of which he had kept a yellowing cutting of a translation from a 1960s *New Statesman*, contained one image of 'astonishing rock-pool clarity' in which bare pebbles and a crystalline sky borrowed the poet's usual function of seeing and 'embracing... incompatibles in one sight'.[14]

By that time Pasternak had been enduring the terror and squalor of 1930s Moscow, shifting from one wretched, overcrowded apartment to another. His marriage became frayed to exhaustion during the war, and in 1946 he met Olga Ivinskaya, the mistress who endured imprisonment on his behalf during the last four years of Stalin's life. While acknowledging her warmth and loyalty, and especially Pasternak's fondness for her daughter, Peter was clearly less interested in that affair than in the vast romantic energy Pasternak channelled into *Doctor Zhivago*. Assuming that much of the novel was a true reflection of the writer's life and thoughts, he took Yuri's late diary entries as a reassurance that Pasternak must have been happy at Peredelkino, harvesting his potatoes and chatting casually to passers-by.

Sometimes Peter felt depressed by the knowledge that, unlike Pasternak, he would never write a worthwhile novel. His blithe assertion that fiction *withers away on the branch* long pre-dated his Pasternak period.[15] In a fit of November gloom after returning from Texas, he decided that he had depended too much on his own emotions as a poet, 'using the self as a metaphor for mankind'. Pasternak's own emotional lyric poetry had been an early manifestation of the genius that had reached maturity in his novel – 'the last stage of being grown up' (Peter now acknowledged to himself), whereas poetry was 'a continuation of the soul, the integrity of childhood'.[16]

After finishing *Knit One, Drop One* he had experimented with another genre, dashing off a brittle society novella, *To the Goat,* at Frank Delaney's request. Elegantly illustrated by André Yaniw, this passed muster as a piece of witty satire when Hutchinson published it in the summer of 1988, earning praise from at least one reviewer for its sharp lyrical style.[17] Two years later he would complete Cyril's unfinished *Shade Those Laurels* in a similar vein. But the big, serious, humane novel he had longed to write since his twenties remained for ever out of his reach.

He had debts to pay to the present as well as to the past, and called his penultimate lecture 'From Aeschylus to James Fenton', praising the grandeur, sharp wit and 'impressive tranquillity' of his former pupil's poems about the Vietnam War. To justify the sweep of his title he explained that Bowra's *From Virgil to Milton* had looked promising when he was young, until he realised that, while good on those two giants, it was 'rather thin in between'. Fenton could be powerfully dramatic and compassionate like Aeschylus, as well as playfully inventive and ironic. His most serious language achieved the impression that 'you, the reader, had written it'. Peter ranked him not only with Auden but, more complimentarily, with Huchel, whom he considered one of the finest post-war poets. In passing he mentioned the sonnet on Bashō in Fenton's Newdigate Prize poem about Japan, without explaining that Bruce Chatwin's death made the connection especially significant for him just then.[18]

John Minton, who had killed himself at thirty-nine, had shared a house for several years with Keith Vaughan, another homosexual, illustrator, depressive and eventual suicide. Perhaps Peter was thinking of Bruce when he noted a remark of Vaughan's about Minton: '"What does it all *mean*" he would repeat year after year, without really wanting to know the answer.'[19]

His last lecture, 'Goodbye to the Art of Poetry', was in heroic couplets. Funny, informal, passionate, and Byronically inventive in its line-endings (apart from the odd, line-filling 'I fear' or 'I assume'), it was a hat from which he drew one rabbit after another. Larkin's perfect poem 'The Trees' mingled with a stretch of Dryden's *Æneid*, a line from the Cretan ballad *Erotokritos* for comparison with the scansion of 'Barbara Allen', and chunks of Mayakovsky, Milton, Shakespeare, Langland, Waller, Tennyson, Yeats. Romantic images of the greenwood, where the individual could express himself freely and *honey of wild bees dripped in the green oak*,[†] alternated with crisp personal judgments about poetry in general and the greatest twentieth-century poets in particular. Yeats, Eliot and Pound came in for high praise, despite acknowledgements of Eliot's decline into dimness and the eccentricities of Pound and Yeats. The lines on *New England Lowell, Russian Pasternak/[who] heard the river heave and the ice crack* introduced considerations of the way in which private events could affect a poet's output, the constant need to cut and revise, and the ultimate impossibility of achieving *the greatest poem... the unwritten one.*

The Eliotian mysticism of his conclusion may have disappointed members of the audience who had come hoping for incisive poetic

---

† Wild bees were known to make honey inside the hollow, sometimes dead trunks of oaks, as in the medieval North European folk-tale Reynard the Fox. Peter's green tree dripping with honey seems closer, however, to the image in Virgil's fourth eclogue of oak trees exuding the insect secretion *roscida mella*, honeydew.

judgments. After asserting that the one centre of English poetry was the individual, obstinate soul, he suggested, echoing the theme of *Burnt Norton*, that the true end of poetry was a meditative silence.

> *There is a silence beyond poetry,*
> *and poetry reaches to that silence*
> *or poetry punctuates a silence,*
> *or it is punctuated with silence.*

Poetry itself (he concluded) was *the silence between lines... the flight of the alone from the alone,* and without that quest for transcendent perfection, poetry would be *as lost as paradise.*[20]

With his farewell speech at Encænia, welcoming Seamus Heaney as his successor, Peter's long connection with Oxford came to an end. Yale, not Oxford University Press, brought out his lectures, *The Art of Poetry*, in 1991. Half-way through his time as Professor of Poetry he had made a last stab at applying for a teaching fellowship, in English Literature at Keble College, but, all other considerations apart, he had clearly been too old at fifty-five. The experience may have rankled, since his occasional snide remarks about 'salaried... fat cats'[21] usually referred to English dons rather than classicists, most of whom he respected and liked.

Assuming that Austin's Farmhouse would sell quickly, he had wondered in the spring of 1989 if he and Deirdre might spend the summer in a North Oxford college flat, enjoying plays, films, concerts, restaurants, gardens and libraries. 'Perhaps I'll buy a new bicycle.'[22] But the move happened only in October, and they spent several months in a flat in Bath before eventually taking possession of Prospect Cottage, a neat, brick-built house at one end of the long village green at Frampton on Severn, Gloucestershire.

Leaving Stonesfield threatened to be an emotional wrench. He would miss the church tower, the scramble down to the river, the sound of trains in the valley and the enfolding woods. One day old Mr. Austin brought his daughter for a look round and told them about Walter the stonemason who had made 'apprentice pieces' for the graveyard in the cobweb-draped shed near the gate. In early May, thinking they would soon be moving out, he felt 'desperate to record white triumphator tulips against wet stone'. While the wall glowed with sun they blazed with light or seemed transparent, but he preferred them as pure, milk-white shapes. Seeing the country that spring with new eyes, he felt that the world had become 'lightheaded with lack of meaning', freed from the weight of significance that Hopkins suggested in the single word 'crushed'.[23]

As the date of the move remained uncertain, he went alone to Greece in a summer heatwave to stay with George Pavlopoulos. On the journey from Athens he stopped off in a chaotic small hotel with stiflingly hot bedrooms, wonky plumbing and a stuffed menagerie that included an owl, a hawk, a thrush and a large, dusty badger. 'But what a view, aspens, mountains & sea.'[24]

In the eleven years since his and Deirdre's Greek trip, he and George had kept in touch. George had even visited England one winter, staying at Stonesfield and rushing childishly outside to enjoy the novelty of snow. None of this prepared Peter for the shock of his transformation since retiring from KTEL and achieving national recognition as a poet. No longer a humble provincial accountant, he had gained a new, dapper authority and begun to attend cultural conferences, sit on committees, visit schools and judge poetry competitions. But their friendship survived the adjustment, and they agreed that they must visit Zakynthos together next time Peter came.

The four-part documentary series *Art, Faith and Vision* went out on Channel Four in July. As dignified as a lecture series, it moved at what now seems an extraordinarily deliberate, gimmick-free pace. Before showcasing the other artists, Peter appeared in the first film mainly on his own. Formal in his three-piece suit, with his pinched, old-fashioned vowels, he visited *Stonehinge*, then *Chreist Church*, where he and Iris held a vague, intermittent conversation in the Upper Library about writers and their souls. Prior Park, in his day 'a philistine academy of ferocious brothers', led him into a lengthy, Betjemanic ramble round the subjects of landscape gardening, Pope, Blake, Bashō, the Radcliffe Camera, the University Museum, Matthew Arnold and Victorian unbelief.

The dynamic subject of the next film was the sculptor Elisabeth Frink. Strong-faced and idealistic, with religious instincts that Peter felt were more genuine for owing nothing to her convent education, she impressed him with her creative worship of the bodies and spirits of heroic humans and animals. During filming, he wrote later, they spent a 'curiously intense few days together', although that seems to have been the limit of their acquaintance. Joined on film by her admiring friend and fellow hippophile Peter Shaffer, they examined her Madonna and Child in Salisbury Cathedral Close and watched a sculpture being cast in bronze. A clip was spliced in of her giant water-buffalo sculptures being hoisted into place in Exchange Square, Hong Kong. She was living at the time with her third husband on a country estate she had bought in Dorset and seemed indestructibly energetic. When she died four years later, aged sixty-two, Peter wrote a lament for her, admiring her *barbarous, ambivalent art/blowtorching big bronzes behind Bulbarrow*, and her particular love of the Riace bronzes, two figures of naked, bearded Greek warriors which had been dredged up from the sea off Calabria in 1972.[25]

25
REED MUSIC

The whole lake is consuming with swanfire:
the surface of green marble, chilly cold,
transmuted when the sun falls, to inspire
mere reed music as the muse loses hold.

'Reed Music', *Reed Music* (1997) 9

The winter they spent in Bath was fun. People still had money to spend, and the shops were bright with gas-log fires. Freed from their possessions they could relax and look forward to their new house, where rooms were being knocked together and an Aga installed in the kitchen at the back. The cat had been expensively boarded out, but Pip, the West Highland terrier, stayed with them in the one flat in which they were allowed to keep a dog. Newly decorated and comfortably efficient, it was in the late eighteenth-century, stone-fronted terrace, Belmont, which descends Lansdown Road behind its high, railed pavement as steeply as a street in Porto or Trieste. Walking Pip up and down the pavements, Peter blandly allowed him to foul doorsteps and left the result where it lay. 'He's a country dog. People will just have to get used to it.'

Bath was more thriving than the shabby wartime city he had known from school. No longer in slow decay, it was now partly a dormitory for Bristol, and housed academics, professionals and wealthy retirees. He and Deirdre went out to restaurants, the cinema and the theatre, and once or twice ran Pip on the grassy slopes which plunge down to the Palladian bridge at Prior Park. The fierce revulsion he had once felt against the Christian Brothers had largely disappeared, although when passing through Lancashire he kept clear of Stonyhurst and refused to set foot inside Gillian's convent near Carnforth, preferring to picnic with her in the grounds.

On August 10 he had had the first of a series of small strokes. He had been scrambling to finish Pasternak, find a publisher for his poetry lectures and sort and pack up his papers, which included a second batch for Bertram Rota to sell to Boston College. But the setback did not slow him down for long. In late September Deirdre drove him to a festival in Flintshire at which he was due to lecture on Hopkins, calling at Frampton and Bath on the way home. On October 1, the day after the St. Catherine's college feast, they shut the door on Austin's Farmhouse and drove south-west. For three weeks they occupied their usual bolt-hole at St. Anthony, part of a converted farm building called the Turnip House, endways-on to the little harbour and the creek. Back in Oxfordshire for Heaney's inaugural lecture they stayed at The Feathers in Woodstock, dealing with removal men at Stonesfield and meeting John Bayley and Iris. They were in Bath by the end of October, took a two-week break at St. Anthony around the end of January and moved to Frampton in mid-March. Because work on the house was unfinished they rented the elegant Orangery at Frampton Court, followed by a fortnight in a cottage in the nearby village of Hempstead, before Prospect Cottage was ready for them in early May.

Gloucestershire society was different from the kind they had been used to in Oxford. It was grander, more leisurely, more aesthetic and less intellectual. They took immediately to the Cliffords of Frampton Court, whose family had lived there since the eleventh century, perpetuating daughters' surnames as Clifford in generations that lacked a male heir. It was Berkeley Hunt country, and Henriette Clifford, the widowed owner of the Court, still hunted, shot and fished in her seventies, while her middle son Rollo farmed. Peter loved the wide spaciousness of Frampton under its big, estuarine sky, where he saw more passing wildfowl than aeroplanes bound for Bristol. He liked the Court Lake, the reed-beds, the tumultuous swan-flights, and the green with its playing children, geriatric strollers and scattering of animal life.

The lines

> *they are tethering a chestnut and white horse*
> *in fresh grass like a pensioned-off racecourse*
> *under the trees, somewhere far down the green*

were perhaps a gesture towards a friend's remembered comment about an aged scholar 'browsing among manuscripts, like a pensioned-off racehorse'.[1]

They had begun to make new friendships or revive old ones while in Bath, visiting the novelist Isobel Colegate and her husband at nearby Midford Castle and Tony Mitchell and his French wife Brigitte at Dyrham Park, where Tony had lived for the past twenty-five years as the National Trust's historic buildings representative for Wessex. At a post-Christmas lunch at the Mitchells' the year after moving to Frampton they met James and Alvilde Lees-Milne, who had motored over (a favourite Lees-Milne expression) from their house at Badminton. Both were in their eighties, and Alvilde, the younger of the two, was frailer than the sprightly, industrious, beadily observant Jim. In spite of another stroke Peter was in fine anecdotal form, and he and Deirdre charmed the Lees-Milnes into a friendship which would draw Jim close to them during the last year of his life.[2]

Peter told them he was three-quarters of the way through a biography of Tennyson. *Boris Pasternak* had come out early in 1990, unluckily coinciding with the first volume of a weightier life by an academic specialist in twentieth-century Russian literature, Christopher Barnes. John Bayley gave Peter a pat on the head for his 'lively and delightful' book, singling out his felicitous translations of some of the poems and his cool assessment of their merits. As an example of Peter's eye for detail, he quoted his story that Pasternak had found the name Zhivago on a Moscow manhole-cover.[3] (The name, suggesting 'alive', was mocked by Nabokov as Mertvago, 'dead'.) Anthony Powell, in the *Sunday Times*, praised his 'illuminating and striking' comments on the development of Pasternak's creative impulse. It was clear, however, that this book, although only slightly shorter than *Tennyson* at 310 pages, was unlikely to succeed in competition with two solidly researched volumes by Barnes.

Tennyson, on the other hand, was Peter's triumph. He had been preparing to write it for years, together with a life of Tennyson's close friend and his own long-standing alter ego, Edward Lear. In spite of the Shakespeare fiasco, Macmillan commissioned both books. Peter explained in his introduction that he had delayed beginning to write until after the third and final volume of the Clarendon Press edition of Tennyson's *Letters* had come out in 1990. Like Christopher Ricks's edition of the poetry manuscripts at Trinity College, Cambridge, it had been essential for his work. Yet he had finished his text by February 1992, thirteen months before the biography came out.

Writing by hand in his attic study at Prospect Cottage, he compressed all he knew and thought about Tennyson, his friends, family, contemporaries and poetic output into a rich Christmas pudding of a book. Like Victorian railway stations, wellingtonias and monkey-puzzles, Tennyson had been part of his background all his life. What educated child of his generation had not learnt the rhythm of 'The Lady of Shalott', or marvelled at the arm clothed in white samite emerging from the lake to seize Excalibur? When he was nine, he remarked (he meant eleven), fifty years after Tennyson died, people had still been alive who had known the poet.[4] His own classical education had not been so different from the one that had inspired 'Ulysses', 'Tithonus' and 'Œnone', followed by the great poet's half-century of experimentation with metre. Tennyson's university friendships, with James Spedding, Arthur Hallam and others, had been as formative as his own. The Apostles (whose friendships in the 1820s, he insisted, were largely innocent of homosexuality) could have been the Opimian

Club, and 'magical 1828', the year in which so many of Tennyson's friends arrived at Cambridge, might have stood for 1955 or 1956.[5]

One of the chief strengths of the book is its emphasis on the early Tennyson, who was still a boy when Keats, Shelley and Byron died, but had matured as a poet by the summer of his twenty-eighth birthday when Victoria came to the throne. While the lives and preoccupations of mid-Victorians have been done to death, less attention has been paid to their post-Regency childhood and youth, between Byron's death in 1824 and Victoria's accession in 1837. Not all upper-class dandyism, greed and dissipation, it was the period of Catholic Emancipation, the first Reform Act and the beginnings of Antipodean colonization, when young men worked hard at the universities, Carlyle taught himself German and wrote *The Life of Friedrich Schiller* and *Sartor Resartus*, and many Victorian attitudes and ideas began to germinate. No longer shy of writing about people, Peter filled the early part of his book with a vast range of pre-Victorian characters, from semi-lunatic members of Tennyson's family to people he might conceivably have met or just missed meeting – among them Wordsworth and the thirteen-year-old Matthew Arnold in the Lake District, and John Clare in a private lunatic asylum at Epping.[6]

It was important, he wrote in his introduction, to understand a poet's social world, and the gallop of his narrative conveys the warmth and eccentricity of Tennyson's. Tiny details, such as Hallam's tendency to flush red in the face when concentrating intensely on something (which Tennyson apparently did not notice, but Peter saw as a warning of the condition that would kill him),[7] balance episodes of deep emotion, such as Tennyson's desolation at Hallam's death. Casual asides broaden our view of the period, so that we learn in quick succession that Tolstoy, like the protagonist of 'Maud', chose to fight in the Crimean War to escape from a sexual crisis, and that Gladstone used to read 'Guinevere' to his 'wicked ladies' before sending them to an Anglican convent to be reformed.[8] Now and again the poet's voice can be heard almost directly, as if on an ancient, crackling gramophone record, intoning the most gruesome lines in his early poem 'St Simeon Stylites' 'with ferocious grimness and roars of laughter', or complaining, once famous, that he feared biographers would rip him open like a pig.[9]

Peter's narrative skill, critical judgments and clear affection for his subject paid off. Reviewers praised his close textual study of 'In Memoriam' and 'Maud', together with his refusal to accept other biographers' speculations about epilepsy, homosexuality, masturbatory guilt, chronic depressiveness and incest. He had given fair, detailed treatment to *Idylls of the King*, calling it 'an extraordinary *tour de force*' as well as the 'huge botch' that one reviewer singled out for quotation.[10] As for the earlier 'Morte d'Arthur', it was 'Virgilian, classic, almost epic', in a tradition that came straight from Milton.[11] After a survey of recent Tennyson biographies, John Sutherland concluded, with only the mildest hint of criticism, that Peter's was the most cheerful to have been published since Hallam Tennyson's *Memoir* of 1897.[12]

Next up on the biographical conveyor-belt was Lear. He and Tennyson, Peter proclaimed, were two of the most interesting people of their century, 'emerg[ing] shyly from its forest of inhibitions to come face to face'.[13] Recalling his trip to Corfu with Takis Sinopoulos and his limerick-swapping sessions in Athens with Seferis and Gatsos, he had longed to describe the foreign backgrounds, delicate visual excitement and humour of Lear's life as a change from the insularity of Tennyson's. His Tennyson research, begun years earlier, had taken him no farther than Cambridge, Lincoln, the Lake District and the Isle of Wight. Lear's illustrated manuscript diaries were in the Houghton Library at Harvard, which he hoped to visit provided he was not knocked out by another stroke.

Throughout writing *Tennyson* he had struggled with illness. 'Peter says he'll be dead in 2 years,' Matthew wrote in his diary on August

14, 1990. In late September, after a Lincolnshire trip, he had another suspected small stroke, which left him (Matthew noted) 'very frail'. Deirdre drove him to Oxford for the St. Catherine's feast, then whisked him off to St. Anthony for a week. At the Cheltenham literary festival he felt too weak to give his talk on Pasternak, and their friend Pauline Rumbold read the lecture for him in her beautiful actress's voice.

Somehow he pulled himself together, although less mobile than before. Train-travel became more difficult than he had expected. From the nearest station at Stonehouse, near Stroud, some trains ran directly to London, but a journey to Oxford involved changes at both Swindon and Didcot, followed by a cross-town trudge to the Bodleian or a longer one to St. Catherine's. In the summer of 1991 he resigned his fellowship of the college and became an emeritus fellow, which placed no obligation on him to go there again. A recent young fellow by special election, the Wordsworth scholar Duncan Wu, wrote inviting him to speak on an arts programme he produced and presented for Radio Oxford. After an interval, for which he apologized, Peter declined:

> Just when you wrote I was unwell & then went away to Cornwall for 6 weeks... But I'm afraid I can't do it, as I am seldom in Oxford now, have resigned from college, & am defeated by the simple logistics of getting from x to y, even within Oxford. I am a rubbish-heap of catastrophes (from which there emerges only a small dry cheep like a lone cicada).

Early the next April, however, he was on a plane to Canada. *Tennyson* was in the publishers' hands, and with his friend and contemporary P.J. Kavanagh and the Ulster poet Michael Longley he had been invited to the Harbourfront World Poetry Festival in Toronto. The Lake Ontario weather was bleak, and their soporifically heated waterside hotel was hemmed in by the glittering, faceless towers of the financial district; but, unlike Austin, this did not depress him. At his reading he found himself billed to follow a militant American feminist poet, whose supporters stormed out noisily after her. Kavanagh felt anxiously protective as Peter limped up on to the platform in his buttoned-up tweed suit. Would the Canadians and Americans sneer at his 'elegiac cadences' and consider him some kind of antiquated joke? He disarmed them at once with an anti-war rhyme of Cyril's, and they flocked round him admiringly in the common-room afterwards. To Kavanagh, his performance was one of magnificent courage, courtesy and grace.

In his free time at the conference he chummed up with Kavanagh and the American poet W.S. Merwin, who had been a friend of Robert Graves in Majorca and of Ted Hughes and Sylvia Plath in Primrose Hill. Eating oysters in a deserted café on the shore of the freezing lake, they held one of those symposia which may have reminded him of Sounion or the Plaka, quoting Theocritus and the Mabinogion and joking about 'Oldtimers' Disease', as Merwin called their shared spasms of memory-loss. Searching for presents to take home, Kavanagh found him wandering vaguely round a display of artistic reproductions. 'I'm looking for an Augustus Egg,' he said, 'to go with Matthew's Francis Bacon.'[14]

∾

He had long realized that there was more to find out about Edward Lear than he had known before giving his Oxford lecture in February 1988. Then, he had been mainly concerned to point out what he saw as the profundities and beauties of Lear's poetry, together with the memorable, 'necessary' quality of much anonymous, light and children's verse, which he thought showed most clearly the basic techniques of what it meant to be a poet. Lear had 'entered an ancient tradition so swiftly that poems by him were recorded as anonymous, orally transmitted children's rhymes while he was still alive.' In ancient Greece he might even have been considered Aristophanes' equal. It was a matter of how you preferred your truths to be purveyed: directly, in emotional, adult language, or indirectly, through the 'tougher language and sad morality of the nursery'.[15] Presenting Lear as symbiotic with Tennyson, to the extent of expressing 'worship' by parodying, as well as illustrating, Tennyson's poems, he credited him with helping to revive the dying plant of nineteenth-century English poetry from the edges, while Tennyson 'like a gardener of genius made the centre flourish again'.[16]

If his defence of Lear's sillier rhymes seems strained, the biography as a whole represents a sympathetic attempt to portray every aspect of a complicated creative spirit. He was not a pioneer in the field: in 1968 Collins had published an authoritative life of Lear by the thirty-one-year-old Vivien Noakes. She had also edited the *Selected Letters* for the centenary of his death twenty years later, had curated a major exhibition of his paintings and had written a study of him as a painter. Weidenfeld had brought out a centenary biography by Susan Chitty, the biographer of Anna Sewell and Charles Kingsley. On the well-known publishing principle that if something has been done already it is always worth doing again, Peter and his editor at Macmillan saw no reason why he should not add to the heap. He was eager to describe Lear's friendship with the Tennysons, and especially his close, confiding relationship with Alfred's wife Emily; his travels in Greece, where he believed Lear always felt most at home, and his long, dependent attachment to his Corfiote manservant, Georgis Kokalis; the 'dew-freshness' of his topographical sketches and the tectonics of his verse. He also felt a remote personal connection with him through the woman he had come closest to marrying, Denis's great-aunt Gussie Bethell. Unlike Chitty and Noakes he flatly refuted the idea that Lear been homosexual, citing in evidence his startling claim that he had contracted 'every sort of syphilitic disease' at the age of twenty or twenty-one (when a young man uncertain which sex he preferred might well have run that risk trying to find out). Lear, he insisted, was a 'warm, affectionate, somewhat frustrated man, who tried to marry but failed, and that is all – there is no evidence whatever of homosexuality in his life.'[17]

A fretfully delicate, depressive bachelor, who wandered rootlessly abroad for much of his seventy-five years, Lear had corresponded copiously with his mainly upper-class English friends. Vivien Noakes lent Peter her photocopies of many of the letters, and he tracked down collections of others in libraries and record offices throughout the United Kingdom. The Tennyson Research Centre in Lincoln had a particularly rewarding cache, which he had already seen but had made little use of in *Tennyson*. In May 1993 he spent a fortnight examining the diaries at Harvard, arriving home the day before his sixty-second birthday and three days after Lear's one hundred and eighty-first.

Lear's life, as recounted by Peter, is an episodic concatenation of emotional and social entanglements, foreign travel, comic incidents and minor mishaps. The narrative is more breathless than that of *Tennyson*, and can sometimes resemble the relentless anecdotes of a witty dinner-party guest who makes one's jaw ache with laughing while one longs for him to stop. The scattiness of Lear's manner was catching, and Peter found it all too easy to pick up. Vivien Noakes in the *Daily Telegraph* kindly called his interpretation 'joyous', and the humorist E.S. Turner gave it a detailed, sympathetic appreciation in the *London Review of Books*. But Penelope Fitzgerald, who was usually so charitable in her reviews, concluded that Peter's amiable, sometimes confusing rambles through the life left no room for an intelligent assessment of the verse. On what basis, for example, could he claim so confidently that Lear, as a poet in the 1880s, had been superior to everyone but Tennyson, and later Hardy? 'What's become of Browning?' she demanded.[18]

༄

Edward Lear came out in January 1995. By then Peter had started work on a life of Milton, another writer he felt he had short-changed in his poetry lectures. Macmillan and Oxford University Press divided the Milton industry between them, publishing biographies, critical works and editions. Although mainly by English Literature academics, they included A.N. Wilson's accomplished *Life of John Milton* from Oxford in 1983. In 1995 Macmillan's scholarly branch published Cedric C. Brown's *John Milton, a Literary Life*, and in 1997 Gordon Campbell's *A Milton Chronology*. In 1996 their commercial list included Peter's *Eden Renewed: the Public and Private Life of John Milton*, which (he acknowledged) made only one or two points not already covered by Wilson. On a postcard to Bertie he wrote that the book had 'near killed' him. It would be the last of his biographies for Macmillan as his health grew more precarious and he turned away from English poets to his early loves among the Latin classics.

During the past few years he had suffered from failing eyesight, diabetic lameness and a hiatus hernia, but no major strokes. In October 1993 he flew out to another Toronto poetry festival, this time without Kavanagh. In England he was a regular at the Cheltenham and Hay festivals and the Thomas Hardy Society's biennial conference at Dorchester, where in 1994 he lectured on his favourite dialect poet William Barnes. At Cheltenham in October 1995 he had been due to promote the Lear book, but found at the last minute that he was also billed to introduce Yevtushenko. Rushing in late, Zhenya hugged him with a cry of 'Brother!', then gave his usual vigorous performance in Russian, helped by his sixteen-year-old son Sasha reading translations of the poems. Peter, feeling weak, sat down to read 'The Man in the Runcible Hat' with his usual rambling digressions and joky asides. John Bayley and Iris Murdoch appeared together in a more distressing state: Iris obstinately mute and confused, while John, trying to hide her dementia, coaxed her fruitlessly to respond to Humphrey Carpenter's interview questions with more than curt monosyllables or vague stares.

&

Early in October 1995 Seamus Heaney was awarded the Nobel Prize for Literature. Asked to comment on the radio, Peter was magnanimous in his praise. 'He really does mean more to us than any other living poet writing in our language... [His work is] strongly worded, it's clear, it's often quite enchanting – it's very beautiful.'[19] Heaney's bog-bound rootedness was not something he had tried to imitate, although an early Heaney phrase, 'reed music', forms the theme of the Frampton poem that gave the title to the last collection of his lifetime.[20] His own reed music, however, was gentler and more resigned than Heaney's. Assuming that Frampton would be his last resting-place, he chose the reed-beds as the scattering-place for his ashes.[21]

'The chronology of this collection of poems is not to be trusted,' Peter wrote in a prefatory note to *Reed Music*, after dating the composition of the last two in the book, 'Conversation with Philip Sherrard' and 'The Graveyard by the Sea', to the summer of 1997, a few months before publication in November. An added, not particularly helpful comment, that he wrote those poems 'after Horace and before Virgil', indicates that he was still in the thick of turning out prose works; *Horace: a Life* had come out earlier that year, while *Virgil: his Life and Times* was published in 1998.

All the poems, however, date from after the move to Frampton, and mark a shift from the metaphysical confusion of *Shadow and Bone* to a luminously transcendent mood. No longer fretful about the nature of the soul or the existence of God and the afterlife, he achieved the Valéry-like calm which can be one of the bonuses of old age. Far from raging against the dying of the light, he seemed positively to welcome its poetic impact. *Reed Music* blends literary influences with sensitivity to landscape and history and a respect for classic forms. Peter's fondness for the sonnet, with strong, monosyllabic line-endings instead of earlier, weak trochees such as 'season', showed a readiness to improve, if not to modernize. Many of the poems are less memorable individually than as a unity, but a few stand out, either as brilliant pastiches or as genuinely original pieces of work.

At St. Anthony he and Deirdre moved up from the Turnip House by the harbour to a separate cottage with its own high garden, level with the church tower and looking out along the brimming green water or muddy trickle of the creek. There and at Frampton he wrote long, formal, Valéry-like poems, copying the decasyllabic rhythm, six-line verses and AABCCB rhyme-scheme of *Le Cimetière Marin*, which sustains them. Their imagery shares little of its sunlit glitter, while their message is more accepting than Valéry's rousing incitement to live. 'Poem for the Time of Year', although subtitled 'Homage to Valéry', begins its second verse with an Arnoldian sigh,

> *Autumn. Only the children in pure ease*
> *cry out at play among the ruined trees*

and its third with an echo of a well-known hymn,

> *Time carries all away, in one immense*
> *motionless waterfall of innocence.*[22]

By the twenty-seventh, the soul's shrinking journey through autumn has ended with *the year's midnight,* when an icy wind blows out of an empty sky, bringing thoughts of death. 'Indian Summer' is more upbeat about *the afterseason of old men*, but quite explicit that, by his sixties, Peter felt age weighing on him. Yet 'Poem for the Time of Day (Gillan Creek)' is an exhilarating meditation on the movement and *self-delighting descant of the sea*, with a possible nod to Yeats's 'A Prayer for My Daughter' as well as to Valéry's *'la mer, la mer, toujours recommencée'*.

> *Listen: the tide: ocean inexorable*

banging the water-doors of his green stable,
but the sea-horses fling their white foam back
galloping loose through light and through half-light,
barren as the spirit they give delight
breathing freedom and death, and leave no track

because the sea is hungry and spirit
breaks loose and then sighs back to rest in it:
and there is nothing that these waters seek
when the gale sweeps them and the Atlantic rain
lashes them and the moon is horned again,
but to lie quiet in the swelling creek.[23]

Historical or semi-historical vignettes ('Elegy for Miss Benton', 'On a Photograph of Highnam Mummers', 'Ghost of an Old Curse') contain surreally juxtaposed images unlike anything in Larkin. The five sonnets in 'Sir Harry Vane, and Postscript' are a bitterly dark meditation on the past, from the bloodshed of the English Civil War to the doom of 1914. Some of the poems in the collection are slight, repetitive or even excruciating, like these lines from 'Four Pictures of a Poet':

The world is flat, and I can roam around
shifting the blue-green jellies of my eyes
to reckon up sunshadow or moon-size
as if I had my feet glued to the ground.[24]

But once away from the subject of himself, Peter could be extraordinarily moving. 'Conversation with Philip Sherrard' is a dignified, long poem, rich in imagery, on the pattern of *Le Cimetière Marin*, while the relaxed blank verse of 'For Angus MacIntyre' has the sparkling intimacy of remembered friendship.

To count intelligence by funniness,
sparkle in the eye, spring in the footstep,
look for the lurching of the coming friend,

> *or to think all prizes were God-given*
> *and fell by nature to one's dearest friends,*
> *was a mistake of course, easy to make.*[25]

Unsentimentally, with warmth and respect, he portrayed Angus as cricket-player, fisherman and dashing young reservist at the time of Suez (*of all Oxford you were the only one/recalled to the Brigade*); then as a wise, affable historian who embraced poetry, from Milton onwards, in the study of humanity that delighted him so much. With almost Yeatsian resonance he praised him as

> *of all men, of all teachers, all friends,*
> *the most hospitable, most compassionate*
> *and the most liberal I ever knew.*

At the memorial service for Angus in March 1995 David Pryce-Jones read the poem, since Peter could not trust himself to do so with a steady voice.

He cried easily by then, as some old men do. In February he had recorded his reading of a 46-line Easter poem for the final programme in a Lenten television series, *Words from Jerusalem*, devised by Joan Bakewell for BBC North. Before his recitation the ninety-year-old Sir John Gielgud, spry, controlled and moving freely, read part of the Easter narrative from St. John's gospel. Peter sat rigidly, twitching, blinking and apparently on the edge of breaking down. As he read, the camera focused cruelly on his puffy, baggy-eyed face, with no hint of background or body movement apart from a slight tilt of the head. When he reached the lines

> *Who lay dead for the long nights that have gone*
> *and through the seventh day that has undone*
> *the working elements of our creation,*[26]

his head bowed at the words *the seventh day* as if to suppress tears. As usual in openly religious poems he ended with an affirmation of belief, and at the lines *I am washed as white as a clean bone/and shall arise out of my death and shine*, he trembled and his mouth worked with emotion. It was clear that he was far from well. But directly after Angus's memorial service Deirdre put him on a train at Oxford to begin a last journey alone to Greece.

26
ABOVE SIGHT

Now I must climb high up the wooden and white
stairway above the brick comfort of this house,
above learning, above poetry, above sight,
to gather thoughts like birds and let them loose.

Viriditas (2001) 49

He was afraid of losing his memory as well as his agility and sight, but he needed to immerse himself for one last time in the country he loved. 'At a deep level' he wanted to see Nikos Gatsos's grave in the remote family village in Arcadia which he had already described from imagination in an elegy for him.[1] He also wanted to see George Pavlopoulos and to visit the Leigh Fermors at Kardamyli, which he called 'the refreshment of a dream deeply buried'.[2] So much of his Greek life was over, with the abandonment of work on Pausanias, the deaths of Seferis, Gatsos and Takis Sinopoulos and the disappearance of almost everything that had once bound him to Athens. For those reasons, and a loathing of pollution, he would not see the Parthenon again, although it still stands proud and clear on fine spring days in March and is spectacularly floodlit at night. But he had already re-rooted at Pyrgos, and was happy planning to visit the Peloponnese and an island or two close to its shores.

Nervous and invalidish at the start of the journey, he gained confidence as he travelled farther away from home. His agent Andrew Hewson met his train at Paddington and drove him to stay overnight with his cousin Zoë Dominic in Kensington. Before he left, Hewson handed him £2,000 in cash, which P.J. Kavanagh had secured for him as a travel grant from the Society of Authors. Zoë took him to Waterloo, found him a disabled person's buggy and put him on a

Eurostar. Then he was on his own, crossing Paris by taxi to the Gare de Lyon, travelling by sleeper to Bologna, then changing trains to head south. He spent several days sightseeing in Ancona before embarking on a ferry crossing which was as calm (he remarked) as if carrying the body of Arthur Hallam.[3] George Pavlopoulos had asked a friend to meet him at Patras and deliver him to Pyrgos, where he would stay.

His account of the trip, *A Bottle in the Shade*, is the most relaxed of his autobiographical writings. He had shed certain inhibitions since writing *The Hill of Kronos*. No longer shy of describing English friends in Greece, he included Joan and Paddy Leigh Fermor, Philip Sherrard (on an elegiac note, since Philip died in London that May; the poem 'Conversation with Philip Sherrard' offers the mystically positive view of old age and dying that Philip would have expected from him),[4] even Bruce. The only person whose identity he continued to shield was Miranda, 'a girl' he had introduced to Bruce and through whom Bruce had become a friend of Joan and Paddy, spending months with them in his last illness and choosing a spot near a ruined church high above Kardamyli where Paddy and Elizabeth buried his ashes.

Georgis (as Peter now called him) drove him south to Kalamata, where he was due to attend an educational conference, before putting him into a taxi for Kardamyli. The new north-south road used to dwindle into a mule-track after passing the Leigh Fermors' headland at Kalamitsi, but it now plunged on twenty-five miles into the Mani past hillsides scattered with holiday homes and through fishing villages which had expanded into resorts. Peter was horrified to see clumps of 'German' houses as the taxi wound down the mountainside into Kardamyli. The main street had filled up with shops, cafés and hotel signs like a village in Provence. He lost his way among new houses on the headland, but once inside the Leigh Fermors' solid stone walls, facing the sunset over the bay, he felt as cherished and enclosed as before.

Paddy was eighty, Joan eighty-three, but both were still spry, smart and lively, deferring to one another with old-fashioned courtesy. Settling into the house, they had elaborated its structure and decoration during the twenty years since Peter's last visit. There were paintings by Nikos Ghika, Takis Sinopoulos and John Craxton, and the large pavilion-study with its conical Turkish fireplace where Paddy read, wrote letters and made a show of planning the final volume about his pre-war walk from London to the Bosphorus. Youthfully energetic, he still travelled to remote places with friends and climbed down the cliff path below the house to swim. Peter felt decrepit by comparison, and worried that Joan and Paddy might find him an imposition. When they told him they were going up the mountain to look for spring flowers he stayed behind so as not to hold them up. When they stepped out on to the terrace to see the stars he did not join them for fear of having to admit that he could see nothing, but was dazzled by the amazing light-show when he groped his way out on his own.

Although he did not want to leave Kardamyli and Paddy's wonderfully eclectic collection of books, he felt more at ease with Georgis, who, slightly lame from a childhood illness, had crippled himself further by falling down a flight of steps in Athens. The sense of equality he felt with Georgis went much deeper and farther back than their present shared difficulty in walking. In spite of Georgis's new membership of the cultural *petit-bourgeoisie* they still spoke to one another as poets, from their hearts. Peter loved his sincere comradeship, emotional openness, reverence for Greek antiquity and tradition and enjoyment of good wine. For his sake he endured Mitsa's sometimes challenging Lenten cooking, and moved out into a hotel only when Charis and his fiancée came to stay for Holy Week.

He and Georgis went on expeditions together in Elis and Arcadia, chattering in Greek as if they had never left off. They decided they were both too unfit to visit Kythera and Antikythera as they had hoped, but they explored round Lepreo near the west coast and round Andritsaina, where in 1963 Peter had nested on a bell-tower to sleep. They found Gatsos's grave in an almost deserted Asea where an old man told them the villages were all going out like lights. At Bassae Peter thought the temple 'ruined and desecrated' by being swathed in a protective tent. At Olympia he found the main street revolting, and would not stop for a drink in the large, overcrowded hotel. Zakynthos, which Georgis knew well, would have been crammed with pink Brits in vests if it had been summer; as it was spring, Peter excoriated them in their absence. His expected 'afterglow of gratitude' for all he had loved in Greece was partly spoilt by the glare of modernity, mass tourism and ugliness. Yet, for all its fogeyish grumbles, *A Bottle in the Shade* distils mellowness, whether he is celebrating friendships, remembering poems (he particularly enjoyed finding Bertolucci's Italian translation of 'Adlestrop' in Paddy's library), recalling details about rural Greece in 1963, or being unexpectedly struck by the beauty and presence of modern Greek young women at a restaurant party near Katakolo after a theatrical performance at Olympia.

∽

He was sixty-four that May, and told Bertie that he was writing enough books to see out the millennium. In 1996 Macmillan published his life of Milton, and Christopher Sinclair-Stevenson published *A Bottle in the Shade*. This latter was not reprinted in paperback, and is one of the rarest and most expensive of his books at second-hand.

For the next two years he limped along in a semblance of writerly normality. Duckworth, with its classical list, commissioned him to write lives of Horace and Virgil, his two favourite Latin poets. He dashed each of these off in a few months, partly from reflections on their translators, partly from half-forgotten memories of school lessons and Oxford lectures. When he was not at work on those or attempting a last, unfinished thriller, he and Deirdre visited gardens, attended literary festivals and gave lunch parties, at which he put himself out to be a genial host. James Lees-Milne, after lunching at Frampton to meet Cyril's biographer Jeremy Lewis, remarked on his amusing imitations of Maurice Bowra and the Queen Mother and the way in which he looked round the company afterwards, expecting a laughing response.[5]

His Oxford connections were shrinking. John Wain died in May 1994, and John Bayley and Iris, that once free spirit, became trapped in a chaotic home life by her dementia. Asa and Susan Briggs had retired from Worcester College to their house in Sussex. Peter preached his last sermon, on George Herbert, at an Easter service in the chapel of Lincoln College in 1997. Deirdre and Matthew sat with the Rector and his wife, Eric and Poppy Anderson, watching anxiously as he reached his conclusion and then murmured apologetically that he hoped that had been all right. 'He made everybody laugh as ever and read well, but with a bit of difficulty,' Matthew wrote in his diary.

In spite of encroaching blindness he had managed a last Canadian visit early in 1996, when invited to give the annual Pascal lectures at the University of Waterloo. The theme was Christianity and the University, and Peter, ambivalent about religion to the last, gave the overall title 'Of what use is Christianity to Humanism?' to his seminars on humanism in poetry and his lectures on Hopkins and Horace. Laser treatment at a Cheltenham eye clinic had continued through the next year, staving off the diabetic retinopathy for which there was as yet no cure. But in June 1997 he suffered an attack so violent that Deirdre feared it might be another stroke. It was a haemorrhage in one eye which left it almost sightless.

Far from retreating into isolation like John and Iris, he and Deirdre kept their social life going. With Deirdre's expert organization, delectable meals appeared for their guests - caviar and cream, calf's liver and a delicious, unidentified pudding when Jim Lees-Milne and

Anthony Hobson lunched there in January 1997. No wonder, Jim exclaimed in his diary, how warm and welcoming he found Deirdre and how much he loved her. After their first meeting at Dyrham he had commented a little spitefully on her looks, but he had been a widower for nearly three years now and had changed since Alvilde's death. That spring, summer and early autumn he saw Deirdre and Peter often. They went to tea with him at Essex House, Badminton, taking offerings of home-made marmalade and biscuits. Peter was helpful too: when Jim shyly sent him the manuscript of a long poem he had written in 1950, he replied on a postcard full of encouraging comments, and when Jim lunched at Frampton three days after Peter's haemorrhage he urged him once again to have the poem published privately. They remained Jim's 'dear Levis' until he fell ill early in November while travelling to Paris with Deborah Devonshire to visit one of his oldest friends, her sister Diana Mosley. Whisked back to England, he lingered on for several weeks as Cyril had done, before dying in hospital at the age of eighty-nine.[6]

The responses of some English classicists to Peter's *Horace* resembled Peter's kindness about Jim's poem. They understood how delicate and out of touch he was, and accepted the book as his personal declaration of a lifelong love of Horace. Peter Jones, in the *Literary Review*, complimented him on the amount of useless knowledge it contained, while Jasper Griffin, in the *Spectator*, remarked on its probable appeal to 'amateurs of poetry'. It took a professor of classics at the Episcopal Academy in Philadelphia to complain of its inaccuracies and deliberately anachronistic viewpoint, sneering about senior common-room fuddy-duddiness while conceding the charm of Peter's allusions to his wide reading and the fineness of some of his translations of the poems.[7]

Virgil: his Life and Times is still more idiosyncratic. In addition to slaughtering long-dead dragons, like the outdated, schoolmasterly theory that Virgilian Roman imperialism anticipated Christianity, it is full of strange quirks and irrelevancies. In the first line of his first chapter, Peter referred confusingly to Virgil's birthplace as 'Mantua, then Mantova'. ('Now' or 'later' Mantova would have been clearer.) Discussing the 'self-echoing' opening of the first eclogue, 'Tu, Tityre', he could not resist dragging in an onomatopœic poem about a lark's song that he had found during his Shakespeare researches and already quoted in his paper on Theocritus at Austin:

> La gentille Alouette avec son tyre-lyre
> Tire l'yre à l'iré, et tiri-lyrant vire
> Vers la voute du Ciel, puis son vol vers ce lieu
> Vire, et desire dire, adieu Dieu, adieu Dieu.[8]

The verse (he asserted) had been written by Charles d'Orléans, and he had found it in a book called *Shepherds' Gowns* [sic]. In an endnote he admitted that he could never remember the reference, but Pauline Tennant (their friend Pauline Rumbold) had kindly found it for him in a book by her grandmother Pamela Grey. In fact it is clear from the spelling and wording of the verse, copied directly from his notebook, that he had taken it from Samuel Johnson's footnote on page 70 of the 1813 edition of *Cymbeline*, which quotes it from Sir Thomas Elyot's *Ortho-œpia Gallica* (1593). Pamela Grey, who confidently attributed the poem to Charles d'Orléans, gave a different version of it altogether in her collection of essays *Shepherd's Crowns*.

While the chapters about the *Æneid* in *Virgil* amount to little more than a serial commentary on the story, the index to the book is monumentally vague. It contains no entry for Virgil himself, and a lazy *passim* for 'Greeks, Greece', 'Horace' and 'Rome'. Homosexuality (which Peter briskly attributed to his subject, without comment)[9] has no entry. Nor have honey and oaks, a favourite, linked motif that Peter borrowed from both the eclogues and the georgics. Ralph Hodgson, on the other hand, merits an entry for his pitying poem about a bullfight, although in Virgil's third georgic the bulls fight one another.

Surprisingly, *Virgil* attracted immediate notice from the *New York Times*, which, while criticizing its failure to say anything satisfactory about either the life or the times, did so fairly compassionately. But the *TLS* published a scathing condemnation by a New Zealand-born classical scholar, Denis Feeney, who had left for the United States after taking a postgraduate degree at Oxford. *Virgil* (he wrote) was so 'self-indulgent and howler-ridden' that he had felt tempted not to review it, and did so only to warn non-classicists who might want a simple introduction to Virgil to avoid it.[10] Luckily for Peter, by the time this appeared he was almost wholly blind.

The eye surgeon who operated on him in Cheltenham in February 1998 prescribed him spectacles with one strong magnifying lens and one black one, but warned him that the good eye would soon deteriorate to the same level as the bad one. He would have only peripheral vision and would no longer be able to read. Deirdre found him an amanuensis, Dot Jackson, who had always loved his work, and who came in once a week to decipher his scraps of poems and type letters to his dictation, replacing his increasingly wild postcard scrawls. She read poetry to him, and at other times he listened to it on tapes.

The laser treatment continued through the spring of 1998, in a rearguard action against Peter's loss of sight. The hills at St. Anthony were now too steep for him, but in late March he, Deirdre and Matthew spent a few days at Salcombe, before an eye operation in mid-April which left him exhausted, bloodshot and little improved. Deirdre told Matthew despairingly that she expected to find him dead at any moment. For his birthday in May, however, they drove to lunch with Julian and Richard at the Walnut Tree near Abergavenny, and in September they visited Dorset and Somerset, stopping off at Eliot's grave at East Coker. In October Peter lectured on Virgil at the

Cheltenham Festival, armed with reminder sheets from Dot containing a few mnemonic words in bold, outsize print. He told Bertie that it had felt bizarre being unable to see his audience, which someone told him afterwards had included crowds of schoolchildren. Having insisted (he said) that Virgil was mainly about sex, he had received a tremendous round of applause at the end.

Poverty was no urgent worry, since he now received a small pension from the Royal Literary Fund. Mark Amory sent him talking books to review for the *Spectator*, which kept him in tenuous touch with the literary world. Cressida's friend Sofka Zinovieff, having seen from his column that he wished he had a recording of Seferis reading his poems, promptly sent him one from Athens. Another friend, John Byrne, a former manuscript expert with Bertram Rota who had handled the sales of both his and Cyril's papers, also found him tapes of poetry. Collections of modern Greek poems, sent with compliments by their authors, continued to arrive at Stonesfield and Frampton, but he could no longer read them and there was no-one able to read them to him. He gave his collection of modern Greek books to a young scholar, Thomas de Waal, whose wife Georgina Wilson was a friend of Matthew's, and with his blessing they later passed them on to the Slavonic section of the Taylorian Library in Oxford.

Early periods of his past still haunted him, and he yearned for contact with Jesuit friends or even news of their deaths. Blindness deprives its sufferers of the middle-aged pleasure of reading newspaper obituaries and skimming death notices, and he persuaded Farm Street with some difficulty to let him know which of the former brethren had died. In long letters to Bertie, typed by Dot, he gossiped about past acquaintances, including several who were in trouble for having molested boys at Stonyhurst and its prep school. ('I grieve for the whole order, don't you?') Bertie could not travel south from Glasgow, but in November 1999 Peter sent him a delighted report of a visit from

Kevin Donovan and Robert Murray, 'the only Jesuit visitors since old Lawn popped in on his motorbike for a glass of beer on his way to take up residence somewhere at the bottom of Cuckoo Hill.'

Other fragments of the past reassembled themselves round him. Walking on the Green, *anchored to earth by dim eyes like torch-light,* he wore *an old brown coat for the year's shortest days/with the wind coming icy out of Wales.*[11] It was the coat Bert used to wear to the races, in heavy, old-fashioned tweed. Until then he had spurned it; now it comforted him, and he wanted nothing else.

Anthony had also re-entered his life, mellowed by his own misfortune. Peter and Deirdre had stayed with him as seldom as possible in Scotland, since, like Bert in middle age, he had reacted to stress by becoming combatively moody and drunk. Honor had kept in touch with them, however, and two weeks after meeting her for lunch in Oxford with her undergraduate daughter Clarissa they were shocked to hear that she had dropped dead from an aneurysm. Anthony retired to Oxford to be near his daughters, then moved out to Chipping Norton, where Peter, Deirdre and Matthew visited him in July 1998. A year and a half later I met him at a New Year's Eve party in Charlbury, where he spoke of his love of fast cars and opera and his ambition to drive himself and his daughters to every opera house in Europe 'if the diabetes doesn't get me first'. He did not mention Peter and I did not catch his surname, realising who he was only after both Peter and he had died.

By 1999 the laser treatment had come to a standstill. Peter found it difficult to recognize faces or even see people's heads, although he sometimes saw objects at the edge of his field of vision while the centre remained a dark blur. He walked with a white stick, had a disabled badge for the car and helped Deirdre push the trolley round the Stroud branch of Waitrose, endearing himself to checkout ladies as the funny, blind gentleman with the beautiful manners. On Matthew's twenty-ninth birthday he began a journal for him in a hard-covered notebook, inscribing the front pastedown in his large, chaotic writing: 'For your 30th birthday April 14th 2000 Out of the North come angels (Maybe Longfellow?)' The first entry begins 'April 14 Here is a year's journal. I hope so because my only ambition is to live another year: it seems to me a preposterous hope, & it does include the millennium. I expect it will mostly be about the weather.'

Matthew was detaching himself from home, and towards the end of the year took up quarters close to Charles and Cressida's house, Wyke Manor, near Pershore. Peter and Deirdre drove to Wyke for Peter's sixty-eighth birthday, and the next day set off on a 'wonderful green journey' to the Isle of Wight. Then for Deirdre's birthday in early December they stayed at Ludlow in a 'heron haunted weir hotel run by large grey cat'. In his journal Peter wrote about the weather, the sounds of geese on a north wind and 'swans wings like wind screen wipers', the springtime burst of pink flowering currant and early summer 'fusillade' of opening rosebuds, the smells of rain and hay and the autumnal smells of trees ('yellow leaves still underfoot by black poplar smelling heavenly'). Sentences wander blindly over the pages, sometimes tangling with one another in indecipherable knots. Very few of the entries are dated.

1 Sept. Blazing day all games over. Pip loiters in shades. Swans straggle. Sky Persian blue & flawless. Lavender breast high at front door.

Misty & no flies or wasps – sun appeared at 12. Early swans passed over & geese in the mist. Pip & I in a daze to P.O. & back. D ill since yesterday (after 3 wks of dentist trouble). Gug [Matthew] in London. In the afternoon we read Basho in bed.

Mist then by 10 a blazing Persian bowl. Green silent[,] swans in line of battle bent. Pip had a few dog and many child friends. D better[...]'

Mist then rain. Cleared by 10.30 & Pip & I met the whole hunt who were coming home from cubbing... No trouble. One elderly whip w[ith] a lame hound (?) alone. I think the [Clifford] family all in strength all chirping Good morning in their saffron coats.

To Tew [to visit Nancy Sandars] by Stow & Cross Hands the perfect sept. journey & the garden like an adventure in the past.

On January 5, 2000, as the Millennium fuss began to subside, he and Deirdre went to lunch with Joan and Paddy at the Mill House at Dumbleton, near Evesham, a remnant of the estate which had belonged to Joan's childhood home, now a hotel. Their fellow-guest was the resourceful, humorous and independent Lady Dorothy ('Coote') Lygon, a girlhood friend of Joan's whom they had come to know well since moving to Gloucestershire. Peter was in fine form, holding forth on the sonnets of the *Pléiade* group of Ronsard and Joachim du Bellay and the place of constellations, comets and meteors in the poetry of Sappho, Propertius and Virgil.[12]

Perhaps because Matthew had also been at the Leigh Fermors' lunch, Peter did not mention it in his journal. 'Dark day with familiar noises & some rain but a waterfall of hoofbeats now & then & chink & cheep of birds,' he noted one day early in January. There were floods, with the Court Lake overflowing and Rollo Clifford trying to hold it back with sandbags. Then 'Frost & blue sky the lakes magnificent & birds the birds like Olympia to Pyrgos.' A few days later he wrote:

... THINGS bulbs [snowdrops?] & violets out[.] But everything says snow is coming. Here I *must* end this journal listening to Manon des Sources over a good fire[.] W[hich may do?] for you though it does not reach the end of the book quite nor your birthday which is on the 14th of April. Here I give up but with much love.

Peter Levi

So this is a journal of 10 [*sic*] months / 14 Jan 2000.

By then, however, he had started another, more personal notebook, headed 'Jan 10th 2000', with his name and the note 'I cannot read the writing in this book but I suppose I can have it read to me.'

I am now read to only in English but am surprised to find I shall pine for Russian & Spanish, not at all for Italian; I often long for Latin & Greek & French but in only modern Greek for the language & my little Persian & less Arabic & Hebrew have vanished like snow I do still long to reread' [two cut-off initials, apparently in Greek].

The jottings continue, without dates:

The landscape I long for is Spanish the ruins & architecture Italian & the rivers & the place to live England 1740 to 1840.

My sweetest recent dreams are a chat with Auden and David Jones and a kind of triumphal arch made of sucked purple red yellow & green boiled sweets.

May 31 1666 Pepys feared blindness like "going into my grave" but died sight sighted [*sic*] in 1705.

Then, after various reflections, comes the pitiful:

Jan 26 2000 Dusk walk w[ith] dog, same terrible shoulder pain, pockmarked paths freezing fog light fading Hell.

Five days after that Deirdre took him to Cheltenham, where he enjoyed a morning stroll. Matthew was at home recovering from flu. In the afternoon he rested, then listened to a tape of Eliot reading his poems and asked Deirdre to read to him from a favourite book by Maurice Baring. Dwelling on the past, he reminisced about Jesuit friends. After supper he listened to one of his talking books, a novel by Bernard Cornwell about India during the Napoleonic War. At about eleven o'clock he felt his way up the narrow staircase to join Deirdre, who had gone on ahead. Matthew heard them chatting and laughing, found he was unable to sleep, and was listening to his radio in the dark some time after midnight when Deirdre came to his door with a torch and said 'I think Peter may have died.'

ENVOI

As he had wished, they had him cremated and scattered his ashes among the reeds. Perhaps to placate something residual in his spirit, Deirdre asked Gillian to arrange a Catholic Requiem for him at Prinknash Abbey, where she had sometimes unsuccessfully offered to take him to hear Mass. Bertie, who had seen so little of him for so long, travelled south to be the celebrant. Afterwards Matthew hosted a wake at a hotel in Painswick, where the Rococo Garden had been one of Peter and Deirdre's favourite places while he was still able to climb the steep slopes.

P.J. Kavanagh described Peter's memorial service in his 'Life and Letters' column in the *Spectator*.[1] It was conducted by Bishop Peter Walker, who had blessed his and Deirdre's marriage, on his sixty-ninth birthday, May 16, in the church of St. Mary the Virgin in Oxford. Like a reprise of his ordination service, the church was crowded with literary, academic, ex-Jesuit and Jesuit friends. Cressida gave a lunch beforehand at the Old Bank Hotel in High Street and Charles filled the church with flowers from Wyke. Georgina Wilson's choir sang Mozart's *Ave Verum Corpus*, and a young Polish violinist she had discovered played one of Peter's favourite pieces, the solo from Vaughan Williams's *The Lark Ascending*. Cressida read from the Song of Solomon and the Book of Revelation, and Peter Jay and Fram Dinshaw each read three of Peter's poems. David Pryce-Jones gave the address, which is printed in the appendix below.

In 2001 Anvil Press Poetry brought out a last volume of Peter's poems, called *Viriditas* in allusion to the Green at Frampton. It contains some short, late fragments, several sonnets in continuation of the mood of *Reed Music*, and a charming re-telling of the Japanese legend of the fishing boy Urashima, who was lured into a kingdom under the sea and emerged to find himself an old man.

One of the sonnets is a declaration of his symbiotic love for Deirdre.

> *Two poles trembling and twirling north to south*
> *whizzing and wobbling in a sea of light*
> *like spheres of fire for ever out of sight,*
> *or like two rivers spouting mouth to mouth,*
> *two springs of ocean, under one sea floor*
> *greening each other's water breast to breast*
> *freezing into one sunset and cold west*
> *and yet still pouring as green oceans pour*
> *as ragged birds pour on through the night sky*
> *and moonlight pours between the mist and cloud,*
> *and high above the wind you hear the loud*
> *concerted creak as Russian swans go by:*
> *we are two oceans, and our breath is single,*
> *and our souls only live when our fires mingle.*[2]

APPENDIX

PETER LEVI: AN ADDRESS DELIVERED IN THE UNIVERSITY CHURCH OF ST MARY THE VIRGIN OXFORD ON 16 MAY 2000 BY DAVID PRYCE-JONES

Occupying the best part of one of my shelves are twenty-eight books by Peter Levi – by no means his whole output – and a dozen or more of those desirable items described in dealers' catalogues as v. scarce. The titles of the latter say something about him: *Pancakes for the Queen of Babylon, The Shearwaters, Comfort at Fifty* (with an annotation in his hand 'Five anti-platonic sonnets'), *In Memory of George Seferis, Orpheus' Head, Music of Dark Tones*. Here's an offprint from the 'Heythrop Journal' of an article on the Podgoritsa Cup, a clear glass patera apparently of uncertain origin. In an offhand footnote Peter likens it to one similar signed by Acaunissa who 'probably worked at Vichy under Hadrian'. Another offprint, this time from the 'Classical Review', opens: 'If we had Cyriaco of Ancona's full and original journal and drawings, his immense importance as an archaeological traveller would be even more obvious to everybody than it already is.' Cyriaco's numerous journeys, Peter continues in his own manner, 'are as hard to unravel as very old cobwebs.'

Who else combines such natural gifts with such learning? Of course he knew the classical languages from schooldays, and he had to learn at least some Hebrew. He had a crack at Arabic – or was it Aramaic? He taught himself Russian to translate Yevtushenko and to write about Pasternak. His modern Greek was idiomatic, and he translated that too. Certain Serbo-Croat poems, he held, occupied an essential place in the history of the epic, and he came to translate them. As for French, he once took a troop of boy scouts from Stonyhurst to the Auvergne, and sent me a postcard with the news that he had led them to sing out of the train window at some station, '*Il est cocu, le chef de gare.*'

As in that remark about cobwebby Cyriaco, Peter really did think that everybody knew what he knew. What often got him into trouble with pedants was a belief that learning mattered not for its own sake but for the illuminations and excitements which emerged from it. A scholar, he once said, is someone who claims to know more about some tiny thing than the only other man to make the same claim. On another occasion, someone to whom I had just sent a book of mine had returned a list of its errors. Peter brushed this off. 'Mistakes are the plums in the pudding.'

He was a poet. I see him as he was when a young man, for whom handsome is too dull a word, and beautiful too feeble. With those dark profound eyes and the eyebrows with a right-angle in them, the intensity of his face expressed the inner spirit. Peter and his looks went beyond the full romantic image of the poet. A bus had knocked him down and almost killed him. In the street passers-by turned to stare at this ethereal El Greco figure, and of course to wonder at the dog-collar. A dandy, out to surprise and shock, he was at the same time a visionary on a mountain-top.

The house of his childhood, in Ruislip, was a place like any other, but it concealed impenetrably the origins of his parents and their many relations. On his father's side, they were originally Jews from Constantinople and Baghdad, settings far more exotic and far-flung than the Middlesex from which his mother, a Catholic, came. Somewhere in the surrounding suburbs, he told me, he had had a revelation that God called him not just to be a Catholic but a Jesuit priest. To a man of reason, faith was 'axiomatic' – the adjective was as unusual as the thought behind it. Father Levi of Campion Hall was a match for Evelyn Waugh's Father Rothschild S.J. Improbability gathered round him. One day the Heythrop Hunt met in the park of Heythrop College, where Jesuits did their theological training, and a jolly huntsman cantered past to call out to Peter, 'Just over from

Ireland, padre?'

A group of close friends tried to persuade him not to take final vows. A kind of medieval disputation occurred. In self-protection, he slipped lower and lower in his chair, until finally he was hiding under the table. There were as many bohemians as believers in the church at Eastbourne when Peter was ordained, a lonely figure face down on the floor, arms extended.

Peter reached maturity at a moment when high culture still meant to quite a lot of people what it meant to him, and there was no pressure to apologise for what is now called elitism. The great Judæo-Christian tradition held art to be an act of rightful worship of God, for purposes of enjoyment and fulfilment and renewal. Peter found in David Jones perhaps the one living artist with a natural affinity. David Jones was also a visionary, and Peter praised him in a wonderful, almost rapturous, sermon he preached after Jones's death, because 'what he accomplished in his art was a direct projection of what he was as a man.' It is not an accident that one of David Jones's most magnificent works of lettering is the ordination card he designed for Peter, with the name of Melchisedek in Greek capitals coloured an unimaginable flamingo pink right across the centre of it, and at the very bottom the dedication in Welsh, 'from David the painter to Peter the poet.'

An early challenge to Peter's high culture came in the surprising form of the Beat Poets, Allen Ginsberg and Gregory Corso, who exploded into Oxford one fine day shouting that has-beens and the walking dead were all around. Impressed as he undoubtedly was, Peter could never have made the sort of concessions they demanded, nor the even simpler concessions inherent in the popular culture of the rest of his lifetime. Too intelligent for nostalgia or regret, he had no interest in fame and fashion. His art was also a direct projection of the man he was.

Peter's poetry was religious in the sense that he celebrates the natural creation. Earth and stone, water and fire, are central to his imagery. Some of his finest poems are addresses to friends, sometimes commemorations of their death, in the form almost of biographies. Other poems tell stories, while several of his travel books are really poems in praise of nature and landscape, in Greece and Afghanistan and England. The shape of the hills, the colours of the seasons, the evocation of history, the mortality inherent in the word 'bone', inspired Peter's special lyricism.

Peter left the priesthood to marry Deirdre Connolly. Theirs was love at first sight. 'Such a relief,' Peter said. They lived in a country cottage, appropriate for a story with a happy ending. Peter was proud of Cressida and Matthew, the children of Deirdre and Cyril Connolly. *Shade Those Laurels* was a comic novel which Cyril had begun, and Peter was to complete and publish it. Like Cyril he had a taste for good food and champagne with friends, and the wanderer from the mountain-tops bloomed into a family man. But Peter actually enjoyed writing, in his case with a fountain-pen, making extraordinarily few corrections on the pages of thick note-books. Concentration led to fluency. From the cottage came poems, reviews, biographies of Horace and Virgil, Shakespeare and Milton, Tennyson, Lear and others. Peter seemed the last true man of letters, always consistent, and bravely sure that his precarious way of life would turn out all right in the end.

I see him head tilted back for one of his long delighted laughs. There was in him all manner of squibs and what the French call *boutades*, but no trace of malice or unkindness. I see him in a café in Athens one hot summer afternoon with Nikos Gatsos and another Greek poet, talking about Pausanias. I see him in that favourite tweed three-piece suit, as green as pea-soup. I see him in the enchanted garden of his own imagination, where all the great things ever made by God and the hand of man are there to be enjoyed. Finally I see him walking in Frampton-on-Severn to post a letter on the evening before he died, and which I received only two days afterwards. Diabetes had by then robbed him of almost all his eye-sight. Looping large over the page, the last words he wrote also say something about the man:

> We are both terribly sorry to hear of your father's death. He was a great favourite of ours and to me an early friend and a bright star that never faded... I share with R.S. Thomas the distinction of being his discovery... I write this without help so the process is very queer like going downhill backwards with your eyes shut.

BIBLIOGRAPHY

Peter Levi's main publications are listed below. The list does not include book-reviews, the majority of his other articles, poems published only in periodicals and some pamphlets.

POETRY

1960 *The Gravel Ponds* (André Deutsch)

1962 *Water, Rock and Sand* (André Deutsch)

1962 *Orpheus' Head, or Dialogue on an Ash-Heap* (privately printed, Oxford)

1965 *The Shearwaters* (Harlequin Poets)

1966 *Fresh Water, Sea Water* (Black Raven with André Deutsch)

1968 *Pancakes for the Queen of Babylon* (Anvil Press Poetry)

1968 *Ruined Abbeys* (Anvil Press Poetry)

1971 *Life is a Platform* (Anvil Press Poetry)

1971 *Death is a Pulpit* (Anvil Press Poetry)

1973 in *Penguin Modern Poets 22: John Fuller, Peter Levi, Adrian Mitchell*

1976 *Collected Poems, 1955-1975* (Anvil Press Poetry)

1978 *Five Ages* (Anvil Press Poetry)

1981 *Private Ground* (Anvil Press Poetry)

1983 *The Echoing Green: three elegies* (Anvil Press Poetry)

1985 *Shakespeare's Birthday* [three elegies] (Anvil Press Poetry)

1989 *Shadow and Bone: poems 1981-1989* (Anvil Press Poetry)

1989 *Goodbye to the Art of Poetry* (Anvil Press Poetry)

1994 *The Rags of Time* [nine elegies, comprising *The Echoing Green, Shakespeare's Birthday* and *The View from the Canal Path*] (Anvil Press Poetry)

1997 *Reed Music* (Anvil Press Poetry)

2001 *Viriditas* (Anvil Press Poetry)

AUTOBIOGRAPHY AND TRAVEL

1972 *The Light Garden of the Angel King: Journeys in Afghanistan* (Collins)

1980 *The Hill of Kronos* (Collins)

1983 *The Flutes of Autumn* (Harvill)

1996 *A Bottle in the Shade: a Journey in the Western Peloponnese* (Sinclair-Stevenson)

LECTURES AND CRITICISM

1970 *Ο τόνος της φωνής του Σεφέρη* [Mr Seferis's Tone of Voice] (privately printed, Athens)

1967 'The Poetry of David Jones', *Agenda* **5:1-3**, 80-89

1974 'History and Reality in David Jones', *Agenda* **11:4/12:1**, 56-59

1975 'In Memory of David Jones' (eulogy published by *The Tablet*; reprinted as appendix to *The Flutes of Autumn*, 1983)

1975 *John Clare and Thomas Hardy* (John Coffin Memorial Lecture, University of London, Athlone Press)

1977 *The Noise Made by Poems* (Anvil Press Poetry)

1990 *Hopkins and his God / Hopkins a'i Dduw* (North Wales Arts Association)

1992 *The Art of Poetry: the Oxford Lectures* (Yale University Press, London)

LITERARY BIOGRAPHY

1988 *The Life and Times of William Shakespeare* (Macmillan)

1988 *A Private Commission: New Verses by Shakespeare* (Macmillan)

1990 *Boris Pasternak* (Hutchinson)

1993 *Tennyson* (Macmillan)

1995 *Edward Lear* (Macmillan)

1996 *Eden Renewed: the Public and Private Life of John Milton* (Macmillan)

1997 *Horace: a Life* (Duckworth)

1998 *Virgil: his Life and Times* (Duckworth)

FICTION

1979 *The Head in the Soup* (Constable)

1985 *Grave Witness* (Quartet)

1986 *Knit One, Drop One* (Quartet)

1988 *To the Goat* (Hutchinson)

1990 Conclusion to Cyril Connolly's *Shade Those Laurels* (Bellew)

TRANSLATIONS

1962 (with R. Milner-Gulland) Yevgeny Yevtushenko, *Selected Poems* (Penguin)

1966 (with R. Milner-Gulland) Yevgeny Yevtushenko, *Poems, chosen by the author* (Harvill)

1971 Pausanias, *Guide to Greece* (2 vols., Penguin Classics)

1976 *The Psalms* (Penguin Classics)

1977 George Pavlopoulos, *The Cellar* (Anvil Press Poetry)

1983 Alexandros Papadiamantis, *The Murderess* (Writers & Readers)

1984 (with Anne Pennington) *Marko the Prince, Serbo-Croat Heroic Songs* (Duckworth)

1985 *The Holy Gospel of John* (Churchman Press, Worthing)

1988 Martine de Courcel, *Tolstoy, the Ultimate Reconciliation* (Scribner's Sons, New York)

1992 *The Revelation of John* (Kyle Cathie)

HISTORY

1961 *Beaumont* (André Deutsch)

1980 *Atlas of the Greek World* (Phaidon)

1985 *History of Greek Literature* (Penguin)

1987 *The Frontiers of Paradise: a study of monks and monasteries* (Harvill)

ANTHOLOGIES AND OTHER EDITIONS

1974 *The English Bible* (Constable)

1974 *Pope*, selected & edited by Peter Levi (Penguin)

1984 Johnson & Boswell, *Journey to the Western Island of Scotland* and *Journal of a Tour to the Hebrides*, edited by Peter Levi (Penguin)

1984 *Penguin Book of English Christian Verse*

OTHER SOURCES

Between the 1960s and the 1980s Peter Levi was a frequent contributor to the poetry magazine *Agenda*. As well as reviews of his individual collections, *Agenda* published general appreciations of his poetry by John Bayley (**6:2**, Spring 1968) and John Bayley, Fram Dinshaw and others (**24:3**, Summer 1986).

Dooley, Tim, in *Dictionary of Literary Biography* **40** (Detroit, 1985) 306.

Gardner, Kevin J., 'Peter Levi: Poet of Winter' in *Renascence: Essays on Values in Literature* (Marquette University Press), **63:3** (Spring 2011) 229 ff.

Haffenden, John, 'Peter Levi: An Interview' in *Poetry Review* **74:3** (1984) 5-21

Hurwitt, Jannika, 'Peter Levi: The Art of Poetry no. 24' in *Paris Review* **76** (Fall 1979) 1-34.

Seymour-Smith, Martin, 'Levi, Peter' in Ian Hamilton (ed.), *The Oxford Companion to Twentieth-Century Poetry in English* (1994) 299-300.

ENDNOTES

PLP= Papers of Peter Levi, John J. Burns Library, Boston College, Mass.
p/m = postmarked

NOTES TO INTRODUCTION
1 *Edward Lear* (1995) 154.
2 To David Pryce-Jones [summer 1973].
3 *Flutes of Autumn* (1983) 151-153.
4 *Flutes of Autumn* 153.
5 Information kindly supplied by Roger Garfitt, Frances Horovitz's widower and literary executor.
6 To Peter ('Bertie') Granger-Banyard [May 1972].

NOTES TO CHAPTER I
1 To D P-J [late 1961].
2 *Flutes of Autumn* (1983) 13.
3 *Flutes of Autumn* 19.
4 'Ghost of an Old Curse', *Reed Music* (1997) 73.
5 *Light Garden of the Angel King* (1984 ed.) 20, 23
6 'Moscow Diary', 19 March 1989, MS 90-15, Box 9 no. 4, PLP.
7 *A Bottle in the Shade* (1996) 199.
8 Caryl Brahms and Ned Sherrin, *Too Dirty for the Windmill* (1986) 2-3. Julian Mitchell used the story about the sixteen children in his *Independent* obituary of Peter, 3 February 2000, and it appears in the article on Caryl Brahms in the *Oxford DNB*. Portrait photographs of Moses and Sultana are reproduced in the Brahms and Sherrin book.
9 Moses Jourado died in Hammersmith in 1922. Until then the Jourado Carpet Company had traded in Newman Street and (later) Oxford Street, London W1. Victoria continued to live at 22 Canfield Gardens, West Hampstead (where she was listed in the telephone directory in 1917) before moving to Chichele Mansions, Cricklewood.
10 See note 8 (unfortunately an unreliable source).
11 CB to PL, 29 September 1958, PLP.
12 *Flutes of Autumn* 24.
13 *Flutes of Autumn* 24.
14 E. Baines, *History, Directory & Gazetteer of the County of York* (1823). International Genealogical Index, Yorkshire (microform). 1841-61 censuses (*www. Ancestry.co.uk*). East Yorkshire Family History Society, *Beverley St Mary's* (1995). Anne Mary Borchert and Joseph Tigar were

married in St. Marylebone in the spring of 1844. Anne's mother Anne, who lived with the couple as a widow, had been born in Southwark.

NOTES TO CHAPTER 2
[1] *Flutes of Autumn* (1983) 11.
[2] *Flutes of Autumn* 31.
[3] 'Self-portrait' in *Light Blue, Dark Blue, an Anthology of Oxford & Cambridge Writing* (1960) 134.
[4] Richard Ellmann, *James Joyce* (1965 ed.) 26.
[5] *Shadow & Bone* (1989) 69.
[6] PL to P. Granger-Banyard (henceforward PB where named in text as recipient), May/June 1985.
[7] *Flutes of Autumn* 32.
[8] *Collected Poems* (1976) 151.

NOTES TO CHAPTER 3
[1] *Flutes of Autumn* (1983) 38.
[2] Prior Park School Magazine, December 1945.
[3] Christopher Logue, *Prince Charming: a memoir* (1999) 14.
[4] *Flutes of Autumn* 57.
[5] *Flutes of Autumn* 60.
[6] *Horace* (1998) 1.
[7] *Art of Poetry* (1991) 50.
[8] *Flutes of Autumn* 60
[9] Madeleine Devlin, *Christopher Devlin* (1970) 95.
[10] *Flutes of Autumn* 60.
[11] *Beaumont Review*, July 1947.
[12] *Beaumont Review*, January 1948.
[13] *Beaumont Review*, July 1948.

NOTES TO CHAPTER 4
[1] *Flutes of Autumn* 66.
[2] R. Butterworth, *The Detour* (2005) 72, 75.
[3] *Flutes of Autumn* (1983) 63.
[4] *Collected Poems* (1976) 225.

NOTES TO CHAPTER 5
[1] *Flutes of Autumn* (1983) 69.
[2] *Flutes of Autumn* 72.
[3] Butterworth, *The Detour* ((2005) 94, 106.
[4] *Times Literary Supplement*, 23 July 2010, 15/2, announcing the discovery by June and Paul Schlueter of the only extant version of this and other

poems in a manuscript in Kassel, Germany.
[5] PL to PB, 23 January 1951.
[6] *Flutes of Autumn* 77-78.
[7] Courtesy of the Rev. Peter Granger-Banyard S.J.
[8] Courtesy of the Rev. Peter Granger-Banyard S.J.
[9] HG to PL, 3 December 1953, PLP.
[10] Letter to author, 1 December 2006.
[11] *The Gravel Ponds* (1960) 41; *Collected Poems* (1976, new ed. 1984) 31.
[12] PL to PB, 'St. Peter C[anisius, 27 April 1953]'.
[13] 'For Angus Macintyre', Reed Music (1997) 77.
[14] PL to PB, 'Pentecost' [1953].
[15] *Flutes of Autumn* 79.
[16] PL to PB, 6 October 1954.

NOTES TO CHAPTER 6

[1] PL to Willie Charlton [autumn 1955].
[2] PL to Nancy Sandars [23 May 1966].
[3] *Flutes of Autumn* 1983 82.
[4] *Downside Review,* October 1955.
[5] PL to John Fuller [spring 1961].
[6] PL to PB, 27 September 1955.
[7] *Gravel Ponds* (1960) 55; *Collected Poems* (1976, new ed. 1984) 41.
[8] PL to PB [March/April 1955].
[9] 'For Denis Bethell', *The Echoing Green* (1983) 12.
[10] EF to PL, 5 June 1955, PLP; cf. PL to Willie Charlton, 19 December 1955.
[11] *Diaries of Evelyn Waugh* ed. Michael Davie (1979 ed.) 735. ES to PL, 15 Sept. 1955, PLP.
[12] PL to PB, 20 February 1957.
[13] PL to PB, 27 September 1955.
[14] Willie Charlton, e-mail attachment, 6 January 2008.
[15] Opimian Club minute-book, '*Falernum Opimianum*', courtesy of William Charlton.
[16] PL to John Fuller, [November 1964].
[17] DB to PL, 20 March 1956, PLP.
[18] *Flutes of Autumn* 89.
[19] Opimian Club minute-book, courtesy of William Charlton.
[20] 'Charterhouse Chronicle', *Catholic Herald,* 11 February 2000.
[21] PL to PB, August 1956.
[22] PL to PB, August 1956.
[23] 'Isis Idol', *Isis* 30 October 1957, 21; Moraes, *My Son's Father* (1968) 180-181.

24 *Gemini*, Spring 1957, 34; *Gravel Ponds* 16 ; *Collected Poems* 14.
25 *Isis* 16 October 1956; *Gravel Ponds* 34; *Collected Poems* 26. *Isis*, 20 November 1956.

Notes to Chapter 7

1 PL to WC, [early November] 1956.
2 CM to PL, 15 April 1960, PLP.
3 *Gemini*, summer 1957; *From the Gravel Ponds* (1960) 21; *Collected Poems* (1976, new ed. 1984) 18. After a scurrilous allusion to Lord Leconfield on a postcard to Julian Mitchell in November 1964 , P wrote: 'I lived near there one winter & wrote a poem you printed about deer & a holly bush.'
4 CT to PL, 6 January 1956 [i.e. 1957]; DB to PL, 3 January 1957; JM to PL, 5 January 1957, all PLP.
5 Lavinia Greacen, *J.G. Farrell, the making of a writer* (1999) 79-89.
6 Notebook entry quoted in PL to Julian Mitchell, ?8 November 1959.
7 *Gemini*, summer 1957; *Gravel Ponds* 37; *Collected Poems* 28.
8 PL to JM, 30 September 1972.
9 Ved Mehta, *Up at Oxford* (1993) 209.
10 L'Aurore Grelottante', *Paris Review* spring/summer 1959; *Gravel Ponds* 17; *Collected Poems* 15.
11 Paul Haddon, interview, 7 November 2007.
12 PL to PB [May? 1957].
13 'For Colin MacLeod', *Echoing Green* (1983) 26.
14 *Flutes of Autumn* (1983) 98.
15 PL to JM, 7 August 1957.
16 PL to JM, [September 1957.]
17 PC to PL, 15 July 1957, PLP.
18 PL to JM, 5 October 1957. SS to PL, 6 January 1958, PLP.
19 Barbara Bray to PL, 1957, PLP.
20 Letters to PL, 18 July, 29 August, 24 October, 15 and 19 November, 19 December 1957, 20 January 1958, PLP.
21 Mary O'Hara, *The Scent of the Roses* (1980) 154.
22 *Isis* 30 October 1957, 21.
23 PL to PB, 25 October 1957.
24 PL to JM, 12 April 1958.
25 *Gravel Ponds* 40; *Collected Poems* 30.
26 Ferdinand Mount, *Cold Cream: My Early Life and Other Mistakes* (2008) 179.
27 *Water, Rock & Sand* (1062) 39; *Collected Poems* 66.
28 Moraes, 'Verses for Peter Levi' in *Poems* (1960) 21.
29 E. Jennings to PL, 23 October, 3 and 8 November [1957], PLP; Jennings,

The Animals' Arrival (1969) 35.

[30] PL to P. Banyard, 7 June [1957].

[31] PL to Julian Mitchell, 1 February 1958.

[32] *TLS* 31 January 1958 ; *Gravel Ponds* 22 ; *Collected Poems* 19.

[33] PL to JM, 30 January 1964.

[34] FW to PL, 20 February 1958, DA to PL, 27 March 1958, JM to PL, 31 March 1958, PLP.

[35] PL to JM, 30 March, ?Easter and 12 April 1958. 'Notes Towards A Novel - Perhaps?', *Isis*, 14 May 1958.

[36] Ginsberg to his father, 24 May 1958, in *Family Business: selected letters between a father and a son* (2001) 110.

[37] Corso to John Wieners, 22 May 1956 in *Accidental Autobiography* (2003) 105.

[38] *Gravel Ponds* 57; *Collected Poems* 42

[39] 'For Gregory Corso', *Gravel Ponds* 57; *Collected Poems* 42.

NOTES TO CHAPTER 8

[1] Paul Haddon, interview, 7 November 2007.

[2] CB to PL, 29 September 1958, PLP.

[3] *The Gravel Ponds* (1960) 47; *Collected Poems* (1976, new ed. 1984) 35.

[4] *Flutes of Autumn* (1983) 79.

[5] JM to PL, 6 October 1958, PLP.

[6] PL to PB, 8 September 1958; to Julian Mitchell [autumn 1958].

[7] *Isis* 12 November 1958, 13. PL identified himself as the author, writing to Julian Mitchell on 18 December that he wished someone would send him his 'Isis Idol' of Dom.

[8] PL to JM, 17 November 1958.

[9] PL to JM, 3, 11 October 1958; *Stonyhurst Magazine* January 1959, 224-5; May 1959, 283.

[10] PL to JM, 11 October 1958; Dom Moraes, *My Son's Father* (1968) 218.

[11] To Julian Mitchell [February 1959]. The masque was privately printed in Oxford in 1962.

[12] *Collected Poems* 44

[13] *Stonyhurst Magazine* May 1959 283

[14] JM to PL, 16 March 1959, PLP; John] David Caute, *At Fever Pitch* (1959).

[15] *Water, Rock & Sand* (1962) 37; *Collected Poems* 64-65

[16] *My Son's Father* 219.

[17] 'The Master', *Fresh Water, Sea Water* (1966) 5; *Collected Poems* 95-96

[18] 'Proposals for a Poetic Revolution', *New Statesman* December 1958; *Water, Rock & Sand* (1962) 12; *Collected Poems* 45.

[19] PL to Julian Mitchell, [January 1959], 17 March 1961.

[20] John Wynne-Williams to Deirdre Levi, February 2000.
[21] *The Shearwaters* (1965); *Collected Poems* 83.
[22] *Collected Poems* 90, 92.
[23] PL to WC [1959].
[24] PL to JM [postcard, p/m 20 October 1959]; JM to PL, 17 November 1959.
[25] E. Fraenkel to PL, 5 November 1959, PLP.
[26] PL to Julian Mitchell 16 January 1960.
[27] CB to PL, 10 January 1960.
[28] *Water, Rock & Sand* 32; *Collected Poems* 61.
[29] *Gemini/Dialogue* January 1960, 49.
[30] PL to JM [p/m 18 February 1960; p/m 17 March 1960].
[31] JB to PL, 10 March 1960, PLP.
[32] JM to PL, 10 March 1960, PL P.
[33] *Water, Rock & Sand* 16-19; *Collected Poems* 48-51.
[34] PL to JM [30 April 1960]; 'John' to PL, 27 March 1960, PLP.
[35] DM to PL [?February 1960]; H to PL, 7 December 1959, PLP.
[36] R M-G to PL 1 April 1960, PLP.
[37] PL to JM, 30 April, 2 May 1960.
[38] PL to John Fuller [September 1960].
[39] PL to JM, 4 September 1960.

Notes to Chapter 9

[1] *Daily Telegraph* 18 August, *TLS* 15 September 1961.
[2] PL to Julian Mitchell, 20 January 1961
[3] PL to P. Banyard, 'April the late' [1959].
[4] PL to Willie Charlton, January [1960]; to Julian Mitchell [April 1961].
[5] PL to JF [January 1961].
[6] *Time & Tide* 27 January 1961.
[7] *Time & Tide*, 31 August 1961
[8] Mount, *Cold Cream* (2008) 189-90.
[9] *Flutes of Autumn* (1983) 125.
[10] PL to JM, 17 March 1961.
[11] PL to Tony Mitchell [summer 1961], papers of Julian Mitchell; *Flutes of Autumn* 126.
[12] *Flutes of Autumn* 113-14.
[13] R.P. Graves, *Richard Hughes* (1994) 396.
[14] *Flutes of Autumn* 112.
[15] PL to John Fuller [?late 1961] and JM [November 1961].
[16] PL to John Fuller [30 May 1962].
[17] PL to Julian Mitchell [8 February 1962].
[18] PL to JM [5 May 1962].

[19] *Art of Poetry* (1991) 203-204.

[20] P. Hancock in *Varsity* (Cambridge) 5 May 1962, 3. Amis, *Memoirs* (2004 ed.) 235-41. PL, *Boris Pasternak* (1990) 65.

[21] 'Echoes of Mayakovsky Square', *Times*, 14 May 1962.

[22] *New Statesman*, 18 May 1962, 731-732. Amis, *Memoirs* 239.

[23] Spender, *Journals* 1939-1983 (1985), 12 & 14 May 1962, 227.

[24] PL to IB [May 1962], IB to PL, 28 May 1962, MS Berlin 168, Bodleian Library, Oxford.

[25] *Observer*, 25 May 1962.

NOTES TO CHAPTER 10

[1] See AC to Sir Isaiah Berlin, 23 October 1961, MS Berlin 165, and David P-J to Berlin, 22 July 1962, MS Berlin 169, Bodleian Library, Oxford.

[2] *Flutes of Autumn* 126.

[3] Obituary of Betty Sandars, *Independent*, 21 July 1995.

[4] *TLS* 19 October 1962.

[5] PL to JM [autumn 1958].

[6] *TLS* 26 October 1962.

[7] *New Statesman* 7 December 1962; *TLS* 22 March 1963.

[8] PL to Connolly [winter 1962/63], Connolly Papers, University of Tulsa, Oklahoma. PL to David Pryce-Jones [early 1963].

[9] PL to Julian Mitchell [3 October 1962].

[10] PL to WC [16 November 1962].

[11] See note 9.

[12] PL to Bertie Banyard [early 1963].

[13] PL to Julian Mitchell [11 January 1963].

[14] PL to David Pryce-Jones [early 1963].

[15] See notes 12 and 13.

[16] PL to WC, April [1964].

[17] JM, diary entry, 21 September 1963.

[18] PL to David Pryce-Jones [5 April 1963].

[19] 'For Nancy and Betty Sandars', *Fresh Water, Sea Water* (1966) ; *Collected Poems* (1976) 106.

NOTES TO CHAPTER 11

[1] *The Hill of Kronos* (1980) 15. See also Robert Butterworth, The Detour (2005) 107, on his parents having to take a taxi to Banbury after being refused a lift with a Jesuit who was catching the same train.

[2] *Hill of Kronos* 17-18.

[3] *Hill of Kronos* 19.

[4] *Birthday Letters* (1998) 3.

[5] PL to NS [18 September 1964].

[6] To David Pryce-Jones [7 January 1964].

[7] *Hill of Kronos* 30-32.

[8] *Hill of Kronos* 116.

[9] *Hill of Kronos* 28. In an interview with John Haffenden, *Poetry Review* **74**.3, 16, Peter said that he met Haldeman on his last night in Athens that summer, perhaps meaning the last night of his first stay there.

[10] *Hill of Kronos* 45, 49.

[11] *Hill of Kronos* 49-50.

[12] *Hill of Kronos* 88-89.

[13] *Hill of Kronos* 70.

[14] PL to JF [winter 1963/64].

[15] Introduction to PL's translation of Pavlopoulos, *The Cellar* (1977) 5. For a fuller version of the conversation, see *Hill of Kronos* 65.

[16] *Hill of Kronos* 71-72.

[17] *Hill of Kronos* 49, 55-73.

[18] *Hill of Kronos* 81.

[19] PL to his mother [August 1963].

[20] *Hill of Kronos* 98.

[21] IB to Noel Annan, 31 August 1973 in *Building: Letters* 1960-1975 (2013) 550.

[22] Artemis Cooper, *Patrick Leigh Fermor, an Adventure* (2012) 283-90, 317, 324.

[23] *Mani* (1958) 30.

[24] *Independent*, 16 February 2000.

[25] *A Bottle in the Shade* (1996) 55.

[26] *Hill of Kronos* 111.

[27] *Hill of Kronos* 104.

[28] *Hill of Kronos* 108-109.

[29] Julian Mitchell, diary, 21 September 1963.

Notes to Chapter 12

[1] PL to David Pryce-Jones [1963/64].

[2] *Agenda*, David Jones Special Issue 1967, 87. See also Jones to PL, 'St Matthew' [21 September] 1967, PLP.

[3] *The Hill of Kronos* (1980) 115.

[4] *Diary* 30 April 1934 (1982) 210.

[5] Postcard [17 November 1963], Connolly Papers, University of Tulsa.

[6] *Spectator*, 13 December 1963.

[7] PL to CC [15 January 1964], Connolly Papers, University of Tulsa.

[8] *Collected Poems* (1976) 114.

[9] PL to JM [30 January 1964].

[10] PL to Julian Mitchell [March 1964].

[11] PL to Nancy Sandars [22 June 1964].
[12] PL to WC [November 1964].
[13] 'The Wreck of the Deutschland' II. xxiv: 'Away in the loveable west, On a pastoral forehead of Wales, I was under a roof here, I was at rest.'
[14] PL to Nancy Sandars [9 November 1964].
[15] PL to Willie Charlton [November 1964] and to PB [?late 1964].
[16] P. Kitchen, *Gerard Manley Hopkins, a Life* (1978, 1989) 156.
[17] PL to D. P-J [November 1964].
[18] PL to Nancy Sandars [9 November 1964].
[19] See note 17.
[20] SO to PL, 10, 27 January 1965, PLP.
[21] PL to NS [17 January 1965].
[22] *Agenda*, David Jones special issue 1967, 80-81.
[23] *Collected Poems* (1975) 201.
[24] PL to NS [17 January 1965].
[25] *Flutes of Autumn* (1983) 126.
[26] PL to David Pryce-Jones [17 February 1965].
[27] See note 26 and PL to Julian Mitchell [1 March 1965].
[28] 'Because we are in a Muslim country.' Vicar Apostolic to PL, 29 April 1965, PLP.
[29] 'Bob' [Murray, S.J.] to PL, 7 July 1965, PLP.

NOTES TO CHAPTER 13

[1] PL to Willie Charlton [September 1965] and Wikipedia entry on George Pavlopoulos.
[2] GP to Deirdre Levi, 7 February 2000.
[3] *Hill of Kronos* (1980) 121-122
[4] See note 1.
[5] PL to Willie Charlton [September 1965; autumn 1965].
[6] *Hill of Kronos* 16.
[7] PL to WC [autumn 1965].
[8] PL to JM [October 1972].
[9] M. Devlin, *Christopher Devlin* (1970); J. Rockett, *A Gentle Jesuit : Philip Caraman*, SJ, 1911-1998 (2004).
[10] PS to PL, 12 October 1965, PLP.
[11] Raine, e-mail to author, 7 July 2009.
[12] MW to PL, 11 October 1965, PLP.
[13] Haddon, e-mail to author, 1 October 2007.
[14] JB to PL, 1 April 1965, PLP.
[15] *Collected Poems* (1976) 126, 124. Interview with John Haffenden, *Poetry Review* 74/3, 1984, 16-17.
[16] Garfitt, e-mail to author, 6 July 2009. See also his memoir *The*

Horseman's Word (2011) 161.

[17] *Times*, 24 August 1968.

[18] P. Jay to PL, 30 November 1968, PLP.

[19] See John Johnson to PL, 27 August 1965, PLP.

[20] *Hill of Kronos* 130.

[21] GD to PL, 6 June 1966, PLP; *Collected Poems* 56.

[22] PL to CC [?December 1966], Connolly Papers, University of Tulsa.

Notes to Chapter 14

[1] PL to JM [12 February 1963]

[2] 'David Archer, Wallpaper Salesman', *Nova* January 1967, 52-3

[3] 'For Dom and Henrietta', *Water, Rock & Sand* (1962) ; *Collected Poems* (1976) 79.

[4] H. Moraes, *Henrietta* (1994) 70. PL to JM [25 November 1965].

[5] YD to PL, 5 April 1966, PLP.

[6] *Hill of Kronos* (1980) 130.

[7] PL to NS [?early 1966].

[8] D de G to PL, 12 January 1966, PLP.

[9] PL to David Pryce-Jones and to Willie Charlton [both early 1966].

[10] *Life is a Platform* (1971) 23-25; *Collected Poems* (1976) 162-163.

[11] *Life is a Platform* 23; *Collected Poems* 162.

[12] PL to David Pryce-Jones [early 1966].

[13] PL to David Pryce-Jones [early 1966]; Sir Patrick Leigh Fermor to author [August 2009].

[14] PL to WC [early 1966].

[15] DC to PL, 4 November 1966, PLP.

[16] *Life is a Platform* 35; *Collected Poems* 169.

[17] *Life is a Platform* 26; *Collected Poems* 164.

[18] PL to JM [24 April 1966].

[19] PL to Willie Charlton [August 1966].

[20] KR to PL, 22 September 1966; AL to PL, n.d, PLP.

[21] PL to NS [?October 1966].

[22] *Sunday Times* 20 November 1966.

[23] PL to CC [December 1966], Connolly Papers, University of Tulsa.

[24] *Hill of Kronos* 125.

[25] PL to CC [Oxford, 30 January 1967], Connolly Papers, University of Tulsa.

[26] GC to PL, 18 September 1966, PLP.

[27] J. L-F to PL [late April 1967]; MP to PL, 8 May 1967, PLP. Miranda's family nickname was Quail.

[28] CB to PL, 18 May 1967; David Pryce-Jones to CB, n.d., PLP.

[29] MR to PL, 1 May 1967, PLP.

[30] Frances Partridge, *Good Company: Diaries 1967-1970* (1994) 9 May 1969.

[31] PL to David Pryce-Jones [August? 1967].

Notes to Chapter 15

[1] JM to PL, 21 May 1967, PLP.

[2] *Hill of Kronos* (1980) 137, 152.

[3] DC to PL, [March] 1967, PLP.

[4] Miss Paterson to PL, 6 June 1967; HM to PL, c. 20 June 1967; C. Clancy to PL, 13 July 1967, PLP.

[5] VH to PL, 10 April 1967; Joan Leigh Fermor to PL [spring 1967], PLP..

[6] PL to an unnamed journalist (copy), 9 May 1967, PLP..

[7] CMW to PL, 3 May 1967, PLP.

[8] LD to PL, 16 November 1966; John Johnson to PL, 12 and 28 October, 9 November 1966; Adrian House to PL, 4 and 8 November 1966; PL to BR (copy) [early November 1966]; Francis Pagan to PL, 1 November 1966, 1 February 1967, PLP..

[9] DA to PL, 11 April 1967, PLP.

[10] AH to PL, 20 April, 5 June 1967; John Johnson to PL, 6 June 1967, PLP..

[11] PL to Betty Radice (copy), 20 July 1967, BR to PL, 24 July 1967, and Andrew Pennycook to PL, 4 August 1967; DA to PL, 9 October 1967, PLP.

[12] DC to PL, 6 November 1967, PLP.

[13] PL to 'John' [David Caute], (copy), 16 June 1967, PLP.

[14] MB to PL, early November 1966; SS to PL, 6 November 1966, PLP.

[15] SS to PL, 27 April 1967, PLP

[16] SS to PL, 6 July, 11 July 1967, PLP.

[17] PL to JC (copy), 16 June 1967; JC to PL, 26 June 1967; VA to PL, 9 July 1967, PLP.

[18] PL to DP-J [early August 1967]. DP-J to PL, 7 August 1967; JB to PL, 16 August 1967; 'John' to PL, 12, 14 October 1967; P to TG, 23 October 1967 (copy); TG to PL, 28 November 1967, PLP.

[19] 'John' to PL, 5 May 1967,PLP.

[20] PL to Nancy Sandars [p/m 15 January 1968].

[21] MB to PL, 14 September 1967, PLP.

[22] Eric Peters, Thames & Hudson, to PL, 20 October, 3 November 1967; RM-G to PL [?early October 1967], PLP.

[23] F. Sweeney to PL, 18, 26 October, 7 December 1967, with copy of telegram from PL on verso of the former; John Johnson to PL, 29 November, 1967, PLP.

[24] *Collected Poems* (1976, new ed. 1984) 209

[25] *Hill of Kronos* 145-46; PL to David Pryce-Jones [November 1968].

[26] PL to CC [postmarked 10 March 1968], Connolly Papers, University of Tulsa; to Nancy Sandars [15 January 1968].

[27] *Hill of Kronos* 149.

[28] *Hill of Kronos* 147; 'Amnesty's Anniversary', *Tablet*, 23 November 1968.

[29] John Johnson to PL, 8 September 1968, PLP.

[30] PL to Willie Charlton [spring 1969].

[31] PL to David Pryce-Jones [November 1968].

NOTES TO CHAPTER 16

[1] Nicholas Shakespeare, *Bruce Chatwin* (1999) 165.

[2] *Flutes of Autumn* 135.

[3] Shakespeare, *Bruce Chatwin* 311.

[4] NS to PL, 8 August 1967, PLP.

[5] *Light Garden of the Angel King* (1972) (Preface) 13.

[6] *Light Garden of the Angel King* 20-22.

[7] *Ibid.* 30-32.

[8] For the 'old-fashioned' idea see, for example, *Encyclopædia Britannica* (1911) under Kabul. Ghirshman, in *Begram* (1946), argued for a site some forty miles north of Kabul, near the present-day Bagram military airbase. Peter Fraser, PL's *bête noire* as director of the British School at Athens from 1968 to 1971, placed the city at Bamiyan, about 150 miles west of Kabul (*Cities of Alexander the Great*, 1996, 142).

[9] Notebooks, summer 1969, Bruce Chatwin papers, MS Eng. e. 3714-3717, Bodleian Library.

[10] Shakespeare, *Bruce Chatwin* 228.

[11] *Light Garden of the Angel King* 40-43, 228-29; Chatwin, *What Am I Doing Here* (1989) 292-23.

[12] *Light Garden of the Angel King* 40, 216.

[13] Also published in *What Am I Doing Here* (1989).

[14] See note 9.

[15] Shakespeare, *Bruce Chatwin* 227; *Light Garden of the Angel King* 58, 52.

[16] *Light Garden of the Angel King* 54-55.

[17] *Ibid.* 57-70.

[18] *Ibid.* 36-38.

[19] *Ibid.* 71-73; Chatwin, *What Am I Doing Here* 287.

[20] *Light Garden* 79-81;

[21] *Bruce Chatwin, Photographs & Notebooks*, ed. D. King & F. Wyndham (1993) 122.

[22] *Light Garden of the Angel King* 133n.

[23] *Ibid.* 128.

[24] *Ibid* 115-16 and 224, note 3; *Bruce Chatwin, Photographs & Notebooks*

125.

[25] *Light Garden of the Angel King* 117-20, 129; Chatwin, *What Am I Doing Here* 292.

[26] *Light Garden of the Angel King* 142, 242; *Life is a Platform* (1971) 41.

[27] *Light Garden of the Angel King* 148n.

[28] *Life is a Platform* 38.

[29] 'For Colin Macleod', *The Echoing Green. Three Elegies* (1983) 28; *The Rags of Time* (1994) 36.

[30] *Bruce Chatwin, Photographs & Notebooks* 130-131; *Light Garden of the Angel King* 154-57.

[31] *Light Garden of the Angel King* 150, 167-180; PL to Willie Charlton [September 1969].

[32] *Light Garden of the Angel King* (1984 ed.) 15.

NOTES TO CHAPTER 17

[1] PL to Willie Charlton [September 1969] and to David Pryce-Jones [autumn 1969].

[2] Myron Gilmore to Isaiah Berlin, 31 March 1965, MS Berlin 173 f.121, Bodleian Library, Oxford.

[3] AL to PL, 2, 18 July 1966, 20 July 1967, PLP.

[4] Stephen Rawles, obituary, 'Professor Anthony Levi', *Independent* 12 January 2005.

[5] *Hill of Kronos* 148. Rather than the elegant-sounding *retiré*, it seems to have been more of an *ypostegon*, a (rooftop) shelter or shed.

[6] PL to D P-J [February/March 1970] and to WC [September 1970]. See also *The Hill of Kronos* 148.

[7] Roderick Beaton, *George Seferis, Waiting for the Angel, A Biography* (Yale, 2003) 5.

[8] *O tonos tes phones tou Sephere* ['Mr Seferis's Tone of Voice'] (Athens, 1970). For a fuller account of the affair of the lecture, see *The Hill of Kronos* 161, 163-165.

[9] Postcard [March 1970], Connolly Papers, University of Tulsa.

[10] *Hill of Kronos* 169.

[11] BC to James Ivory, 21 May 1970, and to Elizabeth Chatwin [July 1970] and 12 August 1970, in E. Chatwin and N. Shakespeare eds. *Under the Sun, The Letters of Bruce Chatwin* (2010) 151, 153, 157.

[12] PL to Willie Charlton [September 1970].

[13] See note 12.

[14] See prefatory note to *Collected Poems* (1984 ed.), 'I do not really think that Life is a Platform; when I named that collection I was more interested in Death being a Pulpit'.

[15] PL to Julian Mitchell, 30 September 1972.

16 *Hill of Kronos* 170; PL to WC [27 September 1971].

17 *Hill of Kronos* 176.

18 PL to WC [27 September 1971]; *Hill of Kronos* 175-176.

19 *Hill of Kronos* 177-79.

20 'Profile: Peter Levi, Romantic at the High Table', *Observer* 1 May 1988.

21 See note 4.

NOTES TO CHAPTER 18

1 'And a lost summer at a dying point', 'Nothing has been written about this life', *Life is a Platform* (1971), 166, 169.

2 'When does it end?'; 'The break of day and the falling of night', *Life is a Platform* 36, 20.

3 *Critical Quarterly*, June 1971 141-148; *Collected Poems* (1976) 209.

4 *Poetry Review*, September 1984, 12.

5 *Death is a Pulpit* (1971) 29.

6 'W.H. Auden' in *Art of Poetry* (1991) 247.

7 Empson to PL [1972] and note in J. Haffenden (ed.) *Selected Letters of William Empson* (2006) 526-529. PL notebook [late 1988], MS 90-15, Box 1, PLP.

8 BC to E. Chatwin, 14 September 1972, in E. Chatwin & N. Shakespeare (eds.), *Under the Sun. The Letters of Bruce Chatwin* (2010) 221. For Peter's account of the escape plan, see *Poetry Review*, September 1984, 10.

9 *Hill of Kronos* (1980) 182.

10 PL to Willie Charlton, April 1972.

11 PL to David Pryce-Jones, [6 December 1972] and [1973].

12 *Collected Poems* (1976) 237.

13 Sir Patrick Leigh Fermor to author [August 2009].

14 *Hill of Kronos* 184-188.

15 *Collected Poems* 206.

16 J. Wain, Professing Poetry (1977) 1-3.

17 'Rivers (*The Thames, August-November 1973*)' in *Collected Poems* (1976) 238.

18 *Collected Poems* 238-241

19 PL to Willie Charlton, 27, 29 October 1972.

20 *Times* 28 May, 14 June 1974.

21 PL to WC [9 August 1974]. He gave the lectures the following summer term.

22 *Hill of Kronos* 190-192.

23 Mischa Scorer, e-mail to author, 24 August 2010.

24 June Henman, e-mails to author, July-August 2010, and photographs, which unfortunately cannot be reproduced here.

²⁵ See note 24.

NOTES TO CHAPTER 19
¹ *Agenda*, David Jones special issue 1973/74, 58.
² *Times*, 14 December 1974.
³ 'He [the priest] has no need of the rubric's nudge: *osculatur altare in medio*. For what bodily act other / would serve here? Creaturely of necessity / for we are creatures.' *Agenda*, David Jones special issue (1967) 7.
⁴ *In memory of David Jones : the text of a sermon delivered in Westminster Cathedral at the Solemn Requiem for the poet and painter, David Jones, on 13 December 1974* (1975); also printed as Appendix to *The Flutes of Autumn* (1983) 187-191.
⁵ *Hill of Kronos* (1980) 201.
⁶ From 'Memoir' in PL tr. G. Pavlopoulos *The Cellar* (1977) 14.
⁷ Oxford Poetry Lecture, 'George Seferis', 12 November 1986, in *Art of Poetry* (1991).
⁸ *Collected Poems* (1976) 218.
⁹ 'Notes about Kant'; 'For Peter and Margaret', *Collected Poems* 237, 248.
¹⁰ *Collected Poems* 232.
¹¹ *Critical Quarterly*, June 1971; *Collected Poems* 216.
¹² *Agenda*, winter/spring 1977.
¹³ 'Christmas Sermon 1967'in *Death is a Pulpit* (1971) 22-23; *Collected Poems* 191.
¹⁴ Introduction to *A Hot Bath at Bedtime* (1977) xxi. Robertson's title-poem is not a description of cosy comfort but an agnostic's plea to be purified in Purgatory before entering the eternal void.
¹⁵ *Collected Poems* 122.
¹⁶ *Goodbye to the Art of Poetry* (1989) 13.
¹⁷ *Collected Poems* 231.
¹⁸ *Private Ground* (1981) 47.
¹⁹ 'Village Snow' in *Private Ground* 22.
²⁰ Copy of typescript of sermon kindly provided by William Charlton.
²¹ *Hill of Kronos* 203.

NOTES TO CHAPTER 20
¹ *Hill of Kronos* 203; *Flutes of Autumn* 154.
² Notebook 1 (1977-80), MS 90-15, Box 1, PLP.
³ *Private Ground* (1981) 29.
⁴ See note 2.
⁵ *The Flutes of Autumn* (1983) 132.
⁶ *Flutes of Autumn* 73-74.

[7] PL to Willie Charlton [September 1970], and postcard [27 April 1977].

[8] Lowell to Elizabeth Hardwick, 31 May 1970, in *Letters* (2005) 539.

[9] 'In Memory of Robert Lowell', *Art of Poetry* (1991) 271.

[10] See note 2.

[11] *Art of Poetry* 270.

[12] *Art of Poetry* 266.

[13] *Paris Review* **76**, Fall 1979, 34.

[14] *Agenda* **24**/3 (1986) 56.

[15] *Ibid.* 64.

[16] *Five Ages* (1978) 15-18, 20-23.

[17] *Grave Witness* (1985) 57.

[18] *Flutes of Autumn* 154.

[19] *Iris Murdoch as I Knew Her* (2003) 43.

[20] *Agenda* **24**/3 (1986) 95.

[21] See note 2.

[22] *Grave Witness* (1985) 59.

[23] *Poetry Review* **74**/3, p.9.

[24] See note 2.

[25] *Oxford University Gazette*, 3 May 1973, 26 October 1978.

[26] *Hill of Kronos* 225, 214-15.

[27] *Times* 7 August 1980.

Notes to Chapter 21

[1] Notebook 1 [1977-80], MS 90-15, Box 1, PLP.

[2] H. Lloyd-Jones, 'Colin William Macleod (26. 6. 43 - 17. 12. 81)' in *Gnomon* **54** (1982) 413-415.

[3] 'The Colors of Spring', *New York Times* 7 February 1982.

[4] Notebook 6 [early 1987?] , MS 90-15, Box 1, PLP.

[5] See note 4.

[6] 'For Colin Macleod', *The Echoing Green. Three Elegies* (1983) 27.

[7] *Five Ages* (1979) 53.

[8] See note 1 (late August 1979).

[9] *Private Ground* (1981) 39.

[10] *Private Ground* 25.

[11] 'Snow is falling, snow is falling' in Henry Kamen tr. Pasternak *In the Interlude – Poems 1945-1960* (1962) 90. Peter quoted this line in his Oxford Poetry lecture on Pasternak on May 12, 1988, without attributing the refrain to Kamen, and with his own prose translation of the last lines of the poem. See *The Art of Poetry* (1991) 201.

[12] *Private Ground* 50, 42, 29.

[13] See note 1 (late 1979).

[14] *Private Ground* 45.

[15] *Flutes of Autumn* (1983) 97.
[16] *Flutes of Autumn* 84.
[17] PL to Willie Charlton, 9 August 1974.
[18] *Echoing Green* 15, 18 ; *Rags of Time* (1994) 23, 26.
[19] *Echoing Green* 26; *Rags of Time* 34.
[20] Notebook 4 [1982-83], 26-27 January [1982], MS 90-15, Box 1, PLP.
[21] *Echoing Green* 28; *Rags of Time* (1994) 36.
[22] See note 20.
[23] See note 1 (late 1980).
[24] *Flutes of Autumn* 154.
[25] 'The Meditated Landscape' *Agenda* 24/3 (1986) 76.
[26] *Flutes of Autumn* 177.
[27] 'For Angus MacIntyre', *Reed Music* (1997) 79.
[28] 'For Caryl Brahms', *Shakespeare's Birthday* (1985) 21-28; *Rags of Time* 49-56.
[29] 'For Alasdair Clayre', *Shakespeare's Birthday* 34; *Rags of Time* 60.
[30] *Shakespeare's Birthday* 38; *Rags of Time* 64.
[31] Notebook 5 [1983-85], MS 90-15, Box 1, PLP.
[32] See note 31.
[33] *Art of Poetry* (1991) 3.
[34] College Literary Society Minutes, summer term 1974, Eton College Archives.
[35] I may have imagined this, but I was certain that I read about it somewhere at the time. Deirdre has no clear memory of it.

NOTES TO CHAPTER 22

[1] *Spectator* 9 June 1984.
[2] *Spectator* 6 October 1984.
[3] See P. Conradi, *Iris Murdoch, a Life* (2001) 438.
[4] 'Oxford victor baffled by fuss', *Guardian* 4 June 1984 3/1.
[5] *Art of Poetry* (1991) 235, 270.
[6] Notebook 5 [1983-85], MS 90-15, Box 1, PLP.
[7] *Flutes of Autumn* 53. The translation was published in the *Irish University Review*, Spring 1971.
[8] *Art of Poetry* 15.
[9] *Art of Poetry* 6.
[10] 'Risks', *London Review of Books*, 1 August 1985.
[11] *Tennyson* 218.
[12] *Goodbye to the Art of Poetry* (1989) 22.
[13] Notebook 6 [1985-88] (late 1987), MS 90-15, Box 1, PLP.
[14] *Art Of Poetry* 256, 262, 270.
[15] See, for instance, W. Geoffrey Arnott, 'Renderings down', *TLS* 12 April

1985.

[16] *San Diego Tribune*, 9 September 1988.

[17] Notebook 6 [1985-88] (December 1985), MS 90-15, Box 1, PLP.

[18] Notebook 7 [1988-89] (1989), MS 90-15, Box 1, PLP.

[19] See note 13.

[20] *Shadow & Bone* (1989) 40, 22.

[21] P. Conradi, *Iris Murdoch, a Life* (2001) 33.

[22] *Shakespeare's Birthday* (1985) 14, 16.

[23] *Echoing Green* (1983) 30; *Shakespeare's Birthday* 26.

[24] *Shadow & Bone* 44, 86.

[25] *Shadow & Bone* 47, 52, 72.

[26] *Shadow & Bone* 16, 117.

[27] Notebook 6 [1985-88] (November/December 1985), MS 90-15, Box 1, PLP..

[28] *Art of Poetry* 88.

[29] *Art of Poetry* 272-292.

[30] *Art of Poetry* 187.

Notes to Chapter 23

[1] Notebook 6 [1985-88], MS 90-15, Box 1, PLP.

[2] S. Schoenbaum, 'Extraordinarily like other men', TLS 20 Jan. 1989.

[3] *Life & Times of William Shakespeare* (1988) 93; 'Shakespeare's Sonnets' in *Art of Poetry* (1991) 128.

[4] *Art of Poetry* 133.

[5] *Daily Telegraph*, reprinted in Powell, *Some Poets, Artists & a Reference for Mellors* (2005) 21.

[6] *Art of Poetry* 134, 137.

[7] *Life & Times of William Shakespeare* 269.

[8] See note 7.

[9] *Life & Times of William Shakespeare* 247.

[10] See note 1 (1987?).

[11] 'What the Rose Said', *Shadow & Bone* (1989) 79; 'For C.C. 80', Viriditas (2001) 36.

[12] 'For Fram and Candia', *Shadow & Bone* 75.

[13] See note 1 (early 1988).

[14] McWilliam, *What to Look for in Winter, a memoir in blindness* (2010) 412.

[15] Interview, *Poetry Review*, September 1984, 15, 17.

[16] See note 1.

[17] *Art of Poetry* 133.

[18] *Shadow & Bone* 30, 85.
[19] *Shadow & Bone* 40.
[20] *Shadow & Bone* 39, 30; 'For Alasdair Clayre', *Shakespeare's Birthday* (1985) 34.
[21] *Shadow & Bone* 62.
[22] *Shadow & Bone* 40, 42.
[23] *Shadow & Bone* 54, 70.
[24] Notebook 7 [March 1988 – July 1989], MS 90-15, Box 1, PLP.
[25] *Reed Music* (1997) 11-17, 47-53, 89-94 and Prefatory Note.
[26] 'Behind the Lines', *TLS* 13 February 1987.
[27] 'Marginal and seminal', *TLS* 24 April 1987.
[28] Collier, *New Particulars Regarding the Work of Shakespeare* (1836).
[29] See notes 24 and 2.
[30] *Guardian*, obituary section, 10 February 2000.

NOTES TO CHAPTER 24

[1] Notebook 7 [March 1988-July 1989], MS 90-15, Box 1, PLP.
[2] See note 1.
[3] See note 1.
[4] Introduction to Robertson, *A Hot Bath at Bedtime* (1975); *Daily Telegraph* obituary of Robertson, 4 Jan. 2005.
[5] *Shadow & Bone* (1989) 100.
[6] See note 1 and 'Austin, Texas', *Shadow & Bone* 98-107.
[7] *Shadow & Bone* 99, 103.
[8] *Shadow & Bone* 104.
[9] See note 1.
[10] *Tennyson* (1993) 47.
[11] All references to the Russian trip, unless otherwise specified, come from the 'Moscow Diary', MS 90-15, Box 9 no. 4, PLP.
[12] *Art of Poetry* 230 (on Seferis), 204 (on Pasternak).
[13] *Boris Pasternak* (1990) 127.
[14] *Boris Pasternak* 172.
[15] See page 395.
[16] See note 1.
[17] Deborah Steiner, 'Ordinary nothingness', *TLS* 19 Aug. 1988.
[18] *Art of Poetry* 27-46.
[19] See note 1.
[20] *Goodbye to the Art of Poetry* (Anvil Press, 1989),9-38 *passim*; also in *The Art of Poetry* (1991) 293-312.
[21] As in *Tennyson* 129.
[22] See note 1.
[23] See note 1. 'Crushed (GMH)' in the notebook refers to the fourth line of

Hopkins's poem 'God's Grandeur'.

²⁴ See note 1.

²⁵ *Rags of Time* (1994), introduction and 83-90.

NOTES TO CHAPTER 25

¹ 'Indian Summer', *Reed Music* (1997) 40; *Flutes of Autumn* (1983) 90.

² Lees-Milne, *Ceaseless Turmoil, Diaries 1988-1992* ed. M. Bloch (2004) 279.

³ *London Review of Books*, 8 February 1990.

⁴ *Tennyson* (1993) 5.

⁵ *Tennyson* 60-61.

⁶ *Tennyson* 127, 156.

⁷ *Tennyson* 60.

⁸ *Tennyson* 224.

⁹ *Tennyson* 110, 284.

¹⁰ *Tennyson* 234, 247; Elspeth Barker, *Independent on Sunday*, 21 March 1993.

¹¹ *Tennyson* 188, 120.

¹² *London Review of Books* 8 April 1993.

¹³ *Tennyson* 250.

¹⁴ Kavanagh, *Spectator*, May 1992, republished in *A Kind of Journal* (2003) 85; letter to author, 23 Oct. 2012.

¹⁵ *Art of Poetry* (1991) 183-4, 176.

¹⁶ *Art of Poetry* 174.

¹⁷ *Edward Lear* (1995) 31.

¹⁸ *LRB* 23 February 1995; *TLS* 3 February 1995.

¹⁹ Interview with Nick Higham, transcribed by Matthew Connolly.

²⁰ 'Reed Music', *Reed Music* 9. Heaney had used the phrase in 'Gifts of Rain' in *Wintering Out* (1972).

²¹ '...The reed beds / where I will that my ashes be scattered,' *Viriditas* (2001) 21.

²² *Reed Music* 11.

²³ *Reed Music* 52.

²⁴ *Reed Music* 21.

²⁵ *Reed Music* 79.

²⁶ *Reed Music* 62.

NOTES TO CHAPTER 26

¹ *A Bottle in the Shade* (1996) 44; 'For Nikos Gatsos', *Rags of Time* (1994) 69.

² *A Bottle in the Shade* 65.

³ *A Bottle in the Shade* 128.

[4] *Reed Music* (1997) 83-88.

[5] Lees-Milne, *Ceaseless Turmoil, Diaries 1988-1992* (2004) 332.

[6] Lees-Milne, *The Milk of Paradise, Diaries 1993-1997* (2005) 251, 255-6, 262-3, 267-8, 276-7, 286, 296. Michael Bloch, *James Lees-Milne, The Life* (2009) 351.

[7] Lee T. Pearcy in *Bryn Mawr Classical Review*, Oct. 4, 1998.

[8] Notebook 6 [winter 1986-87], MS 90-15, Box 1, PLP. *Virgil, his Life and Times* (1998) 29.

[9] *Virgil* 93.

[10] *TLS* 25 June 1999.

[11] *Viriditas* (2001) 25, 69.

[12] Leigh Fermor in *Independent* obituary section,16 February 2000.

NOTES TO ENVOI

[1] Reprinted as 'Remembering Peter Levi' in *A Kind of Journal, 1987-2002* (2003) 167-170.

[2] *Viriditas* 15.

Index

The initials 'S.J.' after surnames distinguish Jesuits who remained (or remain) members of the order from others who resigned from it.